THE LONDON SECUR

THE LONDON
SECURITIES MARKETS

S M Haslam, MA ACA
S G G Peerless, MA FCA

The Institute of Chartered Accountants
in England and Wales
Chartered Accountants' Hall
Moorgate Place
London
EC2P 2BJ
1990

Chartac Books
The Institute of Chartered Accountants in
    England and Wales
Chartered Accountants' Hall
Moorgate Place
London EC2P 2BJ

British Library Cataloguing in Publication Data
Haslam, Simon S.M.
    The London securities market : organisation, regulation,
    auditing and financial reporting.
    1. Great Britain. Securities markets
    I. Title   II. Peerless, Simon G.G.   III. Institute of Chartered
    Accountants in England and Wales
    332.64241

ISBN 1 85355 132 5

Cover design by Progress Graphics
Typeset by J&L Composition Ltd, Filey, North Yorkshire
Printed in England by Biddles Ltd, Guildford

Contents

Appendices

Preface

We have prepared this book in the hope that it will provide a practical guide to the operations of the London Securities markets which will be of interest to a wide range of people. Our intention has been to give practical information on the day-to-day operations of the participants in these markets that will be of relevance to those involved in the financial management and control of businesses involved in the markets. In addition, we have included detailed guidance on the controls appropriate to those operations and the regulatory, accounting and auditing aspects of each element of the industry. This will, we hope, be of particular assistance to those who are auditors of a firm in the industry, for whom there is currently little or no published guidance on the detailed audit work appropriate to this highly specialised type of business, and also of use to financial controllers, office managers and internal auditors. Although written from the standpoint of the external auditor, the chapters have been structured so that the more detailed regulatory and audit matters may readily be omitted by those for whom they hold no particular fascination.

This book is in no small measure due the the considerable efforts of a number of people without whose assistance this book would not only have been a lot less complete, but probably a lot less readable and no doubt still in draft. Amongst those involved the authors must especially thank John Waddington, Paul Leech, Julian Pilkington and Paul Tickle.

We have in a number of areas expressed views on either the current industry practice, our personally preferred approach or our views on possible developments in particualr circumstances. However, we realise the industry is still evolving after the radical changes resulting from Big Bang, the Financial Services Act and the 1987 crash, whilst new regulations will shortly be arriving from Brussels, the three-tier system of rulebook regulation being introduced by the Securities and Investments Board and the International Stock Exchange's proposals on TAURUS. We have discussed the way we see these progressing in the appropriate chapters of the text, but out views on these developments are likely to be quickly overtaken by events and the reader should keep himself up to date on the progress of these matters.

Whilst every care has been taken to ensure the accuracy of the contents of this book, no reponsibility for loss occasioned to any person acting or refraining from acting as a result of any statement contained in it can be accepted by the authors or publishers.

Simon Haslam
Simon Peerless
September 1990

PART I

1 Introduction

1.1 The purpose of the book

1.1.1 Over the last ten years there have been substantial changes in the United Kingdom's securities industry. These changes have been driven both by internal forces within the industry, by government and by other external influences; the combination of which has resulted in an entirely new regulatory structure for the industry under the Financial Services Act 1986. We have witnessed new methods of transacting securities business, through electronic share-dealing systems, and changes in the composition and structure of firms actually transacting such business, particularly through the acquisition of stockbroking firms by major banks and international securities firms. These changes have had a fundamental impact on the operations and financial management of many businesses in the securities industry.

1.1.2 Concurrent with these changes have been a number of regulatory developments affecting the role of the auditor. These have largely been responses to a number of well-publicised investment business collapses which have caused losses of large sums of money to members of the general public. Regulatory developments have in turn led to greater demands on the work and reports of auditors of securities businesses in an attempt to prevent recurrences of these failures. Accordingly, the auditor of a securities business does not have responsibilities solely to the shareholders or proprietors of the business, but also has reporting responsibilities to the regulators of the securities industry. In extreme cases, the auditor is now empowered to report matters of concern directly to the regulator, without the prior consent of his client.

1.1.3 These changes, both to the industry and to the role of the auditor indicate a need for a book covering the practical aspects of the operation of the London securities market. Such a volume could also meet the need for the auditor to have a source of guidance on the operations of securities businesses, the framework within which they currently operate and the audit techniques that may be appropriate in that environment. It is the intention of this book to provide such a source.

1

1.2 Its scope

1.2.1   This book seeks to explain the operations of the London securities markets for accountants, financial controllers and others, whilst also providing practical guidance for auditors of securities businesses. In the interests of providing this guidance in a manageable form, the book's contents are organised around those matters that are of direct relevance to an auditor. It is not, however, a textbook of auditing *per se* and assumes that those readers interested in the auditing aspects will be broadly familiar with the planning and conduct of an audit of a standard commercial enterprise.

1.2.2   To obtain a proper understanding of the London securities markets, it is necessary that the nature and practice of the organisations involved are understood and the environment, both trading and regulatory, is appreciated. It is these particular aspects of the securities industry that this book addresses, namely the peculiarities of dealing and settlement with their associated terminology, together with the framework of rules and regulations governing the industry. These are particularly important to the auditor as an understanding is vital to the effective performance of his engagement.

1.2.3   The book generally reflects the SRO rules, guidelines and other material as they stood in March 1990. However, two significant subsequent changes have been incorporated – the amendments to The Securities Association's rules on safe custody issued in June 1990, and the publication of the Auditing Practices Committee's Auditing Guideline on communications between auditors and regulators in July 1990.

1.3 Its structure

1.3.1   To set the market in context, the book commences with an overview of the regulatory framework that now governs the operation of all businesses within the securities industry. There follows an explanation in some detail of the financial regulations imposed upon securities businesses by that framework. Together with the financial regulations, the book also sets out the responsibilities imposed upon auditors by the Financial Services Act and by various bodies charged with the responsibility for day-to-day regulations. These include in particular those arising from section 109 of the Financial Services Act which gives auditors the right to make *ad hoc* reports to regulators. For a more detailed guide to the Financial Services Act itself, the reader is advised to consult other appropriate sources.

1.3.2   Chapter 4 sets out the overall approach to the audit of a securities business, setting the matters specific to such an audit in the context of normal auditing practice and the matters addressed by general audit textbooks. That chapter also considers particular accounting treatments that may be necessary within the securities industry.

1.3.3   The more detailed aspects of the securities business are then considered. The chapters in Part 2 in each case commence with an overview of a particular aspect of the business operations which will be of interest to general readers, followed by a review of the auditing objectives relevant to that area, the internal controls that might assist in the achievement of those objectives and finally guidance on the audit tests and procedures that might be appropriate. These detailed areas commence with the business of a standard UK 'stockbroker', that is a firm which is a member of the London Stock Exchange. The book goes on to describe the main categories of transactions and balances which will be found within a stockbroker and includes a summary of taxation and related duties that are likely to affect a securities business.

1.3.4   In Part 3, the book addresses a number of more specialised business areas or business types, and finally the book includes in its appendices suggested wordings for an unqualified report to each of the regulatory bodies and a pro-forma engagement letter for a client who is a member of The Securities Association.

1.3.5   It must be emphasised that the auditor must ensure he consults an up-to-date copy of the rules of the relevant regulatory body when carrying out any audit. He should also ensure he has read any guidance notes, as well as rule amendments that may have been issued but which have not yet been incorporated in the text of the rulebook, that accordingly he has an up-to-date file of notices of rule changes and that he considers the impact on his client of any absolute or temporary concessions granted in the particular case by the regulator.

1.4   A hope

Hamlet, in a somewhat different context asked the question, 'How his audit stands who knows save heaven?'

The authors hope that, at last, the auditor of a securities business will, with the assistance of this book, find that some of the uncertainties implied by that question are reduced.

2 The Regulatory Framework

2.1 Introduction

2.1.1   It is beyond the scope of this book to consider in detail the regulatory structure for investment businesses established by the Financial Services Act 1986 (FSA). However, the auditor of an authorised investment business must have some understanding of the principles of this regulatory framework as set out in this chapter. Not only does he need to be aware of the implications that the various rules have for his client, so as better to understand the business that he is auditing, but also of the ways in which the regulatory system affects his role, powers and obligations.

2.1.2   The following summary of the structure created by the FSA is intended merely as an overview of its principal features. The auditor should have access to the text of the FSA itself and to more detailed legal analysis of the statute to enable him to consider the extent of his, and his client's, obligations under the FSA. He may in exceptional circumstances need to seek legal advice on the interpretation of some sections of the FSA. The auditor's own role in the regulatory system, his responsibilities and his relationship with the regulatory bodies is covered in chapter 3.

2.1.3   Under the FSA, any individual, partnership or body corporate carrying on investment activities by way of business in the UK must be authorised. 'Investments' are defined in schedule 1 to the FSA to include shares, warrants, debt securities of all kinds, unit trusts and other collective investment schemes, futures contracts, options on investments or on currency or precious metals, and most life assurance contracts. Contracts for the future delivery of any type of asset are included where the contract is for investment purposes; and many banking instruments such as swaps, forward rate agreements, interest

4

rate caps and collars, etc., fall within the definition of investments as being either an option or a 'contract for differences'.

2.1.4 Investment activities are also widely defined:

- the purchase or sale of investments, as principal or agent, or arranging such transactions;
- investment management;
- giving advice on investments.

2.1.5 The operation of a collective investment scheme is also an investment activity. A collective investment scheme is an arrangement, of which a unit trust is a particular example, where assets of any kind (not restricted to investments) are held under a pooling arrangement to enable the participants to share in the profits arising from the assets.

2.1.6 There are numerous exemptions to the definition of investment activities – for example, a person buying and selling investments on his own account is exempt unless he is making a market in the investments or otherwise holds himself out to the public as a dealer in the investments.

2.1.7 In order to determine whether or not authorisation is needed the person must consider:

- whether its activities involve investments;
- whether the activities constitute investment activities and, if so, whether any of the detailed exemptions apply;
- whether the investment activities are carried on as a business in, or from, the UK.

2.1.8 Certain persons are exempted from the requirement to be authorised; these include the Bank of England and certain other international institutions and official bodies. Two other classes of exempt person of particular relevance to the securities industry – appointed representatives and listed institutions – are discussed in section 2.7 below.

2.2 Regulatory structure for authorised businesses

2.2.1 At the heart of the regulatory structure lies the Securities and Investments Board (SIB). The Secretary of State for Trade and Industry is given extensive powers by the FSA to regulate the investment industry, but is empowered to delegate many of these powers to the

Table 1   The SROs and the activities they can authorise

	TSA	IMRO	FIMBRA	AFBD	LAUTRO
	The Securities Association	*Investment Management Regulatory Organisation*	*The Financial Intermediaries, Brokers and Managers Regulatory Association*	*The Association of Futures Brokers and Dealers*	*Life Assurance and Unit Trust Regulatory Organisation*
Main types of member	Securities market participants	Institutional investment managers and unit trust managers	High street investment and life assurance advisers	Futures and commodities market participants	Insurance companies, unit trust managers and friendly societies
Main investment activities covered	Dealing, arranging deals and advising on deals in equity and debt securities and stock exchange options	Discretionary investment management, unit trust management	Advising on, dealing (other than as market maker) and arranging deals in securities and options thereon, unit trusts and life assurance policies	Dealing, arranging deals and advising on deals in financial and commodity futures and options	Marketing of life assurance and authorised unit unit trusts

(handwritten: SFA)

	Corporate finance and venture capital	Acting as trustee of a unit trust	Investment management of funds invested solely in the above
Ancillary activities covered when carried on in conjunction with a main activity above	Investment management, marketing and advising on transactions in unit trusts	Advising on, and arranging, deals in investments	Dealing in securities
	Dealing, arranging deals and advising on deals in financial futures and options		

Note: TSA and AFBD have announced their intention to merge, and detailed proposals are expected in late 1990 or early 1991.

SIB. Thus the SIB, although a private limited company rather than a government department, has statutory powers.

2.2.2   Although the SIB is itself able to authorise any investment business, its main function is to oversee the system of 'practitioner-based regulation' whereby investment businesses are authorised through membership of the self regulating organisation (SRO) responsible for regulating that type of investment business.

2.2.3   The five SROs, and the types of business with which they are concerned, are set out in Table 1. Each SRO has been 'recognised' by the SIB, which first ensures that the governing structure of the SRO, its rulebook and its procedures for monitoring and enforcing its rules are sufficient to ensure that authorisation by means of membership of that SRO gives a similar level of protection to investors as would direct authorisation by the SIB.

2.2.4   Each SRO is limited in the scope of investment business it is empowered to authorise. Thus a firm seeking authorisation will apply to the SRO which covers the particular aspect of investment business which the firm intends to carry on. In some cases, a firm will need to apply to more than one SRO – for example, a firm wishing to transact both commodity futures business and securities transactions will require authorisation from both the AFBD and TSA. However, the need for dual memberships does not often arise, as the SROs are able to authorise investment business outside the main scope of their authorisation if it is carried on as an ancillary business by a firm whose primary business is within the main scope of that SRO's authorisation. For example, TSA may authorise a member firm to carry on financial futures business provided the firm's main business is dealing in securities. Only in a few special cases, such as building societies, is direct authorisation by the SIB appropriate.

2.2.5   The original concept of practioner-based regulation was of a relatively simple but restrictive set of SIB rules which could be applied to any investment business. Each SRO would then develop less restrictive rules that would apply to its own particular type of investment business; because these rules would apply to particular types of business only, they would be written in terms of the market-practice in that business. By taking account of market-practice, they could provide adequate investor protection without being as onerous as the SIB's rules of more general application.

2.2.6   The expected benefits have largely failed to materialise, for a variety of reasons. First, the SIB, on the basis of legal advice, gave a narrow interpretation to the requirement for SRO rulebooks to give 'equivalent' investor protection; equivalence was to be tested on a rule-by-rule basis, rather than by judging whether the investor protection afforded by an SRO rulebook *overall* was equivalent to SIB's. Not only did this result in SRO rulebooks that were, to a large extent, reproductions of the SIB's rulebook; it also meant that where a relaxation of the rules was justified in a particular type of transaction, the SIB's rulebook itself had to incorporate the relaxation of the rule so as to enable the SRO to follow it. As a result, the SIB rulebook had to become a compendium of detailed rules applicable to different types of investment business. This in turn highlighted areas of the rules where the established market-practice differed from one type of investment business to another.

2.2.7   Another factor was the impact of section 62 of the FSA. This originally stated that any customer of an investment business had a claim in damages for a loss suffered as a result of a breach of the SIB or SRO rules. There was considerable concern that professional investors and others 'in the market' would attempt to exploit technical rule breaches as a means of recovering losses arising from poor investment decisions. This led to the rules being drafted in a legalistic way, with an emphasis on detailed procedures to be followed rather than as broad principles and objectives, to minimise scope for dispute as to whether a breach had in fact occurred. Section 62 has now been amended to apply solely in circumstances where losses have been suffered by *private* investors.

2.2.8   Finally, the scope of authorisation of each SRO, originally intended to overlap as little as possible, was widened considerably. It became apparent that multiple SRO membership merely added to the administrative burdens of firms offering a wide range of investment services, notwithstanding the arrangements whereby a firm which is a member of more than one SRO is 'lead regulated' by one of the SROs. As a result of this widening of the scope of individual SROs, their rulebooks have to cover a wider range of investment business.

2.2.9   Following amendments to the FSA in the Companies Act 1989, the SIB and SROs are redrafting their existing rulebooks using a 'three-tiered' approach. The first tier consists of ten general principles issued by SIB covering the whole range of investment regulation. A breach of one of the principles would not be grounds for an action for damages under section 62, but could be the basis for disciplinary action. However, the main purpose of the principles is to assist in the interpretation and understanding of the more detailed rules, and to ensure that investment business is conducted following simple concepts of 'good market practice' rather than careful adherence to the letter of detailed regulations.

2.2.10   The second tier, some 60 designated rules, often referred to as the 'core rules', will represent the basic rules in each area of the regulations and would be adopted verbatim by each SRO (though the SIB would allow some exceptions to this).

2.2.11   The third tier will be the detailed rules, supported where appropriate by codes of practice, drafted by each SRO, to apply the core rules to the specific circumstances of the types of investment business for which that SRO is responsible. Considerable variation in the third tier rules is, therefore, to be expected. Drafts of these rules are expected to be published by the individual SROs in late 1990.

2.2.12   There is also provision for the SIB to publish codes of practice amplifying statements of principle or core rules. Such codes of practice would not have the status of rules, but non-compliance with a code of practice could be taken into account in determining whether a breach of a rule had occurred or not.

2.3   SIB and SRO rulebooks

2.3.1   Both the current and redrafted versions of SIB and SRO rulebooks address two main considerations; to ensure that all investment businesses are 'fit and proper' and to regulate the way they conduct business.

Fit and proper

2.3.2   First, the SIB (or the SRO) must ensure that authorisation is granted only to those persons who are 'fit and proper' to carry on investment business, and that authorisation is withdrawn if they no longer meet the test. The concept of 'fit and proper' has three main elements; honesty, competence and financial soundness. The Financial Regulations set out in great detail the requirements for accounting, record-keeping and capital adequacy necessary to meet the test of financial soundness. These are of particular relevance to the auditor of an investment business and are dealt with in detail in chapter 3.

2.3.3   The concepts of competence and honesty are less precisely defined. Every person involved in the ownership or management of an investment business must submit a detailed application form setting out their previous experience in the industry and details of any legal actions or disciplinary proceedings against them. The regulatory bodies also consult their records of investor complaints and their investigations. It is clear from recent Authorisation Appeals Tribunal proceedings that any lack of candour on the part of the applicants is regarded as prima facie an indication of dishonesty. Once any doubts as to the honesty or competence of the applicant have been raised, the burden of proof is on the applicant to show that the doubts are unjustified rather than on the regulatory body to prove a lack of honesty or competence.

2.3.4 Similar considerations of honesty and competence apply to each trader and representative of an authorised firm, that is anyone who has authority to enter into investment transactions for the firm, or has direct dealings with customers. All such traders and representatives must apply individually for registration to the regulatory body. Examinations are increasingly used to test competence in different areas of investment business.

2.3.5 When a UK investment business is a branch of an overseas investment business regulated in its home country, the SIB or SRO may rely, to a greater or lesser extent, on the monitoring carried out by that business house's national regulator; the SIB has entered into Memoranda of Understanding with the regulators in major overseas financial centres setting out the agreed basis for this monitoring and the exchange of information between regulators. The monitoring of conduct of business remains the responsibility of the SIB or SRO.

2.4 Conduct of business

2.4.1 The second main concern of the SIB and the SROs is to regulate the conduct of business by investment firms. The aim is to ensure that each authorised firm:

(a) observes high standards of integrity and fair dealing and complies with best market-practice;
(b) acts with due skill, care and diligence in providing investment services; and
(c) deals fairly with its customers.

2.4.2 One of the main threads that runs through the Conduct of Business Rules is the fiduciary duty the authorised person owes to its private customers; that is, the authorised person is expected to act as the agent of its customer in protecting the latter's interests, and not to take advantage of the customer or profit at his expense.

Conduct of business rules

2.4.3 The main areas covered in the Conduct of Business Rules are as follows:

2.4.4 *Integrity* A firm must not claim to be independent or impartial when it

11

is not; and must not give or offer gifts or inducements which might cause detriment to any of its customers. Its charges must be reasonable, and it must not generate commission by unnecessarily frequent dealing for a customer.

2.4.5   *Skill, care and diligence*   A firm must carry out its instructions promptly, and must obtain the best price or other terms that are available for its customer. It must not give advice that it believes is unsuited to the particular needs of the customer, and, in the case of private investors, must know enough about their circumstances as to be able to make a reasonable judgement on the suitability of a particular transaction.

2.4.6   *Advertisements*   A firm must ensure that any advertisement promoting the services of the firm, or advertising a particular investment product or transaction, or any research circular it issues, is fair and not misleading, provides adequate information for investors, and any prediction or forecast is reasonably justified and supported by appropriate explanations.

2.4.7   *Information for customers*   Certain types of investment business require a written agreement to be sent to the customer setting out the contractual terms under which investment services will be provided, which must be signed and returned by the customer. Where a private investor is intending to deal in more risky investments, such as futures or options, he must receive and sign a statement setting out and drawing his attention to the particular risks involved. Customers must be given a contract note for each transaction carried out for them, and must be given details of all commission and other remuneration received by the firm in relation to the transaction.

2.4.8   *Fairness to customers*   A firm may not deal for itself ahead of transactions for clients in the same investment; nor deal for its own account ahead of the distribution of research material, with the knowledge of price-sensitive information which that material contains.

2.4.9   *Conflicts of interest*   Where the firm has a material interest in a transaction, the interest must be disclosed to the customer unless the firm has procedures such as 'chinese walls' (chapter 20) to ensure that the interests of the customer are not adversely affected.

2.4.10   *Cold calling*   A firm may not call a customer other than by invitation unless the customer has agreed to such calls, or the investment transaction can be cancelled by the customer in a 'cooling-off period'.

2.4.11   *Internal organisation*   A firm must ensure it carries on investment business only within the scope permitted by its SRO. It must maintain compliance procedures (usually under the control of a compliance officer) to ensure its employees are aware of, and comply with, the requirements of the conduct of business rules, and must ensure that complaints from customers are properly handled and resolved.

In-house rules for personal dealing by employees are also required to prevent any conflicts of interest to the detriment of the firm's customers arising from such dealings.

2.4.12   *Life policies and unit trusts*   Under the 'polarisation' principle, a firm must choose between providing independent advice, with an obligation to consider the products of all insurance companies or unit trust managers in deciding on the best investment for its customer, or to be 'tied' to a single insurance company or unit trust manager, selling only the products of that company.

2.4.13   *Corporate finance*   Less stringent regulations apply to a firm when providing corporate finance advice or similar services to a corporate finance customer.

2.4.14   Needless to say, the conduct of business rules are very detailed and contain many exemptions for special situations. Broadly though, many of the protections that are considered necessary for private investors are waived for experienced investors and, to an even greater extent, market professionals and other firms carrying on investment business.

2.4.15   It is outside the scope of the audit to check that the authorised firm is complying with the conduct of business rules. However, in extreme circumstances, breaches of the conduct of business rules can have audit implications. For example:

(a) claims for damages from customers as a result of rule breaches may be material, individually or in aggregate, to the accounts; and

(b) persistent or serious rule breaches may lead to material fines, or restriction, suspension or withdrawal of authorisation, with 'going concern' implications.

2.14.16   Therefore, the auditor of an investment business must have a general understanding of the principles of the rules, and satisfy himself that his client has suitable procedures for monitoring compliance, for recording and investigating complaints and must ensure that his client is not recklessly ignoring the rules or deliberately evading his responsibilities. He should in this context consider whether any serious complaints have been made by customers.

2.5 Monitoring and enforcement

2.5.1 A substantial proportion of the resources of each SRO is directed towards the monitoring and enforcement of compliance with its rules by its members. In addition to regular financial returns, annual accounts and audit reports submitted to the SRO (chapter 3), the enforcement teams of each SRO carry out routine inspection visits covering all SRO members. For example, each TSA member can expect to be visited by an enforcement team at least every year, with a visit lasting up to two ays or more. Whilst minor rule breaches found during these visits may result in no more than an oral reminder or unofficial letter from the SRO, formal warning notices are often issued and it is essential for an investment business not to underestimate the potential gravity of such a warning.

2.5.2 The SIB, under the FSA, and the SROs, under the terms of their rule books, have exceptional powers to deal with investment businesses which, in their view, are placing investors' money or assets at risk. An 'intervention notice' issued by the SIB or an SRO may:

- instruct an authorised firm to cease particular classes of business, or to cease business altogether, for a specified time;
- prohibit an authorised firm from disposing of certain assets;
- require certain assets to be transferred to a nominated trustee;
- require certain assets to be retained in the UK.

2.5.3 The use of these powers can effectively close down an investment business with a few days' or even hours' notice; the SIB or SRO cannot be held liable for damages if the use of the powers is later shown to have been unnecessary or based on wrong information, provided the SIB or SRO acted in good faith. Authorised firms and their professional advisers must, therefore, act immediately they know, or have reason to believe, that an intervention notice has been or is likely to be issued, if they wish to appeal against the issue of the notice.

2.6 The International Stock Exchange

2.6.1 Having described in outline the structure for authorising investment business, we now turn to another part of the framework, that responsible for ensuring a proper and orderly market exists for transacting business in securities. It should be noted that the FSA has made a distinction between the *authorising* of investment businesses and the *regulation* of organised investment exchanges.

2.6.2   The London stock market is regulated not by TSA but by the Stock Exchange, now called The International Stock Exchange of the United Kingdom and the Republic of Ireland Limited, or 'ISE'. Membership of TSA in itself carries no rights of access to the ISE. Separate membership of the ISE is, therefore, required for any firm carrying on a traditional stockbroking or market-making role. However, a number of TSA members have not applied for membership of ISE but carry on other investment business, such as corporate finance advice or venture capital business, that does not require them to transact share dealings on the ISE. Conversely, membership of TSA is not essential for ISE members, some of whom have found IMRO more appropriate to their business. However, the ISE is not an SRO and cannot confer authorisation to conduct investment business on its members.

2.6.3   The ISE no longer imposes its own capital requirements on members, but relies on the SROs to monitor capital adequacy. Its rulebook deals with matters relating to the execution and settlement of bargains, the SEAQ price-quote system, the reporting and checking of bargains, the Talisman settlement system, etc. These are all discussed in more detail in chapter 5.

2.6.4   The ISE also has default rules setting out the way in which bargains are to be settled when a member is declared in default; these rules override the normal insolvency rules to ensure that market obligations are settled in an orderly manner and that the default of a member has the minimum impact on the operation of the Exchange. These are discussed in more detail in chapter 7.

2.6.5   The ISE itself is a 'recognised investment exchange' (RIE) regulated under the FSA by the SIB. In order to be recognised, it must have appropriate rules and procedures, and adequate finance and monitoring resources, to maintain an orderly exchange. The ISE is also the competent authority under EC legislation for supervising quoted companies and thus responsible for conferring listed status on securities which are permitted to be traded on the exchange and for monitoring compliance with the Listing Agreement by such companies.

Other recognised investment exchanges

2.6.6   Other RIEs under the FSA include:

LIFFE – the London International Financial Futures Exchange
LTOM – the London Traded Options Market (which is part of the ISE).

The various London commodities exchanges are also RIEs, as are two overseas exchanges – NASDAQ in the USA and the Sydney Futures Exchange – and an independent options market, OM Ltd.

2.6.7   Each RIE has its own rules regulating the way transactions are executed and reported by its members. However, some of the above exchanges are not responsible for overseeing the *settlement* of transactions dealt on the exchange. For example the International Commodities Clearing House Limited (ICCH) operates a clearing house for LIFFE. ICCH is also regulated by the SIB, under the FSA, as a 'recognised clearing house'. The role of the ICCH is discussed in more detail in chapter 18.

2.7   Exemptions from authorisation

2.7.1   To conclude this chapter, we discuss briefly two exemptions from the need for investment businesses to obtain authorisation that are relevant to firms operating in the securities industry.

Listed money-market institutions

2.7.2   The first special exemption from the need for authorisation applies to money-market institutions which are included on the list maintained by the Bank of England under section 43 of the FSA. These 'listed institutions' are, instead, regulated by the Bank of England under rules set out in the 'Grey Book' issued jointly by the Treasury and the Bank (last revised in April 1988). A listed institution is exempted from the FSA in respect of any transaction which is a wholesale money-market transaction, as defined in the 'Grey Book'.

2.7.3   This definition is, in some respects, wider than the FSA definition of investment transaction and includes:

— sterling wholesale deposits;
— foreign currency wholesale deposits;
— foreign exchange;
— gold and silver bullion;
— short-term certificates of deposit, local authority and other public sector debt (but not gilts);
— options or futures on the above;
— forward rate agreements, interest rate swaps and similar contracts.

2.7.4   The transactions must be with another listed institution, or be in 'wholesale size' – above £100,000 (or with underlying value above £500,000 in the case of futures, options and similar trans-actions). However, smaller transactions are permitted with a counterparty who has previously dealt in wholesale size with that listed institution.

2.7.5 The Bank of England expects all participants in the wholesale money market to apply for 'listed' status even if they do not need exemption from the FSA – for example, if they are already a member of TSA. In such cases, the listed institution may choose whether to comply with TSA's capital requirements or those of the 'Grey Book' in relation to its wholesale market transactions.

Authorised representatives

2.7.6 Another important exemption, under section 44 of the FSA, is for appointed representatives. An appointed representative is a self-employed person who arranges investment business on behalf of his principal. The most frequently quoted examples are of sales forces in some life assurance companies or of unit trust managers, where the salesmen are not employed by the principal company but are under contract to procure business for it. Being self-employed, the representatives would require separate authorisation if the section 44 exemption were not available.

2.7.7 Another important example of the application of this exemption are the associates or 'half-commission men' working for some firms of broker-dealers. These associates are not employed by the firm but have a formal arrangement whereby the associate obtains business for the firm from his list of customers; in exchange the firm provides dealing facilities and pays the associate a share of the commission it charges (traditionally 50 per cent, hence the phrase 'half-commission men', although considerable variations in individual arrangements are found).

2.7.8 The principal firm is responsible for ensuring that its appointed representatives comply with all the relevant requirements of the conduct of business rules; the contract with the representative must, to comply with section 44, enable the principal to restrict the type of business carried on by the representative.

2.7.9 This exemption is also occasionally used by an authorised firm to enable subsidiary companies to carry on investment business without each requiring separate authorisation. However, the investment business that an appointed representative may carry on is narrower in scope than that possible under full authorisation. The representative is only permitted to arrange deals between his customers and his principal or other investment firms, and to provide advice on such transactions.

2.8 Other relevant statutes and regulations

2.8.1 Many other statutes and regulations impact upon the business of a securities firm. The more significant are discussed briefly below.

The Takeover Code

2.8.2 The City Code on Takeovers and Mergers (usually known as the Takeover Code) governs the conduct of all participants in a takeover of a 'Plc' in the UK, whether or not the Plc is actually listed on the ISE. Its importance is discussed further in chapter 20. Whilst the Takeover Code originally had no statutory backing, the SROs have now incorporated a requirement for their members to comply with the Code, and prohibit knowingly acting for any other person (whether authorised or not) who fails to comply with the Code.

2.8.3 As well as governing conduct during a takeover, the Code sets out the circumstances in which one company acquiring shares in another is obliged to launch a full takeover bid.

Companies Act requirements for notification of interests in shares

2.8.4 Further protection for companies against unwanted takeovers is provided in the shareholding disclosure requirements of sections 198–220 of the Companies Act 1985. Any shareholder, or group of connected shareholders, holding in excess of 3 per cent of a public company must, within two days, notify the company of their holding. This also applies to beneficial holders of shares held via nominees. In addition, the company may, under section 212 of that Act, require any shareholder on the register to disclose whether he is holding the shares on his own behalf or for another and, if the latter, to identify that other. Listed companies frequently use section 212 notices to try to identify potential stake-building in the company under nominee names. Broker-dealers and investment managers, in addition to ensuring that notification is given of large holdings, must also respond to section 212 notices addressed to their nominee companies or to their clients.

Money laundering

2.8.5 There is a growing international consensus that money laundering of funds from any illicit source should be countered by concerted international action.

2.8.6 The Drug Trafficking Offences Act 1986 contains provisions making it a criminal offence to assist in any way in the investment, or transfer of funds, or other transactions relating to the proceeds of drug trafficking. Those involved in any aspect of the financial markets must, therefore, be on their guard against this possibility, and ensure that they make sufficiently detailed enquiries about prospective customers.

2.8.7 Similar provisions are contained in the Prevention of Terrorism (Temporary Provisions) Act 1989 in relation to funds for terrorist organisations.

Codes of practice

2.8.8 Several codes of practice are issued by the ISE, Bank of England and the SIB. Although these do not have regulatory force, they are regarded as indicative of the expected standards to be followed in the market. These codes include:

- Equity market makers
- Wholesale markets in sterling, foreign exchange and bullion.

Misleading statements and practices

2.8.9 Section 47 of the FSA makes it an offence for anyone (whether authorised or not) to make any statement which is misleading or false, in relation to investment transactions or to engage in any course of conduct intended to give a false impression as to the market price of an investment.

International regulation

2.8.10 The securities industry is becoming increasingly international and few firms in the industry are able to ignore regulatory requirements imposed by countries where counterparties or customers of the firm are located. For example, the USA imposes its own rules on the sale of investments to US citizens, and authorisation by an SRO may not be sufficient to carry on business with the USA.

2.9 The proposed EC investment services directive

2.9.1 As part of the EC legislation process towards achieving the Single European Market from 1992, the draft Investment Services Directive is currently proceeding through the European Parliament.

2.9.2 This directive will enable an investment business authorised in one member state to operate in any other, without requiring further approval from the 'host' country – an arrangement known as the 'passport' concept. Minimum standards for authorisation will be established.

2.9.3 Capital requirements for such businesses are set out in a second directive, currently also in draft – the Investment Services Capital Adequacy Directive. Whilst this sets up a capital adequacy framework similar to that in the UK under the FSA, significant changes from the actual levels of capital required may be expected.

2.9.4 Whilst capital adequacy will be monitored by the investment firm's home country, it will be subject to the conduct of business rules of the host country. There are presently no provisions in the directives for harmonising these rules; thus a firm carrying on business in more than one EC country will be subject to different conduct of business rules in each country. However, it is expected that economic and commercial pressures will lead to a convergence of these rules.

2.9.5 Investment firms which are also banks will, it seems, be able to operate throughout the EC under the provisions of the Second Banking Directive. This directive originated the 'passport' concept adopted by the Investment Services Directive, whereby a bank authorised in one member state needs no further approval to be able to operate throughout the EC. However, the substantial differences between banking supervision and investment business regulation will lead to complex interaction between the banking and investment services directives.

2.9.6 A number of other EC directives and proposed directives are also of relevance to firms in the securities industry, including an Insider Trading Directive making insider trading a criminal offence throughout the EC (largely on the lines of current UK legislation); and the UCITS Directive, permitting the marketing throughout the EC of UCITS (or undertakings for collective investments in transferable securities) which are authorised in a single member state.

3 Financial Regulations and the Role of the Auditor

3.1 Introduction

3.1.1 The section of an SRO's rules which is of prime relevance to the auditor of an authorised firm is the financial regulations. Although the rules of each SRO cover much the same ground, the detailed requirements differ from one SRO to another, and the auditor must have a thorough understanding of the regulations applicable to his audit client. The main areas covered in each SRO's financial regulations are:

3.1.2 *Accounting records* – the requirements are more detailed, wider in scope, and generally require records to be much more up-to-date than the equivalent requirements of the Companies Act.

3.1.3 *Clients' money and asset rules* – which require the segregation of money held on behalf of clients in client bank accounts separate from the firm's own money; and similar segregation of clients' investments and other property held in safe custody from the firm's own assets.

3.1.4 *Capital adequacy* – which comprise complex rules for calculating an authorised firm's capital requirement and its qualifying capital available to meet the requirement, to ensure that it has sufficient resources commensurate with the type and scale of business carried on. This capital test must be satisfied *at all times*, not merely at the year-end or other reporting dates during the year.

3.1.5 *Regular financial returns* – which must be submitted to the SRO showing that the capital adequacy test has been met, and giving further information to enable the regulators to monitor the firm's compliance with financial regulations; there are tight deadlines for submission of these returns.

3.1.6   *Audited annual financial statements* – which are distinct from the statutory financial statements and must be in a form complying with the SRO's rules. These must be submitted to the SRO within a time limit, usually three or four months after the year-end, depending on the SRO; in addition to giving an opinion on the truth and fairness of the balance sheet and profit and loss account, the audit report must include opinions on compliance with certain other financial regulations and with the client money and client asset rules.

3.1.7   *Notification rules* – under which the firm is obliged to notify the SRO immediately of any breach of the financial rules such as a shortfall of qualifying capital below its capital requirement, the inability to reconcile its client money account, or where the auditor intends to qualify his report. Other matters such as a proposed change of auditor are also to be notified.

3.1.8   The next section examines the financial regulations in more detail; to avoid confusion, this deals with only one SRO, TSA, which is generally the most relevant to the securities industry. However, it should be noted that the overall impact of the rules of the other SROs is similar. The final section of this chapter sets out the principal aspects of the auditor's role, his rights and responsibilities, and is applicable to the auditors of members of any SRO or the SIB.

3.2   TSA financial regulations

3.2.1   The financial regulations of TSA are contained in chapter III of its rulebook.

Accounting records and controls (rule 20)

3.2.2   The member firm must maintain up-to-date records describing all transactions, receipts and payments and movements of share certificates and other documents of title; these must be sufficient to enable management to:

   (a) identify, quantify, control and manage all risk exposures (and must contain formal exposure limits authorised by management to enable this to be done);
   (b) make timely and informed decisions;
   (c) monitor the performance of all aspects of the business on an up-to-date basis;
   (d) monitor the quality of the firm's assets; and

(e) safeguard those assets, including assets held on behalf of customers and others.

The records must also *at any time* disclose with reasonable accuracy the financial position of the member firm and demonstrate compliance with the capital requirements, and must enable returns to be completed accurately and submitted to TSA within the timescale permitted.

3.2.3 The rules do not specify how quickly transactions must be entered in the records nor how instantly compliance with the capital requirements, at a specified time, need be capable of being proved. However, it is clear that TSA expect broker-dealers and market makers to have a reasonably accurate daily indication of their capital adequacy position, and to be able to make more detailed calculations within two or three working days. The capital requirement resulting from market-making positions and other positions in investments must be monitored at all times (i.e. during the course of each day), since the capital requirement will change with every transaction entered into and also with changes in the market value of the investment positions held.

3.2.4 The member firm is also required to establish adequate systems of internal control, and to document all accounting systems and internal controls. Although the rules themselves give no indication of the level of detail of the documentation that is required, TSA issued draft guidance in November 1989 (Board Notice 152) and is expected to confirm this guidance, in an amended form, shortly. The draft guidance states that the documentation of accounting systems should provide an overview of how accounting information is captured from primary documents, validated and incorporated in the balances subsequently disclosed in the financial reporting statements. The documentation of internal controls should focus on the key manual and computer procedures and controls designed to safeguard the assets, to ensure that all transactions are authorised and are accurately recorded and to maintain the integrity of the records and the prevention of their unauthorised alteration or destruction. Relatively minor systems need not be covered. An organisation chart, identifying those responsible for each individual function, should also be maintained.

Clients' money and clients' property

3.2.5 The rules regarding clients' money are dealt with in detail in chapter 11 and those covering safe custody of client property (such as share certificates and other documents of title) are discussed in chapter 12. The fundamental principle is that all clients' assets must be held in such a way that they are clearly separated from the firm's own assets and not mixed with them. Clients' money must be held in specially designated client bank accounts, and there are detailed rules governing what may or may not be paid into, or out of, these accounts. Further rules apply to money received and held in the course of settling client bargains. Detailed records and regular reconciliations are required to demonstrate that the rules are being complied with.

3.2.6   Clients' share certificates that are not registered in the client's own name must be held in designated accounts with approved custodian banks, or else in the firm's nominee name segregated from the firm's own securities. Again, detailed records and reconciliations are required to ensure that no mixing occurs between clients' securities and those belonging to the firm.

Capital adequacy

3.2.7   The relevant details of TSA's capital adequacy requirements are discussed in the chapters dealing with specific aspects of investment business. In summary, the capital requirement has three elements: the base requirement, the position risk requirement (PRR), and the counterparty risk requirement (CRR). Less stringent and simpler rules apply to two special categories of TSA members, corporate finance advisory firms and venture capital firms (rules 110 and 111).

Base requirement (rule 61)

3.2.8   The base requirement is, broadly, equivalent to three months' expenses of the authorised firm; on the basis that this would enable the firm to cease trading and close down its business in an orderly fashion without becoming insolvent. It is based on the total expenses shown in the firm's last audited annual accounts, although certain expenses may be excluded from the calculation. There is an absolute minimum figure for most types of firm of £10,000.

Position risk requirement (PRR) (rule 62)

3.2.9   The position risk requirement is a measure of the risk inherent in any position in investments held by the member firm – that is, any situation in which the member firm is exposed to the risk of price movements in an investment. This subject is dealt with in more detail in chapter 14.

3.2.10   The simplest calculation for equities and debt securities is a percentage (which varies with the type of security) of the current value of each position, whether long or short, aggregated over all securities positions to give the total PRR. However, more complex methods are permitted which reduce the PRR to take account of the hedging and portfolio effects of holding positions in a range of different securities. Additional PRR is required to recognise the risk inherent where substantial positions are held in a single security.

3.2.11   Additional PRR calculations apply to positions in other investments, including options, futures and interest rate swaps. A PRR is also calculated on the overall foreign currency exposure of the firm.

3.2.12   The position risk requirement will change as a result of both transactions in investments and changes in the market value of positions held. This capital requirement must, therefore, be monitored continuously, requiring complex computer systems for recording and evaluating dealing for market makers and other active principal dealers.

Counterparty risk requirement (CRR) (rule 63)

3.2.13   The CRR is intended to be a measure of the capital required to reflect the credit risk of default by a counterparty. Although its basis of calculation is complex, it can nevertheless only represent a broad estimate of this risk. This subject is dealt with in more detail in Chapter 10.

3.2.14   In respect of both 'market' and 'client' counterparties for normal securities transactions, a CRR does not usually arise until settlement has remained outstanding for fifteen, or in many cases, thirty days after the due settlement date. For counterparties (both debtors and creditors), where payment is made against delivery of stock, the CRR is a percentage of the loss the firm would suffer if it had to 'buy in' or 'sell out' the stock, based on the current market value of the stock in question. The percentage increases the longer settlement is delayed, up to 100 per cent by ninety days after the due settlement date.

3.2.15   For counterparties who do not settle against delivery of stock, but who are expected to settle the balance on their account at the end of each Stock Exchange dealing account, the CRR is the full amount of any debit balances outstanding for more than thirty days since settlement was due. The firm may, however, offset the value of any shares held as collateral. A CRR also arises on credit items outstanding for more than thirty days representing sold bargains where the customer has not delivered the stock certificates. The CRR in this case is a percentage of the exposure (the excess of the stock value over the monetary credit balance still due to the customer in respect of that bargain), increasing to 100 per cent depending on the age of the original bargain. Generally, debits and credits on the same customer account may be offset and regarded as settled, except that no offset is allowed against a credit item which the firm believes arises from a short sale by the customer.

3.2.16 Further rules apply to options dealing, foreign currency transactions, stock lending and borrowing, interest rate swaps and other types of transaction.

3.2.17 In order to comply with TSA's present accounting rules, the member firm must be able to monitor significant changes in its CRR daily, and calculate CRR accurately if required at the close of business on any day. This requirement places very significant burdens on the accounting systems of member firms; in order to calculate CRR relating to any bargain, details of both cash movements and stock movements are required. For all but the smallest operations, this can only be carried out efficiently if a computerised, integrated stock–accounting system is used, with details of stock due to and from the member firm, and subsequent stock movements, being recorded on the same computer system as cash balances and movements. The internal disciplines over completeness and accuracy of stock entries must be as rigorous as for cash items.

Qualifying capital (rule 50)

3.2.18 The member firm must, at all times, have an excess of qualifying capital over its total capital requirement.

3.2.19 Qualifying capital consists of share capital and reserves (or, in the case of a partnership, the net aggregate balances on partners' accounts); in addition, long-term subordinated loans and bank or group company guarantees can be treated as qualifying capital provided they meet TSA's requirements (and in some cases only with specific TSA approval). Qualifying short-term subordinated loans may be used to meet only the PRR and CRR elements of the total capital requirement, and undrawn subordinated loan facilities may be used to meet only that part of the PRR and CRR that arises from issuing market operations (that is, transactions relating to the issue of securities, which are discussed in more detail in chapter 20).

3.2.20 All intangible assets and most types of fixed or unmarketable assets must be deducted from qualifying capital, together with various categories of debtors which are not covered by the CRR calculations.

3.2.21 A gearing restriction also applies under which at least 20 per cent of total qualifying capital must be in the form of share capital and reserves, after deducting intangible assets, thus limiting the amount of qualifying subordinated debt which can be employed.

Financial statements and returns

3.2.22 Member firms (other than those carrying out certain restricted activities) must submit the following financial statements and returns to TSA within the time limits stated.

	Number of reports per year	Time limits
Audited annual financial statements	1	3 months
Annual reporting statement	1	3 months
Quarterly reporting statement	4	20 business days
Monthly reporting statement	8	10 business days unless otherwise agreed with TSA*
Monthly position risk statement	12	10 business days** unless otherwise agreed with TSA*
Fortnightly position risk summary	24	2 business days

* *TSA will not agree a time limit of more than 17 business days.*
** *20 days in the case of the monthly position risk statements coinciding with quarterly reporting statements.*

3.2.23 The audited annual financial statements submitted to TSA within three months of the balance sheet date are similar in format and content to the financial statements required under the Companies Act. Although TSA does not require member firms which are companies to submit their actual Companies Act financial statements for this purpose, in practice most firms will prepare a single set of financial statements, meeting both TSA and Companies Act requirements, any additional information required solely for TSA purposes being removed before the financial statements are filed with the Registrar of Companies.

3.2.24 The annual and quarterly reporting statements include a full profit and loss account, balance sheet and calculation of capital requirements and qualifying capital. The monthly reporting statement is similar, but omits the profit and loss account and detailed balance sheet. The monthly position risk statement is a detailed calculation of all elements of the position risk requirement, whereas the fortnightly position risk

27

summary shows the position risk requirement calculated for each type of investment, but without the supporting calculations.

3.2.25　The format of the annual reporting statement is identical to the quarterly reporting statement, but is submitted at the same time as the audited annual financial statements. It, therefore, takes into account any adjustments that come to light in the preparation of those financial statements and as a result of the audit.

3.2.26　The member firm must prepare a reconciliation showing all adjustments from the last quarterly return of the year (coinciding with the balance sheet date) to the annual reporting statement, and between that annual reporting statement and the audited financial statements.

Accounting principles

3.2.27　The annual financial statements must be drawn up following the accounting principles and rules of schedule 4 to the Companies Act 1985 (even if the member firm is not a company), and UK SSAPs, and must give a true and fair view of the result for the period and the state of affairs at the end of the period. In addition, transactions must be accounted for so as to reflect their substance and financial reality, and not merely their legal form. All foreign currency balances must be translated into sterling using closing mid-market exchange rates or, where appropriate, the rates of exchange under related forward contracts.

3.2.28　Additional accounting rules apply to the financial returns made to TSA but need not be adopted in the audited, annual financial statements. These additional rules include:

(i)　use of a trade date rather than settlement date basis of accounting;
(ii)　accounting for all investment positions on a mark-to-market basis, using a prudent approach to assessing market value and following specific methods set out in the rules;
(iii)　the inclusion of all counterparty balances on a gross rather than netted basis; the only netting permitted is where balances with the same counterparty can be settled net under an express written agreement; and
(iv)　accounting for 'repos' (or stock repurchase agreements), and stock lending and borrowing as financing transactions rather than as sales and subsequent repurchases of stock.

3.2.29　It will normally be appropriate for these policies to be adopted in the audited financial statements, with the exception of (ii) since marking to market is not generally considered an appropriate accounting policy for investments held other than as part of a market-making book or actively traded portfolio. This is discussed in more detail in chapters 4 and 14.

3.3 Auditors and audit reports

3.3.1 Every member of TSA (whether a company or an unincorporated business) must appoint an auditor. To be eligible to act, the auditor must be a member of one of the following bodies:

- The Institute of Chartered Accountants in England and Wales
- The Institute of Chartered Accountants of Scotland
- The Institute of Chartered Accountants in Ireland
- The Chartered Association of Certified Accountants.

and must be independent of the member firm. TSA may also call upon the auditor to demonstrate that he has the appropriate knowledge and experience to carry out the audit of a member firm.

3.3.2 TSA requires the member firm to obtain a letter of engagement from the auditor setting out the terms of his appointment. The auditor must be given access to any accounting and other records he requires, and be given all information or explanations he considers necessary. The auditor must also be authorised, in the engagement letter, to provide any information to TSA it may request and to communicate to TSA details of any matter relevant to TSA's regulatory functions. An example of a suitable engagement letter is shown at appendix II to this book.

3.3.3 The auditor is also specifically required to make at least two visits to the member firm before making his report. The first visit must be during the year under audit, and must include a review of the member firm's accounting records and systems of internal control. Both visits must be followed by a meeting with management to discuss the points that have arisen, unless the auditor confirms in writing that no significant matters for discussion have arisen. The rules also require further meetings between the management of the member firm and its auditors to discuss the implications of any systems changes made by the member firm; in practice, it is helpful to discuss proposed as well as actual changes.

3.3.4 Rules 90.03 and 90.04 set out the matters on which the auditor is required to report. An example of an unqualified audit report on a TSA member firm is shown in appendix I. Exhibit 1 to this chapter sets out the documents that will usually be submitted to TSA as the financial accounts package.

3.3.5 The auditor of a corporate member firm must bear in mind the distinction between the annual financial statements submitted to TSA and the financial statements required by the Companies Act. Although the two sets of financial statements will be very similar and, in some cases, identical, they are formally separate documents. Similarly, the auditor makes two distinct reports, one to the members and one to TSA.

3.3.6 The matters on which the auditor is required to report can be divided into two groups; those which are essentially the same as matters covered explicitly or implicitly in a Companies Act audit report; and those that are specific to TSA audit reports. The first category, which we will refer to below for convenience as the 'statutory report', includes:

(a) whether the auditor has received all the information and explanations required for the purposes of his audit;
(b) whether the financial statements give a true and fair view of the state of affairs and results for the year;
(c) whether proper returns have been received from branches not visited by the auditor; and
(d) whether the financial statements are in accordance with the accounting records.

The second category, to which we refer for convenience as the 'regulatory report' includes:

(a) whether proper accounting records have been maintained (to be interpreted in the context of TSA's strict accounting record requirements and therefore going beyond the normal Companies Act audit opinion);
(b) the adequacy of systems for agreement and reconciliation of balances and securities positions with banks, counterparties and clearing houses;
(c) the adequacy of systems for the safe custody and control of title documents;
(d) the adequacy of procedures for investigating old counterparty balances;
(e) the adequacy of procedures for monitoring counterparty and position risk;
(f) the adequacy of systems for dealing with clients' money and client property, and the member firm's compliance with the requirements of the related rules at the balance sheet date.

30

(g) whether the calculations of the total capital requirement and qualifying capital have been properly prepared;

(h) whether the calculation of adjusted annual expenditure (on which the capital requirement for the forthcoming year will be based) is correct; and

(i) whether the reconciliation of the audited financial statements, via the annual return, to the year-end quarterly return has been properly prepared.

3.3.7   It should be noted that some firms of auditors add wording to amplify the audit report opinions in respect of the adequacy of systems and internal control (chapter 4, paras 4.6.16 to 4.6.19). This is illustrated in the specimen audit report in appendix 1.

3.3.8   The member firm itself must carry out an annual review of its accounting systems and internal controls and confirm to TSA, within five months of the balance sheet date, that the systems and controls are adequate and comply with the requirements of the rules. The member firm must at the same time state whether or not it has received a management letter from its auditors commenting on the auditors' review of systems and controls. If such a letter has been received, the firm must confirm to TSA that all recommendations made by the auditors are being put into effect or have been agreed by the auditors as not being essential. The auditors should ensure, therefore, that any management letter is sent to the member firm early enough to allow proper consideration before the above report to TSA is made. It is also helpful if the management letter distinguishes between those recommendations that the auditor considers essential for the systems to be regarded as adequate, and those that are of less importance, or concerned with improving efficiency.

3.3.9   As discussed in chapter 2, the auditor is not required to consider the member firm's compliance with the conduct of business rules except to the extent that breaches may impact upon the financial statements. Examples of this might be claims by clients for losses suffered as a result of a breach of the rules; fines imposed by the SRO; and, in extreme cases, the going concern implications of the business being curtailed or suspended by the exercise of an SRO's intervention or disciplinary powers.

3.4 The role of the auditor

3.4.1   As discussed above in relation to TSA, the auditor is required to express opinions on the quality of systems and compliance with rules, in addition to the statutory report on the member firm's financial statements. Similar considerations apply to all SROs, since every authorised firm (except for category A FIMBRA members) must have an auditor whose reporting responsibilities extend beyond the normal Companies Act requirements.

3.4.2 The auditor should also be aware of certain other factors which substantially affect the role and responsibilities of the auditor of an authorised firm.

3.4.3 The SROs have a duty under the FSA to monitor their members in order to ensure that they continue to be 'fit and proper' under the terms of their membership, and to take prompt action to protect the interests of investors where necessary. The SROs regard the auditor as an essential element in the process of monitoring the financial aspects of the 'fit and proper' test and they place great reliance on an unqualified audit report.

3.4.4 Three significant differences in the regulatory structure from that applying to audit reports under the Companies Act must also be borne in mind. Firstly, the report is not available to the public since only the authorised firm itself and the regulatory authorities will have access to it. Additional detail may, therefore, be given to amplify a qualification which might not always be appropriate in the statutory audit report.

3.4.5 Secondly, the regulatory report contains a number of separate opinions on different aspects of the financial regulations, and some rule breaches will be more significant than others. However, it is for the SRO rather than the auditor to assess the significance of a breach of rules, since the auditor only reports on compliance, or otherwise, with the rules. Thus some audit qualifications will be of lesser importance than others, but cannot be omitted on these grounds alone.

3.4.6 Thirdly, a qualification in the regulatory audit report will often not be the only communication between the authorised firm, its auditors, and the regulator, particularly where serious rule breaches have occurred. The authorised firm will usually have been obliged to notify the SRO under its notification rules in advance of the submission of the audit report; and the SRO will often wish to investigate matters in more depth either by its own enforcement staff or through a detailed report from the auditors or another firm of accountants appointed for the purpose of a special enquiry. The audit report is thus often merely a formal record of matters of which the SRO is already aware, and into which further investigation has been or will be made.

3.4.7 It is often in an authorised firm's best interest to establish an informal dialogue with its SRO, involving its auditor as appropriate, as soon as a major problem develops, rather than maintaining a strictly formal stance. This can help to convey a willingness to resolve the difficulty, and the SRO may be persuaded that it is unnecessary to respond with formal disciplinary and enforcement procedures. Nevertheless, care should be taken that the authorised firm's position is not prejudiced should such formal procedures be subsequently initiated.

3.4.8 The auditor must also be mindful of the fact that, whilst the SROs are immune from damages (in the absence of bad faith) in connection with action they may have taken, or refrained from taking, in the event of an investment business subsequently collapsing, the auditor has no such protection. There will be instances, therefore, where the auditor will need to qualify his report even though he knows that the SRO is aware of the situation and intends taking no action.

Ad hoc reports under section 109 of the Financial Services Act

3.4.9 The auditor of an authorised firm has a right, overriding any duty of confidentiality he has to his client, to ensure that, if he becomes aware of some matter relating to an investment business, whether or not that business is his client, that is relevant to the regulators, the matter is reported promptly to the appropriate regulator.

3.4.10 Section 109(1) of the FSA sets out the right of the auditor to make such a report notwithstanding his duty of confidentiality, or any other duty, owed to his client. It also provides for the issue of rules or guidance by the auditing profession specifying the circumstances in which auditors should be expected to make such a report. Guidance has been issued in July 1990 by the Auditing Practices Committee of the CCAB in the form of Auditing Guideline 309 'Communications between auditors and Regulators under sections 109 and 180(1)(q) of the Financial Services Act 1986', which should be studied by the auditor of any investment business.

3.4.11 Section 109 sets out the following tests to be satisfied before the auditor may take advantage of its protection:
   (a) the auditor must be the auditor of an authorised business (although not necessarily of the person to which the information to be communicated relates – see section 109 (3));
   (b) the communication must be in good faith;
   (c) the information or opinion reported must relate to a matter of which the auditor has become aware in his capacity as auditor of that authorised person (but see below);

(d) if the regulator to whom the report is made is the SIB, the matter must relate to one of the SIB's functions under the FSA; and

(e) if the report is to an SRO, the matter must relate to either

    (i) the SRO's function of determining whether a person is 'fit and proper' (note that 'fit and proper' includes financial solvency, as well as competence and integrity – *see* chapter 2); or

    (ii) the SRO's function of monitoring compliance with its conduct of business rules.

3.4.12   It is not clear how condition (c) above which states that 'the auditor must have become aware of the matter in his capacity as auditor', is to be interpreted. A narrow interpretation might be that section 109 applies only to matters coming to the attention of the auditor whilst actively engaged in the audit of that client. However, the Audit Guideline suggests that all partners in the audit firm are to be regarded as being in the capacity of auditors from the date of appointment onwards, whether or not they are actually engaged on that client's audit. The Guideline thus suggests it would be prudent for the firm to ensure that all partners were aware of the need to be alert for possible reportable matters and to establish adequate systems of inter-office and inter-department communications to ensure that such matters are brought to the attention of the auditor. However, this is a difficult legal area and it is suggested that legal advice be sought before relying on Section 109 in these circumstances.

Circumstances in which an *ad hoc* report should be made

3.4.13   The APC Auditing Guideline sets out in paragraphs 29 to 39 the criteria for determining when the auditor should consider taking the initiative by making an *ad hoc* report and the procedures to be adopted. These are summarised below, but reference to the Guideline itself is essential when deciding whether particular circumstances justify the auditor taking the initiative and in deciding on the procedures to be followed.

3.4.14   The test to be satisfied before the auditor takes the initiative is that there must have been an adverse occurrence or adverse change in the circumstances of the business; or a change in the auditor's perception of an existing situation; this must either have given rise to a material loss (or indicated that a reasonable probability exists that a material loss may arise) or indicate that there is evidence of dishonesty, serious incompetence or a serious failure to observe rules and regulations for the conduct of the regulation business; and the auditor must consider that investors' interests might be better safeguarded if the SRO were aware of the position, even if only to organise protective action.

3.4.15 Circumstances that might give rise to a reporting situation include:

- the auditor becoming aware of a serious breach of the accounting records rules;
- the auditor discovering a failure to comply with the rules of the relevant Regulator which may have material consequences (e.g. accounting records not kept in accordance with the clients' money rules);
- the auditor forming an opinion that there is a serious breakdown or failure of accounting or internal control systems;
- the auditor forming an opinion that a previous or current financial return to the regulator is materially misleading;
- the auditor becoming aware that management do not intend to report a significant matter required under the notification rules;
- the auditor becoming aware that, as a result of losses, the authorised firm can no longer meet its capital adequacy requirements;
- the auditor believing that the authorised firm is on the point of financial collapse.

3.4.16 Before deciding that an *ad hoc* report must be made, the auditor should ascertain that the client has not already reported the matter to the regulator. The auditor should also consider whether the need to inform the regulator can be met by including the matter in the auditor's routine annual report.

3.4.17 It should be noted that, in almost all circumstances where an *ad hoc* report may be contemplated, the member firm will, itself, be under an obligation to report the matter to its SRO under the SRO's notification rules.

Procedures to be adopted in making an *ad hoc* report

3.4.18 In exceptional cases, such as where the auditor has cause to doubt the honesty, integrity or competence of the management of the authorised firm itself, or where the management are taking reckless or imprudent business decisions, it may be that the interests of investors would be prejudiced if the management of the authorised firm were given warning that the regulators were to be informed. In these rare circumstances, the auditor should report directly to the regulator without first raising the matter with his client. The auditor should also report direct to the regulator when speed is of essence and there is insufficient time to follow the procedures outlined below, for example if the business is about to cease being authorised.

3.4.19 In all other cases, however, the auditor will wish to act in a way that best preserves the professional relationship with his client. If a matter arises that the auditor believes may need reporting to the regulator, it is important that he first discusses it with his client, to ensure that he is aware of all relevant facts, and to suggest that the client himself should promptly report the matter to the regulator. In almost all situations, the client will have a clear obligation to make such a report under the notification rules of the SRO. If the client has reported the matter, through the usual channels, the auditor should obtain from the authorised business a copy of the notification to the regulator and a copy of the regulators' written acknowledgement, sufficient to establish that the matter has been properly reported.

3.4.20 If the client refuses to make this report, and the auditor believes, after full consideration of all the circumstances, that it is a matter which must be brought to the notice of the SRO and which cannot sensibly be addressed by the auditor submitting or accelerating his routine report, the auditor should (except in cases of extreme urgency) formally request, in writing, that the client report the matter to the regulator within a specified time, sufficient for the business to obtain appropriate advice, but short enough to ensure that the risk of damage is limited. If the client still refuses to make this report, or fails to do so within the specified period, the auditor should raise the matter with the non-executive directors or audit committee of the client, if any. If they take no action to ensure that the matter is reported, or in the absence of such directors or committee, the auditor should himself report the matter to the regulator.

3.4.21 It is essential for the auditor to assess the degree of urgency in the SRO being informed; this will vary according to the nature of the matter to be reported.

3.4.22 Where the client agrees to notify the SRO, the auditor must ensure that this is in fact done by inspecting a copy of the letter sent and the acknowledgement received from the SRO.

3.4.23 The auditor should also consider the implications of the matter for the routine annual report, whether an *ad hoc* report is made or not. The fact that a matter has already been reported to the regulator does not permit it to be omitted from the annual audit report.

3.4.24 The auditor must ensure that his decision will stand up to future examination on the following considerations:

- what he knew at the time;
- what he reasonably ought to have known in the course of his audit;

- what conclusions he should have drawn;
- what action he should have taken.

3.4.25   The audit firm should establish procedures whereby any decision on whether an *ad hoc* report should or should not be made should be taken in consultation with other partners not involved in the audit, if possible with securities industry experience, who can review the matter from a more detached viewpoint and ensure that the reasons for the decisions made are properly documented. Consideration should also be given to the need to take legal advice on the applicability of section 109 before any report is made.

Practical implications

3.4.26   The APC Guideline emphasises that the auditor need not extend the scope of his audit work solely with the aim of detecting matters that would lead to an *ad hoc* report.

3.4.27   In order to prevent delay in identifying any reportable matters, the auditor may, however, wish to check, as a matter of routine, at the commencement and completion of each visit of the audit team to the client's premises, that there are no obvious matters of which he should be aware and which have not already been reported to the SRO under its notification rules. This brief check might include confirming with the relevant officials that:

- all returns to the regulators have been submitted on time;
- that the capital requirement is met, both at the date of the last return and currently;
- that all ledger postings, ledger balancing, reconciliations and other checks are up-to-date and correct;
- that there have been no major breaches of conduct of business rules as far as the compliance officer is aware.

3.4.28   The auditor will also need to ensure that, if any potentially reportable matter comes to light, it is considered immediately by the partner responsible for the audit, who can decide on what further action is to be taken.

3.4.29   All staff employed on the audit of an authorised firm should be made aware of the circumstances in which an *ad hoc* report is required and the importance of bringing any such potentially reportable matter to the immediate notice of the manager and partner responsible for the audit. The audit partner will also need to be aware of any other work carried out for the authorised firm by other departments of his firm and to ensure that all those involved are aware of the need to keep the audit partner informed of any potentially reportable matters and any other matters relevant to the audit.

Information provided to the auditor by the SRO

3.4.30 Section 180(1)(q) of the FSA also permits the regulatory bodies to pass information to the auditor of an authorised person. The Guideline notes that the regulators will take the initiative in passing information if they believe it could significantly affect the form of the auditor's report or the way he carries out his reporting responsibilities. The auditor is entitled to assume, in the absence of such communication, that the regulator has no information of which the auditor should be aware in this context. There is no need, therefore, for the auditor to make a general enquiry of the regulator prior to completing his audit.

Exhibit 1
Contents of annual financial statements and associated information to be submitted to the Securities Association, for an Incorporated Member Firm

Report to the Securities Association

Financial statements in compliance with the Companies Act 1985

> Directors' report
>
> Auditors' report to the members
>
> Profit and loss account (not consolidated)
>
> Balance sheet
>
> Source and application of funds statement
>
> Accounting policies
>
> Notes to the accounts

Additional information required by Regulators in particular circumstances (e.g. TSA rule 30.01(h) and SIB Compensation of Investors rule 4.02)

Adjusted annual expenditure calculation

Reconciliation of audited financial statements with annual reporting statement

Reconciliation of annual reporting statement to quarterly reporting statement at balance sheet date

Annual reporting statement

Quarterly reporting statement at balance sheet date

4 The audit approach

4.1 Introduction

4.1.1   As the reader will already have appreciated, the business of a securities firm is in many ways extremely specialised, employing a variety of technical terms, unusual procedures and frequently an absence of the tangible output an auditor might expect from a manufacturing business. However, the basic purpose of the audit of a securities firm is no different from any other enterprise and the majority of audit techniques required for an effective audit will be familiar to any experienced auditor. Similarly, the auditor's duty to detect fraud within an investment business is no greater than in any other audit, although this is an area where public expectation is high and the auditor should be aware of any further professional guidance that may be forthcoming. He should also be aware of the greater opportunities that may exist for fraud in such businesses and therefore the risk that fraud may have a material impact on the financial statement.

4.1.2   Accordingly this chapter, and those that follow, are focused on those areas where different audit techniques are required for, or where the application of a standard technique needs a certain degree of guidance or modification for it to be applicable to, the circumstances of a securities firm.

4.2 The audit opinion

Statutory

4.2.1   Under the rules of each of the SROs, the auditor of any securities business is required to report on whether the accounts of the business drawn up for the reporting date give a 'true and fair view' of the state of affairs of the firm, together with various related matters such as receiving proper explanations, receiving returns from branches etc., which are broadly equivalent to the auditor's duties under the Companies Act 1985. The latter applies to UK companies only, while the SRO rules are applicable to *all* members of that SRO, whether or not the member is incorporated and whatever its nationality.

4.2.2   Since there is no difference between the SRO audit rules for incorporated or unincorporated entities, no distinction needs to be drawn between the two types of organisations for the purpose of reporting to the SRO. The auditor of a business which is a UK company will also need to issue a report to the members of the company, but this opinion should flow from the work carried out to support the 'regulatory' report given to the SRO.

Systems

4.2.3   The rules of each SRO require the auditor to review and report on various aspects of the firm's systems, principally those for handling clients' money and property, although some SROs also require reports on systems for agreeing and reconciling balances with counterparties and monitoring investment positions and counterparty risk exposures. This requirement to report on systems is totally independent of whether or not the auditor would normally seek to place reliance on those systems, for the purposes of reaching his 'statutory' audit opinion, or has already decided that he cannot place such reliance on them. In consequence, therefore, the auditor needs to ensure that the scope of his work is sufficient for him to gain the audit evidence necessary to make these additional 'regulatory' reports.

4.2.4   TSA, in addition, requires auditors to 'review the firm's accounting records and systems of internal control' (TSA rule 80.01), without any limitations on the systems which should be examined. The results of this review do not have to be reported to TSA, although any shortcomings identified must be reported to, and discussed with, the firm's management. In turn, management must inform TSA if they have received a report from the firm's auditors containing recommendations on internal control and must state whether or not the recommendations are being implemented. It should be noted that TSA have the right to inspect any such management letter from the firm's auditor.

Regulatory reporting

4.2.5   In addition to reporting on various aspects of internal control, the auditor is also required to report on the computation of the regulatory capital adequacy at the balance sheet date together with other specific matters, such as compliance with the client money and property rules at the balance sheet date. SROs may also impose additional reports for particular categories of investment business.

4.2.6   In each of the chapters that follow, the audit work necessary to form these opinions will be discussed in the context of a particular activity or balance sheet heading.

4.2.7   To enable these various reporting requirements to be considered in context, appendix I sets out pro-forma unqualified reports suitable for submission to each of the SROs.

4.3   Knowing the client's business

4.3.1   As for the audit of any business, the auditor will need to ensure that he understands the business areas in which his client operates, so that he can plan and carry out an effective and efficient audit. This understanding should encompass the operational structure of the firm as well as the systems used by the firm to record and process transactions.

4.3.2   The auditor will also need to take steps to ensure that he is aware of any recent or forthcoming developments in the industry which may affect his work, such as the move to 'dematerialisation' expected to occur in 1991 and 1992.

4.4   Planning, controlling and recording the audit

4.4.1   The guidance given by the Auditing Guideline, 'Planning, controlling and recording', is wholly relevant to the conduct of an audit of a securities business. The auditor should also have regard to the draft Auditing Guideline, 'The implications for auditors of the Financial Services Act 1986', published as an exposure draft in February 1988 which gives guidance on a number of issues relating to the audit of investment businesses.

Planning

4.4.2   As discussed above, the auditor is required to express opinions on a number of matters that extend beyond what would normally be needed to express a 'statutory' audit opinion. It is essential that all such reporting requirements are carefully considered at the planning stage to ensure that the necessary audit work is carried out in an efficient manner. The use of the relevant SRO model report (appendix I), as a checklist will be helpful to ensure that all aspects of the reporting obligations have been considered.

4.4.3 There are various other requirements of the SROs with which the auditor or the member firm must comply, namely:

- the audit report must be submitted to the SRO within either three or four months (depending on the SRO), of the period end;
- each SRO requires the firm to obtain from the auditor a written engagement letter setting out certain specific rights and duties of the auditor, which must be acknowledged in writing by the firm;
- TSA specifically requires the auditor to make two visits to the firm, one of which must be during the year (i.e. the conventional interim visit); other SROs allow the auditor to decide whether or not to make an interim visit.

Controlling and recording

4.4.4 In most cases, the auditor's normal procedures for controlling and recording his audit will be entirely appropriate to the securities business. However, it may well be the case that a standard audit file layout, appropriate for the average commercial client, will need amendment for use on a securities industry audit.

4.4.5 The auditor should be reminded, however, of the 'ad hoc' reporting requirements imposed by the Financial Services Act (chapter 3) and of the fact that each SRO has reserved the right to appoint a 'second auditor' to report to the SRO on the accounts or any other financial information submitted by a member. The SRO member is, furthermore, required to ask its own auditors to afford all possible assistance to the second auditor. This 'second audit' should not be seen necessarily as critical of the incumbent auditor, but can be used to investigate, for example, periodic returns submitted to the SRO that do not coincide with a financial year end. Nonetheless, it is important for the auditor of a securities firm to be conscious that his work may be subject to greater scrutiny by third parties and therefore, in particular, to make sure that all audit judgements are fully documented.

4.5 Materiality

4.5.1 In the context of the audit of a securities industry firm, there are a number of factors, in addition to those that are common to any audit engagement, that need to be taken into account in forming a judgement on what would constitute a material error.

(a) Typically, much securities business is transacted on an agency basis so that, for example, the purchase of shares on behalf of a customer results in a balance due from the customer, a balance due to the market maker, and only a small figure for commission (say 1/2 per cent) being credited to the profit and loss account. Thus errors which are material to the profit and loss account may be totally immaterial within the relevant balance sheet caption.

(b) As well as expressing a 'statutory' audit opinion to the SRO on the truth and fairness of the financial statements, the auditor must report on the proper calculation of both the firm's regulatory capital requirement and its actual regulatory capital at the period end and for some SROs, on the excess or deficiency of regulatory capital at that date. This reporting requirement constitutes an additional criterion for materiality since the regulatory capital excess could be a very low figure even where total profits and shareholders' funds are large. These circumstances might, therefore, require a much lower level of materiality, in order to isolate errors of measurement or analysis, than that adopted for 'statutory' audit purposes.

(c) Activity in the securities industry is potentially very volatile, with income and consequently profits often showing large variances from one period to the next.

4.5.2 Despite these difficulties, it is still essential for the auditor to make an initial estimate of materiality for the purposes of planning his audit, both in terms of what figures are to be subject to detailed audit testing, and for the sample sizes of such detailed testing.

4.5.3 In order to take account of these special circumstances, the auditor will normally start by setting the level of materiality to be used in planning and carrying out the audit by reference to forming his 'statutory' audit opinion. Of the four commonly used bases for determining materiality (turnover, profit before tax, total assets and shareholders' funds), the first two are likely to be inappropriate due to their high potential variability from one year to the next. The level of total assets is also unlikely to prove a satisfactory measure, because it may vary enormously from day to day. In addition, for an agency business, errors which are insignificant to a balance sheet caption could cause a material impact on the profit and loss account.

4.5.4 Similarly, shareholders' funds will tend to give an unhelpful solution because capital is frequently very small by comparison with both total assets and total revenue. Accordingly, the most useful measure will frequently be the total operating expenses of the business. This gives a broad measure of the absolute size of the business and generally provides a more consistent result from one period to the next than other parameters.

43

4.5.5   Given the relationship between balance sheet and profit and loss account, the auditor may wish to use two materiality measures, one for the profit and loss account, and a second for the balance sheet. It may be appropriate to use a multiple (say twenty times) of the profit and loss account materiality for use in testing for classification errors in the balance sheet.

4.5.6   There would normally be no change to these levels of materiality for the purposes of the auditor's report on capital adequacy, although it may be appropriate for the auditor to take account of the likely level of 'surplus' regulatory capital in determining planning materiality for this purpose. Thus, if the firm only has a small surplus over its minimum regulatory capital, and this situation is likely to persist for some time, then a lower level of materiality may be appropriate. However, if the year-end figure happens to be reduced, for example because of an unexpected level of counterparty risk requirement at the balance sheet date, it would not normally be necessary to reduce the level of materiality and consequently to perform significant extra testing. The level of regulatory capital surplus will also be relevant in determining whether errors identified during the audit require adjustment.

4.5.7   One final problem associated with materiality arises in the context of reporting on compliance with the client money and property rules at the period end, where all errors must be reported to the regulator except where they are 'trivial' and have been promptly rectified. This matter is considered in more detail in chapter 11 on 'Clients' Money'.

4.6 Audit evidence

4.6.1   It is necessary for the auditor to obtain relevant and reliable audit evidence sufficient to enable him to draw reasonable conclusions thereon. This will normally be accumulated from a combination of:

- an assessment of accounting systems and internal control;
- analytical review;
- other substantive tests.

4.6.2   The chapters which follow give specific guidance on the importance of each of these sources of evidence in the audit of particular business areas, as well as on particular audit techniques that may be relevant. One specific audit objective in each area, which has not been repeated in each chapter, in the interests of brevity, is that the auditor should ensure proper accounting records have been maintained. This assessment must have regard not only to the conventional requirements of the Companies Act, but also to the greater standards imposed by SROs as discussed in chapter 3. The significance and volume of cash and other flows of money within the securities industry means also that the auditor should review the controls over receipts and payments in respect of each area of the operations of the firm. The receipts and payments objective is considered in detail in paragraph 9.8.6 onwards of chapter 9 and has not been repeated in other chapters, but reference should be made as appropriate. In the remainder of this chapter, a number of general issues are discussed.

Internal controls

4.6.3 As discussed above, TSA imposes a requirement for the auditor to make two separate visits to the firm, the first of which 'shall be during the period subject to audit and shall include a review of the firm's accounting records and systems of internal control'. This requirement means that the auditor of a TSA member will need to look at all elements of the firm's control procedures, even if his initial assessment is that such controls will be too weak, or their operation inadequately documented or evidenced, to enable reliance to be placed upon them in forming his 'statutory' opinion.

4.6.4 Irrespective of the particular reporting requirements of the relevant SRO, the auditor will need to consider the firm's internal control structure in order to:

- determine the extent to which internal controls and compliance testing may be combined with, and reduce, substantive testing for the purposes of forming his 'statutory' opinion;
- meet specific regulatory reporting requirements.

Regulatory reporting on internal controls

4.6.5 The work necessary to meet regulatory reporting requirements arises because there are certain systems on which the auditor must report specifically to the SROs, as follows:

- the systems for complying with the client money and property rules;
- the systems for the safe custody, identification and control of documents of title;

together with (depending on the particular SRO), some or all of:

- the systems for the agreement and reconciliation of balances and securities positions with counterparties, banks and clearing houses;

45

- procedures and controls for reporting and investigating the ageing and analysis of balances with counterparties;
- procedures for monitoring the firm's investment position risk and counterparty risk exposures and providing appropriate levels of management with the information necessary for them to make relevant, timely and informed decisions to control such risks.

Assessment of internal controls

4.6.6   For the reasons set out in paragraph 4.6.5 above, it is important at an early stage of the audit to place a high priority on the assessment of internal control procedures, covering both clerical and computer systems. The two reasons advanced for considering internal controls should not be looked at in isolation. In particular, the assessment of controls for regulatory purposes can enable the auditor to identify controls on which he can rely and thereby reduce the level of substantive testing – or at least identify specific improvements to, or changes in, control procedures that would then enable reliance to be placed upon them.

4.6.7   It should be noted that, in the past, evidence for the effective application of internal controls within securities businesses has not been easy to obtain because of the tendency of many firms to rely on close personal supervision by partners and directors, rather than detailed reporting procedures. Whilst such supervision can be effective as a method of controlling a business, it is not simple to audit nor susceptive to the examination of objective documentary evidence, and it can be difficult to spot errors where supervision is in fact less than effective. The last few years have seen changes in the quality of internal controls and significant improvements in the way that they are demonstrated, particularly in the larger securities businesses. However, informality continues to be characteristic of the smaller owner-managed securities business.

4.6.8   There can be no prescriptive approach to assessing internal controls; the auditor should document the controls that are in existence and then assess their reliability and effectiveness according to the nature of the business. In documenting controls, the auditor may be able to make use of the documentation prepared by his client, for example to meet TSA or IMRO requirements for firms to prepare and maintain up-to-date documentation of their accounting procedures and controls.

4.6.9   As for any audit, the assessment of controls will need to encompass both the general control environment (which includes such matters as management's attitude to risk and control and the recruitment and training of quality staff) and the specific application controls that exist over a particular accounting procedure.

4.6.10 Because the auditor of a firm in the securities industry will be measuring the existence and effectiveness of many controls against pre-determined standards laid down in the SRO rulebooks, and because control procedures will tend to be broadly similar in all securities businesses of the same type, one approach to assessing controls which may prove effective is based on the use of Internal Control Questionnaires (ICQs) to assess both clerical and computer controls.

4.6.11 Such ICQs should be based on highlighting key control objectives in the various areas and then listing questions which should be addressed in assessing whether those objectives have been met. This approach is clearly only appropriate where the auditor has sufficient experience of the securities industry to formulate the appropriate questions. It is also important that ICQs are completed by senior members of the audit team with prior experience of the client or the industry sector, so that the responses given by the firm's staff can be properly assessed.

4.6.12 It is important that, whatever method of assessing controls is used, the process is completed as early as possible in the audit so that key control procedures can be identified and an assessment made as to whether they are strong enough for reliance to be placed on them. As well as noting controls upon which it is reasonable to rely, and thereby reduce substantive testing, the auditor should also note at this stage the controls that are in place to ensure that the systems for which a specific report is required are receiving satisfactory attentions from the firm.

Testing of controls

4.6.13 Where the auditor has identified control procedures upon which reliance can be placed for the purpose of reducing the substantive testing needed to form the 'statutory' opinions, he must design and carry out suitable tests to ensure that the controls were indeed operating on a satisfactory basis to justify that reliance.

4.6.14 Where the auditor is examining the systems in response to his regulatory reporting obligations, he must bear in mind that his opinions must address the operation of the relevant systems throughout the accounting period under review. They cannot, therefore, be restricted to the particular times when the auditor has carried out his tests of the systems. However, it will clearly be impractical to test the operation of systems on a continuous basis during the year and the auditor, therefore, needs to draw a proper balance between the costs of carrying out tests on procedures over an extended period and the requirements of the SRO. To this end, the auditor will need to examine the general control environment within his client and assess its effectiveness in ensuring the continuous operation of application controls.

4.6.15   It is in this context that the auditor must determine his level of testing of such systems. Given the general control environment in most securities businesses, and the poor cost-effectiveness of large scale tests of, for example, CRR calculations, testing of such systems will normally be confined to the selection of a small number of transactions for the purposes of 'walking through' the system and reviewing the existence of the appropriate reconciliations. This latter exercise will establish that the firm has carried out a calculation of CRR, client money, etc., with the necessary frequency, and the 'walk through' will confirm the basic mechanics of the system.

Reporting to the SRO on systems

4.6.16   The auditor must then decide on the appropriate wording for his report on systems, and the suggested wording of an unqualified report is included at appendix 1. It is designed to indicate to the reader the limitations inherent in all internal control systems and audit reports thereon, without being so verbose that it detracts from the clarity of the opinions being expressed.

4.6.17   It is clearly recognised by the rules of the SROs that the implementation and maintenance of proper systems of internal control is a duty imposed on the management of the firm. In carrying out this responsibility, management must make estimates of, and judgements on, the benefits and costs of particular control procedures and draw an appropriate balance between them. This is equally applicable in determining the procedures for safeguarding clients' money and assets.

4.6.18   The objectives of such internal control systems and the related pro-cedures are to provide management with reasonable, but not absolute, assurance that assets for which the firm has responsibility are safe-guarded against loss from misappropriation, unauthorised use or removal. Such systems are also designed to give management reason-able, but not absolute, assurance that transactions are executed in accordance with established authorisation arrangements and are recorded properly and comprehensively to permit the preparation of financial statements in accordance with statutory and regulatory requirements.

4.6.19   All systems of internal control and related procedures will, by their very nature, contain inherent limitations. For example, an individual charged with the responsibility for reviewing bank reconciliations each week may be distracted from his task on one particular occasion, and therefore fail to notice that an incorrect balance has been entered on the reconciliation. Similarly, for reasons of practicality and to enable an audit to be completed at a reasonable cost within the context of the requirement to determine whether the accounts give a true and fair view (which is not, of course, an absolute assurance), the auditor must restrict his tests on the operation of systems of internal control to their operation on certain occasions during the period. The auditor, therefore, may not test all aspects of a particular system at the same instant during the period. In consequence, errors or irregularities may occur and not be detected during the course of his normal audit work. Equally, there is the risk that systems which have been satisfactory at the time of the auditor's examination may subsequently become inadequate because of changes in conditions or because the degree of compliance with them may deteriorate. It is therefore important for these limitations to be referred to in the audit report.

Analytical review

4.6.20 The extent to which analytical review techniques can be used will depend greatly on the particular aspects of the securities business with which the firm is concerned and the extent to which it has developed good management information systems. For instance, the auditor of a firm operating in the fund management sector with stable charging structures may be able to obtain reliable audit evidence for the level of income by reference to the value of funds under management.

4.6.21 However, for brokerage and market-making business it is unusual to find relationships between figures being audited and other data which are sufficiently predictable for audit purposes and where the other data used for the predictions can be verified more easily by substantive testing than the figures subject to audit. Reasons for this include the fact that commissions and margins are negotiable on each deal, within wide parameters, and that volumes of business and therefore balance sheet totals vary significantly from day to day. This means that month-end or Stock Exchange account-end statistics (the only times when balance sheets are usually prepared), can be quite misleading as to the overall level of activity. The problems are even more pronounced for principal dealing businesses since, even if the dealing margin could be predicted, there are likely to be significant holding gains or losses on positions arising from market price fluctuations, both of the market as a whole and of individual securities.

Substantive testing

4.6.22   As indicated above, the level of the auditor's substantive testing will be determined by the amount of reliance that has been placed on internal controls. It is important to bear in mind though that securities businesses have large volumes of high value transactions, and are also responsible for assets belonging to their customers. Furthermore, the innovative nature of market practitioners often results in a wide variety of unusual transactions that cannot easily be brought within the normal control routines. Therefore, the auditor will normally have to carry out a comprehensive range of substantive tests even in cases where the internal control systems are reliable. Details of appropriate substantive tests are included in later chapters.

4.7   Computer aspects

4.7.1   The securities industry is one where the development of sophisticated computer systems has been an important management objective for many years; initially in the larger stockbroking and fund management groups but increasingly in the smaller advisory businesses. As a result, most of the accounting records are likely to be computerised, together with many of the control procedures, which may not, therefore, exist in 'hard copy' form.

4.7.2   Accordingly, the auditor must ensure that his audit approach recognises the importance of the computer and does not rely on the accuracy and reliability of its output without adequate testing. Other textbooks are readily available to explain the techniques of computer auditing, such as the review of the installation and application controls or the development of computer interrogation routines. Therefore, all that is attempted here is to alert the auditor to certain specific aspects affecting the audit of computer-based accounting systems within the securities industry. In particular, as with the audit of any business which uses sophisticated computer techniques and routines, the auditor of a securities business will need to involve appropriate computer specialists in his audit team, and to ensure a close liaison between those specialists and the rest of the team.

4.7.3   As discussed above, each SRO requires audit reports covering certain systems operated by the firm, while TSA requires a review of all controls. Accordingly, all aspects of the relevant system must be reviewed, not just those of a clerical nature. However, it will not be sufficient to examine only application controls within the particular systems since, unless there are also adequate general (or installation) controls (for example over program changes or access to data), the application controls could be circumvented. It will generally be appropriate for all aspects of the computer controls to be reviewed as a single exercise. It will also make for greater audit efficiency if the audit of the computerised elements and the audit of clerical procedures are closely integrated, not least to enable the auditor to be aware of the extent to which apparent weaknesses in computer processes are compensated for by clerical controls and vice versa.

4.7.4   The SROs also place considerable importance on the need for the accounting records of a firm to possess an 'adequate audit trail', which is defined in terms of being able to:

- trace any particular transaction through the system;
- produce relevant totals of individual balances and the items making up those totals;
- provide prompt access to any particular record.

4.7.5   These attributes must therefore be taken into account by the auditor when making his report on the maintenance of 'proper accounting records'. The auditor should pay particular attention to the procedures which can give rise to items being 'back-dated' or 'value-dated', not least because there is a general requirement that businesses should be able to produce accurate financial information as at any date. While SROs are not normally unreasonable with such a request, they can ask a firm to produce a full financial statement as at some recent past date which is not related to the firm's normal accounting reference date or its internal management accounting cycle.

4.8 Clearing firms

4.8.1   An increasingly common practice within the securities industry is the use of 'clearing firms' to handle back-office processing. This can provide considerable benefits in terms of risk-management, flexibility of costs, expertise, and range of services provided. At one end of the spectrum, the clearing firm will execute bargains, issue contract notes, settle bargains and provide all necessary working capital for the settlement process and may even take a degree of financial responsibility for any bad debts that may be experienced. At the other extreme, the clearing firm simply provides the clerical staff support to enable settlement to take place in much the same way as firms make use of a bureau for payroll production.

4.8.2   The different types of clearing firms and the services they offer are discussed in more detail in chapter 23. That chapter also discusses the roles and responsibilities of the introducing firm and the clearing firm together with the audit implications.

4.9 Reporting

Audit qualifications

4.9.1 Under the regulations of the SIB and the SROs, the firm is obliged to notify the relevant SRO once the auditors have decided to qualify their regulatory report (whether or not a qualification of the statutory audit report is involved). It is therefore important that the auditor should have a clear procedure for determining *when* he has actually decided to issue a qualified report. In many cases, this decision will not occur before the formal 'sign-off' of the qualification by the engagement partner.

4.9.2 Any procedure should recognise that, in certain circumstances, the decision to qualify cannot be made until the actual signing of the accounts, since until then it is possible for the directors to accept the auditor's views and amend the accounts (in the case of a disagreement), or for further audit evidence to become available (in the case of uncertainty).

4.9.3 By contrast, if the auditor identifies a failure to maintain adequate systems for, say, client's money where the SROs require such systems throughout the period, the decision to qualify his report will not be altered by subsequent rectification. The wording used in the qualified report will, of course, reflect the extent to which the failure has been rectified subsequently. Therefore, in cases where a systems failure is identified that is likely to lead to a qualification of the auditor's report to the SRO, the audit partner should be consulted immediately for a decision on whether qualification is in fact appropriate, rather than leaving the matter until the conclusion of the audit. It should be noted that a qualification may affect an audit report relating to the year subsequent to that currently being audited. For example, whilst carrying out audit work relating to the year ended 31 December 1989, the auditor may identify systems failures that existed during 1989 and were not rectified until later in 1990, resulting in qualification of the audit reports for both years.

4.9.4 In general, given the specific nature of the matters being reported on, it is likely that qualified reports to SROs will be much more frequent than qualifications on Companies Act accounts. Furthermore, it will generally be helpful to both the SRO and the audit client if the wording of any qualification is very specific as to the nature of the problem, and if some indication can be given of the remedial actions taken by the audit client. The SRO is likely to ask either the auditor or his client for further details of the matters giving rise to any qualification and these questions can be minimised by making disclosure in the report as full as possible.

Reporting under the Financial Services Act

4.9.5   The right of the auditor under section 109 of the FSA to notify regulators of matters that come to his attention during the course of an audit is discussed in chapter 3. As discussed in that chapter, it is important that the necessary procedures are in place within the audit firm, to ensure that any relevant matters are promptly brought to the attention of the engagement partner so that appropriate action can be taken. These procedures might include:

- briefing of all engagement staff prior to the start of the audit;
- inclusion in the audit planning document of any matters to which staff should be alert;
- in the first few days of the audit to carry out an initial overview of all areas to be audited, to ensure early awareness of any major problems such as a breakdown in accounting routines.

4.10 Accounting policies

4.10.1   Due to the specialised nature of the securities business, there are a number of areas where standard accounting practice is not readily applicable.

4.10.2   Most investment businesses which are limited companies will pre-pare their financial statements in compliance with schedule 4 to the Companies Act 1985, although those companies which are also banks or insurance companies will follow the rules in schedule 9. The schedule 4 formats are more appropriate for a manufacturing or trading company than a securities business, although there is generally little difficulty in adapting the headings to suit that type of business. Thus, for example, firms will usually refer to 'amounts due from market and client counter-parties' rather than 'trade debtors'.

Valuation of investments

4.10.3   A securities firm may hold investments for a variety of reasons. For example, the regulatory capital requirements not infrequently result in firms having capital funds that are not directly employed in the working capital needs of the business and which will be deployed in long-term investments. Firms involved in venture capital and corporate finance will often acquire stakes in new corporate ventures or other unlisted companies in need of equity finance, either as a long-term investment or with the intention of selling the shares when the new or re-financed venture has proved itself, such as when the company's shares are floated.

4.10.4   Securities firms will also invest on a short-term basis, perhaps to take advantage of a short-term market opportunity. Finally, market makers and other principal dealers buy and sell securities as an essential part of their trading business.

4.10.5   Investments held as fixed assets will normally be shown in the balance sheet at their acquisition cost rather than market value, although market value may be required for the financial reporting statements submitted to the SRO. Provision is only made for a diminution in value that is expected to be permanent. However, determining when a fall in value is to be regarded as permanent requires a considerable element of judgement.

4.10.6   The special case of fixed interest securities, such as gilts, where the intention is to hold until maturity, should be accounted for on a 'yield to maturity' basis, where the premium (or discount) in the purchase price above (or below) par is amortised over the remaining period to maturity.

4.10.7   Investments held as current assets, other than trading positions which are discussed below, are normally shown in the balance sheet at the lower of cost and market value, calculated on an individual basis.

Market makers and dealers

4.10.8   Greater difficulties arise in complying with schedule 4 in the case of market making and principal dealing companies, where the requirements of the schedule can conflict with a fair presentation of the financial statements. Some particular problem areas are considered below.

Valuation of securities positions
4.10.9   Where securities positions are held, not for investment purposes but as actively traded portfolios by a market maker or active dealer in those securities, whose purpose is to make profits from the fluctuation of market prices, the 'lower of cost or market' accounting

policy is no longer appropriate as a measure of performance in the accounting period, as it fails to show the true results of the trading activity.

10.10   Where the business of the company is to take advantage of short-term movements in security prices, these movements must be reflected in the profit and loss account as they occur, not deferred until the securities are subsequently sold. The original cost of the securities, and profits calculated only when the security is sold, are meaningless as far as the dealers are concerned and cannot be said fairly to represent the trading results for the period. Instead, an accounting policy of 'marking to market' should be adopted, whereby all positions (both long and short) in readily marketable investments should be valued at their market price at the accounting date, and the resulting gain or loss recognised in the profit and loss account.

10.11   This approach may not be appropriate for positions in investments for which there is no liquid market and no reliable quoted market price, unless such investments form only a small proportion of an otherwise liquid trading book.

10.12   Marking to market is becoming widely accepted as an appropriate accounting policy in such circumstances, and for a company acting as a market maker, or with a similarly high level of turnover, it is generally accepted that the resulting profits are 'realised' for the purposes of the Companies Act.

Options and futures positions

10.13   A similar mark to market approach will normally be appropriate for trading positions in financial futures and options. However, the valuation policy adopted for positions in such contracts will depend on whether they are being used to hedge another investment position, or are being used purely as a trading instrument.

10.14   If the underlying asset or liability being hedged is valued in such a way that profits or losses are taken immediately, then the hedging contract should be valued in a similar way. However, if profits or losses on the underlying instrument are deferred, so that it is shown at the lower of cost and market value, then the same policy should be adopted for the hedging instrument in order to ensure that, so far as possible, profits and losses on the two instruments are recognised over the same period.

10.15   Profits or losses on trading positions in futures and options, on the other hand, should normally be recognised immediately, by marking the positions to market. If a position is merely a short-term investment of

surplus funds, then it may be more appropriate to value it at the lower of
cost and market value.

Turnover

4.10.16 A further difficulty in complying with the Companies Act formats
concerns the presentation of the trading account. For a market maker,
the total proceeds of investments sold in the period is a largely
meaningless figure which is not generally readily available and is in any
event not regarded as 'turnover' in any commercial sense. Instead, most
market-making businesses regard turnover as comprising the gross
profits less losses derived from trading activities before deducting any
expenses. This is consistent with the Companies Act definition of
turnover, '... the amounts derived from the provision of goods or
services falling within the company's ordinary activities ...', since the
market maker is regarded as providing market-making services rather
than merely 'providing' shares. This view is also consistent with the
market maker's obligation to buy as well as sell at his quoted prices so
that it is the profits from trading, rather than the gross sale proceeds,
that are derived from the provision of market-making services.

Interest

4.10.17 An additional and related difficulty with the Companies Act formats
concerns the treatment of dividends and interest received and paid on
bull and bear positions respectively, together with interest payable on
borrowings used to fund positions. These are all elements of the gross
profit so far as the market maker is concerned and the true profit or loss
on a series of transactions can only be calculated after taking account of
them all. Thus, to treat them as 'other income' and 'interest and similar
charges' below the trading profit line in the profit and loss account
would misrepresent the true trading results of the business. It is
therefore general practice for market makers to take these items into
account in arriving at trading profit. In the case of interest charges,
however, it is important to distinguish between borrowings specifically
funding a trading position and those generally financing the business as a
whole. Interest paid on the latter should not be deducted in arriving at
trading profits but should be included under the format heading 'interest
payable and similar charges'.

EC Bank Accounts Directive

4.10.18 The EC Bank Accounts Directive was adopted in December 1986 and is
designed to impose a consistent format for the accounts of all banks and
similar entities based in the EC – similar to that already existing for
most companies through schedule 4 to the Companies Act 1985. The
Companies Act 1989 implements the Directive by making provision

for the necessary changes to schedule 9 to the Companies Act 1985 to be introduced by Statutory Instrument, which must be effective for all accounts in respect of accounting periods beginning on or after 1 January 1993.

10.19   The Department of Trade and Industry (DTI) published a document inviting comment on particular aspects of the Directive and the way in which it will be operated within the UK. Of particular interest to securities businesses is the suggestion by the DTI that the scope of the new requirement could be extended to include certain securities companies. Although this is not envisaged by the Directive, it is felt in certain quarters that the new banking company requirements will be less inappropriate for the accounts of a securities business than the existing schedule 4 requirements. No final decision has been taken at the time of writing, however, it would ensure proper comparability between securities business owned by banking groups and those that are independent. The DTI has yet to determine what definition would be appropriate for securities companies producing accounts in accordance with the revised schedule 9. It should be noted that if this route is followed by the Statutory Instrument, it will be mandatory, since the Directive does not include any provision for giving an option to follow either schedule 4 or the new schedule 9.

10.20   The main advantage to securities companies of being able to follow the banking company requirements would be the removal of any doubt as to the acceptability of the accounting policy of marking to market. However, the banking company formats would result in significant changes to the presentation of the balance sheet and profit and loss account of a securities company, in many ways less suited to the nature of their business, and would also require more detailed information concerning asset and liability maturity analysis, position risks and off-balance-sheet exposures.

Statement of Recommended Practice

10.21   An exposure draft of a Statement of Recommended Practice (SORP) on the valuation of securities in the financial statements of banks was published in late 1989. The draft SORP, entitled 'Securities', is specifically designed to influence the financial statements of banks and banking groups, and addresses both the treatment of securities held in the course of banking activities (such as government securities held by the Treasury department of a bank) and securities held in the course of securities dealing activities, where they are carried out by a bank itself or by a subsidiary or fellow subsidiary of a bank (in so far as the consolidated accounts of the group are concerned). It is expected that the SORP will be issued in its final approved form in late 1990.

4.10.22 The draft SORP does not apply directly to securities firms which are not banks (or members of banking groups); however, for the same reasons noted in paragraph 4.10.19 above, certain commentators have suggested that the scope of the SORP should be expanded to cover all securities firms, whatever their ownership. In any event, the SORP will provide a persuasive influence on the accounting policies and treatments adopted by all securities businesses.

4.10.23 The main recommendations of the draft SORP that are of relevance to securities businesses encompass:

— trade–date accounting;
— valuation policy;
— income recognition;
— account disclosure;

each of which is discussed below.

4.10.24 Trade–date accounting refers to the inclusion of the purchases or sales of securities in the financial statement with effect from the instant that the transaction is executed, and is contrasted with settlement–date accounting under which transactions are only reflected in the financial statements on and after the due settlement day. Trade–date accounting would normally be followed by UK securities businesses, but banks and some foreign-owned organisations have often adopted the settlement–date basis. The draft SORP recommends the use of trade–date accounting only.

4.10.25 The draft SORP contains two basic valuation policies for securities positions held. Fixed asset investments should be carried at cost, less any permanent diminution in value. All other investments should be marked to market as described earlier in this chapter. The SORP will thus regularise what is already standard practice within the industry. Some doubt remains in the draft SORP on the treatment of investments in venture capital and similar holdings, since it is not entirely clear whether they are properly classified as fixed assets. The general view is that such investments are held for resale, as and when a suitable profit can be achieved, and therefore, it is arguable that the investments are current assets (albeit that more than one year may elapse between purchase and sale), however, it would generally be regarded as imprudent to value such holdings at market value, or at the directors' estimate thereof.

.10.26　The draft SORP clarifies existing practice on the recognition of dividend and interest income arising on security positions held. It recommends that dividends should be recognised from the date the dividend has been declared, although accepting that recognition on an 'ex dividend' basis would be acceptable. For interest income (on government and corporate loan stocks, convertibles and preference shares), the SORP recommends that the accruals basis be adopted so that the interest is accrued from day-to-day.

.10.27　The majority of the recommended disclosures within the draft SORP accord with what is already normal practice. However, two particular aspects may give practical problems to securities businesses. Firstly, the draft SORP requires the cost of securities valued on a mark to market basis to be disclosed – a figure which is not generally available within a securities business without an inordinate amount of manual analysis, and a figure which is unlikely to add to the understanding of the reader of the accounts. Secondly, the draft SORP requires dealing profits to be analysed between 'clean' profits (i.e. the difference between purchase and sale price after eliminating any element of dividend or accrued interest in the price) and net dividend/interest income – although again this analysis will be difficult, and the analysis is of uncertain benefit to the reader of the accounts.

Financial reporting statements submitted to SROs

.10.28　As well as financial statements drawn up in accordance with the Companies Act 1985, all SROs require their members to submit annual financial statements to the SRO drawn up in accordance with the rules of the SROs. These are discussed in chapter 3.

PART II

5 The London Stock Exchange

5.1 Introduction

5.1.1 In order to audit effectively the business of a broker–dealer engaged in Stock Exchange transactions, it is important to understand the framework within which the broker–dealer operates and the background to some of the industry terminology and processes. This section on the audit of Stock Exchange transactions therefore starts with an introductory chapter on the London Stock Exchange, its history and its present operations.

5.2 Historical background

5.2.1 The International Stock Exchange of Great Britain and the Republic of Ireland (ISE) is the official name by which the London Stock Exchange is now known, a market that can trace its origins to one of the ubiquitous London coffee houses of the seventeenth century. By the nineteenth century, there was a well-established formal market place, with its own buildings and facilities to support the buying and selling of shares in companies and to finance the capital investments made in the UK, typified by the building of the UK railway network, and the equally large investments made by the UK in overseas operations. Similar exchanges had sprung up in various other major cities around Great Britain and Ireland, such as Birmingham and Manchester, to provide a market place for shares in local companies. By 1900, the structure of the market was well established with member firms divided between brokers – who acted solely as agents on behalf of investors wishing to buy or sell shares – and jobbers, who acted as 'wholesalers' of shares and who were prohibited from having any direct contact with the investing public.

5.2.2　By the 1970s, the provincial stock exchanges had combined with the London market to form a single unified Exchange. By this stage, the Exchange had built up a complex rulebook covering the admission of firms to the Exchange, the way in which deals should be transacted and, in particular, setting the minimum level of commissions which could be charged to investors. This attracted the attention of the Office of Fair Trading in the late 1970s and resulted in an action against the Exchange under the restrictive practices legislation on the basis that the rulebook constituted an unfair restriction of competition.

5.2.3　By this time, there were around 350 member firms on the Exchange, predominantly partnerships, with membership restricted to persons who had become individual members of the Exchange. This, therefore, excluded organisations such as banks and overseas institutions from becoming members.

5.2.4　To avoid the costs and inevitable disruption of the court action proposed by the Office of Fair Trading, the Stock Exchange reached an agreement with the Government of the day, under which the Exchange agreed to abolish the rules prohibiting external ownership of member firms and those requiring a minimum level of commissions to be charged on all transactions.

5.2.5　This agreement led inexorably to the major changes in the structures and practices of the Exchange made during 1986 known collectively as 'Big Bang'. In summary these were:

- the admission to the Exchange of UK clearing and merchant banks, overseas banks and overseas broking firms, either by the acquisition of existing partnerships or by recruiting individuals to set up totally new businesses;
- the replacement of the predominantly small, partnership member firms with corporate entities;
- abolition of the rules enforcing 'single capacity', which meant a firm had to choose between acting as a broker (and thus only acting as an agent for investors) or as a jobber or market maker (and thus only acting as a principal dealer and prohibited from direct contact with investors);
- the abolition of standard commission rates;
- the introduction of an electronic, screen-based dealing system in place of dealing on a physical trading floor.

These last three points are discussed in more detail in chapter 6.

5.3 The present market structure

5.3.1　The ISE now comprises four separate markets:

- UK Equities;
- UK Government Securities ('Gilts');
- International Equities;
- Traded Options (known as the London Traded Options Market or 'LTOM').

5.3.2　The first of these markets, which accounts for the greatest number of transactions on the ISE, can be further sub-divided:

- Listed Securities;
- Unlisted Securities Market;
- Irish Smaller Companies Market.

5.3.3　Listed securities comprise the largest sub-division, popularly known as the 'main market', on which all the major UK and Irish companies are traded. For historical reasons, the ISE has always been the recognised stock market for Irish companies, and the ISE operates a local 'branch' in Dublin which is bound by the same dealing rules as London. A number of overseas companies have also gained a 'listing' in the UK and, for the purposes of the rest of this book, such overseas companies can effectively be treated in the same way as UK stocks. Listed securities also include certain fixed-interest debt securities issued by major UK companies and local authorities.

5.3.4　The Unlisted Securities Market (USM) was set up in 1979 for companies that wished to raise smaller sums of money, release a smaller percentage of total equity or that have too short a trading record for a full listing. The Irish Smaller Companies Market is the equivalent to the USM, but for Irish companies only. Dealings in listed securities and the USM take place through an electronic screen based price transmission system known as SEAQ (Stock Exchange Automated Quotation), the operations of which are described in more detail in chapter 6.

5.3.5　In order to provide users of the market with indicators of overall market-price movements, a number of performance indices are made available on a daily, or more frequent, basis. The most widely used is the Financial Times/Stock Exchange 100 Share Index (FTSE) which is based on the prices of the leading 100 shares traded on the ISE and which is calculated and published on a continuous basis during the trading day.

5.3.6 The UK gilts market is operated by the ISE, but is closely regulated by the Bank of England since the prime purpose of this market is to provide funding for the UK government. Although this requirement has temporarily ceased with the fiscal surpluses of recent years, the Bank of England still needs to ensure that the market remains viable and in good order. For, even at times of fiscal surplus, the level of redemptions of existing stock may exceed the extent to which the Government wishes, or is able, to reduce the National Debt and therefore further issues of government stocks still occur. Dealings in gilts are also discussed in chapter 6.

5.3.7 The International Equities market is a development of the electronic share price information service (SEAQ – described in more detail in chapter 6), which was produced at the time of Big Bang for the UK equity market. The ISE became aware that a considerable number of international banks and securities houses had branches or subsidiaries based in London, and that there was a considerable amount of dealing in the shares of major international companies (listed on exchanges in USA, Japan etc.,) between firms in London. To ensure that this trading was carried out in an efficient manner, and to attempt to ensure that as much of the trading as possible remained in London (rather than being directed to other financial centres), the ISE set up a dealing system known as SEAQ International. On this system, securities firms can display the prices at which they are prepared to buy and sell various designated international stocks, and a buying broker can call up the 'page' for a particular security and see the prices offered by as many as ten different firms. SEAQ International can now offer share prices for the leading shares of virtually all the major European markets. It should be noted that securities do not need to be 'listed' in London to be eligible for trading on SEAQ International.

5.3.8 The final component of the ISE is the options market, which is now primarily the traded options market, although a certain level of dealing in 'traditional' options still takes place. LTOM is the only ISE market that still transacts deals on a physical trading floor, as opposed to using electronic screen and telephone based systems. Since the traded option market opened in the late 1970s, it has grown to the stage where options can be bought or sold on the majority of the top 100 shares as well as on the FTSE Index itself. The options market is described in more detail in chapter 18.

5.3.9 In early 1990, it was announced that LTOM proposed to merge with LIFFE, the financial futures market in London, described in chapter 19, in order to produce a single market for all derivative products in London and to enhance the overall position of London relative to other

European centres. At present, details of the merger have not been made public, but it is unlikely that it will result in major changes to the day-to-day operations of LTOM.

5.4 Member firms

5.4.1 Before an organisation can participate directly in the ISE (i.e. have direct access to the SEAQ dealing services, enter the ISE trading floor for options business and have access to the Talisman settlements mechanism), it must join the ISE as a member. Membership is granted to companies, partnerships or branches using much the same criteria as those used by SIB and the SROs. Each member can conduct business in one or more of a range of activities. Some of these can be combined within the same entity, whereas others must only be carried out in a separate subsidiary. In outline, the main categories of activity are:

5.4.2 *Broker–dealers.* This is the most general category, which permits the firm to transact business as an agent on behalf of customers in any of the four markets described above. It also allows the firm to act as principal, buying and selling shares or options for its own account, either to customers or to other member firms, but without the special privileges and obligations of market makers.

5.4.3 *Market makers – equities.* The role of these entities is described in more detail in the next chapter, but in essence they are the 'wholesalers' of the market place, having taken on much of the role of the pre-Big Bang jobbers. In return for certain special privileges, the market maker undertakes to quote prices at all times in the stocks for which he chooses to be designated and cannot refuse to deal with a broker-dealer at those prices. A single firm can choose to be a market maker in some chosen equities only, and can act as a broker-dealer in all other securities.

5.4.4 *Gilt edged market makers ('GEMMS').* These entities are the equivalent in the gilt market to market makers in the equity market, but must be approved by the Bank of England. The GEMM is allowed to deal in government stock directly with the Bank of England, and is also required to take up stock when it is offered for sale by the Bank. Under the Bank's rules, GEMMs must be separately capitalised companies, which may only trade UK Government Debt and other sterling debt instruments.

5.4.5 *Clearing firms.* These entities are of relatively recent creation, dating from 1986. They exist to provide dealing and (principally) settlement services for other member firms and must be members of ISE to obtain access to Talisman. Based on a long established American practice, they enable a member firm to dispense with its own 'back office' or settlements function. Instead, the originating member firm (or 'introducing firm') will carry out a trade and then pass on all the relevant details to the clearing firm. The clearing firm despatches the contract note to the customer and effects settlement, both with the customer and the market. Clearing members can provide their services in two main ways, categorised for regulatory purposes into Model A (at present, the more common form), where the clearer acts as the agent of the introducing firm and assumes no legal responsibility for completion of the bargains to either customer or market; and Model B, where the clearer takes full legal responsibility for each trade once transacted and bears any bad debts that arise. The use of clearers is discussed in more detail in chapter 23.

5.4.6   *Stock Exchange Moneybrokers.*   These entities are required to be separately capitalised companies whose activities are restricted to those of moneybroking. Their role is to provide liquidity in the dealing system by acting as a middleman for the lending of securities between long-term institutional holders of securities and market makers who have, for the time being, sold more shares than they have bought. Stock Exchange moneybrokers also provide a source of finance for market makers who have bought more shares than they have sold.

5.4.7   *Inter-dealer brokers (IDBs).*   These entities, which are also required to be separately capitalised companies, are a key factor behind the willingness of market makers to quote prices for large blocks of securities, and their role is described in more detail in the next chapter. In brief, they provide a service whereby market makers can offer to buy or sell large quantities of shares to other market makers on an anonymous basis.

5.4.8   *Option dealers.*   These entities are businesses whose activities are restricted to the traded options market where they trade as principals for their own account. They may trade either as market makers, in which case they are granted certain privileges in return for an obligation to quote prices, much as in the equity market; alternatively, they may trade as what are termed *locals*, in which case they are able to participate in the market when and if they so choose. Both categories provide the market depth and liquidity to ensure the options market remains a useful medium for the investor. Option dealers will only participate in the equity market for those shares in which options are traded.

5.5 Users of the ISE

5.5.1 The customers, or users, of the ISE fall into a variety of categories and can be identified according to the way in which they deal, or the way they settle their transactions. Generally, member firms will refer to their customers as clients, but to avoid confusion between references to the client of the auditor and the client of the broker–dealer, we have followed the usage of the SRO rulebooks and refer to clients of member firms, throughout this book, as customers. The one exception to this is reference to 'clients' money', a term enshrined in the SIB rulebook and the FSA itself, and one which we have therefore retained.

5.5.2 The essential feature of all customers is that they wish to either buy or sell securities listed on the ISE and therefore wish to make use of the central market to carry out transactions in securities at the most advantageous price. Only member firms of the ISE have direct access to the SEAQ dealing services, other than the widely available 'SEAQ Level 1' which merely gives the current price for a security without any details of which market maker is offering that price or the size of transaction for which the price is valid. Therefore, customers of member firms will include not only private individuals and the major domestic financial institutions, such as unit trust management companies, insurance companies and pension funds, but also overseas investors, including overseas stock-trading firms wishing to purchase UK shares for their own customers.

5.5.3 Customers can deal in two principal ways:

- through a broker–dealer who will act as agent on behalf of the customer in ensuring that the best possible transaction price is obtained for the customer, and will charge the customer an appropriate commission;
- through a market maker – the customer can contact a market maker directly and deal as a principal with the market maker. The market maker will not assume any responsibility for the customer being offered the best possible price and therefore such customers will normally only be well-informed investors such as financial institutions or overseas stockbroking firms who are competent to make their own decisions on the fairness of a price quoted to them. Such customers will not be charged any commission by the market maker and therefore it may be most efficient for the customer to deal in this way despite the greater responsibility he has to assume for his own transactions. If a private investor were to contact a market maker, SRO rules would oblige the market maker either to act as a broker–dealer (and thus undertake to find the best price) or else to refrain

from dealing. Most would take the latter course, or refer the investor to their 'own' broker–dealer arm.

5.5.4　The relationship between a broker–dealer and its customer will be defined in a written agreement with the customer and will fall into one of three broad categories:

- *Advisory*. This is the most common situation, and for such customers the broker–dealer will advise on the merits of a proposed transaction, its appropriateness in the context of the customer's requirement for investment performance (for example, income generation or capital growth) and the degree of risk associated with the particular security (is it a reliable 'blue chip' share or is it a highly speculative stock?). In many instances, the initiative for dealings by an advisory customer will be taken by the broker–dealer, who will contact the customer with a proposed transaction which can then be accepted or declined by the customer.

- *Discretionary*. Here, the customer gives the broker–dealer full power to invest a specified amount of money in shares of the broker's choosing, and to sell and buy shares within the portfolio without the prior consent of the customer. The firm will base its decisions on what the customer has told it about overall investment objectives and the desired level of risk as contained in a written customer agreement.

- *Execution only*. In this case, the customer takes his own decision on the merits of a particular transaction, and only contacts the broker–dealer to transact the bargain at the best possible price.

5.5.5　The relationship between ISE member firm and customer is regulated by the conduct of business rules of the SRO of which that firm is a member. These rules lay down the type of written agreement that must exist between the firm and the customer, the record-keeping requirement in respect of customer orders and their execution and all other aspects designed to ensure that the customer is properly treated. The auditor need not be unduly concerned about the conduct of business rules except in so far as they affect such matters as whether or not a customer can benefit from the client money and property rules, or in so far as a breach of the rules may give rise to a contingent liability for the firm, for example as a result of legal action by an aggrieved customer.

5.5.6　The various categories of customer are discussed in more detail in chapter 9.

5.6 Stock Exchange rules and regulations

5.6.1   The ISE has two sets of Rules – the 'Blue Book', entitled *The Rules of the International Stock Exchange* and the 'Yellow Book' entitled *Admission of Securities to Listing*. The latter deals with the role of the ISE as the body responsible for granting listings to companies, and therefore sets out the requirements that must be met before a corporate entity can be granted a 'listing' or 'quotation'. It also sets out the continuing requirements that must be complied with by a company if the listing is to be retained covering, *inter alia*, such matters as the disclosure of information to shareholders and the ISE, and the way in which share transfers must be processed. Each company wishing to gain a listing, and each listed company, is required to appoint a member firm of the ISE as its broker, and that broker is primarily responsible to the ISE for ensuring that the listed company complies with the Yellow Book.

5.6.2   The Blue Book contains the rules and regulations governing the admission of member firms to the ISE and their conduct in dealings with customers and other member firms.

The rulebook is in two volumes, the first containing the rules themselves, and the second containing more detailed regulations such as the requirements of the Talisman system (described in chapter 7 below). In summary, the contents of the Blue Book are as follows:

Rules
0   Council and Discipline
1–2 Membership
3–4 Dealings
5   Quotations
6–8 Settlement
9   Default

Regulations
A Miscellaneous
C Dealings
D Company Information
E Settlement
F Financial, Complaints and Default
G & J Miscellaneous
(Sections B, H & I are no longer in use)

5.6.3   Rules section 0 sets out the legal structure of the ISE, the arrangements for its government and the disciplinary power that the ISE has over its members, both at a corporate level and for individuals.

5.6.4   Rules sections 1 and 2 detail the membership requirements of the
         Exchange, which are broadly similar to those for TSA, the main
         difference being that applicants for ISE membership will have to
         demonstrate their ability to interface with both SEAQ and Talisman,
         and their possession of suitably experienced dealing and settlement
         staff.

5.6.5   Rules sections 3 and 4 lay down the rules for transacting business on the
         various markets of ISE, including the obligations of market makers. In
         particular, this section sets out the requirement for a broker-dealer to
         obtain 'best execution' for his customer (i.e., the lowest possible
         purchase price or the highest possible selling price) and also provides a
         definitive set of procedures for each market which, if complied with,
         provide a defence against any claim from a customer that best execution
         was not obtained.

5.6.6   Rules section 5 sets out the securities that can be dealt in by ISE
         member firms, and effectively provides the interface between the 'Blue
         Book' and the 'Yellow Book'. Member firms cannot trade in any
         security unless sanctioned by the rules and thus, for instance, trading in
         the 'grey market' for securities after their issue has been announced but
         before they are formally issued and listed, is generally prohibited except
         when given permission on a case-by-case basis. This section of the
         rulebook does allow certain categories of unlisted shares to be traded,
         albeit on a restricted basis. This section also sets out the conditions that
         must be complied with if unlisted securities are to be traded.

5.6.7   Rules sections 6–8 deal with the settlement of ISE traded securities,
         either through Talisman or otherwise.

5.6.8   Rules section 9 sets out the procedures to be adopted in the event of
         default (i.e. insolvency) of a Member Firm. Generally, the default
         mechanisms are automatic in the event of a firm failing to meet its
         settlement obligations to the market on the due date, irrespective of
         whether or not the firm is technically insolvent within the meaning of the
         Insolvency Act 1986. Insolvency legislation specifically allows special
         rules to be applied in the event of the insolvency of a member of a
         Recognised Investment Exchange, in order to prevent a 'domino' effect
         through the market whereby the default of one firm causes the default of
         a second and so on. The effect of Section 9 is to set out these special
         rules and should therefore be considered by the auditor in the event of a
         potential bad debt arising on the 'market side' of a transaction. This is
         considered in more detail in chapter 7, but is only likely to be relevant
         where a member firm is actually ruled to be in default.

5.6.9   The main area of the regulations likely to be of relevance to the auditor
         is section E. This sets out, in considerable detail, the rules governing
         the use of Talisman, and also the procedures for claiming benefits
         (principally dividends, rights and calls) that arise on unsettled transac-
         tions. These matters are discussed in more detail in chapter 7.

5.7   Planned changes

5.7.1   The ISE is concerned to ensure that the London market retains its role
         as one of the leading financial centres in the world, and as the pre-
         eminent stock market within Europe. The development of SEAQ
         International is seen as a key part of this strategy. However, London
         now lags behind other centres in the settlement system used for equity
         transactions and this is believed to be a potential handicap to London's
         position in the 1990s.

5.7.2   Accordingly, the ISE is developing a system to be known as TAURUS,
         which is designed to eliminate virtually all of the paper that is currently
         involved in the settlement process by moving to a 'book entry transfer'
         system for shareholdings. Under this system, the company's register will
         be split up between different TAURUS account controllers (TACs)
         who will be the large banks, brokers and similar bodies. The share
         certificate will cease to be a legal document of title. Thus the investor
         buying shares will no longer receive a share certificate, but the holding
         will be maintained on his behalf by his broker or other custodian. The
         owner, though, will still continue to receive dividends and annual
         accounts and be able to exercise his vote. With the full introduction of
         TAURUS, the share certificate will cease to have any legal status, and
         share ownership will thus become 'dematerialised'. In parallel with
         TAURUS, the ISE proposes to move from the existing 'account' system
         of settlement, described in chapter 7, to a rolling settlement basis.
         Under this, each trade will be due for settlement five days (to be
         reduced eventually to three days) after the day of dealing.

5.7.3   TAURUS is being designed to replace the existing share ownership and
         transfer processes by electronic means, and thus will complement the
         existing Talisman system, rather than replacing it. Accordingly, broker-
         dealers will continue to report and settle bargains through Talisman in
         the same way as at present. However, the introduction of TAURUS will
         mean significant changes in the day-to-day operations of a broker–
         dealer and consequently in certain aspects of the audit approach. These
         changes are outlined in the paragraphs that follow. These cannot
         describe every detail of TAURUS, not least since many details are still
         unpublished, but are intended to provide a working overview.

5.7.4   At the time of writing, much of the detailed development of TAURUS remains to be clarified. The comments below are based on the outline description of TAURUS and its facilities set out in a document issued by the ISE entitled *Project TAURUS – a prospectus for settlement in the 1990s*. This document also sets out an outline timetable for the issue of more detailed TAURUS description and the implementation of TAURUS and other related matters. The key stages of this timetable are:

September 1990   Detailed specifications of TAURUS published with full user documentation.
March 1991   Electronic network system in place for full testing of TAURUS.
October 1991   First live operation of TAURUS.
Late 1991   Introduction of same-day checking.
May 1992   System testing for rolling settlement and delivery versus payment (DVP).
October 1992   Top 100 shares on TAURUS, introduction of rolling settlement and DVP.
December 1992   Full TAURUS operation for all listed securities.

5.7.5   Under TAURUS, details of shareholding in dematerialised form will be maintained on behalf of shareholders by TAURUS account controllers (TACs) linked through a network to the central TAURUS system. There will be two main types of TAC, company and commercial.

Commercial accounts will be operated by banks, stockbrokers and other institutions independent of the listed company itself. There will be two types of commercial account:

- **Designated** – who will supply the registrars of each listed company with the details of buyers and sellers of their stock, changes to standing details, and off-market transactions on a daily basis via Talisman and TAURUS.
- **Undesignated** – who will provide each registrar monthly with an up-to-date copy of their portion of the register. Companies may in some circumstances wish to know the details of their shareholders more promptly – for example in a takeover bid. This need is met by requiring undesignated account controllers to meet the requirements of LCAS (Listed Companies Access Services). This will mean, for example, that they will be required to respond overnight to *ad hoc* requests from companies for updates on their shareholdings in a takeover situation.

The conditions under which an organisation may become an account controller have still to be specified but are expected to include capital,

74

regulatory and technical requirements. Firms acting as TACs will be required to meet stringent standards of system integrity and robustness. The company account will exist for each listed company and will be used by investors who do not wish to use the commercial accounts. It will be funded by the listed company concerned and the service, it is said, will be free to the investor. The user of the company account service will continue in many ways as at present, except for one key distinction, an investor using the company account system will receive a share advice, but this will not be a document of title.

5.7.6   In simplistic terms the flowchart sets out the events when an investor buys shares under TAURUS.

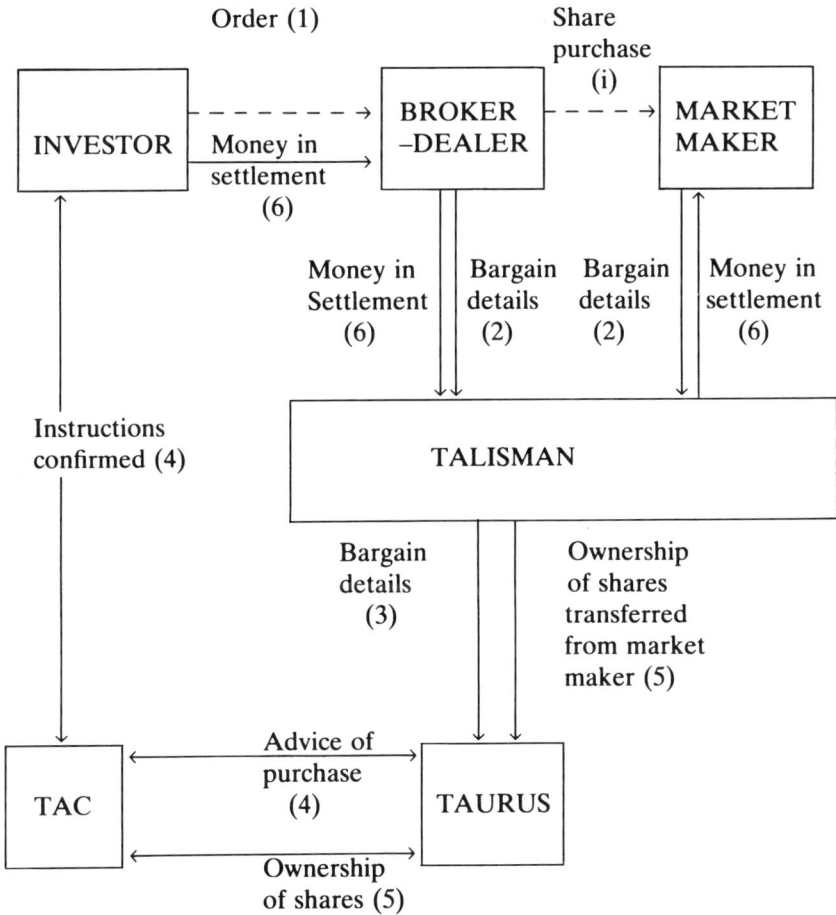

```
        Order (1)                        Share
                                         purchase
                                         (i)
┌────────────┐      ┌──────────┐      ┌──────────┐
│            │--------→│ BROKER   │----→│ MARKET   │
│  INVESTOR  │ Money in │ –DEALER  │      │ MAKER    │
│            │ settlement │        │      │          │
│            │  (6) →   │          │      │          │
└────────────┘      └──────────┘      └──────────┘
      ↑           Money in   Bargain  Bargain  Money in
      │           Settlement details  details  settlement
      │             (6)       (2)      (2)       (6)
   Instructions        ↓↓              ↓
   confirmed (4)    ┌──────────────────────────────┐
      │            │          TALISMAN             │
      │            └──────────────────────────────┘
      │           Bargain        Ownership
      │           details        of shares
      │             (3)          transferred
      │                          from market
      │                          maker (5)
      ↓           Advice of       ↓↓
┌────────┐  ←──  purchase  ──→  ┌──────────┐
│        │         (4)          │          │
│  TAC   │                      │  TAURUS  │
│        │  ←──  Ownership  ──→ │          │
└────────┘     of shares (5)    └──────────┘
```

1. As at present, the investor gives an order to the broker–dealer who transacts a bargain with the market maker.
2. Both broker–dealer and market maker submit bargain details to Talisman for checking, and any queries are resolved. The broker–dealer must also submit full details of the buyer and his TAC (including the customer's reference number).
3. Talisman submits details of the buyer and the shares purchased to TAURUS.
4. TAURUS submits the investor purchase details to the relevant TAC. The TAC must then *confirm these with the investor* and then positively confirm acceptance of the transaction to TAURUS.
5. Talisman apportions shares on the due settlement day from the market maker's account in Talisman (exactly as at present) and passes the details to TAURUS. TAURUS in turn electronically registers the shares with the TAC, transferring the legal ownership to the investor.
6. Payment by the investor to the broker–dealer takes place as at present, as does cash settlement via Talisman between the broker–dealer and the market maker.

The reverse process takes place on a sale, and clearly there are numerous variations on the basic flowchart depending on the TAC used, the nature of the investor etc.

5.7.7   TAURUS and the TACs will process all other shareholder transactions, such as dividend payments, bonus and rights issues and will also provide mechanisms for shareholder voting and takeovers etc. Details of the precise mechanisms for these remain to be finalised, but the essential characteristic is to minimise the flow of paper between different securities industry participants.

5.7.8   As mentioned above, the advent of TAURUS will also bring about various other changes:

  • *Same Day Checking.* At present, as described in chapter 7, bargains dealt between ISE member firms are 'checked' by means of an overnight comparison process. It is intended that by late 1991, bargain details will be checked on a 'real time' basis, enabling any queries to be resolved and corrected on the day the bargain was dealt.
  • *Delivery Versus Payment.* The present Talisman system does not provide any guarantee that securities paid for on a particular day will, in fact, irrevocably be delivered to the purchaser, and problems can arise if one firm becomes insolvent part way through a business day. It is proposed to establish a system of guaranteed

payment and delivery so that the payer of funds will be guaranteed that the shares will be irrevocably apportioned to him, and conversely that the deliverer of securities will be guaranteed receipt of funds.

- *Rolling Settlement*. The basic process of rolling settlement is self-evident and it is hoped that its introduction will greatly streamline the staffing and processing within back offices. However, it will also require a major change in settlement practices by private investors and thus is likely that its introduction will cause problems for investors who have been accustomed to buying and selling shares within the Stock Exchange Account without any need for payment. The first problem is likely to be addressed by a much greater use of 'margin trading' under which a broker–dealer will advance part of the purchase consideration to the investor against the provision of collateral. Margin trading is discussed in more detail in chapter 9.

6 Dealings in Equities and Gilts

6.1 Introduction
6.2 The equity dealing cycle
6.3 Market making
6.4 The inter-dealer broker
6.5 Other aspects of dealing

6.1 Introduction

6.1.1 The starting point for all transactions is the execution of a deal, and therefore, it is appropriate that we should start our detailed examinations of the operations of a broker with consideration of the dealing system. The dealing system used in the London market for equities is an electronic screen/telephone based system under which the prices quoted by market makers for each share are displayed on computer terminals in the offices of all broker-dealers. The market maker is then obliged to deal at his quoted price with any broker-dealer that telephones him.

6.1.2 For gilt-edged stocks, the process is not so sophisticated since there is no mechanism operated by ISE to list all the prices for any particular stock. Instead, a broker-dealer has to ascertain prices by telephoning a number of market makers. To ease the process, individual market makers have established their own systems to disseminate prices electronically to selected broker-dealers and customers. Otherwise the dealing process is broadly similar.

6.1.3 In the rest of this chapter, the dealing process and the role and responsibilities of the market maker are explained in more detail. The mechanics of dealing in traded options and financial futures are considered in chapters 18 and 19 respectively.

6.2 The equity dealing cycle

6.2.1 In order to consider the steps that take place in the initiation and execution of a bargain, it is worth following through a hypothetical stock transaction. This starts with a customer telephoning his broker with an order to purchase, say, 10,000 shares in ABC Plc. This order forms a binding oral contract between the customer and the broker. This order will be recorded on a dealing ticket by the broker together with the time the order was received to facilitate subsequent monitoring of the best execution rules by the brokers' own compliance staff or by the regulators. The order will normally be stated either to be 'at best', i.e. to buy the shares at the lowest possible price, or to be at a stated price (e.g. to buy the shares at 200p, or lower). Whichever type of order is given, the rules of both TSA and the ISE oblige the broker-dealer to find the best possible price for the customer, except where the broker-dealer has expressly agreed with a customer that there is no duty of best execution.

6.2.2 Having received the order, the broker-dealer will call up the relevant page for ABC Plc on his SEAQ (Stock Exchange Automated Quotations) terminal. SEAQ is an electronic system into which all market makers input the prices at which they are prepared to deal, together with the number of shares for which that price holds good. SEAQ automatically sorts prices so as to show the market maker giving the highest 'bid' price (i.e. the price which he is prepared to pay to the broker-dealer selling shares) and the market maker giving the lowest 'offer' price (i.e. the price at which he is prepared to sell shares to the broker-dealer buying shares). Note that the difference between the bid and offer prices quoted by a market maker provides him with his profit margin, known as the 'market maker's turn'. Where two market makers quote the same price, SEAQ will give precedence to the market maker prepared to deal in the larger number of shares, and failing this, precedence is given to the first market maker to quote that price.

6.2.3 To illustrate this, the SEAQ screen for ABC Plc will appear as follows:

ABC Plc

A, B	195 – 198	C
A	195 – 200	5 × 5
B	195 – 200	10 × 10
C	193 – 198	10 × 10
D	193 – 200	25 × 25

The line at the top of the screen (shown in yellow, and known as 'the strip') shows what SEAQ has determined to be the best price – in this case, both A and B are bidding for stock at 195p but B is given precedence (by being the name shown closest to the price in the centre of the strip) since he is prepared to deal in 10,000 shares, compared with A's quote for only 5,000 shares. The amount a firm is prepared to deal in is shown in the right hand column of figures where the two figures shown represent the size (in thousands of shares) for which the firm is prepared to sell shares and to buy shares – the two figures are allowed to be different.

6.2.4   It should be noted that SEAQ offers three levels of service. Level one is for the general investing public, and merely shows the best price quote for each stock without any details of the market makers concerned. Level two is the service used by broker-dealers and gives the information set out in paragraph 6.2.3. Level three is the service provided for market makers and includes the facility to input new price quotes.

6.2.5   Having called up the SEAQ page, the broker can immediately see that the lowest offer price (i.e. the price at which he can buy shares) is 198p, which is quoted by market maker C. Since C is prepared to deal in 10,000 shares, which is all that the customer wishes to buy, the broker-dealer will telephone C and buy 10,000 shares. If the customer wished to purchase more than 10,000 shares, then the broker-dealer would contact C and also probably B and D (because they are showing a willingness to deal in some size) to determine which one was offering the best price in the required quantity.

6.2.6   As indicated earlier, under ISE rules, market makers' prices for most securities on SEAQ are 'firm', and therefore C must deal at that price once telephoned by the broker-dealer. The only exceptions to this rule are that market makers are not obliged to make firm prices to each other, and, when ISE announces that 'fast market' conditions apply, market makers' prices are deemed to be only 'indicative'. A 'fast market' means that prices are changing rapidly, and therefore it may not be possible for market makers to change their quotations fast enough. When this occurs, firm prices can only be obtained by telephoning the market maker directly.

6.2.7   Once the deal has been contracted between the broker-dealer and market maker C, both parties set in motion the recording and ultimate settlement of the transaction. For the broker-dealer, the next stage is to complete the dealing slip with the time of execution, the price of the transaction and the identity of the market maker, following which the dealing slip will be input to the broker-dealer's computer for processing.

6.2.8   This processing is designed to produce three results. The first is to send details of the transaction to an ISE computer system known as 'Charm Checking', which is described below. The second is to produce the 'contract note' to be sent to the customer. For the customer, the contract note is the documentary evidence that the bargain has been transacted and informs him of the total amount that will be payable by him. It also gives the customer the opportunity to identify any errors in the bargain (e.g. the wrong number of shares purchased, the wrong name etc), and therefore it is essential that the contract note is despatched as soon as possible. Most brokers will despatch contracts on the day the bargain was transacted, although it should be noted that TSA rules require the contract note to be despatched no later than the day after dealing. The third result of this processing is to record the transaction in the broker-dealer's accounting records and initiate the settlement process.

6.2.9   The broker-dealer's master record of his transactions will be the 'bargain journal', a daily listing of all bargains transacted that day. For each bargain, the bargain journal will record the customer, the market maker and all other details of the transaction. At the end of each account, the broker-dealer may also produce a 'list-book', which is a listing of all bargains in stock sequence. Given the inevitable size of such a listing, nowadays it is usually only produced for stocks that cannot be settled through Talisman.

6.2.10   Similarly, the market maker will also complete a dealing slip with the details of his sale to the broker-dealer for input to his records. This process is increasingly being simplified by the dealer responsible for the transaction entering details of the bargain directly into the computer. This is done to shorten the time between effecting a transaction and including it in the accounting records. For the market maker, the minimisation of the time lag is crucial since the first result of processing the transaction is to report the details to the ISE, which must be effected within a very short space of time.

6.2.11   This trade reporting is mandatory for all transactions in order to enable the ISE to publish bargain details to the outside world and to facilitate the identification and monitoring of abnormal price movements by the ISE's surveillance staff. It has to be effected within (at present) three minutes of the transaction being executed. However, although transactions are all reported immediately, only those in the securities of larger companies listed on ISE are made public at the time through an electronic data feed known as TOPIC. Full details of all trades are published the following day in a publication called the Stock Exchange Daily Official List (SEDOL) which gives, for each listed share, the prices at which all bargains in that stock were transacted during the previous day. The market maker also reports the bargain to Charm Checking and updates his own accounting records.

Charm Checking

6.2.12   This provides a central mechanism for all broker-dealers and market makers to confirm that they have correctly recorded all transactions executed. As noted above, after each bargain has been carried out, both the broker-dealer and the market maker electronically send the details to the ISE so that it can to be processed through a matching mechanism known as Charm. Essentially, Charm ensures that the details input by both parties to a transaction are in agreement on such matters as number of shares, price, share descriptions, date of bargain and date of settlement etc. The whole checking process is discussed in more detail in chapter 7 on Talisman settlement.

Commissions and charges

6.2.13   The broker-dealer will charge commission to the customer, either at a standard rate or at a specific rate negotiated at the time of the deal. Typically, commission rates for institutional customers will average 0.2 per cent of the value of the transaction, irrespective of bargain size. Typical rates for private customers will operate on a sliding scale with a rate of (say) 1.5 per cent on the first £10,000 consideration, 0.75 per cent on the next £20,000 and 0.5 per cent on the balance, usually with an overriding fixed minimum charge. Whatever the charge, it will be shown on the contract note sent to the customer as an addition to the price of a share purchase, or as a deduction from the proceeds of a share sale.

6.2.14   Since commission rates are freely negotiable, it is important that the management of a firm should establish control procedures to ensure that all commissions to which the firm is entitled have been charged, and dealers do not give excessive discounts. These control procedures include the following:

- review of all contract notes by senior staff;
- exception reporting of all instances where commission falls below a specified level;
- reporting of average commissions actually charged to each customer and by each dealer over a period of time, for comparison with pre-set standards.

6.2.15   Where the customer has been introduced to the broker-dealer through another business (such as a chartered accountant, a solicitor or a financial intermediary), then the broker-dealer will pay a proportion of the commission charged to the introducer. This is generally known as 'returned commission'. The existence of such commission share must be disclosed on the contract note. Similarly, commission shares may be paid to employees of the firm who introduced the customer to the firm.

6.2.16   The contract note will also show other charges:

- On purchases only, *ad valorem* stamp duty at a rate of 0.5 per cent which will, in due course, be paid over by the broker-dealer to the

Government either in the form of stamp duty charged on an executed share transfer or as stamp duty reserve tax, if no share transfer document is executed. It will normally be collected from the broker–dealer through Talisman (dealt with in greater detail in chapter 13 on taxation). This charge is expected to be abolished in late 1991 to coincide with the introduction of TAURUS (*see* chapter 5).

- On all bargains (whether bought or sold) in excess of a minimum value, a levy of 10p for the Panel on Takeover and Mergers. This is collected by the broker-dealer and paid over to the Panel on Takeovers and Mergers on a quarterly basis to assist in the funding of its operations.
- Certain firms may impose additional charges in particular cases, such as an administration charge, a recharge of traded option clearing house fees etc.

6.3 Market making

6.3.1 As we have already seen, market makers act as the buying or selling counterparty for virtually every investor who wishes to deal on the ISE. Under ISE rules, each market maker is required to quote both bid and offer prices at all times in the securities in which he is registered, for a minimum number of shares. This number of shares is set by the ISE dependent on the particular share concerned and its normal price. As indicated above, the market maker must deal at those prices with all other member firms, with certain specific exceptions. As well as the main ISE rules governing market makers, the ISE has also published a code of conduct for market makers which set out their obligations in greater detail and also ensures that market makers compete fairly and equally. Compliance with this code of conduct is obligatory and any breaches can give rise to disciplinary action.

6.3.2 Each security traded on SEAQ is classified in one of the following categories:

- alpha
- beta
- gamma
- delta

The categorisation is set by the ISE, taking account of such matters as the number of market makers registered to deal in the stock, the total market capitalisation of the company and daily turnover in the stock (i.e. number of shares and value). The categorisation is independent of whether a share is fully listed or is traded on the USM.

6.3.3　Alpha is the categorisation for the largest and most actively traded companies, with the majority of other sizeable listed companies being beta. The gamma classification is used for all other stocks where there are at least two market makers prepared to quote prices. Securities classified as delta are those with only a single market maker or where no firm is prepared to act as a market maker. In the latter case, dealings can only take place on a 'matched' basis; this means that an investor wishing to buy shares can only do so if his broker can find another investor willing to sell.

6.3.4　The main distinctions between the classifications are the way in which prices are quoted and the way in which transaction details are published. For alpha and beta shares, the prices shown on SEAQ are binding on market makers who must therefore deal at that price or better with any broker-dealer. For gamma and delta shares, the SEAQ prices are 'indicative', i.e. they serve as the starting point for negotiation. However, it should be noted that a market maker in a gamma stock must give a firm quotation (i.e., both a bid and an offer price) at which he is bound to deal in response to a telephone call from a broker-dealer.

6.3.5　The extent of real-time publication of bargains transacted is also dependent on the category of a stock. The objective of the ISE is for the size and price of all bargains to be published within five minutes of execution in order to provide maximum transparency of market activity to the investing public. However, it is recognised that immediate reporting of particularly large transactions or deals in less actively traded securities could have a significant impact on the willingness of market makers to quote prices for sizeable quantities of shares, since this would allow other market makers to adjust their prices in anticipation of the position being unwound, and lead to the original market maker incurring losses. Accordingly, the real-time trade reporting system specifically omits trades outside certain parameters and these omitted trades are merely featured in cumulative volume reports published during the day on TOPIC.

6.3.6　Trade information is also published on a daily basis in hard-copy form in the Stock Exchange Daily Official List (SEDOL), an ISE publication which lists, for every quoted stock, each successive price at which bargains have been transacted during the day. It also shows what might appear to be a closing bid and offer price for each stock, although the spread between SEDOL published bid/offer prices is considerably wider than that which would appear on the SEAQ screens. Despite the different bid/offer prices, the mid-point of the price spread will be consistent between SEDOL and SEAQ.

6.3.7   The audit of market making businesses and more detailed descriptions of the market making process are set out in chapter 16.

6.3.8   The reader should note that the services offered through SEAQ, and the rules for trade publications undergo regular review and at the date of writing, consideration is being given to introducing a 'limit order' facility whereby investors could record a standing instruction to buy or sell shares at a pre-determined level.

6.4   The inter-dealer broker (IDB)

6.4.1   IDBs (of which there are only two in the equity market) are used by market makers who wish to reduce a large position built up through normal dealing activities, without revealing their identity to other market makers. By making it easier for market makers to unwind positions efficiently and confidentially, IDBs make an important contribution to the overall liquidity of the market. If a large position taken by a market maker became known, other market makers could adjust their own prices in that stock so that the original market maker could only close his position at a loss. Thus, if market makers did not have a route for closing out positions without risking adverse price movements, they would not be prepared to quote prices to investors in large quantities, and consequently the liquidity of the overall market would be reduced. IDBs are, therefore, used only by market makers and access to IDBs is prohibited to anyone else. Market makers choose which IDB screens they will have in their dealing-room, and are then restricted to dealing with those IDBs.

6.4.2   The IDB is purely a 'middle man' and is not permitted to take positions except as a result of errors. If an IDB has to take a position as a result of a dealing error, it must immediately take steps to close that position by displaying the relevant information on its screens.

6.4.3   As an example, suppose market maker A wished to buy 10,000 XYZ plc at 150p. He would telephone his selected IDB with these details who then displays this information on his screens (omitting the name of the market maker to ensure confidentiality) which will then be seen by all other market makers dealing in XYZ plc who have that IDB's screen. Market maker A is known as the 'initiator' or the 'passive' party to the deal.

6.4.4   On seeing these details on the screen, market maker B may decide that he wishes to sell 10,000 XYZ plc at 150p. He becomes the active party or aggressor or responder, and telephones the IDB to arrange completion of the deal. To ensure confidentiality even during settlement, the deal is transacted by the IDB as principal with each of the two market makers.

6.4.5   The IDB is, therefore, a notice board where both parties to the transaction remain anonymous. IDBs make their profit by charging a 'turn' on the deal, which is calculated as a fixed percentage of the 'passive' price and is charged to the initiator. Thus, in our example, B will receive 150p per share, while A might pay 150.125p per share.

6.4.6   IDBs must accept full responsibility as a principal on both sides of a transaction. They must operate on a matched basis at all times, and must immediately cover any exposure arising as a result of a misunderstanding or of a market maker failing to deliver stock. Unlike market makers, IDBs are not permitted to borrow stock. If the delivery of stock purchased by an IDB is delayed, the IDB may delay delivery on its matching sale, although it will remain ultimately responsible should the seller default on the transaction.

6.5   Other aspects of dealing

6.5.1   While the transaction described in section 6.2 above represents a 'standard' equity bargain, there are many variants which may be encountered. The more common transaction types are described in outline below.

6.5.2   The originator of an order will, as described above, normally be the customer. However, the broker-dealer may take the initiative by proposing a transaction to the customer, in which case the 'order' takes effect when, and if, the customer accepts the proposed transaction. In other cases, the customer may have given discretion to the broker-dealer to deal without prior approval from the customer, in which case the 'order' takes effect when the broker decides to effect a particular transaction for the customer. Discretionary dealings are discussed in more detail in chapter 22.

Principal dealing

6.5.3   Instead of acting strictly as agent to a customer by passing the order from the buying customer to the market maker using the SEAQ screen, the broker-dealer may choose to deal directly with the customer by agreeing to sell the shares to the customer himself as principal. Under ISE rules, this can only be done if the price at which the broker-dealer sells to the customer, taking commission charges into account, is more advantageous to the customer than the best price shown on SEAQ, this rule being established to ensure that the market making system is not undermined. Under normal agency law, dealing as principal with a customer in this manner is only permitted if sanctioned, in advance, by the customer. Such permission is usually included within the Customer Agreement Letter. If the broker-dealer does not already own the shares he has sold, he is taking a risk that subsequent adverse price movements will not occur on the shares. However, the broker-dealer may be content to run this risk given the potential profit opportunity if the price moves favourably.

6.5.4   One variant of this is the 'riskless principal' trade, where the broker-dealer will undertake to buy, as principal, from one customer and immediately sell the same shares to another customer or a market maker. This deal will usually originate from one customer where the broker-dealer knows there is another customer wishing to deal in the opposite direction. Technically, the broker-dealer is fully on risk at the moment of the first deal, but in practice neither deal will be executed until the broker-dealer is satisfied that both parties are prepared to enter into the transaction. The broker-dealer will not usually charge any commission on either of these deals, instead making his profit from the price differential.

Agency cross

6.5.5   This transaction is broadly identical to the riskless-principal trade described above, where a broker-dealer has two customers wishing to deal in opposite directions in the same share. However, in this case the broker-dealer is legally acting as the agent to both parties and therefore can only deal in this manner when he has permission from both customers. The broker-dealer will charge a commission to both customers.

Direct contact with market maker

6.5.6   Instead of dealing through a broker-dealer, investors may choose to make direct contact with a market maker. This will typically be the case where the investor is a sophisticated investor, such as an insurance company or fund manager, who is sufficiently aware of market prices to make his own assessment of whether the price that will be offered is the best that could be obtained. In such dealings, the market maker will not normally take any responsibility for giving 'best execution' to the customer, and equally will not usually charge commission to the customer.

Automatic execution

6.5.7   A number of services are available which enable the broker-dealer to simplify the dealing process for smaller transactions, by automating the dealing process and the role of the broker-dealer in obtaining the best possible price for the customer. This service is offered by SAEF (an acronym standing for Small-order Automated Executions Facility) operated by the ISE and also by proprietory systems from a number of individual market makers.

6.5.8   Under any of these services, where an order received from a customer is no larger than the maximum order size specified for a security traded in the service, the broker-dealer enters the number of shares to be traded into the computer terminal of the dealing service located in his office. This automatically executes a trade at the current best price shown by SEAQ without further manual intervention. Under SAEF, the counter-party is the market maker actually giving the best price at the time, while the proprietory services result in a deal with the market maker providing the service, but at the same best price. In all cases, the input to Charm checking is automatic.

Gilts

6.5.9   Transactions in gilts are dealt in broadly the same manner as those described in section 6.2 above, the only difference being that there is no equivalent of the SEAQ screen showing the prices of all the market makers. Instead, the broker-dealer will either telephone two or more gilt edged market markers (GEMMs) to obtain their quotes, or call up the relevant 'pages' in the TOPIC screen information service which are published by the individual GEMMs.

6.5.10   Gilts prices are quoted and calculated in a different manner to those for equities. Firstly, prices are quoted in pounds per £100 nominal amount of stock, with prices between whole pounds being quoted in fractions of a pound. By long established custom, the minimum price variation is 1/64 of a pound, and all prices are quoted in multiples of 1/64, using simplified fractions (e.g. 3/8 instead of 24/64) where appropriate. Secondly, the quoted screen prices are 'clean prices'. This means that the basic price is adjusted for the amount of accrued interest earned by the stock, calculated from the date of the last interest payment to the due settlement date of the transactions (usually the next business day after the transaction date).

6.5.11   Thus suppose an investor wants to buy £20,000 nominal of Treasury 12 3/4 per cent 1992 stock. The best price quoted for the stock is £82,17/64, the date of the purchase is 17 May 1990 and the stock last paid interest on 22 December 1989. The price that will be paid by the investor is computed as follows:

		Consideration
Clean price £20,000 × £82 17/64 per £100		16,453.12
Accrued interest		
Days from last interest date (22/12/1989)		
to settlement date (18/5/1990)	147	
Interest rate (nominal rate)	12.75%	
Principal	£20,000	
		1,026.99
Commission say		100.00
Total purchase price		£17,580.11

5.5.12   If the purchase is made after the date on which the stock is quoted ex-interest, the buyer is not entitled to receipt of the next dividend to be paid. Accordingly, for such a purchase the adjustment is to reduce the price by the accrued interest between the settlement date and the next payment date.

5.5.13   This adjustment for accrued interest is analogous with the operations of the Accrued Income Scheme for the taxation of holdings in gilts (and other fixed interest securities). The accrued interest purchased or sold is treated as part of the income of the tax payer for income tax purposes and not as part of the capital cost.

5.5.14   The other feature of the gilts market is that the great majority of deals by value are transacted on a principal to principal basis directly between the large investing institutions and the GEMMs without the intervention of broker-dealers.

Auditing

5.5.15   All the matters relevant to the audit of the dealing cycle are considered in more detail in the chapters that follow, under either customers (chapter 9), market balances (chapters 7 and 8) or principal dealing and market making (chapter 14).

7 Talisman settlement

7.1 Introduction

7.1.1 Talisman is the centralised stock-settlement system operated by the ISE which is able to settle most UK and Irish registered securities as well as a number of Australian and South African securities. Settlement can occur in pounds sterling, US dollars, Irish punts or Australian dollars. 'Talisman' itself is an acronym which stands for Transfer Accounting Lodgement for Investors and Stock Management.

7.2 The Talisman settlement process

Overview

7.2.1 The main steps in the Talisman settlement process are:

- checking
- deposit
- apportionment.

Before describing each of these in detail, we shall first discuss the settlement process in overview.

7.2.2 The key to the whole process is an ISE nominee company called SEPON Limited (SEPON stands for Stock Exchange Pool Nominees), which has a shareholding account in the register of every participating company. Within SEPON, for every security in which they deal, every member firm which acts as a principal or as a market maker has a specially designated trading account of their own. Here, such firms hold stock and give instructions to withdraw it when necessary, in settlement of sold bargains.

7.2.3 During the course of settlement, stock is deposited by selling brokers with the Talisman centre and registered into the name of SEPON. SEPON keeps its own record of which firm 'owns' stock, distinguishing between holdings as agent on behalf of customers and holdings as principal. Initially, sold stock is held to the order of the broker for the selling customer, but on account day it is transferred to the trading account of the buying market maker. With bought transactions, when physical stock becomes available, it is transferred to the account of the buying customer, at which point it is transferred out of SEPON and into the buying customer's name. The trading accounts within SEPON therefore provide a record by principal or market maker of the securities in which they have dealt and hence will show the movement of stock during the settlement process. It is this pooling of stock in the SEPON accounts which is the cornerstone of the Talisman system and is explained in more detail below.

7.2.4 All bargains have firstly to be reported to the checking service by the buying and selling firms which ensures that bargain details are agreed by both parties. The checking service is also a means of reporting transactions to the ISE's Surveillance Department.

7.2.5 Once a bargain has been matched by the checking service, a 'sale docket' is issued to the selling broker by the Talisman Centre. This docket subsequently acts as identification when the share certificate is deposited at the ISE's settlement office.

When stock is deposited by the selling broker, it is first checked for good delivery (i.e. that the share certificate is valid, is for the right class of share, has the same seller's name as the transfer documents etc.) and then passed to the company's registrar for registration into SEPON – initially, to the account of the selling broker. Although legal title passes to SEPON on registration, no share certificate is ever issued to SEPON. SEPON is, however, entitled to all benefits (such as dividends and bonus issues) arising from ownership of the security as nominee for the benefical owner. As we have seen, the beneficial owner at any time may be the original seller, the market maker or the buyer. As discussed below, the Talisman centre ensures that the correct party receives any relevant benefits. It should be noted that the only benefit which cannot be passed on through SEPON is voting rights, and this may occasionally present problems. Most of the time, such voting rights will simply lapse. However, it is conceivable that they may be exercised if all market makers with a holding at SEPON in a particular stock agree on how voting rights should be exercised.

7.2.6 On account day, delivery takes place. The stock is transferred to the principal's or market maker's trading account within SEPON and the selling broker receives payment from the Talisman centre on the principal's or market maker's behalf. The stock in the trading account is then allocated or 'apportioned' to any sold bargains that may have been made by the market maker. Once apportionment has taken place, the stock is held by SEPON to the order of the various buyers. The buying broker will have supplied registration details to the Talisman Centre (e.g. name and address of the buying customer) at some time on or after the checking stage and these will be used by Talisman to prepare bought transfers. Following apportionment, the bought transfers are lodged with the company's registrar for registration, legal title passes from SEPON to the buyer and a new share certificate is issued by the company's registrar.

If the broker wishes, he can instruct Talisman not to lodge the bought transfers for a specified time after apportionment – either forty-eight hours (called 'forty-eight hour hold') or ten days (called 'ten day hold') – to enable the broker to determine whether the customer has paid for its shares. If payment has not been made, the broker can then instruct the share to be registered in the broker's nominee name to enhance the remedies avaiable against the customer's non-payment.

7.2.7   The settlement process and likely timescale at each stage is summarised in Figure 7.1 opposite.

7.2.8   The legal status of Talisman is that of a clearing agency settling trans-actions between two counterparties. If one of the counterparties goes into default, Talisman assumes no liability. As is discussed in more detail in paragraph 7.4.24 below, when a member firm of the ISE goes into default, all transactions relating to that firm are reversed from Talisman's records and settled individually between the two counterparties.

7.2.9   The range of services offered by the Talisman centre and the procedures adopted by brokers and market makers are very much wider than those described in the above overview, and these are discussed below. In addition, it should be noted that a three-volume Talisman reference manual and a code of good practice for Talisman settlement are available from the ISE and these should be referred to where further details are required.

Checking procedures

7.2.10   The purpose of the checking service (sometimes known under its original title of Charm checking or simply Charm) is to obtain an agreed transaction record upon which future processing and settlement can be based. It should be noted that bargains checked through Charm do not automatically settle through Talisman. All bargains in UK and Irish securities (including government stocks), dealt by ISE member firms, have to be reported and matched in this manner.

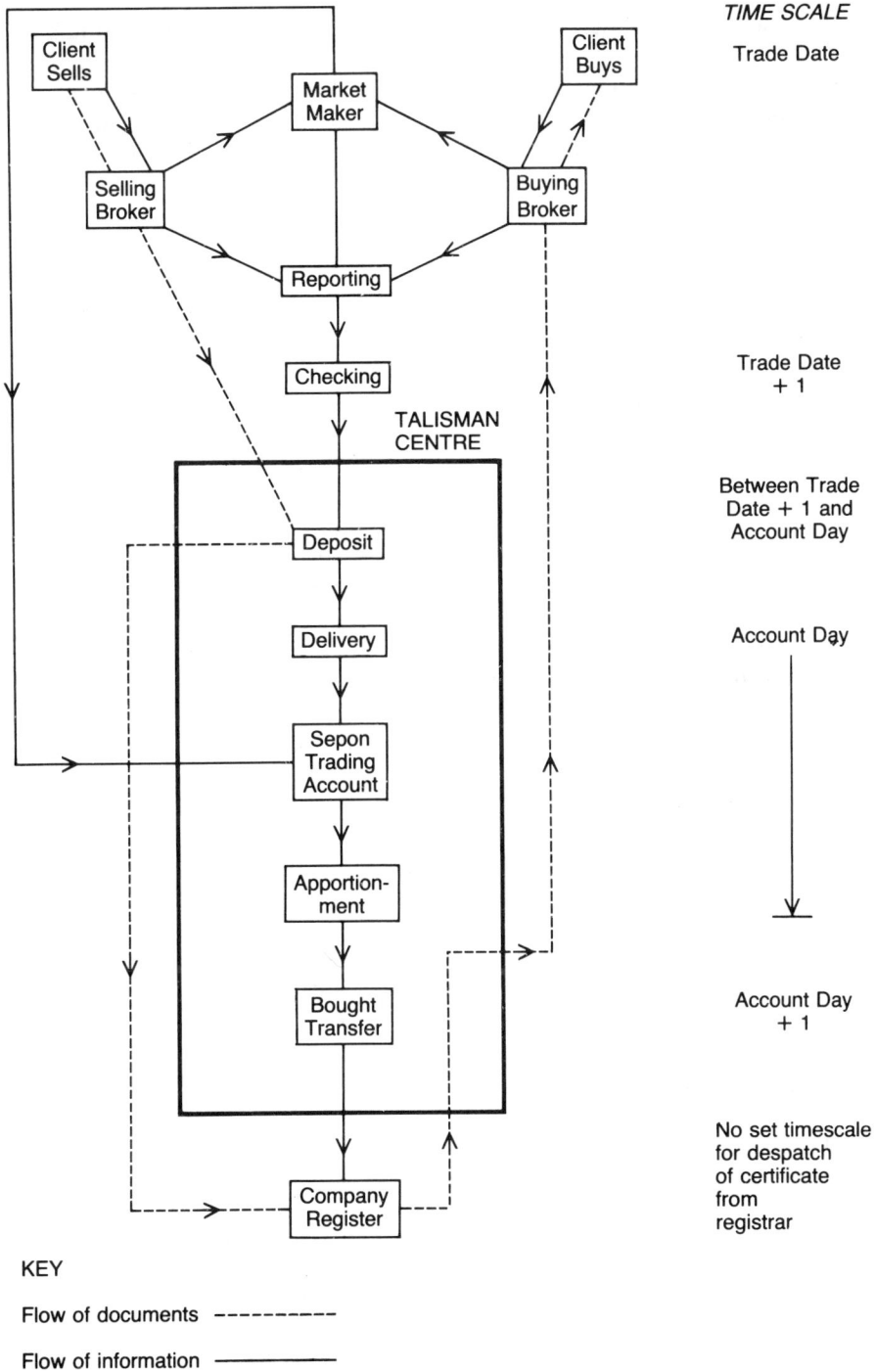

TIME SCALE

Trade Date

Trade Date
+ 1

TALISMAN
CENTRE

Between Trade
Date + 1 and
Account Day

Account Day

Account Day
+ 1

No set timescale
for despatch
of certificate
from
registrar

KEY

Flow of documents ----------

Flow of information ——————

Figure 7.1 How Talisman works.

Even where the underlying security is eligible for settlement through Talisman (now 99 per cent of quoted UK registered shares), it is possible for both counterparties to request that settlement takes place outside Talisman. In that case, once a bargain has been matched, it will be removed from Talisman's records. Non-Talisman settlement is discussed in chapter 8.

7.2.11   Thus all bargains dealt between ISE member firms are notified to the checking service and details are compared. On a daily basis, firms are informed of their matched, unmatched and rejected transactions. Bargains remain on these reports until they are matched (usually two or three days at most).

7.2.12   The following key print outs are available from the Checking Service every day:

- *Matching Report* – details all bargains input by the firm which were agreed by counterparties on the previous business day.
- *Unmatched/Alleged Report* – details those bargains input by the firm but not agreed by the counterparty ('unmatched'), and those input by other counterparties who claim to have dealt with the firm but which the firm does not agree ('alleged').
- *Rejections Report* – details the bargains input by the firm which have been rejected due to errors on the input document.

7.2.13   Each morning, firms act on these reports either by contacting the counterparty to agree upon bargain details, or by re-inputting the bargain to correct the rejection. In order to agree bargain details, the original dealers may need to be contacted, which means that matching may not be instantaneous. Nevertheless, experience indicates that few items should remain unmatched or alleged for more than two or three days. It should be noted that the ISE impose fines on member firms if the percentage of their unmatched bargains exceeds laid down standards.

Deposit of stock

7.2.14   Deposit is the term used for the lodgement of certificates and transfer forms at the Talisman centre prior to the settlement of brokers' sold bargains. For such bargains, it is the responsibility of the selling broker to collect the certificates and signed sold transfer forms from his customer.

7.2.15   Stock for UK settlement is deposited in what is known as a 'deposit set' which consists of the sale docket (issued by Talisman at the checking stage), a sold transfer form signed by the selling customer (to show he approves the transfer), and the share certificate. It is possible to effect a part deposit (deposit less than the bargain quantity), or to request a balance certificate (where the certificate quantity exceeds the bargain quantity).

7.2.16 Deposit must take place before the sold bargain can be settled. After the stock has been deposited, there is a book entry transfer to the principal's or market maker's SEPON trading account which is known as 'delivery'. Delivery takes place on the settlement due date or the day following deposit, whichever is the later. Once delivery has taken place, the selling broker is paid by Talisman on behalf of the purchaser. Following delivery, the stock then becomes available for apportionment.

Apportionment

7.2.17 Apportionment is the daily process whereby stock in a principal's or market maker's trading account at SEPON is allocated to his open sold bargains or stock loan returns to moneybrokers (*see below*). Every evening at the Talisman centre, open bargains and stock-loan returns which are ready for apportionment are formed into an apportionment queue (generally bargains are settled in date order, although this can be changed at the option of the market maker). Stock is then apportioned to items in this queue until no more stock is left in the trading account or all outstanding transactions are satisfied. The apportionment process may result in the last transaction apportioned being only partially satisfied. In this case, the satisfied part of the transaction appears on the relevant apportionment schedule as part-apportioned and the balance is accorded a higher priority in the next apportionment run.

7.2.18 The buying broker may request that, on apportionment, the Talisman centre produces a stock note upon which a claim can be made on his customer. The stock note guarantees that stock has been apportioned to a particular bargain and can therefore be used by brokers as documentary evidence of the transfer. It can then be sent by the broker to his customer to support his claim for payment of the amount due. In practice, a stock note is only requested for cash against documents (CAD) customers where the customer only settles upon transfer of the stock and not on the designated account settlement day. It should be noted that this procedure is becoming less common following the introduction of Institutional Net Settlement as discussed below.

7.2.19 Following apportionment, there may be a balance of stock left in the market maker's SEPON trading account which means that he has been a net buyer of that type of security. This stock position may be financed by borrowings using the stock as coliateral. Alternatively, following apportionment, there may be transactions which cannot be satisfied because the market maker has been a net seller of that stock. In this case, stock may need to be borrowed in order to satisfy outstanding transactions.

Apportionment reversals/bad delivery

7.2.20 Although, as we have emphasised, Talisman checks that the certificate and transfer deposited by the selling broker constitute good delivery before they are processed, it occasionally happens that when the stock reaches the registrar the transfer cannot be effected. This might be because the shares are 'frozen' under a court order prohibiting any transfer, or because the shares have already been sold against a letter of indemnity. Since Talisman operates on the basis that all deposits processed by them will be honoured, this rejection by the registrar gives rise to a problem since the buying broker may well already have had the shares apportioned to him, and thus effectively created more shares than the company has issued. To ensure there is no financial exposure to the Talisman system as a result, the selling broker is required to pay a deposit to Talisman equal to the market value of the stock rejected by the registrar. This deposit is adjusted each day so that it always reflects the current market value of the stock, and is only repaid when the selling broker has resolved the problem with the registrar and the selling client so that transfer of the shares can be effected. Effectively, the deposit would allow Talisman to buy an equivalent number of shares in the market to fulfil the delivery. This deposit mechanism is known as 'deficit redemption', and the aggregate of any deposit paid will be held in the 'deficit redemption account' of each broker with Talisman.

7.2.21 The other instance where the normal deposit/delivery/apportionment cycle can be interrupted arises if, for some reason the buying broker or the market maker does not pay the amount due to Talisman by the specified deadline (10.00a.m. of the day of apportionment). In this case, Talisman stops the apportionment process, does not send the bought transfer details to the registrar and makes a book entry transfer within SEPON back to the selling market maker or broker's account. Simultaneously, it will seek repayment of the sale proceeds from the selling firm until the matter can be resolved. This process is known as reverse apportionment and reverse delivery and is rare – only normally being encountered in the event of the default of a member firm.

Stock-loan agreements

7.2.22 Another important part of the service offered by Talisman is the matching and settling of stock-loan agreements between moneybrokers and market makers. The role of the moneybroker is discussed in more detail in chapter 14. In summary, stock is borrowed where the market maker has been a net seller in a particular security and does not own enough shares to satisfy all its sold bargains. In order to satisfy these buyers it may borrow the stock. Having decided its borrowing requirements, the market maker contacts one of the designated moneybrokers (who will also be a member of the ISE). The moneybroker will, in turn, borrow the shares concerned from an institution such as an insurance company or pension fund. Both the moneybroker and the market maker give Talisman details of the agreement; it is then matched through the Checking service before being passed forward for settlement. The stock is deposited at the Talisman centre by the moneybroker on or before the agreed settlement date and on the due settlement day is then delivered into the market maker's SEPON trading account. When stock is delivered to the market maker's SEPON account, the market maker makes a payment to Talisman as collateral for the stock loan which is passed on to the moneybroker and thence the institution. This collateral payment is calculated on a daily basis on the market value of the stock borrowed, and any resulting surpluses/shortfalls are repaid.

7.2.23 As stock subsequently becomes available in the market maker's SEPON trading account (due to purchases by the market maker and deposits of stock by selling brokers), borrowed stock can be returned to the moneybroker and cash collateral repaid. Talisman treats outstanding stock loans in the same way as unsettled sales and therefore automatically transfers the stock back to the moneybroker and the cash to the market maker. These transactions are known as stock-loan returns.

7.2.24 It should be noted that such stock lending facilities are only available to registered market makers and cannot be used by principal dealers to settle short positions.

Collateral

7.2.25 Talisman also allows market makers to finance, on a secured basis, stock held in their SEPON trading accounts without having to withdraw the stock physically. This financing requirement may be satisfied by borrowing money either from a moneybroker or a bank. The loan will be secured by pledging the stocks held by SEPON, and is evidenced by the issue to the lender of a Talisman Short Term Collateral Certificate which specifies the value of stock so pledged. Such certificates are re-issued on a daily basis and therefore can only be used to secure overnight borrowings.

Benefits

7.2.26   A further feature of the Talisman settlement system is in the area of dividends, rights, and other customer entitlements (collectively known as 'benefits'), where a centralised claiming and distribution service is provided. The Talisman centre has full details of every bargain, and can therefore identify the beneficial owner of all benefits arising from stock ownership. Benefits received by the Talisman centre arising out of its SEPON holding are passed immediately to the entitled party. Where, through delays in registration, benefits are paid by a company to a seller who is not entitled to the benefit, Talisman identifies this, raises a claim form and passes it to the relevant broker so that the benefits can be reclaimed and passed to the entitled party.

7.2.27   The ISE tries to avoid this problem by determining when a security is sold with the entitlement to an impending dividend (know as 'cum-div') or other benefit and when the security is sold without that entitlement (know as 'ex-div' in the case of the impending dividend). Generally, a security will be traded on a cum-div or cum-benefit basis, i.e. the buyer gains full rights to every benefit associated with the share from the moment of purchase. However, shortly before a dividend is due to be paid, ISE will decree that it should only be traded 'ex-div' – the timing of this change being such that, provided all bargains are settled on their due date, the cum-div buyer will be the registered owner of the shares and thus receive the dividend directly from the Registrar. However, not all bargains will settle on the due date and therefore some transfers will not have been affected in time. The registrar will therefore have paid the dividend to the seller, even though, as he sold cum-dividend, he was not entitled to it. Talisman is able to match bargain dates with benefit dates and hence ensure that benefits flow through to the correct party.

7.2.28   As an example of how benefits are treated by Talisman, a dividend that had been paid by a company to the wrong person because of a delay in registration would result in claims being automatically raised for and against the buying and selling brokers respectively. These are posted to a cash distribution schedule (produced for information purposes and to which postings can be made daily, up to and including the dividend payment date of the security), as 'claims raised'. These schedules are sent to firms whenever there is a change in the level of claims outstanding either for or against them. Cash distribution claims are usually settled three days after the pay date of the underlying dividend with a net payment or receipt being made through Talisman.

7.2.29   Another type of benefit which may arise is where there has been a takeover and this has transformed the nature of the stock. Typically, there may be a cash alternative as part of the offer for the original stock of the company being taken over. All such situations are identified by Talisman and 'stock situation notices' are sent to firms detailing the terms of the offer and how outstanding positions in the old stock will be settled.

7.2.30   The old bargain is removed from the standard Talisman bought and sold stock accounts (listings of bargains awaiting settlement – discussed in more detail in paragraph 7.3.9 below) and placed in a 'transformation account'. This account is then allocated to the various elements of the new bargain (in line with the stock situation notice), which could be any combination of the following:

- bought/sold stock account (for Talisman settled stock);
- linked settlement account (for non-Talisman settled stock);
- cash offer settlement account (for the cash element of the offer).

The proceeds of the offer are deposited by the selling firm and Talisman ensures that the correct combination of stock and money is delivered to the buying firm.

Institutional Net Settlement (INS)

7.2.31   This was introduced in August 1988, and enables institutional investors to settle all Talisman bargains dealt with member firms with a single daily net payment.

7.2.32   Bargains to be settled through INS are dealt and submitted to the ISE by the broker-dealer in exactly the same way as any other bargain. The member firm has to inform Talisman that the bargain will settle through INS and also has to provide details of the customer settlement consideration (i.e. the amount the institution actually pays or receives, taking account of commission and dealing expenses).

7.2.33   The day after the bargain has been matched, the institution will receive from Talisman confirmation of the transaction and the fact that it will be settled through INS. Talisman maintains separate bought and sold stock accounts of outstanding transactions for each INS participant and details of these are despatched to both the institution and the member firm. The INS bought and sold stock accounts show customer settlement consideration and, as submitted to the broker, are shown from the perspective of the customer (opposite to the main bought and sold stock accounts). In addition, it should be noted that they are provided to the broker for memorandum purposes only, i.e. they merely reflect the fact

99

that the customers concerned are to settle bargains shown as outstanding in the customer accounts of the broker by a payment or receipt from Talisman.

7.2.34 For sold bargains, the institution delivers the stock to the member firm who is required to deposit it with Talisman in the usual way. For bought bargains, Talisman raises a guaranteed apportionment schedule which is despatched to the institution and serves as a guarantee that stock has been apportioned to it (and hence takes the place of a stock note). The institution then makes a net financial settlement with Talisman based on the day's apportionments and deliveries.

7.2.35 For the member firm, two cash movements take place for each apportionment and delivery. Firstly, there is the usual cash movement which clears the main bought and sold stock accounts. This is based on the bargain consideration (quantity x price). Secondly, there is an opposite cash movement equal to the customer settlement consideration. This clears the memorandum INS bought and sold stock accounts. The member firm would normally use the clearance of the INS stock account to settle the customer ledger balance in respect of that institution.

7.2.36 These two cash movements, which take place simultaneously, give rise to a net receipt for the member firm which represents its commission plus VAT on that transaction.

7.2.37 INS has meant a great reduction in the amount of paperwork at institutions and member firms. This is because stock notes are no longer required as proof of apportionment, and claims and cheques do not have to be raised for every bargain dealt.

TAURUS

7.2.38 Over the past few years, attempts have been made to further develop the Talisman system with the eventual aim of achieving a 'paperless' London settlements system. To this end, the ISE is proposing to develop TAURUS, which is discussed in more detail in chapter 5. This will not change the basic operation of Talisman described above, but will replace the physical delivery of shares and transfers by selling customer and the delivery of shares to buying customers with entries within TAURUS.

7.3 Accounting

7.3.1 Due to the high proportion of securities business that is settled through Talisman, it is very important that accounting procedures and controls in this area are clearly set out and well maintained. The extent to which member firms rely on Talisman varies, although there are two basic approaches which are commonly adopted.

7.3.2 The first is to use Talisman as a bureau handling the detailed accounting entries for all relevant business, with the firm merely maintaining appropriate control accounts which are reconciled to the detailed Talisman records. In this case, the firm will need to maintain its books of prime entry (e.g. bargain journal and cash books) in such a way that totals relating to Talisman bargains can easily be identified and posted to the control accounts on a regular basis.

7.3.3 The second approach is to duplicate, in whole or in part, Talisman's detailed record-keeping within the firm's own books of account which will therefore show every open bought and sold transaction.

7.3.4 The approach adopted will usually depend on the nature of the member firm's accounting system. A predominantly manual system will tend to lead to the control account approach, since otherwise a large amount of work is necessary to provide records of individual outstanding bargains. Alternatively, a computerised system will usually be able to provide detailed open item listings without significant extra cost. In practice, larger firms tend to adopt the second approach as this usually enables better control over large bargain volumes. The first approach is more usually adopted by smaller firms.

7.3.5 As well as the nature of the accounting system, a second factor in determining the amount of detail that the accounting records should contain is the reporting requirements that firms face. Most firms using Talisman will be members of TSA and the presentation of Talisman balances is covered by TSA Financial Regulations rule 30.02a (iii) which states that 'all balances with counterparties must be reflected at their gross amount. Netting of balances with the same counterparty will not be permitted unless an express written agreement exists between the parties to the transaction which provides for the settlement by transactions on a "net" basis.'

7.3.6 This requirement to show balances gross means that a firm will usually maintain separate accounts for debits (sold bargains) and credits (bought bargains). Presentation of Talisman balances in the financial statements follows market practice which means that, in line with the above rule, they should be shown gross.

7.3.7 For TSA reporting purposes, further analysis is required which may require even more detailed accounting records. In particular, where a firm has been trading with member firms which are affiliated companies (e.g. subsidiaries, parent company and subsidiaries of the parent company), this needs to be disclosed separately both in TSA reporting statements and in the firm's financial statements prepared under the Companies Act. It should be noted that the number of brokers with affiliates which are also member firms is quite small and hence this is not likely to be an extensive problem. A further regulatory reporting requirement is to show separately balances which have been outstanding for more than thirty days from the relevant settlement date. This will not necessarily require the more detailed accounting records envisaged by the second approach because the bought and sold stock accounts produced by Talisman are aged.

7.3.8   Accounting for Talisman is reasonably straightforward so long as postings (both bargains and cash) are kept up-to-date. Because of the large volumes processed, daily reports are produced by Talisman for distribution to firms showing current positions and movements on the previous day. The most important of these are:

- *Bought Stock Account.* This is a list of bought bargains which are open for apportionment at the specified date. On a daily basis, firms normally receive a control account statement showing the account balance brought forward and the aggregate figures for new matched bargains and apportionments, with a full open item listing only being received once an account.
- *Sold Stock Account.* This is a list of sold bargains which are open for delivery at the specified date. As for the bought stock account, full listings are normally received once an account, with control account statements on a daily basis.
- *Stock Delivered Schedule.* This shows for each bargain the quantity of stock delivered in satisfaction of sold bargains, as well as recording any bad deliveries (i.e. rejected stock), that occurred on the previous day.
- *Apportionment Schedule.* This gives details of each stock which has been apportioned or part apportioned on the previous day.
- *Net Payment Account* and accompanying *Payment Account Control Statement.* As discussed below.
- Detailed reports relating to benefits, in particular:
  - bargain transformation list
  - cash offer settlement detailed list
  - linked settlement account
  - cash distribution account.

Although there are other reports distributed to broker-dealer firms by the Talisman system, those listed above are the most important reports necessary for the day-to-day control of the Talisman settlement process within a member firm.

7.3.9 As discussed above, once bargains have been matched, they are added to a list of outstanding transactions maintained within the system. Sold transactions are added to the sold stock account and bought transactions to the bought stock account. Hence stock accounts represent agreed unsettled bargains.

7.3.10 Transactions will be removed from the stock accounts when they have been settled (i.e. on apportionment or delivery). Hence the apportionment and delivery schedules provide the information necessary to clear down the Talisman accounts maintained by the firm. Where the firm only maintains control accounts, then it is merely total apportionments and total deliveries that are posted.

7.3.11 The Talisman bought and sold stock accounts should be reconciled to the firm's own accounting records on a regular basis. How frequently this is done will depend on the size of the firm and complexity of its operations. Where a large number of transactions are processed, a daily reconciliation should be performed in order to ensure that a large backlog of disagreed items does not build up. However, as a minimum (even where volumes are low), reconciliations should take place at the end of each account period.

7.3.12 The state of the Talisman reconciliation is usually a good indicator of whether the settlements department of a firm is operating efficiently. This is because, in order to produce a regular reconciliation without a large number of reconciling items, all parts of the settlement process, from initial checking through to delivery and apportionment, must be under tight control.

7.3.13 A typical format for the reconciliation of the Talisman bought stock account would be as follows:

Balance per Talisman produced bought stock account	X
add bargains apportioned overnight (not notified to the firm until the subsequent morning so not yet reflected in the firm's records)	X
add unmatched bargains	X
add transformed bargains removed from the Talisman produced bought stock account and moved to the linked settlement and/or cash offer settlement accounts	X
less 'new time' bargains which have been matched but are excluded from the firm's ledgers until the next SE account	(X)
Balance per member firm's bought stock control account	X

7.3.14 Similarly, a typical format for the reconciliation of the Talisman sold stock account would be:

Balance per Talisman produced sold stock account	X
add bargains delivered overnight (not notified to the firm until the subsequent morning so not yet reflected in the firm's records)	X
add unmatched bargains	X
add transformed bargains removed from the Talisman produced sold stock account and moved to the linked settlement and/or cash offer settlement accounts	X
less 'new time' bargains which have been matched but are excluded from the firm's ledgers until the next SE account	(X)
Balance per member firm's sold stock control account	X

Net payment account

7.3.15 Settlement is made with Talisman on a daily basis. Each morning firms receive a net payment account and accompanying payment account control statement. These give the net amount to be settled that day, together with an analysis of how it is comprised. Settlement is on a net basis which means that one cheque is drawn (either by the firm or Talisman). Most of the settlement is usually made up of apportionments and deliveries which took place on the previous night.

7.3.16 However, there are other types of balances which may also be settled; the most significant of these are as follows:

- cash distributions payable and receivable – these are dividends being claimed from, or paid to the firm, in respect of their customers' trading or in respect of their own principal or market making trading;
- stamp duty – this is presently payable by the firm to Talisman on most customer bought transactions. It is discussed in chapter 13. The customer is charged the $\frac{1}{2}$ per cent on the original contract note and the firm pays this over on apportionment;
- XSP settlement – the cash settlement for bargains not eligible for Talisman settlement, but transacted between member firms, can be made through Talisman. This is discussed in more detail in chapter 8.

7.3.17 A typical firm's net payment account statement and payment account control statement are reproduced below. It should be noted that only the items most likely to be found on these reports are discussed in the example. For an explanation of less common items, the reader should refer to the *Talisman Reference Manual* (published by and obtainable from the ISE).

Payment account control statement

	Reference	Debit £	Credit £
Bad delivery	– bargains		
Stock apportioned			125,000
Apportionment reversal			
Stamp duty			625
Stock delivered		150,000	
INS bought settlement total			
INS sold settlement total			
Cash distributions	– paid		1,000
	– received	4,000	
Cash settlement items			
Cash fractions	– rights and caps		
Linked settlement differences			
Cash offer settlement	– paid		
	– received		
Deficit redemption	– charges		
	– releases		
Free name charges on delivery			
Stock loan stamp adjustments			
Credit vouchers			
Centre inter firm adjustments			
Balance transferred to net statement			27,375
		154,000	154,000

Firm's net payment account statement

	Debit £	Credit £
Balance brought forward		128,777.70
Payments/receipts	128,777.70	
Net agent Talisman settlement transferred	27,375.00	
XSP payable		2,000.00
XSP receivable	10,900.00	
Balance carried forward to next statement		
(due to be paid to firm)		36,275.00
	167,052.70	167,052.70

7.3.18   As can be seen, the payment account control statement gives rise to a balance which is transferred to the net payment account. This latter report starts with the balance brought forward from the end of the day before yesterday and which was settled yesterday. Next comes the balance being transferred from the payment account control statement. Finally items being settled through XSP are brought in. This leaves a net balance due to be settled with Talisman. On this particular day, the firm will expect to receive a cheque for £36,275 from Talisman.

7.3.19   The usual process is to credit this to a Talisman payment control account (TPCA) in the firm's records and to then clear this down to zero by journal entry by posting to the relevant parts of the accounting records on a daily basis.

In this particular case, the postings would be:

1. Dr Cash book	36,275	
Cr TPCA		36,275

being the cheque received from Talisman.

2. Dr TPCA	150,000	
Cr Talisman sold stock account		150,000

being that part of the settlement relating to the delivery of sold bargains.

Where detailed stock accounts are kept by the firm, the Talisman stock delivery schedule will provide a detailed analysis of bargains which need to be closed down on the ledgers. Otherwise, the posting is made to the Talisman sold stock control account.

3. Dr Talisman bought stock account	125,000	
Cr TPCA		125,000

being that part of the settlement relating to the apportionment of bought bargains.

Where detailed stock accounts are kept by the firm, the apportionment schedules will provide a detailed analysis of bargains which need to be closed down on the ledgers. Otherwise the posting is made to the Talisman bought stock control account.

4. Dr Stamp control account	625	
Cr TPCA		625

being the $\frac{1}{2}$ per cent stamp duty on the apportioned bargains.

When the contract note was raised, the customer would have been charged stamp duty and the stamp control account would have been

106

posted with a credit. On apportionment and payment of the stamp duty to Talisman, this account is cleared to zero.

5. Dr Customer A	1,000	
Cr TPCA		1,000
6. Dr TPCA	4,000	
Cr Customer B		4,000

Posting 5 represents dividends incorrectly paid by the Registrar to customer A which Talisman is now claiming from the firm. The firm will need to claim this from the customer which it does by debiting his account. The reverse has occurred in posting 6 with the firm receiving dividends which are due to customer B. In both cases the firm will have been warned by Talisman that payments and receipts in respect of claims would be made, ensuring that the relevant customers could be notified.

7. Dr TPCA	10,900	
Cr residual (Non-Talisman) sold stock account		10,900
8. Dr residual (Non-Talisman) bought stock		
account	2,000	
Cr TPCA		2,000

being that part of the settlement relating to non-Talisman items which have been settled through XSP (discussed in chapter 8 on non-Talisman settlement). The residual bought and sold stock accounts are similar to the ones maintained for Talisman items.

The TPCA is thus cleared down to zero:

TPCA

Posting 2	150,000	Posting 1	36,275
Posting 6	4,000	Posting 3	125,000
Posting 7	10,900	Posting 4	625
		Posting 5	1,000
		Posting 8	2,000
	164,900		164,900

A firm does not necessarily need to maintain a control account to record these postings. Where manual accounting records are kept, it may be appropriate to keep an analysed cash book which shows how the Talisman cheque is broken down. This may then be posted in total to the ledgers on, for example, an accountly basis. However, with the large number of journals needed even for the simple example given, it is clearly important that the net Talisman receipt/payment is in some manner analysed on a daily basis.

7.4 Audit

7.4.1   In carrying out an audit of a firm's Talisman balances, there are two types of audit objective that must be addressed.

7.4.2   *Statutory reporting objectives*
These may be listed as:

(i)   debtors and creditors in respect of Talisman balances are genuine and are completely and accurately included in the balance sheet;

(ii) adequate but not excessive provisions have been made for amounts which may prove to be irrecoverable;

(iii) balances due to and from Talisman are presented in the balance sheet in accordance with the rules of TSA, accounting standards and the Companies Act, as appropriate.

By considering these objectives, the work performed will enable the auditor to decide whether Talisman balances are presented in the accounts in a 'true and fair' manner.

7.4.3   *Additional reporting objectives*
These are specific matters which auditors are required to report on under the Financial Regulations of TSA as follows:

(i)   whether the systems for the agreement and reconciliation of balances with Talisman are adequate and such procedures are carried out at appropriate intervals (rule 90.03d(i));

(ii) whether adequate procedures and controls are in operation for reporting and investigating the ageing and analysis of balances with Talisman (rule 90.03d(iii)).

7.4.4   The accounting systems for processing financial transactions with Talisman are identical for both purchases and sales of stock. Therefore, it is sensible to adopt a single approach to the audit of both debit and credit balances. This is also justified by the good quality of the external audit evidence which enables balances to be ascertained with a high degree of precision. In spite of this, it is still necessary to consider fully the firm's internal control procedures because of the additional reporting audit objectives discussed above.

7.4.5   As a result of the reliance placed by firms on the completeness and accuracy of Talisman accounting, the auditors of the ISE, as part of their annual audit report to the shareholders of the ISE, make specific comments on the operation of controls within Talisman. The ISE accounts, which are made up to the end of March, are available by May or June of each year. It is important that the auditor of any ISE member firm has considered the contents of this report as part of the planning of his audit.

7.4.6   As already noted, Talisman also operates balances in US dollars, Australian dollars and Irish punts which function as for sterling balances. It should be noted that the same procedures apply to auditing currency balances as apply to sterling balances.

Internal control

7.4.7   The following control objectives are appropriate for the recording and settlement of balances, and relate to both purchases and sales. The control procedures set out below relate specifically to Talisman, but also include other controls which may exist in respect of the completeness, accuracy and validity of balances and which occur more through the manner of dealing than through controls over Talisman.

7.4.8   *Control objectives:*

(i) *All bargains are completely and accurately recorded.*
(ii) *All recorded bargains are genuine.*

Possible errors under this heading are:

- validly transacted bargains excluded from the accounting records;
- bargain details incorrectly recorded (e.g. wrong counterparty, incorrect description of share, etc);
- spurious bargains recorded, especially sales to conceal irrecoverable debit balances;
- bargains alleged by counterparties not genuine;
- bargains posted twice.

7.4.9   Control procedures which may exist to ensure that all bargains are both accurately recorded and genuine are:

— dealers independent of: Contract issue
                            'Checking' department
                            Talisman reconciliations
                            cashiers
                            cheque signatories
                            transfer department;
— contract department;
— all bargains reported to the Checking Service;
— all unmatched/alleged bargain reports effectively and promptly followed up;

— all bargains recorded checked back to dealing slips;
— all dealing slips signed by dealer as valid, and unsigned slips not processed;
— regular reconciliation of Talisman bought and sold stock accounts with firm's records;
— experienced staff controlling Talisman settlement process;
— evidenced management review of Talisman reconciliations;
— matching adjustments reviewed regularly by a designated official (especially price adjustments);
— review of rejection and warning reports, checking reconciliation reports and previous account's unmatched deletion report;
— all 'suspense' accounts such as matching alterations, contract suspense etc regularly analysed and cleared to zero (preferably on a daily basis);

7.4.10 *Control objective: All payments to, and receipts from, Talisman are properly recorded*
Possible errors under this heading are:

• bought/sold stock account balances mis-stated;
• unreconciled payment control accounts.

7.4.11 Control procedures which may exist to ensure that payments/receipts are properly recorded include:

— regular reconciliation of Talisman bought and sold stock accounts;
— regular bank reconciliations;
— daily analysis of the Talisman payment control account;
— control over signing of cheques;
— experienced staff controlling Talisman settlement process;
— evidenced management review of Talisman reconciliation.

7.4.12 *Control objective: All apportionments of bought stock and all deliveries of sold stock are properly recorded*
Possible errors under this heading are:

• bought/sold stock account balances mis-stated;
• incorrect amounts paid to/received from Talisman centre;
• claims not made from customers when due.

7.4.13 Control procedures which may exist to ensure that apportionments/ deliveries are properly recorded include:

— regular reconciliation of Talisman bought and sold stock accounts;
— experienced staff controlling Talisman settlement process;

— evidenced management review of Talisman reconciliations.

Analytical review

7.4.14   Analytical procedures will be of limited use as a tool for gaining positive assurance as to the completeness and accuracy of Talisman balances. This is because there is no clear mathematical relationship between Talisman balances and such figures as bargains transacted or customer balances. Moreover, as will be shown below, direct substantive testing is normally a quick and simple method of obtaining a high degree of audit confidence.

7.4.15   As part of the overall accounts appraisal, however, it is nonetheless a worthwhile exercise to understand the influences affecting the balance sheet by reviewing the following:

- the relationship of total Talisman balances to equity turnover in the dealing account preceding the balance sheet date;
- the relationship of Talisman debtor to customer creditor balances and vice versa.

Substantive testing

7.4.16   Substantive tests on the completeness and accuracy of Talisman balances will comprise requesting the ISE to confirm in writing all Talisman balances, reconciling these balances to the firm's accounting records, and investigating all unmatched and alleged bargains shown in the Checking report as at the balance sheet date.

Confirmation of balances by the Audit Services Department of the ISE

7.4.17   The ISE has requested each member firm to give it a permanent authority to allow disclosure of any information that may be required by the firm's auditor. The request for confirmation of balances should be despatched at least two weeks prior to the balance sheet date because of the need for Talisman to process additional copies of reports for the auditor. Requests can be made in arrears, but in such cases a considerable charge will be levied by Talisman on the member firm. It may also be necessary to request other reports from Talisman, for example bought and sold stock account listings in customer order. These can be obtained in either document form or as a computer tape. Any such request should accompany the request for confirmation of balances.

7.4.18   Once a reply has been obtained, it will be necessary to reconcile the certificate balance to that shown in the firm's books of account. It should be ensured that all balances reported by Talisman are reconciled to the relevant part of the firm's accounting records. Even where the firm's ledgers show the correct balance, the operating cycle within Talisman means that a reconciliation along the lines set out in section 7.3 above will be required. It is important that all items appearing in the reconciliations should be verified adequately and appropriate adjustments made in the member firm's accounts.

Unmatched/alleged bargains

7.4.19   To ensure that all bargains, and only genuine bargains have been included in the Talisman balances, it is necessary to examine the reports of unmatched and alleged bargains produced by the checking service. The required report will be that issued on the morning subsequent to the balance sheet date, although it may also be necessary to examine reports for the days after this to follow up on the resolution of unmatched items. It is usually sufficient to obtain copies of the reports annotated by the firm's staff, although in this case it is clearly necessary to verify that all pages are available.

7.4.20   All bargains shown as unmatched (i.e., where the firm has input a bargain but it does not agree to the details input by the counterparty) should be checked for correction by the firm. Such items will normally be indicated by a manuscript comment on the report, for example 'his way', indicating that the firm has accepted that the details input by itself were incorrect. Similarly, all bargains shown as alleged (i.e., where the counterparty has input a bargain, but does not agree to the details input by the firm) should be investigated.

7.4.21   All adjustments made by the firm should then be followed up to ensure that the appropriate alteration has been made in the financial statements. In order to check the accuracy of the adjustments made, the matched bargain reports for subsequent days should be examined to locate the correct, now matched, bargain.

Bad debts

7.4.22   Because of the checking system, all balances with Talisman represent bargains that have been confirmed by the counterparty. Accordingly, a bad debt should only arise where a firm defaults. The identification of any provisions against Talisman balances will accordingly consist of identifying any firms in default either prior to the year-end or in the period between the balance sheet date and the date that the audit report is signed.

112

7.4.23 The auditor should also review the potential exposure on bargains within Talisman that have not settled by the time the auditor concludes his audit work, since a large exposure could give rise to a bad debt if there were a subsequent default of that member firm. This can be achieved by reviewing the 'CRAS' report produced by Talisman for the purpose of computing a firm's Counterparty Risk Requirement (see below), which will identify bargains where there has been a significant change in market price of a security since the time of the original bargain and where therefore the firm would be exposed to loss if the other member firm defaulted.

7.4.24 The procedures adopted when a firm goes into default depend on whether the firm was an agency broker or a market maker.

(i) If an agency broker goes into default, then all of its Talisman balances are reversed out of its books via a process known as 'issuing the reads'. It is then up to the respective market makers to settle with the customers of the defaulting agent on an item-by-item basis. This process is allowed because of the legal status of Talisman which merely serves as a clearing house between two firms – the broker on the one side and the market maker on the other. If the broker drops out (because of default) then the individual for whom he was dealing (the customer) takes his place.

(ii) If a market maker or principal trader goes into default, then all outstanding transactions, whether through Talisman or directly with firms, are closed out at the prices prevailing when the default was called (known as the 'hammer price' because default used to be called by the bringing down of a hammer). Hence the settlement price will vary from the original bargain price, which means that a potential loss may arise if the price has moved adversely. The extent of the loss will be determined by the ultimate proceeds from the liquidation of the defaulting firm.

7.4.25 It should be noted that defaults are very rare and, with the new capital adequacy requirements of TSA, should remain so. Nevertheless, before conducting the audit of an ISE member firm, the auditor must ensure that he is aware of any firms in default so that doubtful balances can be identified and a reasonable assessment of loss can be made.

Disclosure of Talisman balances

7.4.26 The detailed disclosure requirements are set out in section 7.3 above and are not repeated here. Usually the analysis and ageing of Talisman balances prepared by the firm will be test-checked by the auditor for completeness and accuracy.

Exposure and cover summary report

Counterparty risk assessment system
Firm

Assessment categories

A = Exposure as deliverer of sold stock which has gone down (to default of buying firm).
B = Exposure as taker of sold stock which has gone up (to default of selling firm).
C = Exposure as taker from client of sold stock which has gone up (to default of client).
D = Exposure as deliverer of bought stock which has gone down (to default of buying firm).
E = Exposure as taker of bought stock which has gone up (to default of selling firm).
F = Exposure as deliverer to client of bought stock which has gone down (to default of client).

Category:	A		B		C		D		E		F	
	No	Amount	No	Amount	No	Amount	No	Amount	No	Amount	No	Amount
Currency:												
£ Exchange rate: 1.000000												
Exposure:	27	9031			20	4428			9	6663	3	3320
Cover:		6810				2181				6636		915

Totals for all categories expressed in sterling

	A		B		C		D		E		F	
	No	Amount	No	Amount	No	Amount	No	Amount	No	Amount	No	Amount
Exposure:	27	9031			20	4428			9	6663	3	3320
Cover:		6810				2181				6636		915

Total counterparty risk requirement: £16,542   Excluding categories C & F: £13,446

Total exposure: £23,443

Total number of assessed bargains: 59

Cover % used: 31–45 days 25.00%, 25.00%   46–60 days 50.00%, 50.00%   61–90 days 75.00%, 75.00%
91–+++days 100.00%, 100.00%

End of exposure and cover summary for

7.4.27   As noted under the additional reporting objectives above, the auditor has to give a specific opinion on the firm's systems for ageing and analysing Talisman balances. This will involve investigating how the firm arrives at its Talisman analyses and ageings and also looking at the extent of management review of these analyses. It should be noted that an increasing proportion of over-30-days items could be the first sign of a settlements department backlog and it should be ensured that such a review is carried out regularly by the firm at a suitably senior level.

7.5   Capital requirements

7.5.1   For capital purposes, Talisman balances are assessed under the counterparty risk requirement (CRR) rules. These are contained in rule 63 of TSA Financial Regulations.

7.5.2   Because the ISE has details of all outstanding bargains dealt by the firm through the Talisman system, they are in a position to provide the firm with their CRR. This actually occurs through the ISE's Counterparty Risk Assessment System (CRAS), whereby member firms are given a daily figure for CRR in respect of outstanding Talisman bargains. Under TSA rule 63.02c, member firms may rely on this information and in practice many firms do. A typical extract from a CRAS report is shown opposite.

7.5.3   CRR is discussed in detail in chapter 10 and therefore is not considered further here. However, it should be noted that firms do not have to rely on CRAS and some firms have introduced their own systems for calculating CRR on Talisman balances.

7.5.4   CRAS categorises each type of exposure and calculates the CRR cover required. In the example given, total exposure is £23,443 for which CRR cover of £16,542 is required. These figures include exposures under what CRAS describes as categories C and F which are provided as an aid to firms in calculating CRR on customer balances. Since CRAS cannot take account of client free deliveries, etc., these categories are unlikely to give an accurate figure. Therefore, if the firm has (as is usual) a separate system for calculating CRR on customer balances, then exposure under categories C and F can be ignored. CRAS output readily enables this to be done, and the example shows CRR, excluding categories C and F, to be £13,446. This figure can then be entered directly into the reporting statements submitted to TSA.

8 Non-Talisman Settlement

8.1 Introduction

8.1.1   As discussed in the previous chapter, most securities transactions between ISE member firms settle through the Talisman system. However there are still some types of securities which do not settle in this way. One alternative is by way of 'tickets', which was the main system for settlement before Talisman was introduced. Tickets, which are also known as 'names' or 'residuals', may be used either for securities which Talisman cannot settle (e.g. Hong Kong stocks), or where a broker elects to settle a Talisman security outside the normal system (e.g. for reasons of confidentiality).

8.1.2   The other major types of UK securities which settle outside Talisman are:

- those which settle on a cash basis, principally UK government securities or gilts, new issues and traded option premiums; and
- transactions with unit trust managers where a customer of a broker wishes to purchase or redeem units and uses the broker as an intermediary rather than dealing directly with the unit trust manager.

8.1.3   It should be noted that even though non-Talisman settlement forms a small proportion of total settlements, it is an area which needs to be considered carefully by the auditor because there is no central settlement system and the firm is therefore required to deal with all aspects of settlement itself. This can lead to a great deal of extra paperwork and therefore is more prone to error.

8.2 Cash settlement and the CGO

8.2.1   'Cash settlement' is the term used for transactions which are expected to settle on the day after the bargain was dealt. The most important classes of equities covered by this form of settlement are:

(i) 'new issue' equities in the first month or so after the initial issue, while they are traded in allotment letter form; and

(ii) premiums due in respect of traded options transactions (discussed in detail in chapter 18).

8.2.2 As far as new issues are concerned, after the bargain is dealt, it is reported to the ISE for Checking in the normal way. After the bargain has been matched, it does not proceed to Talisman. Instead, member firms settle for cash with the market maker on the following business day, usually through the XSP system described in section 8.3 below. This rapid settlement is possible because allotment letters are usually renounceable, which means that ownership is not registered and can be transferred merely by signing the back of the certificate *The CGO*, thus effectively producing a 'bearer' document. This of course means that physical security over such document is essential.

The CGO

8.2.3 The other significant type of stock which settles on a cash basis is UK government bonds (otherwise known as gilts). The due date to settle a transaction in a gilt is the morning after the bargain was dealt. In order to facilitate gilt settlement, the Bank of England has developed the Central Gilts Office (CGO) service. This provides a computerised book-entry transfer system for gilts and a number of other fixed-interest stocks and eliminates the need for paper transfers, certificates and cheques in the execution of transactions between members of the CGO. The service ensures that stock moves only against assured payment, thereby eliminating settlement risk in transactions between members.

8.2.4 The range of membership of the CGO is quite wide. Gilt-edged market makers, inter-dealer brokers, broker-dealers, ISE moneybrokers, Discount Houses, institutional investors and banks are all eligible for membership provided they can meet certain conditions. All CGO members have accounts within the CGO system in which a record of their stock balances is held. These balances represent prima facie evidence of title to stock, but it should be noted that member-to-member deliveries between CGO accounts are notified to the Registrar who maintains the stock registers which constitute the prime record of legal title. Where one side of a transaction is not a member of the CGO, then a conventional paper transfer has to be effected through the Registrar. The Registrar function of the Bank of England (the Registrar for all gilts and some corporate bonds) will be moving from London to Cheltenham, but this is not expected to make a tangible difference to the registration and settlement process.

8.2.5 The CGO service is based on the concept of book-entry transfer.

117

Records of members' stock balances are maintained in CGO accounts and one member can deliver stock to another by entering the relevant instructions to the system at the CGO terminal in his office. Movement of stock is dependent upon both the giver having sufficient stock on his account and the taker positively accepting the offer of stock. An irrevocable payment instruction guaranteed by the payer's bank is generated simultaneously with (but in the opposite direction to) the movement of stock between accounts. Once stock is credited to a taker's CGO account, it becomes available for onward delivery. It should be noted that stock certificates are not issued in respect of holdings on CGO accounts.

8.2.6 A key aspect of the CGO service is the assured payment arrangement. This is effected by each CGO member nominating an account at a designated settlement bank through which payments and receipts are passed. The buyer's settlement bank gives an unconditional undertaking that, as soon as the CGO transfers stock from the seller to the buyer, it will effect payment the same day to the seller's settlement bank. Any exposure to the buyer's settlement bank is covered by a charge in its favour over stock held in the buyer's CGO account and over moneys receivable by the buyer for any stock subsequently transferred out of his CGO account. Thus the buyer and seller of the stock are protected by the assurance of the movement of stock across CGO accounts, and the commitment to make the payment occur simultaneously.

8.2.7 Settlement of payments takes place towards the end of each day between transferee's banks across bank accounts at the Bank of England, with the CGO providing the necessary information. The CGO also provides schedules for each bank, setting out the final net payment position for each of the bank's CGO member customers. These schedules enable the banks to make the relevant postings to their member customer's accounts.

8.2.8 When a CGO member wishes to withdraw stock from the CGO system, a stock transfer form (STF) has to be lodged at the CGO where it is validated (to ensure that there is sufficient stock in the transferee's account), and then it joins the queue of stock movements to be effected on that particular day. Where the consideration on the STF exceeds £100,000, the STF must be accompanied by an assured payment (in favour of the CGO) drawn on the CGO member's settlement bank. The assured payment provides confirmation for the CGO that the settlement bank concerned is content for its CGO member customer to withdraw the stock from his account. The payments are transferred back to the settlement bank of the CGO member. For deliveries where the consideration is below £100,000, assured payments are not required.

118

8.2.9   It is clear, therefore, that the CGO with its book-entry transfers and
         assured payments greatly eases the settlement of gilts transactions
         between members. For brokers, it is important that stock is received
         promptly from non-CGO customers so that next day settlement can be
         effected. In many cases this is eased by customers maintaining stock in
         safe custody accounts with the broker.

Accounting

8.2.10   It is usual for all bargains which settle on a cash basis to be recorded on
         what is known as a cash jobbers ledger, which is usually separate from
         the residual jobbers ledger discussed in section 8.3 below. This will
         normally be structured in ISE member firm code order and therein on
         an open item basis.

Accounts presentation

8.2.11   The disclosure requirements are very similar to those set out below for
         tickets and residual jobbers balances. Cash jobbers fall into the category
         of balances that need to be shown gross because transactions settle on
         an item by item basis.

8.3 Tickets

The settlement process

8.3.1   As discussed in the previous chapter, all transactions between member
         firms must first be reported to the Surveillance Department of the ISE
         and then sent for checking. Having been agreed in checking, equity
         bargains are then either passed on to Talisman, or back to the firms for
         settlement through the ticket system.

8.3.2   The ticket settlement process starts with the buying broker raising a
         ticket (stating stock, quantity, price, name of purchaser and name of
         broker) which he passes to the market maker. This will usually be done
         at the end of an account when the buying broker goes through his
         ledgers and raises tickets for all such bought transactions. It should be
         noted that the prime objective of the ticket system is to keep paper-
         flows to a minimum. If therefore, during the account, the buying broker
         also has sold bargains in the same stock with the same market maker, he
         will match them up first, and only despatch a ticket for the net quantity
         of stock bought. For these matched-off bargains (known as cross-office
         bargains or tickets), stock received from the selling customer will be
         immediately applied in fulfilling the buying customers' bargains.

8.3.3   The market maker will have been buying and selling that stock during the course of the account and it is his responsibility to match up buyers and sellers. It should be noted that under the Talisman system, this matching of buyers and sellers takes place in the SEPON trading accounts and therefore greatly reduces the amount of paperwork and effort required to settle a bargain as compared with the ticket system. Having performed this matching process, tickets received from buying brokers are passed on to selling brokers by the market maker, thereby informing the seller of the identity of the ultimate purchaser. Settlement is then carried out directly between the buying and selling brokers. The passing of tickets does not itself achieve delivery of stock, it merely informs member firms with whom they should settle. Settlement of stock and money is discussed in more detail below. It should be noted that the ISE is shortly to stop this passing of tickets around the market. It is proposed that in future, tickets will be settled 'as dealt', i.e. each bargain will be settled directly between the broker and the market maker which should greatly simplify the accounting and control of the settlement process, although it will mean more actual deliveries. However, since readers may still encounter unsettled transactions from the earlier methods of dealing with tickets, we have set out the mechanics of this below.

8.3.4   There are a number of problems which may arise in practice with this process.

   • Buyers and sellers may have transactions of differing amounts of stock so that individual tickets cannot simply be passed on. In this case, the market maker will have to 'split' tickets which means replacing the ticket raised by the buying broker with more than one raised by himself. The buying broker will not know that his ticket has been 'split' until he starts to receive stock in smaller quantities than the original purchase.
   • The market maker is unlikely to have equal numbers of buyers and sellers to match up. Where he has too many buyers (i.e. he has a short position in the stock), he will be holding tickets which he cannot pass on. These tickets are commonly called 'names over' and the market maker will hold them until he has bought or borrowed further stock. Where he has too many sellers (i.e. he has a long position in the stock), the market maker has to raise tickets himself for the net amount he has purchased in the account. In this situation, selling brokers simply deliver stock to the market maker.
   • It is probable that the prices of the bought and sold transactions matched by the market maker are different. This will be due both to the market maker's spread and price volatility during an account. In this case, settlement between the buying and selling brokers will take

place at the price on the ticket (i.e. the buying broker's price). If the buying price was above the selling price, the selling broker will receive more than the transacted price for his stock. The broker pays this difference (known as the 'jobber's difference') to the market maker. The converse applies where the buying price is lower than the selling price.

8.3.5   It should be noted that tickets can be passed around the market. In particular, if a broker is a seller in one account but a buyer in the next, and the ticket he received on the original sale had not been settled, he could pass that ticket back to the (possibly different) market maker in the next account rather than raise a new ticket, and settle the buying customer against the selling customer as explained above.

8.3.6   Because of this movement of tickets around the market, the buying broker can lose track of unsettled tickets. To ease the settlement process, and so that the buying broker can identify the holder of his ticket, in order to demand delivery, a 'names over return' exercise is carried out quarterly at the instigation of the ISE. Each member firm lists out all the tickets it holds for each issuing broker which are over one account old at the reporting date. This list is then delivered to the issuing broker who checks it against his open, bought tickets. Any open, bought tickets not reported to a firm by any other broker are reported to the ISE for further investigation.

8.3.7   This procedure should provide an effective control over tickets. In the past, it has fallen short of its potential, mainly because of the absence of any penalties for non-compliance with the exercise. However, with increased control awareness within member firms, it is a procedure which is now much improved.

8.3.8   Each ticket should be settled directly between the buying and selling broker. This occasionally occurs in practice with the selling broker delivering the stock, with the ticket, directly to the buying broker and receiving payment in return. However, most tickets are actually settled through XSP (Cross-Centre Stock Payments), whereby the selling broker passes the stock certificate, transfer deed and bought ticket to the ISE, receiving payment as part of its Talisman settlement the following morning.

The ISE sorts the stock and tickets received and delivers them on to each buying broker the following day. The buying broker also pays the ISE as part of its daily Talisman settlement. The manner in which tickets settle through the Talisman net payment account is illustrated in section 3 of the previous chapter.

Accounting for tickets

8.3.9   In order to control the settlement process relating to tickets, most member firms find it necessary to maintain two ledgers – a 'residual'-jobbers ledger and a ticket ledger. The residual-jobbers ledger is so called because it is used mainly for the initial posting of all 'residual' bargains dealt with other member firms. These are all defined as non-Talisman bargains which are due to settle on the ticket system.

8.3.10   It should be noted that the residual-jobbers ledger can be used for transactions other than those requiring tickets, including moneys due to/ receivable from other member firms in respect of conventional options, as described in chapter 18. In addition, it may be used for recording transactions with market makers who are not members of the ISE, for example bullion dealers for transactions in Krugerrands. Practices vary among member firms, and it is important to identify all the various types of balance on a particular residual-jobber ledger.

8.3.11   Therefore, when a bargain requiring a ticket is dealt, the initial posting on the transaction date is usually to the residual jobbers ledger. On production or receipt of a ticket, the balance is subsequently transferred to the ticket ledger which is usually kept in stock code order. Because tickets usually pass on an accountly basis, such items should clear from the residual jobber ledger promptly. The journal clearing the residual jobbers ledger will be for the monetary amount on the ticket produced or received. Therefore, on bought bargains the broker raises the ticket for the whole amount and the residual jobbers ledger clears down to nil. On sold bargains, the broker will receive a ticket which, as discussed above, will probably be at a different price to that at which he dealt. The value on the ticket is therefore posted to the ticket ledger and the difference (known as the 'jobber's difference') is left on the residual jobbers ledger. The aggregate of the differences is then settled with the market maker on the relevant account day.

8.3.12   A similar accounting process is carried out by the market maker, and the jobbers differences are agreed between the respective parties so they can be settled on the designated account day. Settlement will usually take place through XSP.

Example

8.3.13   The following example illustrates how tickets are created, and balances raised in the ticket ledgers:

Day 3 of Account Broker A buys 5,000 XYZ plc (a non-Talisman stock) @ 90p from market maker M for customer 1.

Day 5 of Account Broker B sells 8,000 XYZ plc @ 86p to market maker M for customer 2.

Day 8 of Account Broker B buys 3,000 XYZ plc @ 92p from market maker M for customer 3.

The bargains are posted on transaction day by the relevant broker to the customers' ledger accounts and to the relevant market ledger (in this case the residual jobbers ledger account for market maker M). It should be noted that all of these bargains are due for settlement on the Monday, six business days after the end of the account.

8.3.14   During the first two or three days after the end of the account, the following events take place.

(i)   Broker A is a net purchaser of XYZ plc, and therefore produces a ticket for 5,000 XYZ @ 90p. The ticket will show the broker's name and ISE reference number, a full description of the shares being purchased, their price, any stamp duty that may be payable by the purchaser, and the total consideration that the broker will pay against the receipt of the shares. This ticket is passed on to market maker M. On production and passing of this ticket, the balance on the residual jobbers ledger is transferred across to the ticket ledger in the books of broker A.

(ii)   Market maker M receives the ticket from broker A and, from his dealings during the account, allocates sufficient sold bargains to make up the total number of shares required by broker A. In this instance, he will pass the ticket to broker B, because he is a net seller of 5,000 shares.

(iii)   Broker B receives broker A's ticket from the market maker. This informs him that he has to deliver 5,000 shares to broker A. He already knows he is due to receive 8,000 shares from customer 2, so 5,000 of these will be delivered to broker A; the balance of 3,000 shares will be used to satisfy the purchase by customer 3.

(iv)   Broker B has entered into two transactions with market maker M which means he is due to receive £4,120 in return for 5,000 shares (i.e. 8,000 x 86p less 3,000 x 92p). The ticket received by broker B shows that he is to deliver 5,000 shares to broker A in return for £4,500. The difference of £380 is the jobbers difference and is due to market maker M. This will be agreed between M and B and settled on account day.

(v)   All that remains is for the delivery of the stock and settlement of the money, which will take place through the XSP system. On account day, customer 2 delivers 8,000 shares to broker B. This

123

is split so that 3,000 are delivered to customer 3 and 5,000 to broker A, at which point broker A pays broker B the £4,500 in settlement.

Accounting entries

In the books of broker A

Market Maker M		Ticket ledger – Stock XYZ	
on production of ticket	on transaction 4,500 day	on production of ticket	
	4,500	(stock due from broker B)	4,500

In the books of broker B

Market Maker M		Ticket ledger – stock XYZ	
on transaction day jobbers difference (due to market maker M)	on transaction 6,880 day on receipt 380 of ticket from broker B	on receipt of 2,760 ticket from broker B (stock due to 4,500 broker A)	
7,260	7,260	7,260	4,500

In the books of Market Maker M

Broker A		Ticket ledger – stock XYZ	
on transaction day	on receipt of ticket 4,500	on receipt of ticket 4,500 from broker A	on passing on of ticket to broker B
		4,500	4,500
Broker B			
on transaction day on passing on of ticket	on transaction 2,760 day 4,500	6,880 jobbers difference 380	
7,260	7,260		

8.3.15 In practice, two separate ticket ledgers may be kept, one for tickets passed (i.e. bought bargains) and one for tickets received (i.e. sold bargains). Usually, a broker will be a net recipient or net producer of tickets for each stock and so it is not appropriate to maintain gross

124

bought and sold balances by stock. Hence at any given time, a stock will either be in the tickets passed or tickets received ledger, but not both.

8.3.16 One exception to this is in the worked example given above where broker B may choose to create an internal ticket to reflect the 3,000 shares to be delivered to customer 3.

Such a ticket would be raised on broker B himself and would simply be shown as a ticket passed and as a ticket received (i.e. shown gross in the ticket ledgers). These are known as 'cross-office' tickets and ensure that when the 8,000 shares are delivered by customer 2, they can be speedily allocated to the 5,000 due to broker A and 3,000 to customer 3. On delivery of stock, cross-office tickets are simply netted off.

8.3.17 Finally, the treatment of the stamp duty on the transaction should be noted. This is usually paid over to the Inland Revenue by the selling broker who executes the transfer deed (thereby transferring it into the name of the buying customer), but the cost is borne by the buying customer. This means that the buying broker has to reimburse the selling broker. The stamp duty is shown as part of the consideration on the ticket and is settled in the same way.

Accounts presentation

8.3.18 The presentation of ticket balances is covered by TSA Financial Regulations rule 30.02a (iii) which states that, 'all balances with counterparties must be reflected at their gross amount. Netting of balances with the same counterparty will not be permitted unless an express written agreement exists between the parties to the transaction which provides for the settlement of transactions on a "net" basis'.

8.3.19 As mentioned above, a firm will usually maintain separate accounts for debits (tickets received) and credits (tickets passed). Thus presentation of tickets as gross balances in the financial accounts will follow normal market book-keeping practice. A particular problem with the grossing of tickets arises with cross-office tickets. As noted above, these tickets have been created internally and do not represent the external assets or liabilities of the firm. The accounting records should enable cross-office tickets to be easily identified and hence netted off for accounts disclosure purposes.

8.3.20 It should be noted that residual jobbers ledgers balances need, in theory, to be split between the element that will be settled net (i.e. the jobbers difference) and bargains where a ticket is outstanding, which should be shown gross. However, it is unlikely that this will be done in practice, since the jobbers differences are unlikely to be material.

8.3.21 For TSA reporting purposes, further analysis is required which may need more detailed accounting records. In particular, where a firm has been trading with an affiliated company (e.g. subsidiaries, parent company and subsidiaries of the parent company), these balances have to be disclosed separately – although they will frequently be immaterial and therefore ignored. A further regulatory reporting requirement is to show separately individual ticket balances which have been outstanding for more than thirty days after the settlement date. The element of the residual jobbers ledger balance that is settled net (i.e. the jobbers difference) and is more than thirty days past settlement date is also shown separately.

8.4 The audit of tickets and jobbers ledger balances

8.4.1 Although the settlement process relating to tickets and cash items has been described separately, it is convenient to consider the audit of these areas jointly. This is because both types of settlement result in balances with member firms and similar audit procedures are adopted irrespective of the way in which the balance initially arose. However, where an audit procedure relates to a particular type of balance, this is highlighted. It should be noted that the jobbers ledger (either cash or residual) can be used as a home for balances with non-member firms. These are considered elsewhere in this book, in particular: overseas brokers (chapter 15), unit trust managers (section 8.5 of this chapter) option dealers (chapter 18) or some other counterparty (treated like a customer as discussed in chapter 9).

8.4.2 The audit objectives may be split as follows between statutory and additional reporting objectives.

8.4.3 *Statutory reporting objectives:*
   (i) Debtors and creditors in respect of tickets and jobbers ledger balances are genuine and are completely and accurately included in the balance sheet.
   (ii) Adequate but not excessive provisions have been made for amounts which may prove to be irrecoverable.
   (iii) Debtors and creditors in respect of tickets and jobbers ledger balances are presented in the accounts in accordance with the TSA's rules, accounting standards and the Companies Act.

8.4.4 *Additional reporting objectives:*
   These are specific matters on which auditors are required to report under the Financial Regulations of TSA as follows:

(i) whether the systems for the agreement and reconciliation of tickets and jobbers ledger balances are adequate and such procedures are carried out at appropriate intervals (rule 90.03d (i));

(ii) whether adequate procedures and controls are in operation for reporting and investigating the ageing and analysis of tickets and jobbers ledger balances (rule 90.03d (iv)).

Internal control

8.4.5   The following control objectives are appropriate for the recording and settlement of balances and relate to both purchases and sales.

8.4.6   *Control objectives:*
(i) *All bargains are completely and accurately recorded.*
(ii) *All recorded bargains are genuine.*

Possible errors under this heading are:

- bargains may be incorrectly stated;
- bargains alleged by counterparties may be genuine;
- bargains may be omitted from the records;
- bargains could be posted twice.

Although it is important for all bargains to be properly and immediately recorded in the ledgers, it is particularly important for cash settlement items. Given the short period of time that elapses before settlement, the firm must be able to ensure the validity of recorded transactions to avoid the risk of settling spurious bargains.

8.4.7   The following control procedures may exist to ensure that all bargains are genuine and are properly recorded:

— dealing room controls, as discussed in chapter 14;
— regular checks between open tickets and the transfer department (which should have details of transactions where re-registration is still outstanding);
— where delivery is made/sought by a counterparty, settlement details are matched to the bargain records in the firm's ledgers;
— regular checks between open sold tickets/open items on cash jobbers ledger with customer accounts;
— all unmatched bargains effectively followed up;
— regular analysis and clearance of suspense accounts;
— 'Names over return' exercises carried out in accordance with ISE requirement and old items agreed with other member firms on a regular basis;

— agreement of jobbers differences with each market maker prior to account day;

— clear distinction made between cross-office tickets and genuine tickets.

8.4.8 *Control objectives:*
(i)   *All sold tickets due are received.*
(ii) *Tickets are raised for all bought bargains.*
(iii) *All tickets are correctly posted from the jobber ledger to the ticket ledgers.*

Possible errors under this heading are:

- balances may be mis-stated;
- delay in the delivery of stock to broker/customer;
- stock may be delivered to the wrong broker/customer.

These are identified as separate control objectives because without the production or receipt of a ticket, the firm will be unable to settle the transaction.

8.4.9 The following control procedures may exist to ensure that these control objectives are met:

— formal procedures in place, governing the automatic raising of tickets;

— each member firm's account in the residual jobbers ledger is balanced by stock quantity, as well as by monetary amount for each stock traded;

— any outstanding stock positions are followed up regularly and promptly;

— regular matching of tickets recorded in the ledger with physical tickets held by the firm;

— the jobbers difference due to/from each market maker is agreed orally or in writing prior to account day;

— where bargains are 'made up' across the office (i.e. where the buyer and seller are both customers of the firm) internal, 'cross-office' tickets are raised;

— regular review of residual-jobbers ledger to ensure that bought bargains are being cleared by the raising of a ticket.

8.4.10 *Control objectives:*
(i)   *Cash receipts and payments are properly recorded*
(ii) *Stock receipts and payments are properly recorded*

Possible errors under this heading are:

- tickets passed/received mis-stated;
- jobbers ledger balances (cash and residual) mis-stated.

8.4.11   The following control procedures may exist to ensure that these control objectives are met:

— segregation of duties between cashiers, transfers' department and jobbers ledger/ticket ledger staff;
— cash receipt compared with open ledger balances;
— regular bank reconciliations;
— prompt completion of the names over returns;
— regular checks between open tickets/open items on jobbers ledger with customer accounts;
— review of all balances (stock and money) remaining unsettled after account day.

Analytical review

8.4.12   Analytical review procedures are unlikely to be of much practical assistance since there are no sources of information within the firm's office which can be used to predict the size of ticket or jobbers ledger balances which are primarily dependent on the level of activity in the preceding account period.

Substantive testing

8.4.13   The principal substantive tests that may be carried out are:

(i) circularisation of member firms to confirm open tickets and jobbers ledger balances; and
(ii) verification of post year end settlement of tickets and jobbers ledger balances.

Circularisation of member firms

8.4.14   It will usually be necessary to perform separate circularisations for the different types of market balances discussed above. The reason for this is that it assists the member firm responding to the circularisation if it knows in which ledger to locate the balance. In addition, it should be noted that letters can be sent out through the XSP system which greatly speeds up the despatch process. It should be noted that TSA rules specifically require all member firms to respond to circularisation requests from the auditors of other member firms, and this can be of benefit if it proves difficult to obtain positive confirmation of a material balance.

Tickets

8.4.15 For reasons of practicality, the circularisation of open tickets is often carried out as at a date subsequent to the balance sheet date with confirmation requested only of those tickets dated before the balance sheet date and still unsettled at the circularisation date. This has the advantage of producing a much smaller list of balances to be covered, but conversely means that the balances settled between the balance sheet date and the circularisation date have to be verified by alternative means.

8.4.16 It is not usually practicable to request that all balances relating to the firm circularised should be confirmed. The sample to be circularised may be selected to cover all tickets in excess of a certain age, and it is important to ensure that tickets with open stock but nil money (for example on bonus issues) are also covered. The circularising firm's ticket ledgers do not always indicate the identity of the member firm issuing the ticket (and almost never the identity of the firm holding a ticket in the case of bought bargains). Moreover, the recipient of the circularisation letter will seldom have the time to carry out a comprehensive check of the completeness of the information on the letter and the auditor should be aware of the restricted audit evidence this circularisation produces. The auditor should also have regard to the results of the names over return, closest to the reporting date.

8.4.17 When preparing the circularisation letter, any reference number provided by the firm being circularised should be included in the letter. This is particularly important for sold tickets, where the sold bargain reference used by the firm being audited should be supplemented by the identification number shown on the ticket itself.

8.4.18 In the event of a non-reply, appropriate alternative verification procedures would include:

- physical inspection of the ticket held by the firm;
- verification of subsequent settlement of the ticket to XSP statements.

To verify tickets settled between the balance sheet date and the circularisation date, a sample of such settled tickets should be selected. For these items, settlement should be vouched to XSP statements to ensure validity.

Residual jobbers ledger

8.4.19   It is important to note that, at any point in time, balances in the residual jobbers ledger will consist of one or more of the following components:

- bargains dealt during the current account for settlement at least ten days in the future;
- differences awaiting settlement in respect of the account just ended;
- differences awaiting settlement in respect of earlier accounts;
- bargains dealt for previous accounts for which tickets have not yet passed (these should be unusual occurrences as tickets usually pass at the end of each account).

8.4.20   As for tickets, it is usual to carry out the circularisation at a date subsequent to the balance sheet date of items which remain unsettled at that date.

8.4.21   The circularisation letter will be used for both unsettled jobbers differences and open bargains for which tickets have still to pass. By performing the circularisation at a date subsequent to the balance sheet date, tickets should have passed for most bargains which means they will have been transferred to the ticket ledger and covered by the separate circularisation of that ledger.

8.4.22   For non-replies, suitable alternative procedures to verify balances will include:

- for unsettled differences – subsequent receipt of cash;
- for open bargains – subsequent transfer of bargains to ticket ledger and subsequent settlement of the ticket;
- for unsettled differences at the circularisation date, any evidence (such a correspondence or discussion with settlements staff) indicating that the counterparty disagrees with the monetary balance.

8.4.23   In order to obtain assurance as to the validity of items settled between the balance sheet date and the date of circularisation, a sample of jobbers differences should be selected and vouched to cash settlement. In addition, a sample of bargains transferred to the ticket ledger should be selected and the corresponding ticket verified as described above.

Cash jobbers ledger

8.4.24   As for tickets and residual jobbers ledger balances, it is normal to carry out the circularisation at a date subsequent to the balance sheet date. The circularisation should cover all open bargains with the member firms selected that were dealt on or before the balance sheet date but not settled by the circularisation date. In the event of a non-reply, suitable alternative procedures will be similar to those discussed above on the tickets and residual jobbers ledger circularisation.

Identification of bad debts

8.4.25 The same considerations as for Talisman balances, which are discussed in the previous chapter, apply here and the audit work consists of identifying any amounts in respect of member firms in default, and any potential exposure to other firms at the completion of the audit.

Accounts presentation

8.4.26 The disclosure requirements relating to tickets and jobbers ledger balances have already been discussed above. The audit work will largely consist of test-checking the analyses prepared by the firm. An area which will require careful attention is the treatment of 'cross-office' tickets which do not constitute external assets and liabilities of the firm. It is therefore important that such items are identified and correctly netted off.

Capital requirements

8.4.27 Outstanding tickets and cash jobbers ledger balances are covered by the counterparty risk requirement (CRR) rules discussed in chapter 10. The element of the residual jobbers ledger balance that is settled net (i.e. the jobbers difference) is treated in the same way as 'settle on balance' (SOB) customers and any element of the balance which is more than thirty days past settlement date should be added to the CRR. The procedures for testing the ageing of SOB customers, set out in chapter 10, are applicable here.

8.5 Unit trusts

8.5.1 Member firms will have two types of dealing with unit trust managers (UTMs). The first is where the UTM buys or sells securities on his own account, or for the account of one of the unit trusts managed by him. The second arises where a customer of the firm wishes to purchase or redeem units in a unit trust and uses the member firm as his intermediary. It is only the second type of transaction that is considered here. Where the UTM is buying or selling shares for his own account, or that of one of his unit trusts, he will be treated like any other customer (discussed in chapter 9).

8.5.2 It should be noted that principal dealers may also have direct dealings with UTMs because some unit trusts are listed on the ISE. As and when principals find they have built up excessively large positions, and the price is favourable, they may buy or sell units direct to the UTMs.

8.5.3 Some firms operate their own 'in house' unit trusts, where the UTM will be the member firm itself, or a company owned by it, and where the investment management of the funds will be carried out by the firm. For the purposes of buying and selling units, the firm will deal with, and account for, the 'in house' unit fund exactly as for external unit trusts, and there will be no difference in the audit work required – albeit that verification of balances may be more straightforward.

8.5.4 The main problem with UTM balances arises from the nature of the settlement process. On a purchase of units, the member firm has to pay the UTM before the relevant certificate is issued. Conversely, on a redemption of units, the firm must deliver the certificate prior to the UTM issuing the cheque. The firm is thus 'out of stock and money' for a considerable period of time – typically at least ten days with UK-based unit trusts, and frequently much longer with overseas trusts. The audit and regulatory capital implications of this are considered below.

Accounting

8.5.5 Most firms will maintain accounts for UTMs within their customer ledgers, with normally one account for each manager but occasionally, where turnover is small, a single account for dealings with all managers. These accounts should be maintained on an open item basis and so will fall within the 'cash against documents' (CAD) section of the customer ledgers, as defined in chapter 9.

Accounts presentation

8.5.6 Disclosure requirements for UTM balances are very similar to those set out above for ticket balances. UTM balances fall into the category that need to be shown gross because transactions settle on an item-by-item basis.

The audit of UTM balances

8.5.7 Since UTM balances are similar in kind to market balances, the audit objectives are similar to those outlined above for tickets and jobbers ledger balances. Many of the control objectives and audit procedures are similar to those set out above and hence only matters specific to the audit of a UTM balance are dealt with here.

Internal control

8.5.8   *Control objectives:*

(i) *All bargains are accurately recorded*
(ii) *All recorded bargains are genuine*
It is important to note that no central checking function exists for transactions with UTMs. Hence procedures should exist to ensure all bargains are confirmed promptly and in writing with UTMs.

8.5.9   *Control objective: All deliveries of stock to UTMs are properly recorded*
This control objective is especially important with unit trust dealings due to the fact that stock and money do not move simultaneously.

8.5.10 The following control procedures may exist to ensure that all deliveries of stock are properly recorded:

— segregation of duties between settlement staff and staff responsible for maintaining accounts with UTMs;
— regular checks between items open with UTMs and items on the corresponding customer accounts (both for stock and money balances);
— regular follow up of unsettled balances.

8.5.11 *Control objective: Stock is received from UTMs in respect of all bought bargains*
This can be a particular problem area, since payment to the UTM takes place before receipt of stock. Once the financial balance has been cleared it is possible that the undelivered stock position may be overlooked.

8.5.12 The following control procedures may exist to ensure that stock is received in respect of all bought bargains:

— segregation of duties between settlement staff and staff responsible for maintaining accounts with UTMs;
— use of stock records to show stocks paid for but not yet received;
— settled bargains are not deleted from open item financial records until stock is received;
— regular follow up of undelivered purchases;
— regular checks between items open with UTMs and items on customer accounts (both for stock and money balances).

Analytical review

8.5.13   Analytical review procedures are unlikely to be effective in this area.

Substantive testing

8.5.14   There are two types of substantive tests which should be performed on UTM balances:

(i) substantive tests on the completeness and accuracy of UTM balances and the adequacy of provisions against UTM balances which will involve a mixture of post year-end settlement testing and circularisation; and

(ii) substantive tests on the adequacy of disclosure.

Circularisation and subsequent settlement

8.5.15   UTMs should be circularised with details of all open transactions, giving both the stock and the monetary balance. UTMs often keep records on a bargain by bargain basis, rather than operating accounts for each counterparty with whom they deal. Therefore, it will be necessary to analyse the monetary balance shown in the member firm's records into individual bargains. Any reference numbers provided by the UTM should be added to the circularisation letter.

8.5.16   As discussed in the section on tickets and jobbers ledger balances, it may be impractical to circularise balances as at the balance sheet date due to the volume of open transactions. Therefore, the circularisation could be carried out at a later date with appropriate testing of balances settling in the intervening period.

8.5.17   In the event of non-reply, alternative verification procedures should be carried out which will include:

- verifying subsequent settlement of the ledger balance;
- ensuring cash was received by reference to cash books;
- ensuring stock certificates are received for all purchases.

A stock agreement may have been carried out by the firm (see chapter 10) providing assurance on the completeness and accuracy of UTM balances. However, since most unit trust transactions are dealt on behalf of SOB customers, the stock agreement may not prove particularly effective.

Bad debt review

8.5.18   For practical purposes, losses are only likely to be incurred by the firm where the UTM refuses to settle at the original dealt price due to dispute over the timing of the transaction.

Such instances should become apparent from the circularisation or tests on post year-end settlement.

Capital requirements

8.5.19   Balances with UTMs will be covered by the counterparty risk requirement (CRR) rules which are discussed in detail in chapter 10. It should be noted that these rules do make an allowance for the distinct settlement procedures in place between member firms and UTMs. Every time a UTM transaction takes place, the firm suffers a free delivery which, under the normal rules, would need to be fully provided against for capital purposes. However, a concession to the normal rules relating to free deliveries means that a firm will not suffer a 100 per cent capital requirement every time it enters into a transaction with a UTM.

8.5.20   The concession applies in either of the following circumstances:

- A firm makes a payment in settlement of a purchase of units from a UTM, in respect of which the certificate is undelivered; or
- a firm delivers units to the UTM in settlement of a redemption (i.e. a sale to the UTM), in respect of which the UTM has not made payment.

8.5.21   In either of these cases, a percentage of the free delivery shall be added to the CRR in accordance with the scale below:

From the date of delivery of, or payment for, the units	% of the free deliver to be added to Counterparty Risk Requirement
Up to 30 days	0
31 to 45 days	25
46 to 60 days	50
61 to 90 days	75
More than 90 days	100

Without this concession, the firm would have to provide against 100 per cent of the free delivery three days after the payment for, or delivery of, the units was made. For all other UTM balances, the normal CRR rules for CAD customers apply.

9 Customer Balances

9.1 Introduction

9.1.1 The customer of a broker-dealer is normally the initiator of a transaction. He will contact the firm who will quote a price for the stock based on current prices being offered by market makers. Under the conduct of business rules, the firm is required to deal at the best price available after enquiring into the prices of a number of market makers (a process known as 'best execution'). In practice this process is eased by the SEAQ screen system (discussed in chapter 6) which shows the best prices being offered by market makers, at a particular time, for standard sized transactions.

9.1.2 It should be noted though that the process of receiving a customer 'order' may differ from that set out above. At one extreme is 'execution only', where the customer receives no advice whatsoever on the merits of his proposed transaction. At the other extreme are discretionary customers who make no (or very few) investment decisions themselves. They merely tell the firm the type of investment portfolio they require (e.g. high income, high capital growth or more usually a balance between the two) and the firm then proceeds to invest in line with these requirements, altering the portfolio as it sees fit. In between these two extremes are customers who have built up a relationship with their broker and who rely on him for investment advice and to take the initiative by making investment recommendations, although the customer still makes the ultimate decision whether or not to enter into a transaction.

9.1.3 Hence, there is a wide spectrum of customer categories, each of which is likely to pay a different amount for the services provided. Some customers will be charged purely on a commission basis, some on a fee basis, and some on a combination of both. Execution only customers will generally be charged the least because they are being provided

137

purely with a dealing service. Conversely, discretionary customers usually suffer the highest charges which are typically calculated as a percentage of the value of the portfolio being administered.

9.1.4 For settlement purposes, there are three main categories of customer, those who settle on a cash against documents (CAD) basis; those who settle on balance (SOB) on the appropriate Account day and those who settle on a rolling balance (i.e. a set number of days after the bargain date).

9.2 CAD customers

9.2.1 These are customers whose accounts are settled against delivery of stock. That is to say, where a customer has entered into a bought transaction, he will only pay the firm when he receives the stock. Conversely, on a sold transaction, the firm will only pay upon delivery of the stock by the customer. Such procedures are generally applied to institutional investors (such as pension funds and insurance companies) who do not wish to be constrained by the rigid settlement rules attaching to SOB (as discussed in section 9.3 below). In addition, it should be noted that settling CAD provides cash-flow advantages to the customer. By settling on the designated account day, customers may be 'funding' the firm if stock has not been apportioned by the market. CAD means that customers do not have to pay until stock has been apportioned and the firm has paid the market.

9.2.2 The settlement process for such customers operates as follows:

(i) For bought Talisman bargains, the firm pays the market on apportionment of stock. As described in chapter 7, after apportionment, stock is sent for registration, which can take a number of weeks. To enable the firm to make a claim on his customer, a stock note is produced by Talisman which acts as a guarantee that stock has indeed been apportioned to a particular bargain and is used as documentary evidence of that transfer into the buyer's name. The customer is informed that stock has been apportioned so that a cheque can be prepared. Usually, a messenger will deliver the stock note by hand to the customer or his agent bank and collect the cheque at the same time. When the certificate is ready, it will usually be sent direct to the customer or to his designated custodian, by the company's registrar. Instructions on this will have been submitted to Talisman when the bargain was first transacted.

(ii) For non-Talisman bought bargains (e.g. gilts and residual stocks as discussed in chapter 8), the firm pays the market upon physical delivery of stock. It is usually the firm's responsibility to complete the registration procedures by sending the stock and the relevant transfer forms to the registrar. Upon despatch of the stock for registration, the firm will make a claim on the customer; usually with a copy of the bought transfer acting as evidence that settlement has taken place.

(iii) For both Talisman and non-Talisman sold bargains, the customer informs the firm when stock (i.e. a share certificate together with the related, signed transfer form) is ready for delivery. The firm raises a cheque and, as above, the transfer of stock and money takes place simultaneously by messenger.

9.2.3 To minimise the risk involved in settling large transactions, both customers and brokers place great store on the simultaneous, or near simultaneous, exchange of stock and money. Where the customer and the broker are based too far away from each other for this to take place by messenger, each will endeavour to use a branch office or a settlement agent bank to effect settlement. Only if this is not practicable will settlement take place by use of the postal service and post-dated cheques.

9.2.4 A further complication is that a single, bought bargain will not necessarily be settled by one delivery of stock. Talisman will part-apportion stock to the bargain rather than waiting for the full amount of the bargain to become available in the relevant SEPON trading account, and it is therefore possible that apportionment may take place in a large number of small 'parts'. Some institutional investors refuse to settle such part-apportionments, requiring the whole bargain to be settled by one payment when delivery is complete. Given that part-apportionments are frequent, this is likely to leave the broker-dealer considerably out of money as he waits for the whole bargain to be apportioned. To ease this problem, most institutional investors will agree to settle part-apportionments above a stipulated minimum size.

9.2.5 It should be noted that the item by item process of settlement described above is changing with the implementation of Institutional Net Settlement (INS). This is a service introduced by the ISE in August 1988, which enables institutional investors to settle with one net payment or receipt, direct with the ISE, all Talisman bargains dealt with any member firm which are settled on a particular day. INS is discussed in detail in chapter 7. INS means that stock notes are no longer required and the amount of paperwork both at the customer and the broker is considerably reduced.

9.3 SOB customers

9.3.1 These are customers whose accounts are supposed to 'settle on balance' on the appropriate settlement day for each Stock Exchange account period. For most stocks, this will be on account day, which is usually the Monday ten days after the last day of dealing for a particular account period. However, for some stocks, such as gilts and allotment letters, the appropriate settlement day is the day after the bargain was transacted. The customer must therefore pay for such purchases and deliver stock for such sales the next day.

9.3.2 SOB means that where a customer has entered into a number of transactions during an account, only the net balance is settled on account day and the customer is required to pay any such debit balances irrespective of whether stock has been delivered. It should be noted that, in order to avoid exposure to bad debts, the firm may choose not to pay a customer on a sold transaction until the stock has been delivered. This is discussed in more detail below.

9.3.3 The SOB classification will usually apply to private investors and to intermediaries such as solicitors and accountants who buy and sell stocks on behalf of their own clients.

9.3.4 In order to minimise the paper-flow between brokers and customers, and to streamline the settlement process, many firms offer safe custody facilities for their customer's physical stock holdings. This usually involves the use of a nominee name into which all customers' holdings are registered. This greatly facilitates settlement, since there is no need for stock to pass between the firm and its customer. In addition, it provides a means by which a firm can ensure that a customer does not sell stock he does not possess. Safe custody and nominee shareholdings are discussed further in chapter 12.

9.3.5 Where nominee facilities are not provided to a customer, the firm will have to handle stock registered in the name of the customer. Where a customer purchases stock and settlement is made through Talisman, the firm must provide Talisman with details of the name into which the stock should be registered. After apportionment, stock is sent directly from Talisman for registration and is then returned to the firm for despatch to the customer. For sold transactions, the firm will receive a certificate and a signed transfer form from the customer which is then deposited with Talisman in order to fulfil the responsibilities of the firm.

9.3.6   The settlement process may be further simplified by customers' maintaining cash deposits with the firm which can be used to settle balances
every account and which will be protected by the client money rules
discussed in chapter 11.

9.3.7   In order to demonstrate how SOB customers settle their accounts, three
different situations are described below. It should be noted that
whenever a customer transacts a bargain, it is allocated to an account
period and thereby the settlement date is fixed. This is notified to the
customer on his contract note. If the customer is selling shares, the
broker will send the contract note to the customer with the relevant
share transfer forms for signature.

(i)   If a customer transacted a single bought bargain during an account,
he is required to send a cheque for the full value of that bargain to
the firm by the designated account day. This applies whether or not
the stock has been apportioned by the market and means that the
customer may pay for something he does not yet possess although
he is protected, in that he does become entitled to all of the benefits
which are attached to the shareholding, such as dividends, from the
transaction date. Moreover, until such time as stock is apportioned, the firm is required to hold the customers' funds in a
suitable client money account, as described in chapter 11. In
practice a large proportion of bargains are apportioned on account
day.

(ii)   If a customer transacted a single sold bargain during an account, he
is required to deliver the stock and signed transfer forms to the firm
on or before the designated account day. On receipt of these
documents, the firm will draw a cheque in favour of the customer.
It should be noted that until the customer delivers the stock, the
firm is under no obligation to pay him. Best practice dictates that
no payment is made until stock has been delivered in order to
minimise the financial exposure of the broker. If, however, the firm
holds the customer's stock in its nominee facility, the firm is able to
make the necessary transfer itself and settlement invariably takes
place on account day.

(iii)   A more complex situation arises where a customer buys one stock
and sells another in the same account leaving a small net balance.
Before allowing this offset between debit and credit and delivering
the bought stock to the customer, the firm must be sure that the
customer possesses stock to deliver on the sale otherwise the firm is
exposed to the risk of a bad debt. This would arise if the customer
were never to deliver the sold stock, and therefore the broker were
forced to purchase the shares in the market to fulfil delivery of the
sale to the market maker. The cost of this purchase would then be

debited to the customer, and if the original purchase had been delivered to the customer, the broker would be exposed to the risk of loss of the entire debit. Avoiding this sort of situation involves having some knowledge of a customer's holdings and not knowingly transacting a 'bear sale' (i.e. a sale by a customer in the expectation of a fall in prices). If the customer does not deliver the sold stock within a pre-set number of days (for example thirty), the firm may claim for the full value of the bought bargain. Alternatively, it may retain the stock certificate in respect of the bought bargain, to facilitate any subsequent legal actions to recover the debt. Overdue balances are discussed in more detail in section 9.8.

9.4 Rolling settlement customers

9.4.1 Rolling settlement describes the situation where a bargain is settled a pre-set number of days after it was transacted. This is in contrast to the account settlement system, discussed above, where bargains are due to settle on the Monday ten days after the last day of dealing, for all bargains dealt in a particular account.

9.4.2 Rolling settlement is already the norm on many overseas stock exchanges (e.g. USA, Japan and Hong Kong). It is proposed that in the near future, rolling settlement will be introduced in the UK as a replacement for the account settlement system. No fixed date has been set for this, but it is expected that it will be introduced in the latter part of 1992, as part of the TAURUS development discussed in section 9.7 of chapter 5.

9.4.3 Rolling settlement is therefore currently of relevance primarily for customers who deal on overseas stock exchanges, although it will undoubtedly be of major importance for the UK market in the future. In practice, rolling settlement is very similar to CAD settlement in that transactions settle on an item-by-item basis.

9.4.4 For bargains dealt on overseas exchanges, firms usually rely on the services of overseas brokers and custodians (detailed procedures for which are discussed in chapter 15). The firm will wait until it has been informed by the overseas broker/custodian bank that a bargain has settled and then make the appropriate settlement with its customer. Settlement takes place a pre-set number of days after the transaction was dealt; exactly how many days depends on the particular overseas market.

9.5 Discretionary customers

9.5.1   These are customers who, having indicated the general nature of their portfolio, leave specific investment decisions to their broker-dealer. They may choose this approach because of a lack of time or insufficient knowledge of investment opportunities. It is clearly important that a customer agreement letter exists for such customers, setting out the general aims and restrictions under which the account is to be operated. It should be noted that such an agreement is a requirement of all the SROs which lay down the minimum contents of agreements. This agreement may set out, for instance, excluded stocks or sectors which the customer does not wish to invest in.

9.5.2   The manner in which such agreements operate varies, although most customers deposit a fixed sum which the firm then invests as it sees fit. Uninvested funds are held on deposit by the firm and earn interest for the customer; once the fixed amount has been deployed, further investment can only take place by selling existing securities. Dividends may be paid away to the customer or re-invested in the portfolio. The customer may be charged commission on each transaction, or a fee based on the value of the portfolio under management, or a combination of both. It is important that, if commission is charged on each transaction, the firm does not 'churn' the portfolio by carrying out an unnecessarily large number of transactions simply to generate commission income for itself.

9.5.3   The customer will require a regular status report on his portfolio. How often this is sent will be one of the terms in the initial agreement with the customer but, under SRO rules, cannot be less than every six months. TSA Conduct of Business Rules (rule 720.03) gives the following specific guidance on the contents of such reports:

    — listing of investments held, together with cost and current value;
    — the amount of cash not invested;
    — a statement of the basis on which the valuation of each investment has been prepared;
    — any investments lent to a third party and any charge to secure borrowings made on behalf of the customer;
    — the income receivable by the customer during the period of account in respect of each investment in the portfolio, together with the amount of any tax credit, tax deducted at source or withholding tax;
    — any interest payments made during the valuation period in respect of sums borrowed on behalf of the portfolio;
    — particulars of each transaction entered into by the firm for the portfolio during the period;

- the remuneration of the firm and companies connected with it in respect of each transaction effected for the portfolio during the valuation period, or a statement of the aggregate amount of such remuneration;
- a statement of any remuneration received by the firm or any company connected with it from a third party (other than another customer of the firm for whom the firm has acted as agent in the transactions concerned), in respect of transactions entered into by the firm for the portfolio.

9.5.4   It should be noted that fund management is discussed in more detail in chapter 22 and reference should be made there as appropriate.

9.6 Loan account customers

9.6.1   A further category of customer are those to whom credit or 'loan account' facilities are extended. In these cases, the firm extends credit on a secured basis against the collateral of the stock purchased by the customer. Such customers may normally be CAD, SOB or rolling settlement and the loan account may apply to individual transactions or to all dealings by the customer. In the US and, occasionally in the UK, these are known as 'margin' account customers.

9.6.2   An example of a loan account transaction would be for the customer to purchase £100,000 worth of stock through the firm, for which he might pay, say, £50,000 with the firm making him a loan for the balance. An appropriate rate of interest would be charged for this credit facility.

9.6.3   Such business involves a different degree of risk for the firm and, therefore, appropriate control procedures need to be in place. A key control and, indeed, a TSA requirement is that there should be a written agreement between the firm and its customer setting out the details of the credit arrangements. In addition, the firm must ensure that it holds the relevant share certificates, registered in its nominee name, so that collateral can be speedily realised without reference to the customer. The firm must also monitor the value of collateral held on a regular basis (at least once per account if not daily), and compare the value of the collateral held with the outstanding loan. Typically, collateral will be valued at a discount to its market value to reflect the costs of sale and the risk of adverse price movement between the time of valuation and any ultimate sale. Under TSA's rules for such business, the usual discount will be the PRA for the security concerned, as described in section 14.6 of chapter 14.

9.6.4   Since loan account customers require the extension of credit by the broker-lender, it may be necessary for the firm to be registered under the Consumer Credit Act 1974. This requires all organisations that grant credit to be registered, and to comply with various detailed requirements, except where the minimum amount of credit extended exceeds £50,000.

9.7   Accounting

9.7.1   Traditionally, CAD and SOB customer balances have been accounted for in different ways. Since CAD settlement is on an item-by-item basis, it is important that accounting records identify each outstanding transaction. This will allow the firm to identify bargains which have not yet settled and also when settlement does take place, ensures that cash can be applied against the correct bargain.

9.7.2   Conversely, since SOB customers settle on a net basis, historically there has been no need to maintain open item ledgers. Firms have traditionally maintained 'rolling ledgers' which means that a net balance is carried down at the end of each account. This net balance should then be cleared by a cheque on the designated account day. However, it is in the firm's interests to be able to identify which bargains make up the balance on a SOB account since this makes it easier to highlight undelivered sales, which may be concealing large and potentially irrecoverable debits relating to purchases. In addition, as noted in chapter 10, open item accounting for SOB customers is also essential for the calculation of CRR. For these reasons, increasing numbers of firms are moving towards open item ledgers for SOB customers. For accounting purposes, balances relating to rolling settlement customers are normally included as part of the CAD records.

9.7.3   A second factor in determining the amount of detail that accounting records should contain is the reporting requirements of TSA. The presentation of customer balances is covered by TSA Financial Regulations rule 30.02a (iii) which states that 'all balances with counterparties must be reflected at their gross amounts. Netting of balances with the same counterparty will not be permitted unless an express, written agreement exists between the parties to the transaction which provides for the settlement of transactions on a "net" basis'.

9.7.4   Hence, CAD customer balances should generally be grossed up for inclusion in the financial statements. However, because SOB customers settle on a net basis, which is usually formalised by the Client Agreement Letter, these balances are shown net.

9.7.5   For TSA reporting purposes, further analysis is necessary. In particular, the accounting records will have to distinguish between:

(i) balances with an affiliate (i.e. subsidiaries, parent company or subsidiaries of the parent company) and with any other type of counterparty;

(ii) balances which will clear by rolling settlement, by Stock Exchange account settlement, or by some other means of settlement; and

(iii) whether the balance has been outstanding for more or less than 30 days from the designated settlement date.

9.7.6   For CAD customers, this should be relatively simple because every open transaction can be allocated to a particular 'slot' in the analysis. This process is usually computerised and is reliant on there being correct standing data on file (i.e. with respect to customer and settlement type).

9.7.7   For SOB customers, ageing is more problematical because of the netting that takes place. It is usually sufficient to determine whether any part of the current net balance arose in the 'less than thirty days' settlement period. Ageing is usually carried out on a FIFO basis except that special allowance must be made for 'closing' bargains (i.e. bought and sold bargains for the same type and quantity of stock in the same account) and 'bear' sales (i.e. where the customer does not possess the necessary stock). Any part of the balance that did not arise in this period is then shown in the 'over thirty days past settlement date' category. An example of how such netting should be carried out is given in section 10.6 of chapter 10.

9.8 Audit

There are two types of objective that the audit of customer balances must address.

9.8.1   *Statutory objectives*
These are as follows:

(i) debtors and creditors in respect of customer balances are genuine and are completely and accurately included in the balance sheet;

(ii) adequate but not excessive provisions have been made for amounts in respect of customer balances which may prove to be irrecoverable;

(iii) amounts due to and from customers are presented in the balance sheet in accordance with the rules of TSA, accounting standards and the Companies Act as appropriate.

9.8.2 *Additional reporting objectives*
These are specific matters on which auditors are required to report under the Financial Regulations of TSA. These are as follows:

(i) whether the systems for the agreement and reconciliation of customers' balances are adequate and such procedures are carried out at appropriate intervals (rule 90.03d(i));
(ii) whether adequate procedures and controls are in operation for reporting and investigating the ageing and analysis of balances with customers (rule 90.03d(iii)).

Internal control

The following control objectives should be considered.

9.8.3 *Control objective:*
(i) All bargains are completely and accurately recorded.
(ii) All recorded bargains are genuine.

Possible errors under this heading include:

- valid bargains excluded from the accounting records;
- bargain details incorrectly recorded (e.g. wrong customer, incorrect description of share etc.);
- transactions which a customer thinks have been entered into have not been properly executed with the market;
- spurious bargains recorded, especially sales, to conceal irrecoverable debit balances;
- bargains posted twice.

9.8.4 Control procedures which may exist to ensure that all bargains are accurately recorded and are genuine include:

— dealers independent from customer ledgers, accounting function and cashiers;
— review of contract notes before despatch;
— prompt despatch of contract note to all customers;
— automatic despatch of contract note/statement segregated from the dealers;
— regular analysis and reconciliation of customers' accounts;
— statements regularly sent to all customers;
— customers' accounts regularly reviewed by account executives;
— prompt clearance of all suspense accounts.

9.8.5 It should be noted that some overseas customers may request that contract notes/statements are not sent to them. Ideally, this should be evidenced by an agreement letter signed by the customer, although this may not always be practicable. All such arrangements should be formally approved by senior management, who should also ensure that the relevant accounts are reviewed carefully by management to ensure that activity is normal and that cash movements are properly authorised.

9.8.6 *Control objective: All payments to, and receipts from, customers are properly recorded and authorised.*

Controls over cash, cheques and the like are important in any kind of business, but especially so in a broker-dealer which may have tens of millions of pounds passing through its accounts each day, even where it is only a small business. It should be noted, though, that a broker-dealer may find it difficult to implement effective controls in this area because of the high volume of cheques which have to be processed in a short space of time (particularly around account day). Nevertheless it is essential that effective controls are in place in order to protect the assets of the business.

Possible errors under this heading include:

- moneys posted to the wrong customer's account;
- moneys paid or received posted for the incorrect amount;
- payments made in error or through fraudulent intent.

9.8.7 Control procedures which may exist to ensure that payment and receipts are properly recorded include:

— division of duties as above;
— cheque signatories presented with backing documentation to validate payments;
— backing documentation cancelled once cheque signed;
— designated cheque signatories exist with appropriate limits;
— cheques produced automatically from settlement details;
— regular bank reconciliations;
— regular analysis and reconciliation of customers' accounts;
— customers' accounts regularly reviewed by account executives;
— statements regularly sent to all customers;
— statements sent automatically to customers, without intervention by dealers, ledger clerks etc.

9.8.8 *Control objective: Deals are not transacted for customers that are bad credit risks.*

Possible errors under this heading include:

- purchases made by customers who are unable or unwilling to pay;
- bear sales (i.e. customer sells stock he does not possess in the expectation of a fall in price), made by customers who are unwilling or unable to buy back the shares concerned in the event of a price rise.

9.8.9 Control procedures which may exist to prevent such errors include:

— all new customers , as a minimum, are cleared with the Stock Exchange Members Mutual Reference Society and/or an appropriate credit rating bureau to ensure no prior bad debt experience;
— a new customer's initial dealings should be carefully monitored and prompt settlement required;
— setting of limits that a customer's balance may not exceed, above which orders are no longer accepted;
— review of balances against these pre-determined limits;
— for new SOB customers, the firm ensures it is aware of existing shareholdings;
— all stock held in safe custody with the firm;
— requirement for SOB customers to keep a cash deposit with the firm before trading can commence;
— compliance with the 'know your client' requirements of the conduct of business rules;
— use of the 'forty-eight hour hold' and 'ten day hold' facilities within Talisman, to ensure that apportioned stock is not registered in the customer's own name until payment in cleared funds has been received.

9.8.10 *Control objective: Customers' balances are settled promptly.*
Possible errors under this heading include:

- debts allowed to become overdue
- overdue debts not followed up.

9.8.11 Control procedures which may exist to monitor and enforce prompt settlement include:

— regular production of aged listings and follow up of overdue items;
— regular review of CRR reports for 'capital expensive' balances (CRR is discussed in chapter 10);
— statements sent regularly to customers;
— mechanism exists to charge account executives with bad debts (or a share thereof) on customers for which they are responsible;
— legal process for debt collection;

— reminder letters sent, or personal contact by account executive if balance still not settled;

— stock held for customers, or awaiting delivery to customers, sold for the customer's account if funds not received within a specified time;

— use of 'forty-eight hours hold' and 'ten days hold' facilities with Talisman as above.

9.8.12 *Control objective: Payments against sales are only made against good delivery of stock.*
Possible errors under this heading include:

- stock delivered by a customer is out of order (e.g. wrong stock, failure to submit certificate for full extent of sale, or transfer form is in a different name to that on the share certificate);
- payment to customer made on instructions of account executive, whilst expected simultaneous delivery of stock not forthcoming;
- proceeds from sales re-invested in purchases thereby clearing any balance, leading to overdue deliveries on sales not being pursued.

9.8.13 Control procedures which may exist to ensure that payment on sales is only made against good delivery of stock include:

- segregation of duties between customer ledgers, cashiers and sold transfer department;
- payment to the customer made only on receipt of stock, confirmed by a release slip being passed from the sold transfer department, who have checked that the stock is in order;
- regular review of undelivered sales on the market ledgers to identify overdue items relating to SOB customers which may be concealing irrecoverable debits within the customer account;
- review of CRR reports for 'capital expensive' balances.

9.8.14 *Control objective: Potential bad debts are identified and, where necessary, adequate but not excessive provision is made.*
Possible errors under this heading include:

- potential bad debts not identified;
- adequate provision not made;
- excessive provision made.

9.8.15 Control procedures which may exist to prevent such errors include:
— regular production of old, open balance listings for management review;
— bad debt provisions approved by suitably senior management;
— regular review of market debit transaction listings (e.g. Talisman

sold stock account) and matching of this to the SOB customer ledgers for identification of irrecoverable debits concealed by undelivered sales;

— where the SOB ledgers are maintained on a 'rolling balance' basis, an analysis of each open balance is performed so that irrecoverable debits do not become concealed in a net balance;

— regular review of CRR reporting by suitable senior management and follow up on 'capital expensive' items.

9.8.16   *Control objective: To safeguard against the possibility of repudiation of bargains by discretionary customers, satisfactory agreements are obtained in all cases.*
Possible errors under this heading include:

- register of discretionary customers not fully up to date (therefore difficult to ascertain whether letters obtained in each case);
- agreement letters undated or unsigned and therefore invalid;
- agreement letters grant discretion to an individual dealer or client executive and not the firm;
- notice for the termination of, and the period covered by, the letter not stated.

9.8.17   Control procedures which may exist to prevent such errors arising include:

— register maintained under the control of senior management and procedures laid down whereby any new or deleted account is reported;

— responsibility for vetting the agreement letter left to this senior management;

— standard form of letter used;

— periodically, account executives are circulated a list of 'their' discretionary customers so that they may:
   (a) add/delete names where applicable;
   (b) consider any amendments that may have occurred to existing arrangements and ensure that agreements are amended accordingly and confirmed in writing by the customers.

9.8.18   *Control objective: Discretionary accounts are operated in a manner which is consistent with the agreement terms*
Failure to meet this objective exposes the firm to legal action from customers and thus to financial loss. Possible errors under this heading include:

- moneys under- or over-invested beyond any set limits;

151

- dealings conducted in investments which are specifically excluded from a customer's portfolio (e.g. written options, tobacco stocks etc);
- failure to send customers' portfolio valuations on a periodic basis;
- failure to match targeted investment objectives (e.g. buying speculative shares for a 'steady income' portfolio);
- failure to charge the correct fees for handling such portfolios;
- incorrect treatment of uninvested balances, interest and dividends.

9.8.19   A control procedure which may exist to prevent such errors arising is:
— regular review of such accounts by senior management as well by the relevant account executive.

9.8.20   *Control objective: Loan account business is operated and controlled on a proper basis*
Possible errors under this heading include:

- loan accounts operated for uncreditworthy customers;
- fall in value of collateral exposing firm to credit risk;
- collateral held in a non-realisable form.

9.8.21   Control procedures which may exist to prevent such errors arising include:

— all customers undergo a credit assessment (as described above);
— credit only given for a pre-set period;
— credit only given up to a pre-set proportion of collateral;
— where collateral falls below agreed minimum multiple of outstanding loan, collateral is sold to bring the accounts into line;
— agreements setting out terms of lending in place for all loan account customers;
— register of loan account customers maintained and additions only permitted after approval from senior management;
— collateral in the form of share certificates held in the firm's nominee name;
— collateral regularly valued and compared to amount of lending outstanding;
— reports of collateral and lending regularly reviewed by senior management;
— where certificates held in the customer's own name, signed sold transfers are also held;
— where certificates held in customer's own name, holdings are periodically checked against the share register to confirm customer has not sold shares through another broker.

Analytical review

9.8.22 There is little scope for analytical review in this area.

Substantive testing

9.8.23 Substantive testing will principally be aimed at meeting the three statutory objectives set out above. The nature of this testing is summarised below:

- Substantive tests on the completeness and accuracy of customer balances will comprise a mixture of the stock agreement and a circularisation of balances.
- Substantive tests on the adequacy of provisions against bad debts will vary according to whether the customer is CAD or SOB. For CAD balances, subject to a number of factors outlined below, potential bad debts can be identified by a review of 'capital expensive' items on CRR reports. For SOB customers, the substantive testing will be a combination of post-balance sheet date settlement work and a check for bear sales. In addition, it is necessary to review discretionary accounts to ensure that they are being satisfactorily maintained and that there are no outstanding claims against the firm for mismanagement of accounts.
- Substantive tests on the adequacy of disclosure will involve test checking analyses to ensure that they meet with the requirements set out in section 9.7 above.

Completeness and accuracy

Stock agreement

9.8.24 As more fully discussed in section 10.3 of chapter 10, the stock agreement can be an important audit procedure for verifying the calculation of CRR and it also provides comfort on the internal consistency of the accounting records and settlement systems of the firm, and their completeness and accuracy.

Circularisation of customer balances

9.8.25 A circularisation carried out at the balance sheet date can provide a particularly effective audit procedure. If it is not carried out at this date, although it then provides little direct comfort on the accuracy of customer's balances, it does provide good, general evidence on the 'collectability' of balances and the accuracy of the accounting system. In addition, it can be used to assess the firm's procedures for agreeing and reconciling balances. It should be noted that where there are a large number of customer balances, a negative circularisation can be a particularly useful procedure.

9.8.26 Firstly, a representative sample should be selected to include all types of customer balances, including:

— private investors
— institutional investors
— foreign customers
— intermediaries (solicitors and accountants)
— discretionary accounts
— loan accounts

9.8.27 A small selection of nil balances should normally be included in the sample and, to be representative, each account executive should have at least one of his customers selected. The following details should be noted for each customer:

— balance on the account;
— bargains not yet settled;
— dividends, rights and calls due;
— share certificates in the course of registration;
— balance certificates in the course of registration;
— share certificates in the firm's possession or under its control;
— note on whether authority/no authority to deal on discretionary basis has been given;
— secured loan account arrangements;
— any outstanding traded options or financial futures transactions (discussed in chapters 18 and 19 respectively);
— any margin held in respect of traded options or financial futures transactions.

9.8.28 The reason such a large amount of detail is required is that settlement involves far more than simply ensuring that correct monetary payment or receipt takes place. By obtaining confirmation on all of the matters noted above, the auditor gains significant comfort on the satisfactory operation of the settlement operations as a whole.

9.8.29 The amount of information required means that the preparation of letters can be a time-consuming exercise and, wherever possible, the firm's staff should carry this out, with audit staff reviewing the letters before despatch. Where it is not practicable to produce all the information in the time available it may be appropriate to perform a more extensive negative circularisation of monetary balances, and, then select a smaller sample of accounts for detailed positive circularisation.

Adequacy of provisions

9.8.30 Bad debt provisions for CAD and SOB customers are dealt with below. The adequacy of provisions for balances derived from traded options and financial futures business are considered in chapters 18 and 19.

CAD customers

9.8.31 An important tool in the review of CAD customer ledger balances is the Counterparty Risk Requirement (CRR) required under TSA regulations. CRR is the means by which member firms are required to provide regulatory capital against the potential risk of default by their counterparties. The higher the perceived risk, the greater the capital requirement. Therefore CRR can be reviewed, and material exposures investigated for the adequacy of any provisions.

9.8.32 The calculation of CRR and its audit is discussed in detail in chapter 10. It is sufficient here to note that the auditor is required to give an opinion to TSA on whether the total capital requirement (of which CRR forms a part) has been correctly calculated. For this purpose, audit work needs to be performed to verify CRR. This work should also enable the auditor to be able to rely on CRR for the review of the adequacy of provisions. If CRR is found not to be correctly calculated then it cannot be relied upon to provide a basis for this review. In this case, a combination of the stock agreement and the late stock agreement (both discussed in chapter 10) should be carried out in order to identify bad debt exposures.

9.8.33 As well as reviewing CRR at the balance sheet date, it is also necessary to keep CRR under review right up to the signing of the audit report. This may reveal transactions which, although not showing a material exposure at the year-end, have subsequently resulted in a material exposure.

SOB customers

9.8.34 For SOB customers, CRR reporting can also be used for identifying exposure to bad debts. However, there are a number of limitations which must be considered before placing reliance on CRR reporting for this purpose. Firstly, there is no requirement to provide regulatory capital on SOB customers until more than thirty days has elapsed from the designated settlement date. Secondly, it may be permissible to offset credit items on the ledger (e.g. undelivered sales), with debits leaving a small net requirement.

9.8.35   The principal, substantive audit procedure involves checking for the
          post balance sheet date settlement of balances. Given that all balances
          should settle on the account day after the balance sheet date, there
          should only remain a small residue of balances requiring further review.
          For balances which have not settled on the designated account day, it
          is necessary to review the composition of the balance. For debit
          components it is necessary to check whether stock has been apportioned.
          If it has, then there may be an exposure if the firm no longer has control
          of the stock (generally, physical possession of the share certificate is
          accepted as 'control', even if it is registered in the customer's name,
          although in the latter case the firm should be aware of the fact that the
          customer could sell the shares through another broker on completing a
          suitable indemnity). Stock may be in the course of registration, in which
          case it will usually come back to the firm prior to despatch to the
          customer. Hence, the firm has a measure of control over the stock (i.e.
          it could refuse to deliver the certificate to the customer until it has
          received payment) which may be sufficient to prevent the customer from
          avoiding payment. However, the firm could not sell the stock without
          either obtaining the customer's signature on a transfer form, or by
          application to the Law Courts. If stock has been registered and
          despatched to the customer, then clearly the firm has lost control of its
          stock and is totally exposed to the risk of the customer's failure to pay.

9.8.36   If stock has not been apportioned then the only risk to the firm is where
          there has been a significant fall in the price of the stock and the customer
          then does not fulfil his commitment to purchase. The firm will then have
          to bear the loss.

9.8.37   As has already been noted above, a major source of risk with SOB
          customers is where a customer has entered into a sold bargain but has
          not delivered stock to the firm. The resulting credit may mask a debit
          balance representing a purchase for which stock has been apportioned,
          or delivered to the customer, and which may not be recoverable. If the
          sold stock cannot be delivered (i.e. a bear sale has taken place) then
          there is an exposure on the concealed debit balance and, indeed on the
          unsettled sold bargains which the firm will have to satisfy – by buying the
          shares in the market. This can be illustrated by the following example.
          A customer account comprises the following:

	Dr	Cr
Buy 5,000 A plc	£7,000	
Sell 2,000 B plc		£10,000
Net balance		£3,000

Suppose the 5,000 A plc have been apportioned and delivered to the customer, and it then transpires that the customer does not own the 2,000 shares in B plc. These shares will, therefore, have to be bought for their current market value – say £12,000, with the purchase price debited to the customer account. This will show the customer owing £9,000, being the £7,000 cost of the shares in A plc and the loss of £2,000 on the shares of B plc. The firm will then take whatever action it can to recover these sums from the customer.

9.8.38   In performing year-end settlement testing, it is important for the auditor to consider undelivered sales and whether they conceal potential bad debts. This can be achieved by first identifying outstanding sold bargains on the market ledgers in respect of SOB customers. The most important source of this information is the Talisman sold stock account, although it is also necessary to consider other forms of market ledgers (e.g. residual tickets and jobbers). It will usually be appropriate to examine items over one account old at the balance sheet date (anything dealt since then will not be due for settlement until after the balance sheet date). These items may be vouched for subsequent delivery. If items are cleared by way of a closing bargain in the next account (i.e. a purchase of the same quantity of the same stock), it is important to review carefully activity in the next account to see whether another sold bargain takes place. This type of customer activity may be aimed at leaving a small debit or even a credit on the ledger at the end of each account in order to conceal an underlying, irrecoverable debit. Alternatively, the item may remain undelivered, in which case it is important to consider whether the customer is capable of delivering the stock.

9.8.39   There are a number of ways of assessing the deliverability of sold bargains:

- by reference to the age of the bargain. Old (say more than thirty days past the designated settlement date), unsettled bargains may be an indication of a bear sale;
- by reference to a customer's investment portfolio; or
- by review of any correspondence between the firm and customer.

9.8.40   If there is any doubt as to the deliverability of stock, the relevant credit should be disregarded in the customer's ledger account and any resulting debit assessed for recoverability.

9.8.41   For undelivered sales, it is also necessary to be aware of any exposure arising from an increase in the price of the stock subsequent to the settlement date. If the customer could not deliver the stock, the firm would then incur a loss on buying in the shares at the current market price (as shown in paragraph 9.8.39). In addition, there is an exposure if the firm has paid cash to the customer in respect of an undelivered sale. Both situations should be identifiable from the firm's CRR reporting, as discussed in chapter 10.

Discretionary balances

9.8.42   If a discretionary account is operated in breach of the customer agreements, or in breach of TSA rules, then the firm may be sued and face financial loss through having to make good losses borne by the customer's portfolio. To assess the risk of such contingent liabilities, the auditor will need to ensure that discretionary accounts are, in fact, being operated satisfactorily. Clearly, management of the firm also has an interest in ensuring that such accounts are not used improperly. It is therefore probable that the compliance officer or other senior management will operate a review procedure for such accounts to identify any improprieties or breaches of the customer agreement. Where this is the case, the auditor will merely need to review the results of this procedure. However, if no such review is carried out by the firm, the auditor will need to conduct his own review. The procedures that the auditor can perform to ensure that discretionary customer balances are being maintained satisfactorily include:

— examining customers' dealing accounts for an unreasonable level of trading (known as 'churning'), or highly speculative dealing (particularly if heavy losses are incurred);
— checking whether the terms of agreement are being adhered to;
— examining correspondence files for any indication that the customer is dissatisfied with the conduct of his account;
— including a sample of discretionary accounts in the circularisation of customer accounts;
— requesting senior management to confirm in the letter of representation that they regularly review all discretionary accounts.

Loan account customers

9.8.43   The tests that can be performed to ensure that loan account customer balances are being maintained satisfactorily and that any appropriate provisions against irrecoverable balances have been made include:

— checking the valuation of collateral held and comparing to loan account balances;
— ensuring that stock is under the control of the firm, either in the firm's nominee company or, if the share certificates are in the name

of the client, that blank transfer forms signed by the customer are held and that the registrars confirm the customer is still the registered owner of those shares;

— ensuring that the loan account is covered by a suitable agreement with the customer;

— including a sample of loan account balances in the circularisation of customer accounts, in order to confirm both the loan account balance and the collateral.

Disclosure of customer balances

9.8.44 The detailed disclosure requirements are set out in section 9.7 above. As noted under the additional reporting objectives in paragraph 9.8.2 above, the auditor has to review the firm's systems for ageing and analysing balances. This will involve investigating the procedures by which the firm arrives at its analyses and ageings and test-checking these as appropriate.

9.9 Capital requirements

9.9.1 As noted above, customer balances are assessed for regulatory capital purposes under the CRR rules (which are discussed in chapter 10). The principal method of test checking CRR for CAD customers is the stock agreement and this is also discussed in chapter 10. It should be noted that the stock agreement only applies to transactions where stock is being purchased or sold. Non-stock items are considered below.

9.9.2 Non-stock items mainly comprise dividends, fees and charges. Such items are not assessed under the CRR rules, but are dealt with under the provisions of TSA rule 50.05 relating to 'non-approved assets' which are deducted directly from the firm's regulatory capital. Under rule 50.05c(ii): 'debtors arising from other investment business shall be treated as non-approved if they have been outstanding for more than 30 days from the date on which they were first recorded in the firm's balance sheet.'

9.9.3 It should be noted that such non-stock items can also arise on the market ledgers, in particular dividends due from member firms in cases where a customer of the selling broker receives a dividend which is due to the customer of the buying broker.

9.9.4 Such non-stock items are generally not large in relation to dealing balances. However, their effect on the capital requirement can be quite significant due to the 100 per cent deduction that is required in respect of them. The audit approach for such items is to substantively test the treatment of a sample of items selected from the customer and market ledgers.

Loan account balances

9.9.5 Loan accounts are not considered under the CRR rules, but are covered by the provisions of TSA rule 50.05 relating to non-approved assets. Under rule 50.05(1), amounts receivable on loan accounts are to be treated as non-approved unless the following conditions are satisfied:

(i) a written agreement exists between the firm and the counterparty stating, *inter alia*, the interest rate on the loan, that the loan is repayable on demand and that the firm has the unconditional right to realise the collateral should the terms of the loan not be complied with; and

(ii) collateral is held against the loan and consists of marketable investments at least equal in value to the indebtedness to the firm when discounted at a rate equal to the basic PRA (before allowances for hedging or diversification) of those securities (PRAs are discussed in section 9.6 of chapter 14).

Where the condition in (i) above is satisfied, amounts receivable shall be regarded as non-approved to the extent that (ii) is not met.

10 The Counterparty Risk Requirement

10.1 Introduction

10.1.1 The purpose of the Counterparty Risk Requirement (CRR) is to seek to ensure that a firm has sufficient capital in place to absorb any reasonably foreseeable level of losses arising from the default of customers or market counterparties. The calculation of CRR involves reviewing every open transaction with any counterparty (both customer and market) and assessing whether a CRR arises.

10.1.2 It should be noted that the CRR rules are not the only capital adequacy requirements relevant to counterparty balances. CRR only relates to outstanding bargains and does not cover non-stock items such as dividends and charges or loan account transactions. These are considered in section 9.9 of chapter 9.

10.1.3 As discussed in paragraphs 9.8.33 and 9.8.36 of chapter 9, CRR can be an efficient way for the auditor to assess exposures to bad debts on CAD and SOB customer accounts. It can also be an effective way for management to identify and control exposures to bad debts.

10.1.4 The CRR calculation is explained in section 10.2. The information required for this calculation is usually derived from some form of stock agreement and this is explained in section 10.3. It should be noted that the stock agreement serves as a useful management tool, and can also be used as an audit test both for verifying CRR and substantiating the counterparty debtors and creditors themselves. The audit objectives relating to CRR are discussed in section 10.4, and other aspects of CRR and the stock agreement in sections 10.5 and 10.6.

10.2 The CRR calculation

10.2.1 The method of calculating CRR is laid down in rules 63.01 to 63.14 of the Financial Regulations of TSA. The rules lay down that the calculation depends on the nature of the counterparty, in particular the manner in which he is accustomed to settle his transactions, and the type of transactions concerned. The rules which are most relevant to broker-dealers are those relating to cash against document (CAD) counterparties (rules 63.02–63.04) and those relating to settle on balance (SOB) counterparties (rule 63.05). The auditor should, however, ensure that he reviews the rest of the CRR rules to determine their applicability to the firm being audited.

10.2.2 CAD and SOB are the two broad categories into which all counterparties are usually split; these are discussed in detail in chapter 9. It should be emphasized that CRR applies to all types of counterparties and therefore market balances also need to be split in the same way. Generally, market counterparties will be CAD because cash settlement coincides with delivery of stock.

10.2.3 Having determined how a particular counterparty is settling his transactions, a fixed set of rules is applied to every open transaction on the account of that counterparty. There are different rules for CAD and SOB counterparties and these are described below.

CAD counterparties

10.2.4 This section explains how the CRR rules for CAD counterparties should be applied. The CRR rules envisage two types of risk on a bargain, 'market risk' and 'free delivery risk'.

Market risk

10.2.5 This is the risk which arises on bargains where no settlement (either stock or money) has yet taken place. The risk arises where there is a change in price of the stock subsequent to the bargain being dealt. In particular, if the customer was not able to settle, the firm would have to adopt the bargain and a loss could be made on unwinding the position.

10.2.6 Where the customer has purchased stock, there is a risk of loss to the firm if the price falls. This would be a realised loss if the customer was not able to pay for delivery of the stock, since the firm has paid for the stock in the market at the original bargain price. If the price has subsequently fallen, the firm would incur a loss on selling the stock.

162

10.2.7   Where the customer has sold stock, there is a risk of loss to the firm if the price rises. This would be a realised loss if the customer was not able to deliver the stock, thereby requiring the firm to purchase the stock itself in order to be able to satisfy the market on the original sold bargain. If the price has increased since the bargain was dealt, then the firm will have to buy the stock in at a higher price and therefore incur a loss.

10.2.8   Corresponding, but opposite exposures will arise on the market ledgers. For example, if the customer has purchased stock and the price has risen, there is a risk of loss to the firm on the market ledger. If the market counterparty defaulted, and the share price has risen, the firm would need to buy the stock in the market at the new higher price in order to satisfy his customer. Thus on a bargain for a CAD counterparty, market risk will always arise on either the customer ledger or the market ledger.

It should be noted that CRR will apply in this manner to a market counterparty irrespective of whether the corresponding customer is CAD or SOB.

10.2.9   The CRR calculation takes no regard of the actual risk of default for any counterparty (whether customer or market) except where the counterparty is a government or quasi-government body, where lower requirements prevail. This means that the same CRR will result from an unsettled transaction with a large, well-capitalised investing institution, a major firm of market makers or a small, speculative corporate customer. CRR therefore solely reflects the theoretical risk of loss if the counterparty should default.

10.2.10   This potential exposure (whether on the customer or market ledgers) is known as the market risk. The CRR for each transaction is calculated as a percentage of the market risk, in accordance with the following table:

Percentage of market risk to be added to CRR

Age of unsettled bargain by reference to normal due settlement day (i.e. designated account day)	Equities (and equity related instruments)	Debt securities and debt related instruments including convertible debt securities
up to 15 days	–	–
16 to 30 days	–	25
31 to 45 days	25	50
46 to 60 days	50	75
61 to 90 days	75	100
more than 90 days	100	100

163

Free delivery risk

10.2.11 This is the risk which arises when settlement of stock and money do not take place simultaneously. This means that the firm is at risk of loss for the full value of the transaction, not just to the extent of market-price fluctuations.

10.2.12 Where a customer has bought stock, a free delivery is defined as taking place where delivery of stock to the customer has occurred without the corresponding payment to the firm. Here, the monetary amount due to the firm in respect of the delivered stock is the value of the free delivery for the purpose of CRR. Delivery is deemed to have taken place upon the physical release of the document of title to the stock to the customer. In the case of Talisman securities for CAD customers, this means the release of the stock note to the customer.

10.2.13 Where a customer has sold stock, a free delivery is defined as taking place where the firm has made a payment to the customer in settlement, but has not received the necessary stock from the customer. Here, the stock due to the firm, valued at the current offer price (as defined in paragraph 14.1.2 of chapter 14), is the value of the free delivery for the purposes of calculating CRR.

10.2.14 Free deliveries are usually added to CRR at 100 per cent of the exposure without any allowance for age because they are considered to represent the greatest risk to the firm. However, the rules acknowledge that simultaneous transfer of stock and money is often not realistic, and hence the following delays are permitted before the addition to CRR is required:

— for bought bargains, the amount due from the counterparty need not be added to CRR until three days after the delivery has taken place; and
— for sold bargains, the free delivery need not be added to CRR until three days after the payment has been made.

Under certain circumstances, only a proportion of the free delivery need be added to CRR. In particular, where amounts are guaranteed by, or subject to, the full faith and credit of a sovereign government or province or state thereof, which is a member of the OECD, then the free delivery need not be added to CRR. Alternatively, where a counterparty is one of the following:

● Recognised Banking Institution;
● UK building societies;

- UK local authorities supra-national organisations;
- UK discount house;
- gilt-edged market makers;
- ISE moneybrokers;
- other securities firms which have regulation applied to them which (in the opinion of TSA) are equivalent;

then only 20 per cent of the free delivery exposure need be added to CRR.

SOB Counterparties

0.2.15   For SOB customer accounts, individual debit items which have been outstanding for more than thirty days from the normal settlement day should be added to CRR, irrespective of whether or not stock has been delivered to the customer. This may be reduced by the mid-market value of any collateral held by the firm, discounted at a rate equal to the relevant PRA for the security (as used for calculating the position risk requirement and discussed in section 14.6 of chapter 14). The firm must be able to exercise control over this collateral, with control being deemed to be lost when stock has been delivered to the customer. In addition, the firm must have an unconditional right to realise the collateral; this right is usually contained in the Customer Agreement Letter.

0.2.16   As noted in section 9.8 of chapter 9, it can be very difficult to determine whether the firm has control over stock relating to SOB customers. In particular, close reference should be made to the terms of agreements with customers and also to stock movements between apportionment, registration and delivery. An approach often adopted by firms is that, so long as the stock certificate has not been released to the customer, the firm has not lost control of the stock. Hence, non-apportioned stock and apportioned stock still in the course of registration (so long as this is returned to the firm prior to despatch to the customer) are classed as collateral for this purpose. However, it should be noted that this interpretation has not been formally sanctioned by the regulatory authorities.

0.2.17   For credit balances which have been outstanding for more than thirty days from the normal settlement day, exposure is defined as the current value of the sold bargains. CRR is then computed by applying the relevant percentage from the 'equity' column in paragraph 10.2.10 to the exposure. If the firm makes a payment in respect of an undelivered sold bargain then a free delivery has taken place and CRR is computed as for a CAD creditor (i.e. the stock due to the firm, valued at the

165

current offer price, is taken as a free delivery). It should be noted that a firm may seek exemption from the requirement to provide CRR against undelivered sales over thirty days old in exceptional circumstances (e.g. delays in delivery arising on the winding-up of a deceased's estate).

10.2.18 The implication of these rules is that a firm must maintain its SOB customer ledgers in the same way as its CAD customer ledgers, in that it must be able to identify individual bought and sold transactions for both stock and monetary balances. However, as noted in section 9.7 of chapter 9, firms have not traditionally maintained open item ledgers for SOB customers.

10.2.19 In order to achieve a practical solution to this problem, TSA rules on CRR in corporate guidance notes giving firms some scope for using their judgement with respect to offsetting credits against debit items over thirty days old. Broadly, the guidance notes recognise that credit items on such accounts will either represent cash or the contract value of sold transactions, and that the stock due to be deducted against such sold transactions may be under the control of the firm, or the firm may be awaiting delivery from the customer. The guidance notes state that, even where stock is not under the control of the firm, it should not be assumed that the relevant credit has no validity as an offsetting item. TSA states that firms should be aware of stock which their customers own and should not knowingly transact bear sales for them, and therefore, a firm should generally know whether or not a customer does in fact own shares which are being sold.

10.2.20 The guidance notes therefore state that it is only if, in the firm's judgement, there is any likelihood that stock will not become available to complete the transaction, that the relevant credit on the account cannot be used as an offset against debit items. Where this is the case, there may be debit items over thirty days old on the ledger which appear to have been settled by sales but which should not be so regarded, and which must be added to CRR. The credits deemed not available for offset in this manner will attract their own CRR in accordance with the procedures described in paragraph 10.2.17.

10.2.21 Hence, there is as apparent conflict between the rules (which require individual debit and credit items to be shown separately), and the guidance note to the rules (which allow for the offsetting of debit and credit items). TSA have made it clear that it is permissible for either approach to be adopted, although in practice most firms adopt the approach prescribed by the guidance note since this recognises the reality of SOB settlement and will tend to result in a lower aggregate CRR. More and more firms are moving towards monitoring SOB accounts by means of open item accounting; however, this is usually accomplished by means of memorandum records so that the customer continues to receive statements on conventional lines. This is not just for the purpose of calculating CRR, but also for the enhanced control that this brings.

Stock records

10.2.22 From the section above, it is clear that the calculation of CRR, for all types of counterparty, requires the firm to be aware of the location of the stock relating to a bargain, i.e. whether it is with its customer, the market, the company's registrar or in the firm's own possession. Traditionally, firms have only maintained memorandum records of stock movements, which have not been integrated with the financial records and this has resulted in a considerable amount of clerical effort to apply the CRR rules correctly. Accordingly, firms are now developing systems that record stock movements as an integral part of their accounting system. This has greatly facilitated management control over businesses, as well as making CRR much easier to compute.

Worked examples of CRR

10.2.23 In order to illustrate how the CRR rules work, three worked examples are set out below. For each example, the CRR calculation is first based on the customer being CAD and then SOB.

Illustration 1

10.2.24 Customer A buys £60,000 of Treasury 9 per cent 1992 stock at a price of £56 1/2 per £100 and commission of 0.2 per cent, a total consideration of £34,578. The bargain was due for settlement on 28 March but had neither been delivered by the market nor settled by the customer by 15 April (when the mid-market price of the 9 per cent 1992 stock had fallen to £53 1/2 per £100).

CAD basis

10.2.25 As no settlement has taken place, the only exposure relates to market risk. Under the rule for CAD debtors, an addition should be made to CRR equal to a percentage of the excess of any amount due from the customer over the mid-market value of securities sold to him.

The current mid-market price of the gilt edged stock is £53 1/2 per £100, and hence the market value of the investment is £32,100.

Hence market risk = £34,578 − £32,100 = £2,478.

Settlement is eighteen days overdue and for gilt bargains this means that 25 per cent of the market risk has to be added to CRR (per debt table in paragraph 10.2.10 above). Hence an addition of £619.50 to CRR is required.

SOB basis

10.2.26 The amount has only been outstanding for eighteen days and therefore requires no CRR.

Illustration 2

10.2.27 Customer B sells 20,000 shares in XYZ plc at £4.20 less commission of £925, a total consideration of £83,075. The bargain was due for settlement on 28 March. Customer B is paid £83,075 on 29 March although he has not delivered the stock to the firm by 7 April, when the offer price for shares in XYZ plc is £4.30.

CAD basis

10.2.28 The payment to Customer B creates a free delivery (since there has been a payment in settlement of a credit balance where the stock remains undelivered). Based on the offer price of £4.30, the free delivery is valued at £86,000. Since the stock has not been delivered within the three days' grace period, this sum is added in full to the CRR.

SOB basis

10.2.29 Treatment exactly the same as the CAD basis.

Illustration 3

10.2.30 Customer C buys 10,000 shares in RST plc at £6.30 together with commission at a rate of 0.3 per cent and stamp duty of 0.5 per cent, a total consideration of £63,504, due for settlement on 29 February. As at 7 April, the customer has not paid, although the stock was apportioned by the market on 31 March. The market price for RST Plc at 7 April is £5.90.

CAD basis

10.2.31 Under the rule for CAD debtors, a free delivery has taken place because the stock has been apportioned but the firm has not received payment from the customer. Apportionment took place more than three days prior to the calculation date and so the whole amount due from the customer (£63,504) is a free delivery and is added to CRR.

SOB basis

10.2.32 The debit balance has been outstanding for thirty-eight days from the relevant settlement date (i.e. 29 February to 7 April). Therefore, so long as it is the only item on the ledger account for that client, it should be added to CRR in full (irrespective of whether apportionment has taken place). As noted in paragraph 10.2.16 above, the firm has not lost control of the stock (which we will assume is still held in the brokers' office) and it can therefore be used as collateral against the outstanding balance. The stock would be valued at the current mid-market price and discounted as described in paragraph 10.2.15. The outstanding balance would be reduced by this amount in arriving at the addition to CRR. Thus:

Debit balance	63,504
Less value of collateral (10,000 shares at £5.90), 59,000	
discounted by the relevant PRA, say, 10.5%	52,805
Resultant CRR	£10,699

10.2.33   As an extension to this illustration, suppose Customer C subsequently sold the following stock in order to finance the purchase:

18 February 5,000 shares in LMN plc at £4.00, less commission of £160
– net proceeds £19,840 (current price £4.40)

3 April   8,000 shares in EFG plc at £2.00, less commission of £175
– net proceeds £15,825

None of the stock relating to these sales has been delivered to the firm by the customer by 7 April. We will also assume now that the firm does not use the shares in ABC plc as collateral against the outstanding balance.

10.2.34   The current balance on the account is a debit of £27,839 (£63,504 – £19,840 – £15,825). Since this net debit can be related back to items more than 30 days past settlement date, it is added to CRR.

10.2.35   Offsetting these two sold bargains is only allowed if, in the firm's judgement, all the sold stock will be delivered by the customer. If the firm has reason to believe that the customer does not own, say, the shares in LMN plc, it could not use the credit on the ledger in respect of that sale to reduce the debit balance. Therefore, an extra £19,840 would have to be added to CRR. The firm may use its judgement in deciding upon the deliverability of stock. Alternatively, it may set an arbitrary time limit (for example thirty days after the due settlement day) after which it will not allow credits on undelivered sales to be used as an offset for CRR purposes.

10.2.36   In addition, if the sale of LMN plc is deemed to be a bear sale, then we note that the sale of the 5,000 shares in LMN plc is more than thirty days past settlement date. Therefore, it also attracts CRR as explained in 10.2.17 above, based on the ledger value of the sale, since no delivery has taken place.

10.2.37 Settlement is thirty-eight days overdue and for equity bargains this means that 25 per cent of the credit has to be added to CRR resulting in an additional CRR of £4,960. Therefore, the total CRR based on the situation set out in paragraph 10.2.33 would be £52,639 (£27,839 + £19,840 + £4,960).

10.3 The stock agreement

10.3.1 The stock agreement consists of reconciling all open money and stock positions in a customer's account to the corresponding positions in the relevant market account, or to stock or cash in transit. It is frequently used by management as a control over the internal consistency, completeness and accuracy of the accounting records and settlement systems of the firm. It is also, usually, the most effective method for a firm to identify free deliveries for CRR purposes, in the absence of integrated stock accounting as described in paragraph 10.2.22 above. Since the exercise of carrying out a stock agreement is relatively time consuming, it may not be used for the daily estimate of CRR used by management for monitoring purposes, but would be used to support the figure for CRR shown on monthly or quarterly returns to TSA. For the auditor, the stock agreement serves to assist in the assessment of the firm's settlement procedures and in verifying CRR calculations and providing audit evidence on market and client cash and stock positions.

10.3.2 As with CRR, the basis of the stock agreement is the relationship between the settlement of stock and money on individual bargains. Every counterparty balance on the customer and market ledgers should have a money position and a stock position, being respectively the cash and stock due to or from the firm. The cash position is usually easy to determine since it is simply the monetary balance on the ledger. The stock position can be more difficult to establish, particularly in the absence of integrated stock records.

10.3.3 Before discussing the stock agreement, it is first necessary to distinguish between the two main types of accounting systems which may be in use. Firstly, there are the integrated stock and money records in which stock movements are recorded as well as money transactions; secondly, there are the non-integrated stock and money records where stock movements are only recorded in memorandum form. As mentioned in paragraph 10.2.22, the latter system is gradually being phased out in favour of the former which provides greater management control and is more reliable. Whichever form of stock records are used, a key part of carrying out the stock agreement will be counting stock physically held in the broker-dealer's office and agreeing these holdings to the relevant parts of the stock records.

10.3.4 In carrying out the stock agreement, it is necessary to consider the following two types of transaction:

(i) 'agency' bargains for which there are two distinct counterparties, a customer and the market, and where each counterparty will have a related stock and money balance; and

(ii) 'principal' bargains where the firm has bought from, or sold to, its counterparty (either a customer or a market maker) direct. Here, only one side of the transaction has a stock and money position since the other side is the firm's own trading position.

10.3.5 Where a firm maintains integrated stock and money records, it is usually easy to determine whether stock is outstanding since every counterparty balance is analysed both by stock and by money. When either stock or money moves, the relevant records are updated. Where such integrated records are available, it is important for the auditor to confirm their reliability, particularly on the stock side since such systems may not incorporate the 'double entry' controls which exist with monetary balances.

10.3.6 The best way to confirm the stock balance on one counterparty account is by reference to the account of the other counterparty of the bargain, the location of which can usually be determined from the bargain journal or list book. In most cases, stock will move on the same day, on both the customer and market ledgers (i.e. for sold bargains when the customer delivers stock, it will be delivered straight on to the market; and vice versa for bought bargains). Therefore, comparison can be made of stock balances on the market and customer ledgers and discrepancies investigated.

10.3.7 A further source of evidence on the adequacy of stock records will come from the various circularisations carried out. As noted in section 9.8 of chapter 9, the circularisation of customer accounts should include stock balances. The same applies for the circularisation of market balances (i.e. Talisman, tickets and jobbers). In addition, the auditor can review procedures for the posting of stock balances to ensure that these are satisfactory.

10.3.8 If stock and money balances on the ledgers are accurately stated, then a full stock agreement, as set out below, is not necessary for audit purposes. In this situation, stock and money balances for particular transactions should be reviewed and tested and the accuracy of the CRR calculation checked.

171

10.3.9   If stock positions are not accurately stated, or indeed if integrated stock and money records do not exist, then an extended stock agreement will probably be necessary for audit purposes. We shall consider stock agreement procedures for CAD and SOB customers separately.

CAD customers – bought transactions

10.3.10   The first step in the stock agreement is to consider bought transactions on the CAD customer ledgers. For each bargain, it is first necessary to determine whether stock has been apportioned by the market. This will involve reviewing the market ledgers to see how much of the original bargain is still outstanding. The identity of the market counterparty may be found by reference to the bargain journal or list book. This should identify whether the bargain is due to be settled through Talisman or directly with another firm. Alternatively, the transaction could have been dealt with with the firm as a principal bargain.

10.3.11   If the item is in respect of a principal bargain, reference should be made to the position agreement for that stock carried out by the firm (as discussed in chapter 14). If stock still has to be delivered by the firm, it should appear as a reconciling item on the position agreement. In this way it is possible to determine the outstanding stock position with respect to the customer ledger balance. The position agreement is audited by the procedures outlined in section 14.5 of chapter 14 and these are not repeated here.

10.3.12   If the item is in respect of an agency bargain, the following information is required from the bargain journal: stock quantity, bargain consideration (quantity × price) and customer consideration (bargain consideration adjusted for dealing costs). It should be noted that the initial monetary balances on the customer and market ledgers will not be the same because the customer balance is net of expenses, whereas the market balance is gross.

10.3.13   The current monetary balances on the customer and market ledgers are then ascertained. A comparison is made with the original balances as noted from the bargain journal. There are five possible results:

(i)   there has been no change in the balances, in which case no settlement has taken place;

(ii)   both customer and market balances have fallen by the same amount, in which case some or all of the stock has been apportioned by the market for which the customer has paid;

(iii) the market balance has fallen but the customer balance has remained the same, in which case stock has been apportioned by the market for which the customer has not paid; alternatively the market may have been paid for stock which has not yet been apportioned;

(iv) market and customer balances have both fallen with the former falling proportionately more than the latter, in which case stock has been apportioned for which the customer has not completely paid; alternatively the market may have been paid for stock which has not yet been apportioned;

(v) the market and customer balances have fallen with the latter falling proportionately more than the former, in which case stock has been apportioned but the customer has paid for more than the apportionment; alternatively the market may have claimed less than it was entitled to following the apportionment that has taken place.

10.3.14 In cases (i) and (ii), no free delivery has taken place and it is simply necessary to calculate the remaining stock balance and perform a market risk calculation on this (as set out in paragraphs 10.2.5 to 10.2.10 above). The stock balance can be ascertained by pro-rating the original bargain consideration over the original stock quantity. If the price has moved from that at which the original bargain was transacted, a market risk will arise and this should be traced through to the relevant CRR report (either for market or customer ledgers depending on where the risk actually arises).

10.3.15 In case (iii), a free delivery has taken place unless the stock (or in the case of Talisman, the stock note) was still in the office of the firm and therefore not yet delivered to the customer. Here, similar considerations to those set out in paragraph 10.3.22 below apply. If the market balance has fallen to nil, then the whole of the customer ledger balance should be treated as a free delivery, unless apportionment took place less than three days prior to the calculation date. If the market balance is not nil, then a partial free delivery has occurred. Here, it is necessary to calculate the outstanding stock on the market ledgers by pro-rating the original stock and monetary balance. A market risk calculation should then be performed on this stock quantity. The stock apportioned is a free delivery and the customer balance should be pro-rated to arrive at the addition to CRR. If the discrepancy between market and customer balances has arisen because the market has been paid for stock which has not yet been apportioned, then CRR is calculated on the market balance as for a CAD customer sold transaction (as discussed below).

10.3.16 In case (iv), a similar situation to that set out in paragraph 10.3.15 has occurred, the only difference being that the customer has made a partial settlement for stock apportioned. Again, it is necessary to consider whether stock (or for Talisman bargains, the stock note) was held in the firm's office at the calculation date. Similar pro-rating calculations to those set out above are necessary in order to arrive at the market risk and free delivery risk arising on the transaction. It is important that in cases (iii) and (iv), enquiries are made into the reason for non-payment by the customer. This may be indicative of a systems failure (e.g. a failure to send the stock note to a customer on apportionment). As in paragraph 10.3.15, if the discrepancy has arisen because the market has been paid for stock which has not yet been apportioned, CRR is calculated on the market balance as for a CAD customer sold transaction.

10.3.17   In case (v), the customer has paid for more than is strictly due. Here, CRR should be computed by comparing the value of the stock not yet delivered to the customer and the residual debit balance on his account.

10.3.18   As noted in chapter 7, many firms make use of the Counterparty Risk Assessment System (CRAS), as provided by the ISE, for their CRR calculation on Talisman balances. TSA rules state that firms may rely on this figure and hence it is not necessary for auditors to test check it. Therefore, where a firm uses CRAS and CRR arises on a Talisman balance, it is not necessary for the auditor to follow it through to the relevant CRAS report. For all other types of market ledger (i.e. jobbers and residual tickets), the market risk should be followed through to the relevant CRR report.

CAD customers – sold transactions

10.3.19   The next step is to consider sold bargains on the CAD customer ledgers. As above, reference should be made to the bargain journal or list book to determine the identity of the market counterparty. In addition, stock quantity, bargain consideration and customer consideration should be noted. If the transaction is a principal bargain, reference should be made to the position agreement for that stock as discussed in paragraph 10.3.11 above.

10.3.20   The current monetary balance on the customer and market ledgers is then ascertained and a comparison made with the original balances extracted from the bargain journal. As above, there are five possible results:

(i)   the balances are the same, in which case no settlement has taken place;

(ii)   both customer and market balances have fallen in the same proportion, in which case the customer has delivered stock for

174

which he has been paid and this stock has likewise been settled with the market;

(iii) the customer balance has fallen, but the market balance has remained the same, in which case the customer has been paid for stock which has not been passed on to the market, alternatively the market may not have paid for stock which has been delivered to it; one further possibility is that the stock was originally delivered by the customer and duly passed on to the market and paid for, but that the stock was subsequently rejected by the market as being a bad delivery (for example, see chapter 7) and therefore returned to the firm and the firm repaid the market;

(iv) market and customer balances have fallen with the former falling proportionately more than the latter, in which case the customer has delivered stock for which he has not been paid in full, alternatively, the market may have paid for more stock than was actually delivered to it – although this is highly unlikely in practice;

(v) market and customer balances have fallen with the latter falling proportionately more than the former, in which case the customer has delivered stock, but he has been paid more than is due on the partial delivery; alternatively the market may not have paid for stock which has been passed on to it;

10.3.21 In cases (i) and (ii), no free delivery has taken place and it is simply necessary to calculate the remaining stock balance and perform a market risk calculation. The stock balance can be ascertained by pro-rating the original bargain consideration over the original stock quantity.

10.3.22 In case (iii), a free delivery has taken place, unless the stock was received from the customer but was still held in the offices of the firm and therefore not yet delivered to the market. This should be established from the memorandum stock records, if available, which can be confirmed by a count of stock in office at the balance sheet date and corroborated by receipt of funds from the market within a day or two. If the stock can be confirmed as being in the office, then no addition to CRR will be required on the customer sale. If the customer balance has fallen to nil, then all of the original stock quantity is classed as a free delivery, so long as the payment was not made within the three days prior to the calculation date. This stock should be valued at its current offer price and vouched to the relevant CRR report. If the customer balance is not nil then a partial free delivery has taken place. It is necessary to calculate the quantity of stock that the customer has been paid for by pro-rating the original bargain consideration over the original stock quantity which is then classified as a free delivery. The remaining stock quantity is assessed according to the market risk rules.

In the unlikely event that the discrepancy between market and customer balances has arisen because the market has not paid for stock which has been delivered to it, then CRR is calculated on the market balance as for a CAD customer bought transaction.

10.3.23   In case (iv), in effect the customer has delivered stock for which he has not yet been paid. Here, the amount of stock that has not been delivered should be computed and a market risk calculation performed on this by reference to the total balance still owed to the customer.

10.3.24   In case (v), a similar situation to that set out in paragraph 10.3.22 has occurred, the only difference being that the customer has delivered some stock in respect of the payment he has received. Again, it will be necessary to consider whether stock was held in the firm's office at the calculation date. Similar pro-rating calculations to those set out above are necessary to arrive at the market risk and free delivery risk arising on the transaction. It is important to enquire into the reasons for free deliveries to determine whether they are indicative of a systems weakness. On the rare occasion that the discrepancy has arisen because the market has not paid for stock it has received, CRR is calculated on the market balance as for a CAD customer bought transaction.

10.3.25   It should be noted that the same considerations for CRR on Talisman balances and the use of CRAS, as noted in paragraph 10.3.18, apply here.

Market ledger – debit items

10.3.26   The next step is to consider debit items on the market ledgers (i.e. customer sold bargains) that have not already been taken into account by the procedures above. It should be noted that all types of market ledgers (i.e., Talisman, jobbers and tickets) should be used for sample selection. The following details should be noted from the bargain journal or list book: nature of the customer, original stock quantity, bargain consideration, and customer consideration. Where the customer is classed as SOB, the subsequent procedures are set out in paragraphs 10.3.28 to 10.3.33 below. If the customer is CAD, then similar procedures to those set out in paragraphs 10.3.19 and 10.3.25 above should be applied.

Market ledger – credit items

10.3.27   The final step in the stock agreement is to consider any remaining credit items on the market ledgers (i.e. customer bought bargains). All types of market ledgers should be used for sample selection. The following details should be noted from the bargain journal or list book: nature of the customer, original stock quantity, bargain consideration, and customer consideration. If the customer is classed as SOB, then it is only necessary to test CRR arising on the market ledgers (since alternative procedures are required for SOB bought transactions as set out in section 10.6 below). If the customer is CAD, then similar procedures to those set out in paragraphs 10.3.12 to 10.3.18 should be applied.

SOB customers

10.3.28 As noted in paragraphs 10.2.15 to 10.2.21 above, there can be problems with the calculation of CRR where firms do not maintain open item ledgers for SOB customers. If open item ledgers are maintained, the stock agreement procedures outlined above can be followed for SOB customers.

10.3.29 However, where open item ledgers are not maintained, and the firm relies on the TSA guidance note on CRR for SOB counterparties, it is usually not practicable to carry out a full stock agreement. Under these circumstances, the correct identification of debit balances over 30 days old needs to be considered by the alternative procedures discussed in section 10.6 below. Nevertheless, it should be noted that it is still possible to use the stock agreement to check the treatment of un-delivered sales for SOB customers.

10.3.30 In order to test this, undelivered, sold bargains relating to SOB customers should be identified. There are two possible sources for such items:

— items noted in paragraph 10.3.26 above; and
— items selected as part of the bad debt review for SOB customers. (paragraph 9.8.40 in chapter 9).

10.3.31 The procedures necessary for considering the deliverability of such sold bargains have already been discussed in chapter 9 and are not repeated here. Where there is doubt as to whether a customer will be able to deliver stock, the relevant credit should be disregarded from the customer's ledger account. Any debit items over thirty days old that this uncovers should be added to CRR.

10.3.32 The next step is to determine whether the customer has been paid any cash in relation to a particular undelivered sale. This will involve reviewing the ledger account and attempting to link payments to individual credit items on the ledger. If cash can be directly allocated to

10.3.31   a particular sale, then that part of the bargain which has been paid for must be treated as a free delivery.

10.3.33   Finally, it is necessary to check the CRR arising on those undelivered sales more than thirty days past settlement date which are not being offset against debit items. Here, exposure is defined as the value of the open sold bargain, at current market price. CRR is then computed by applying the relevant percentage from the table in paragraph 10.2.10 to the exposure.

Other aspects of the stock agreement

10.3.34   The procedures discussed so far have involved considering bargains on the ledgers (both customer and market), calculating any applicable CRR on those bargains and following that through to the relevant CRR report.

10.3.35   In order to check the completeness and accuracy of CRR reporting, it is also necessary to test-check items on CRR reports back to the underlying counterparty ledgers. This involves selecting a sample of items shown as free deliveries on the CRR reports in order to ensure that the underlying transaction is actually a free delivery. In addition, it is necessary to select a sample of items showing a market risk on the CRR reports and checking them back to the underlying ledgers.

10.3.36   It should be noted that detailed testing in both directions may not be necessary if it can be demonstrated that CRR reports contain appropriate control totals which can be reconciled or agreed back to the underlying ledgers.

10.3.37   As a manual exercise, the stock agreement can be very time consuming since it involves selecting an item on one ledger, locating it on another ledger by way of the detailed bargain journal or list book, and then assessing whether CRR has been correctly provided on that transaction. It is therefore, clearly an area where computer assisted audit techniques can be used to cut down on the amount of detailed manual work. In particular, it may be possible to interrogate accounting records and match bargains on market and customer ledgers. Such an interrogation could effectively validate the CRR calculation by way of a 100 per cent stock agreement.

10.3.38   A further point to consider is that both CRR and the stock agreement provide significant audit comfort on the internal consistency of the accounting records and settlement systems of the firm.
    If a significant number of invalid ledger items are found when carrying

out a sample stock agreement for CRR verification, this may raise doubts as to the accuracy of the accounting and settlement records and in this case a more extensive stock agreement should be considered.

10.4 Audit objectives

0.4.1   The audit objectives relating to CRR are to confirm that:

(i)   the CRR element of the firm's Total Capital Requirement as at the balance sheet date has been properly calculated in accordance with the rules of TSA (rule 90.04a);

(ii)   adequate procedures have been established for monitoring the firm's counterparty risk and providing appropriate levels of management with the information necessary for them to make relevant, timely and informed decisions to control such risks (TSA rule 90.03d(iv)).

0.4.2   The second objective means the auditor must be satisfied that CRR is being calculated regularly and promptly, and is no more than prudent management would dictate, i.e. that the business is operating within its regulatory capital constraints, and effective credit control is being maintained. The majority of these issues should be addressed as part of the work on assessing the adequacy of credit control procedures discussed in chapter 9. It is important to note that the rules require firms to have the capacity to make the CRR calculation each day, no matter what other credit control procedure are in place, however, in some cases a detailed, daily calculation may be unnecessary – except in an emergency (e.g. a large movement in share prices) – with suitable estimates being used instead. TSA is proposing that, from late 1990, daily calculations will be necessary for all firms.

10.4.3   The rigorous nature of the CRR calculation, which requires every open transaction on the counterparty ledgers to be considered, means that the auditor may use CRR reporting as a means of identifying exposures to bad debts on customer accounts. This is possible because, by definition, the higher the CRR on a particular transaction, the greater the exposure to the firm. As noted in chapter 9, it is reasonable for the auditor to rely on CRR reporting as a means of identifying bad debt exposures, so long as he is satisfied with the adequacy of the underlying systems and the accuracy of the CRR figures. However, the auditor should remain alert to the possibility of a debt becoming doubtful before its reaches the CRR computation – for example a customer going bankrupt the day after a deal was transacted.

10.4.4   If the systems for calculating CRR are found not to be reliable, the auditor will need to consider qualifying his systems report to TSA and may have to rely on the stock agreement procedures set out in section 10.3 above, both to identify potential bad debts and to form an opinion on the accuracy of the CRR calculations at the balance sheet date.

10.5   The late stock agreement

10.5.1   So far, the discussion on the stock agreement has been directed primarily at how it can be used to verify CRR reporting. Accordingly, for audit purposes, the stock agreement need only be performed on a sample basis.

10.5.2   However, it is possible that this work may reveal inaccuracies in the reporting of CRR. As well as the implications for the auditor's opinion on the calculation of the Total Capital Requirement, this also means that CRR reporting cannot be relied upon for the review of bad debts on the CAD ledgers. Where the CRR calculation cannot be relied upon to provide evidence of bad debts, the auditor must look for an alternative way of carrying out this review.

10.5.3   One alternative is to increase the scope of the stock agreement at the balance sheet date and look at all open transactions on the customer and market ledgers over a pre-determined size. Bargains from the last account period before the balance sheet date, could generally be omitted from this stock agreement because they will not be due for settlement until after this date and hence are unlikely to give rise to an exposure.

10.5.4   Another alternative is the 'late stock agreement'. Here, a date after the balance sheet date is selected (usually two or three accounts later) and a stock agreement is performed at this date, but only with respect to bargains that arose before the balance sheet date and which remain unsettled.

10.5.5   This should lead to a much reduced level of testing compared to an extended stock agreement carried out at the balance sheet date. This is because a large number of items outstanding at the balance sheet date will have settled in the intervening period. It will be necessary to verify, for a sample of items, that bona fide settlement has taken place between the balance sheet date and the date of the late stock agreement. Such verification will usually be to cash books and stock delivery schedules.

0.5.6   It should be noted that the late stock agreement, whilst providing evidence for bad debts, will not provide any comfort on the CRR at the balance sheet date. Hence, if it is necessary to re-perform CRR calculations in full because of errors or inadequate control procedures, a full stock agreement may still have to be carried out.

0.6   Other aspects of verifying CRR

0.6.1   The discussion so far has been about how the stock agreement can be used to verify the calculation of CRR on standard dealing transactions. There are, however, certain parts of the CRR calculation which the stock agreement cannot verify; in particular, 30 days past settlement date debit balances on SOB ledgers, where the firm does not maintain open item ledgers for SOB customers.

0.6.2   Before discussing the audit of these balances for regulatory capital purposes, an example of how ageing should take place on an SOB account where open item ledgers are not maintained is set out below.

The current date is 11 October and customer A has entered into the following transactions:

Deal Date	Settlement Date	Bought or sold	Quantity	Stock	Price £	Consideration debit (credit) £
5 Aug	23 Aug	B	10,000	DEF	2.20	22,198
23 Sept	11 Oct	B	10,000	XYZ	1.50	15,300
6 Oct	25 Oct	B	20,000	ABC	2.50	50,400
8 Oct	25 Oct	S	20,000	ABC	2.60	(52,000)
9 Oct	25 Oct	S	5,000	RST	0.60	(2,949)
11 Oct	25 Oct	B	8,000	LMN	1.50	350
						45,299

On 11 October, Customer A paid £15,000 to the firm, leaving a debit balance of £30,299 on his account.

0.6.3   Credits should be matched with debits on a FIFO basis. In addition, special allowance should be made for 'closing' bargains (bought and sold bargains in the same stock dealt in the same account period). Of the above transactions, the two bargains in ABC dealt on the 6 and 8 October are closing bargains. In the netting process, these two bargains will be shown as a net credit of £1,600.

0.6.4   Hence, there are the following three credits on the account, totalling £19,549, which are available for offset against debits:

(i) the cash receipt of £15,000;

(ii) the £2,949 in respect of the sale of RST dealt on 9 October, which can only be used as an offset if the firm is certain that Customer A can deliver the stock);

(iii) the £1,600 profit in respect of the closing bargains in ABC.

10.6.5 Matching on a FIFO basis, this £19,549 will be offset against the bargain in DEF dealt on 5 August.

    This leaves £2,649 in respect of this bargain unsettled. Hence the £30,299 debit on the account can be analysed as follows:

Bargain date	Settlement date	Stock	£
5 Aug	23 Aug	DEF	2,649
23 Sept	11 Oct	XYZ	15,300
11 Oct	25 Oct	LMN	12,350
			30,299

10.6.6 The only element of this balance which is more than 30 days from the settlement date is the £2,649 relating to DEF, which was due for settlement on 23 August and hence is 49 days old. Therefore £2,649 is added to CRR.

10.6.7 The audit work on checking CRR on SOB customer accounts consists of test-checking the netting and ageing computations carried out by the firm. Where this results in debits going back more than 30 days, the addition to CRR should be verified. It should be noted that the deliverability of stock on sold bargains needs to have been considered before any netting can be carried out for CRR purposes. This will involve first carrying out the work detailed in paragraphs 9.8.40 to 9.8.42 of chapter 9.

11 Clients' Money

11.1 Introduction

11.1.1 One of the major implications for member firms of the SIB regulations is the requirement for segregation of clients' money. Previously, member firms were permitted to amalgamate all money held on behalf of clients with the firm's own money, and thus to use one client's money to pay for another client's stock purchases, or to fund the firm's own business. However, in practice most member firms would arrange to place any substantial sum held for a client in a separate bank deposit account and would not mix it with the firm's own money.

11.1.2 In the early 1980s, requirements for segregation of clients' money were introduced for dealers in securities outside the ISE under the Prevention of Fraud (Investments) Act 1958, and these requirements were extended to all authorised investment businesses under the FSA.

11.1.3 The main consequences for member firms were the increased need for working capital, since clients' money could no longer be used, and the need for complex accounting systems to identify the amounts held for different purposes for each client. Whilst some regard was given to the particular difficulties that arise in identifying client money in the course of settlement of bargains through the ISE settlement process, the rules have nevertheless placed a considerable additional administrative burden on member firms.

11.2 Outline of the rules

11.2.1 The purpose of the client money regulations is to provide protection for money held on behalf of, or payable to, clients of the firm if the firm itself goes into liquidation.

11.2.2 Client money is any money received from, or on behalf of, a client which relates to an investment transaction. Thus, money received from a client to pay for the purchase of shares is client money until the firm pays it on to the market or, if the firm has dealt as principal, until it has delivered the stock to the client.

11.2.3 Similarly, on a client's sold transaction, money received by the firm from the market is client money until it is paid over to the client. Where the firm has bought as principal from the client, the amount payable to the client becomes client money as soon as the stock is delivered by the client to the firm.

11.2.4 Money held by the firm for a client which is not earmarked for use in settling a bought bargain that has already been dealt is termed 'client free money'. This will often arise where a client pays a lump sum to the broker to be invested on a discretionary basis, or where the broker-dealer manages a portfolio for a client and retains a proportion of the portfolio in cash as a deliberate investment policy.

11.2.5 In order to separate client money from the firm's own assets in the event of a liquidation, all client money must be held in specially designated client bank accounts. In some cases, firms will open separate bank accounts for each client, especially where large deposits are involved, though this is not required by the rules. A pooled client bank account is permitted, but the firm must maintain strict procedures to ensure that no firm's money is paid into the client bank account and that the amount of money withdrawn from the account on behalf of any particular client never exceeds the funds held in the account for that client – it is not permissible for one client effectively to borrow from another.

11.2.6 However, for practical reasons, less strict rules apply to client money that is not free money, but is earmarked for settlement of a bargain dealt on behalf of the client. This money, termed 'client settlement money', may be held in a client settlement bank account under rules which allow settlement money of one client to be used to settle a bargain for another. These rules are discussed in more detail in section 11.5 below.

11.2.7 Regular reconciliations are required of both client free money and client settlement money accounts to ensure that the firm has complied with the segregation requirements.

11.2.8 The firm is obliged to pay interest on client free money, but not on settlement money. The detailed requirements for this are set out in section 11.4.

*Business customers are to be treated as free hearty —
only Market Professionals are exempt from protection & %*

11.2.9 The client money rules apply only to money held or received for private customers and those business customers who have requested this protection, although it should be noted that the rules of the SROs differ in some details in this area. However, any money received from, or held by, a member firm on behalf of an intermediary must be regarded as client money unless the intermediary has confirmed that the money is not client money of any of his clients.

*(loose
)
True*

The statutory trust

1.2.10 Merely holding clients' money in a separate bank account of the firm would not, in itself, provide the protection that is intended; a liquidator might still be able to regard such accounts as being assets of the firm. The client money rules achieve protection for clients against a liquidator by establishing a statutory trust, under which all money in a client bank account set up in compliance with the rules is held by the firm on trust for its clients. Even this status only safeguards the funds actually in the trust account at the time of liquidation. If there is a shortfall as a result of the firm withdrawing client money in breach of the rules, clients have no preferential claim in the liquidation for this shortfall.

1.2.11 Notice of the trust status must be given to the bank where the client account is held; this prevents the bank subsequently claiming an offset between the client account and the firm's own overdraft at the bank. In addition, the bank may itself be liable for payments made out of the client account in breach of the trust, if it knew them to be wrongful or in circumstances where a reasonable banker would have made enquiries; for example cheques paid out of the client account which appear prima facie to be for personal expenses.

1.2.12 In order to maintain the validity of the statutory trust, and thus protect the funds from its creditors, the firm must comply with the detailed rules on clients' money. Clearly, failure to pay one client's money into the client account would exclude that money from protection of the trust, but it is also important to be aware that the mixing of firm's money with clients' money in the client account is also a breach of the rules and could enable a liquidator of the firm to challenge the validity of the trust and thereby establish a claim to money in the client account. It is therefore *not* acceptable for a firm to maintain a surplus of its own money in the client account as a safety margin.

1.2.13 In some cases, a bank account is opened in the client's own name, with the firm having a mandate to operate the account. Such an account is the client's own, and the money therein belongs to the client; it is not the firm's client money, and is not subject to the rules.

The rules

11.2.14 The SIB's clients' money rules are divided into the following four sections:

1 *Citation, Commencement, Interpretation and Application;*
2 *Clients' Money* – containing the definition of clients' money, the statutory trust, and rules for payment of interest;
3 *Banking and Accounting* – containing the rules for dealing with clients' money;
4 *Supplementary* – dealing with introductions to unauthorised persons and overseas branches.

For technical reasons, sections 1 and 2 of the SIB rules apply to *all* authorised businesses; whereas section 3 and 4 may be replaced by equivalent SRO regulations. In the case of TSA, rules 100.02 to 100.12 replace SIB's sections 3 and 4, although the wording is largely identical.

11.2.15 This chapter is written in the context of a broker-dealer and references are to the rules applicable to TSA member firms. Rules for other SROs are in most circumstances identical.

11.2.16 Further guidance on the operation and purpose of the regulations is given in the SIB Explanatory Memorandum contained in chapter VI of the SIB rulebook. TSA has also issued operational guidance on settlement accounts as part of its original rulebook, but this guidance has not yet been updated for subsequent, significant rule changes.

Scope of the rules

11.2.17 The client money rules cover all client money, in whatever currency, held by the firm, its UK branches or its agents. Particular problem areas are:

(a) Appointed representatives (e.g. associates and 'half-commission men') – any client money held by them is regarded as client money of the firm, and the firm is responsible for ensuring compliance with the rules. Client bank accounts must be in the name of the firm, not the representative. There is nothing to prevent the firm opening a special client account for the representative to operate on its behalf, provided the firm takes full responsibility for compliance with the rules.
(b) Clearing firms – where the member firm uses the services of a clearing firm to settle transactions on its behalf (as described in chapter 23), money held by the clearing firm remains client money

of the firm; the introducing firm has a continuing obligation as a member of TSA to ensure that the rules are complied with, notwithstanding the fact that many of the detailed records and operations are outside their direct control. A firm using a clearing firm should therefore ensure that its contract with the clearing firm gives it the ability to monitor compliance, the right to insist on changes to meet the requirements, and a claim to damages if the clearing firm fails to comply.

(c) Foreign settlement agents – again, the client money rules apply. If the agent operates a separate bank account handling client money, this must be in the name of the firm. This situation may arise for example where a UK firm with a US parent uses its parent to clear US trades.

(d) Overseas branches of a UK member firm – client money held by overseas branches does *not* fall under the regulations, except where the branch's business would constitute investment business carried on in the UK if the branch were a separate legal entity. The purpose of this is to exclude genuine overseas business, but to prevent firms from evading the client money rules by passing UK business through an overseas branch. The definition is, however, complex and depends on the legal interpretation of 'carrying an investment business in the UK' contained in the FSA itself.

11.3 Systems requirements for client money

11.3.1   The auditor must have detailed knowledge and understanding of the client money rules. However, the rules as drafted are difficult to interpret in terms of the actual operations and systems that are required in a broker-dealer's office. This section, and the four following, are an attempt to set out the requirement of the rules in terms of the main objectives that an average broker's system must achieve under the following broad headings:

Section 11.3 — general requirements, client bank accounts and client free money;
Section 11.4 — interest;
Section 11.5 — settlement money;
Section 11.6 — margin money;
Section 11.7 — warnings to customers.

The suggestions made are not intended to be prescriptive – many different practical solutions have been adopted by different firms – nor do they encompass all the detailed requirements of the rules.

Identification of clients entitled to segregation of funds (SIB rule 2.1 and TSA rule 100.02)

11.3.2   The client money regulations do not apply to money held for business customers who have agreed to opt out, nor to professional customers (individual SROs have minor rule variations here). However, money of another authorised business (e.g. an intermediary) might be client money of *its* customers and must be treated as such unless the firm is informed in writing to the contrary. Note that money held for a customer that is not client money *must not* be mixed with client money and the firm cannot opt to treat it as such.

11.3.3   A separate ledger will normally be maintained for clients whose funds are segregated, or else their accounts will be 'flagged' in some way.

Requirements for client bank accounts (TSA rule 100.03, 10.01; SIB rule 1.2, practice note to rule 2.11)

11.3.4   Client money may only be held at an 'approved bank' – in the UK, all authorised banks and certain building societies; outside the UK, a branch of a UK bank, an EC credit institution or any other bank approved by TSA – except where such bank has been specifically excluded by SIB.

11.3.5   The bank account must be a current or deposit account (not a building society share account) and its title must contain the description 'client account'. The bank must have been informed of the trust status of the account and requested to confirm this. These requirements also apply to the client settlement accounts and client margin bank accounts dealt with in sections 11.5 and 11.6 of this chapter.

11.3.6   Client money may only be held outside the UK with the permission of the client; and where an overseas bank cannot confirm the trust status of the account (because of a different legal framework), clients must be warned of the lesser protection and their agreement to the use of the overseas account must be obtained.

Receipts of clients' money (SIB rule 2.1; TSA rule 100.04, 100.05)

11.3.7   Client money is any money held or received by the firm in relation to any investment agreement with a client and which is not immediately due and payable to the firm itself. No formal definition of 'due and payable' is given, except that the obligation of the firm in respect of which the money is received must have been performed.

11.3.8   Client money received, either from a client or on behalf of a client, must be paid immediately into a client bank account; if a single receipt contains both client money and non-client money (for example a daily settlement cheque from Talisman), it must be paid initially into a client bank account and the non-client money portion subsequently withdrawn, no later than the time the cheque is cleared.

11.3.9   Any receipts from clients who are entitled to segregation of funds must therefore be examined to determine whether they:

— are free money, to be paid into a client account;
— represent an amount due and payable to the firm, to be paid into a firm's account;
— may be paid directly into a client settlement bank account in accordance with settlement money rules (see section 11.5 below);
— represent margin to be paid into a client margin account under the margin account rules (see section 11.6 below);
— or are a mixture of any of the above.

1.3.10   Receipts from market counterparties will normally be dealt with through the settlement account (see section 11.5 below). Those that are not, and which relate (in whole or in part) to a client entitled to segregation of funds, must be paid into a client account, unless the money is to be used to settle an amount due and payable to the firm, or unless it can be transferred to a settlement account or margin account in respect of another transaction of the same client.

1.3.11   Dividends received on safe custody or nominee shareholdings relate to clients entitled to segregation of funds and must be paid into a client account (unless forwarded directly to the relevant client).

1.3.12   Dividends and other claims paid or received as a result of late registration of stock sold 'cum-div' (or 'cum-rights') relate to the settlement of the transaction and are client settlement money which may be dealt with either through a client settlement bank account (or, in the case of foreign settled bargains, a firm's bank account) or, if preferred, a normal client bank account.

1.3.13   Where the firm provides investment services for intermediaries and other authorised persons such as fund managers, money received from or for such persons is treated as client money, unless notification in writing is received that the money is not client money in the hands of the authorised person.

Amounts payable by the firm to a client (TSA rule 100.04 b, c)

11.3.14 The firm must not delay in settling amounts due to its clients; these amounts must be paid to the client as soon as they become due and payable; alternatively, if the firm has instructions to retain the money, it must be transferred to a client bank account as soon as it becomes due and payable.

11.3.15 The rules do not define when a sum becomes 'due and payable'; but the firm must not delay payment once the client has carried out his obligations and the stated settlement date of the contract has arrived.

11.3.16 Thus a firm need not pay a client who has sold stock but has not yet delivered the stock certificates, even if settlement day has passed; but when the client subsequently delivers the certificates, the firm must make payment immediately. Note that if the client delivers the certificates before settlement day, the firm is under no obligation to make payment until the settlement day itself.

Transfers of client's money to settle debt due to the firm (TSA rule 100.05)

11.3.17 Money may only be withdrawn from a client's account to settle fees or commissions due to the firm, if these are in accordance with a previously agreed scale (perhaps set out in the customer agreement), or the client has been given time to query them. Fees or commissions *must* be withdrawn from the client bank account as soon as the firm is entitled to withdraw them under the rules. Other amounts due to the firm must be withdrawn as soon as, but no sooner than, the firm becomes entitled to payment.

11.3.18 Regular transfer must, therefore, be made of commissions or fees from client account to the firm's account, and amounts due to the firm on purchases of stock must be transferred to the firm's account as soon as, but not earlier than, delivery of the stock to the client. No transfer may be made unless the particular client has sufficient free money within the account to cover the transfer.

Other payments into and out of client bank accounts (TSA rule 100.04 d, 100.5 b)

11.3.19 Client money may only be paid to the client for whom it is held, or on his instructions, or in accordance with an agreement with him. Before any payment is made, the particular client's free money balance must be checked to ensure sufficient funds are available.

1.3.20 The firm may pay its own money into the client bank account to make good a deficiency arising from a breach of the rules, or if the bank insists on a certain minimum balance before opening the account. The firm may withdraw this minimum balance if it is no longer required, and also any other firm's money paid into the account, either in error or in accordance with the interest rules or settlement and margin account rules (see below).

Clients' money reconciliations (TSA rule 100.106, practice note to rule 100.03c)

1.3.21 Reconciliations must be carried out, at least every five weeks, between the client bank account cash books and bank statements. At the same time, the total amount shown as being held in the client bank accounts must be agreed to the list of balances of client money held for each client.

1.3.22 Although the rule, read strictly, requires a single overall reconciliation of client money, in practice this can be split up into separate reconciliations if this is more convenient, provided these are all carried out as at the same date and any reconciling items that affect more than one separate reconciliation (e.g. transfers from one client bank account to another) are properly matched.

1.3.23 All differences and reconciling items must be properly investigated and errors corrected promptly – it is insufficient merely to transfer firm's money to make up a shortfall, and any surplus cannot be assumed to be firm's money. TSA must be notified promptly of any inability to reconcile clients' money.

Accounting records for clients' money transactions (TSA rules 100.10, 20.02 and guidance note on accounting records)

1.3.24 TSA rules and guidance notes lay down the following specific requirements for proper accounting records of all client money transactions:

(a) for each amount deposited or withdrawn from the client bank account (other than settlement and margin bank accounts), there must be a record of;

- the name of the client in respect of whom the deposit or withdrawal was made;

- the corresponding account entry in the firm's client accounts (in

191

the case of clients' money), or any other relevant accounting record (in the case of other moneys deposited or withdrawn from the client bank account);

- the date of the deposit or withdrawal;

- the name of the person to whom moneys withdrawn were paid or transferred;

- the name of the person from whom amounts deposited were received;

(b) for each client bank account, there must be a record of the interest earned on the account and the date that any such interest was credited to the account;

(c) for each customer in respect of whom moneys are held in the client bank account, there must be a record of the amount of interest which the firm is liable to pay the customer and the date it is either paid to the customer or credited to his account.

11.4 Interest on client money

11.4.1 Strict rules (SIB rule 2.3, 2.2(4)) cover the requirement for firms to pay interest on money held for clients. Interest must be calculated at least every six months, on the daily balance of each client's free money, and either paid to the client or credited to his account. The rate of interest must be no less than the normal deposit account rate for small deposits at the bank at which the client money is held. If the firm is able to earn a higher rate of interest on the clients' bank account, it may retain the margin itself; there is no obligation to pay all interest earned on the account to the clients whose money is held in the account (although some firms make a practice of so doing). On the other hand, interest must be paid to clients at the minimum rate specified even if, for some reason, the firm has actually earned less interest – for example, if the firm for practical reasons holds some client money on a non-interest-bearing current account.

11.4.2 All interest received on clients' bank accounts must be held in those accounts until the interest due to clients has been calculated. The firm may then transfer any surplus interest to its own account. Paragraphs 35-39 of the SIB Explanatory Memorandum (in Chapter VI of the SIB rulebook) give an example of interest calculations. If a client's free-money balance falls to nil, the interest due to them must be calculated and paid immediately, unless:

(a) the firm believes it likely that the client will again have free money before the next interest accounting date; and

(b) the client has not requested immediate payment of interest due.

11.4.3   Where a client earns interest of less than £10 in an interest period, the interest need not be paid; but if it is not, it must be accumulated until the total for that client exceeds £10 (in which case it is paid or credited to the client and the process then repeats itself.) Until this happens, an amount equal to the accumulated total must be held in the client bank account. However, if before the interest accumulated for a client reaches £10, the client withdraws all his free money and the firm believes it is unlikely that the client will deposit more free money, the client's entitlement to the accumulated interest is lost and the firm may transfer the amount from the client bank account to its own account. The accumulated total of interest amounts under £10, not yet paid to clients or credited to their accounts, must be retained in the client bank accounts and must be taken into account in the client money reconciliations.

Composite rate tax on interest

11.4.4   As discussed in chapter 13, the treatment of interest on general or pooled clients' bank accounts received from the bank or other deposit taker is a complex issue and it will normally be appropriate to take advice on a case by case basis. However, generally it will be possible to receive and pay interest without any deduction for composite rate tax (CRT) or on account of income tax.

11.4.5   Where the account is not a general, pooled client bank account but is a client bank account identified as holding money for a specific client (or more than one specified client) the above exemption is not applicable, and it is probable that interest will be received and paid net.

1.5. Settlement accounts

11.5.1   The strict application of the payment and withdrawal provisions set out above are not always feasible during the settlement of securities transactions, as a result of the netting of receipts and payments to Talisman, the large number of transactions involved, and the existing state of technology available.

11.5.2   The 'settlement account' procedures provide an alternative method of segregation, which firms may (but are not obliged to) adopt when clients' money held by them becomes involved in the settlement process. These procedures cannot be used in relation to free money, to which the strict segregation requirements set out above always apply.

11.5.3 Sections 11.5.7 to 11.5.27 describe the procedures applicable to bargains settled in the UK. Section 11.5.28 then describes the further relaxation permitted in relation to bargains settled overseas, reflecting the additional complexity of international settlement and the varied systems that apply (as discussed in chapter 15).

11.5.4 The UK settlement account procedures allow the netting of clients' money, between one client and another, during a prescribed period either side of the settlement date. Clients' money in the course of settlement is allowed to be paid into and pooled in one settlement bank account. Although this bank account is a client bank account held on trust for clients in the same way as the normal client bank accounts described in section 11.3, amounts may be withdrawn from the settlement bank account without any requirement that withdrawals are in respect of the same client as the deposits. It is therefore possible that one client's purchase will be paid for by another's money in the short term.

11.5.5 A restriction does apply where the firm is acting as principal and buying from, or selling to, the client on its own account. In this case clients' money may not be used to finance the firm's own transactions but must be held in the client settlement bank account until the securities are delivered and the transaction completed. Hence these transactions must be separately identified and a record kept of the corresponding movements or allocation of stock.

11.5.6 In order to ensure that the correct balance is held in the settlement account, a daily calculation of the assets and liabilities representing the balance on the account must be made, and any shortfall in the actual balance 'made good' from the firm's own money. In addition, the account must be reconciled to bank statements at least every five weeks, as with other client bank accounts, although more frequent reconciliations may be appropriate to maintain proper control over the account if the number of transactions is high.

UK settlement account

11.5.7 A UK settlement account may be used for all settlement money relating to transactions to be settled in the UK – it is irrelevant for this purpose where the transaction was dealt or whether the stock itself is a UK or overseas security.

11.5.8   When a customer has entered into a bought bargain, any free client money held for that client, or received from him, may be transferred into the settlement account. This transfer may be made immediately (whatever the settlement date), except in the case of Talisman settlements, where the transfer to the settlement account may not be made until after the last dealing day of the account.

11.5.9   Receipts from market counterparties, in respect of sold bargains for segregated clients, are also paid into the settlement account, but market receipts relating to other clients must be dealt with through the firm's bank account. In practice this can cause considerable difficulty, particularly in relation to receipts from Talisman.

11.5.10   Funds in the settlement account may be withdrawn when required to settle any UK settled transaction for a segregated client, but again, not for transactions for other clients.

11.5.11   Payment must also be made promptly to the client on his sold bargains – within one day of it being 'due and payable' to him – that is, within one day of his delivering stock (however, for this purpose delivery of Talisman stock by the client *before* the due settlement day is treated as a delivery *on* settlement day). Alternatively, the amount due to the client may be transferred to a 'free-money' client bank account; or, if it is required to settle another bargain for the same client, it may be retained in the settlement account.

11.5.12   The above rules apply only to receipts and payments relating to bargains for clients entitled to segregation of client money. These bargains must, therefore, be separately identified.

11.5.13   Amounts that are due to or from clients or the market which relate to dividend claims, rights and calls claims (i.e. resulting from delays in registration and settlement) should be treated as part of the settlement process of the bargains involved and dealt with through the settlement account. Similar items relating to safe custody nominee shareholdings are not settlement money, as they have nothing to do with the settlement of a transaction; they must accordingly be dealt with through ordinary clients' bank accounts.

UK Settlement Account Required Balance Calculation

11.5.14   A *daily* calculation of the required balance on the account must be carried out to ensure that sufficient funds remain within the account; any shortfall must be made good by an immediate transfer from the firm's own bank account. A surplus may be withdrawn, but only to the extent that it represents firm's money that has previously been used to 'top up' the account. It should be noted, though, that any surplus or deficit can result only from a breach of the rules. The daily balancing is described in rule 100.07i.

11.5.15 The totals of the following balances covering all counterparties have to be extracted daily.

A (i) amounts due to Talisman and other market counterparties in respect of segregated clients' bought bargains; plus
(ii) amounts due to segregated clients in respect of their sold bargains;

C (i) amounts due from Talisman and other market counterparties in respect of segregated clients' sold bargains; plus
(ii) amounts due from segregated clients in respect of their bought bargains (excluding any amounts more than thirty days overdue on agency, but not principal, bargains to the extent that the firm has paid the market counterparty);

(in practice, A(ii) less C(ii) may be calculated together as the net balance on the clients' account; however, the adjustment for items over thirty days may need to be calculated separately).

B the contract value of the firm's sales as principal to segregated clients, where either the firm has not yet delivered the stock or the client has not paid; and

D amounts payable by the firm on its purchases as principal from segregated clients where the firm has not yet received the stock.

11.5.16 In the case of Talisman securities, the firm is not deemed to have 'received' the stock for the purposes of calculating D until the stock is transferred by Talisman to the firm's stock account; merely receiving certificates and signed transfers is not sufficient.

11.5.17 If the firm arranges a deal as agent between two customers, one of whom is entitled to segregation and the other not, the 'non-segregated' customer must be included as a market counterparty in A or C as appropriate. The balance on the settlement account is then required to be $(A+B) - (C+D)$.

11.5.18 The formula may, quite validly, produce a negative figure. If the firm has an overdraft facility on the client settlement account, there is no objection to the account being overdrawn to match a negative formula balance. However, banks will not always agree to overdraft facilities on such accounts, and TSA have made it clear that there is no obligation to overdraw the settlement account if the formula produces a negative balance.

.5.19 The purpose of excluding client debtors more than thirty days overdue from C is to ensure that the firm, rather than other clients, bears the risk of default by a client. This adjustment only applies therefore, where the market counterparty has been paid, and does not apply to transactions where the firm is acting as principal since in these transactions the funding of one client by another is never permitted. This is illustrated in example 1 below.

.5.20 To see how this formula operates, consider the following examples (in each case the client is entitled to segregation of funds). Commission and other charges have been ignored for this purpose although the treatment of these items is discussed below.

.5.21 *Example 1*

Client 001 buys stock for £1,000, the firm acting as agent.
    Initially, £1,000 will be included in A(i) and £1,000 in C(ii), giving net clients' money of nil. If the client pays the £1,000 before the market settles, C(i) becomes nil and clients' money £1,000. When the market settles, all items become nil.
    If the market were to settle before the client pays, A(i) becomes nil and clients money – £1,000, indicating that the client has effectively been funded from other clients' money. But if the client has not settled after thirty days, C(ii) becomes nil and thus the funding of the client from other clients' money is reversed, the firm having to make up this account from its own account.

.5.22 *Example 2*

Client 002 sells stock for £2,000, the firm acting as agent.
    Initially £2,000 will be included in C(i) and A(ii), giving net clients' money of nil.
    If the stock is delivered and money received from the market, C(i) becomes nil and hence clients' money is £2,000.

.5.23 *Example 3*

Client 003 buys stock for £3,000 from the firm acting as principal.
    Initially, £3,000 will be included in C(ii) and B, giving net clients' money of nil.
    If the client pays before the stock is delivered, C(ii) becomes nil and clients' money £3,000. This will then become nil when the firm delivers

197

the stock to the client and becomes entitled to the money. If, on the other hand, the firm delivers before the client has paid, C(ii) and B each remain at £3,000 and clients' money is nil; the firm is not entitled to use other clients' settlement money to settle the debt to itself.

11.5.24   *Example 4*

Client 004 sells stock to the firm as principal for £4,000.

Initially, £4,000 will be included in A(ii) and D, giving clients' money of nil.

If the client delivers, D becomes nil and clients' money £4,000; the firm is thus obliged to pay this into the client settlement account immediately. If the client is paid before he delivers the stock, both A(ii) and D become nil; thus the payment is not permitted to reduce the overall balance on the settlement account, i.e. no borrowing of other clients' settlement money is permitted.

11.5.25   The accounting system will thus need to be able to distinguish Talisman (and other market counterparty) balances relating to segregated clients from those relating to other customers.

11.5.26   The rules do not make it clear whether commission, stamp duty and other changes due from the client relating to the bargain are to be deducted in calculating A(ii) and added in calculating C(ii), or are to be excluded from the calculation. The rule merely states; 'the total sum . . . in respect of . . . transactions' which would seem to encompass commissions and other charges; but this leads to the somewhat illogical situation of other clients' money being used to fund the commission, etc., due to the firm. To illustrate this, suppose in example 1 above, commission and charges amounted to £50 then the amount due from the client would be £1,050. C(ii) is thus £1,050 and the client money £1,000−£1,050 = −£50; i.e. other clients' money can be used to pay the commission and charges to the firm. A similar situation arises on sold bargains, where A(ii) is reduced by the amount of commission and charges. In practice, both interpretations are encountered.

Principal settlement account

11.5.27   Where a firm does not carry out agency business but always carries out bargains as a principal, the firm may use a single settlement account for both UK and foreign settled bargains. Such an account is described as a principal settlement account and must comply with the same rules as the UK settlement account.

Foreign settlement

1.5.28   For transactions settled outside the United Kingdom a 'client settlement (foreign) bank account' may be used. Whilst the rules for foreign settlement and UK settlement appear virtually identical, there is a major distinction. Under the foreign settlement rules, the balance on the foreign settlement account is calculated, in the same way as for UK settlement, but in this case at least every five business days, and the account 'topped up' as necessary with firm's money. *No movement is then permitted* on the foreign settlement account until the next balance calculation date. All foreign settlements, and receipts of clients money for settling foreign transactions (including transfers from clients free-money accounts) are made to, or from, the *firm's* bank account. The effect of this is to 'freeze' an amount of money until the next balance calculation date which represents the money held for clients on the calculation date but which may bear no relationship to what should be held for clients on the following day. However, it is open to the firm to decide to calculate the balance on the account less than one week after the previous calculation. TSA rules go one step further, and permit the 'frozen' amount to be held in the form of collateral rather than money (rule 100.08g).

11.6   Margined transactions

11.6.1   Special rules also apply to client money which relates to 'margined transactions'. These are any transactions in options, futures or other 'contracts for differences' where the customer may be required to pay margin. This definition therefore includes all LIFFE futures and options positions, together with LTOM options.

11.6.2   It also includes SE traditional options *written* (but not purchased), most overseas traded options and futures, and 'over the counter' contracts such as currency options and FRAs if there is a provision for the payment of margin or deposit of collateral.

11.6.3   All client money relating to margined transactions must be dealt with through a special client-margin bank account. A separate margin account must be maintained for transactions in instruments not traded on an exchange and this money must not be mixed with that relating to 'on-exchange' margined transactions. An 'off-exchange' margin account is therefore required for traditional options contracts.

11.6.4   The required balance must be calculated every day for each margin account, based on the previous day's close of business positions and monetary balances.

11.6.5   The first step in calculating the required account balance is to calculate
          for each customer the following figures:

(a)   his *equity balance*, that is the mark-to-market value of the futures
      and options position (treating profits as positive and losses as
      negative), together with the monetary balance on the customer's
      account and the value of approved collateral the customer has
      provided to the firm; that is, the total amount that would be payable
      to, or by the customer, if all his positions and accounts were closed;
      and

(b)   the total initial margin due from the customer under the rules of the
      exchange (i.e. the margin required under the rules of the exchange
      on the opening of a position, see chapters 18 and 19).

The greater of (a) and (b) is referred to in the rules as the customer's
'required contribution'.

11.6.6   The total of required contributions for all customers is then compared
          with the firm's overall equity balance (value of positions plus monetary
          balance) at the exchange and intermediate brokers, plus the value of
          approved collateral deposited with the firm by customers, and either
          retained by the firm or deposited in turn with the exchange or inter-
          mediate brokers.

11.6.7   The excess of customer's required contributions over the firm's equity
          balance and collateral must be represented by cash held in the margined
          client bank account (or accounts). If there is a shortfall, the firm must
          make it up with its own funds. On the other hand, a surplus may be
          transferred into the firm's account, but only to the extent that it
          represents firm's money previously transferred into the margined client
          account to make up a shortfall.

11.6.8   The rules relating to margined transactions are dealt with by TSA under
          rule 100.09 of the financial regulations and rules 960 to 1080 of the
          conduct of business rules. This later section contains most of the
          segregation requirements.

11.6.9   Care should be taken when a TSA member uses an intermediate broker.
          In such circumstances the firm should maintain a file of letters sent to
          exchanges, clearing houses and intermediate brokers notifying them of
          the requirements of TSA rule 1010.01 or 1020.02. For each new
          intermediate broker to be used, consideration should be given to
          whether it meets the requirements of rule 1020.01 (i). If the inter-
          mediate broker does not meet this requirement, an agreement under
          1020.01 (ii) is required with the broker; and the customers must give

written consent to use of the broker – customers having given such consent must be clearly identified in the firm's records.

1.6.10 Each exchange, clearing house and intermediate broker typically maintains two or three separate dealing accounts:

(i)   for dealings of firm's clients entitled to segregation;
(ii) for dealings of firm's clients not entitled to segregation;
(iii) for the firm's own dealing.

((ii) and (iii) need not be separated, but control is enhanced if separate accounts are used).

11.7   Warnings to customers

11.7.1 The final requirement of the client money rules (TSA rule 100.12) is for a firm to give a warning to a segregated customer before introducing them to an overseas branch of the firm, or another investment business which is unauthorised (and therefore presumably operating overseas), drawing the customer's attention to the fact that the branch or other firm is not governed by the client money rules and thus that the customer's money may not be as well protected.

11.7.2 The wide definition of 'introduce' given in TSA rule 100.12(c) should be noted – even if the customer is merely given the name of the other investment business this could be regarded as an introduction for the purposes of this rule.

11.8   Audit

11.8.1 The only statutory audit objectives relating to client money are to ensure that adequate provision is made for any liabilities arising out of breaches of the rules, and that interest earned by the firm is properly accounted for; together with normal audit objectives relating to bank balances in relation to those client bank accounts which are included in the balance sheet (see paragraphs 11.8.28 and 11.8.29).

11.8.2 The auditor's work must, however, be directed towards two regulatory audit objectives:

(i) the firm had systems to have enabled it to comply with the client money rules throughout the period; and
(ii) at the year end the firm was in compliance with the client money rules.

Audit approach

11.8.3   In order to form an opinion on the adequacy of systems, the auditor must consider each requirement of the rules, and ensure that the client did, in fact, have systems capable of meeting the requirements. This review of the systems should be supported by walk-through tests to ensure that the auditor has a proper understanding of the system. For the purposes of this objective, however, the auditor need not consider how well-controlled the systems are; but he will usually want to assess the strength of controls over the accuracy and completeness of recording of client money transactions in the context of the second regulatory audit objective, discussed below.

11.8.4   The work to support the opinion on year-end compliance with the rules will largely consist of verifying the client bank account reconciliations and balancings (including settlement and margin accounts, as well as all client bank accounts). In addition, the auditor must satisfy himself as to the accuracy and completeness of the accounting records supporting the reconciliations and balancings. This may entail both substantive testing of the records, and an assessment and testing of the internal controls over those records.

11.8.5   In forming his opinion on compliance at the year-end, the auditor may ignore errors or breaches of the rules which satisfy all three of the following conditions:

(i)   the error or breach is 'trivial';

(ii)   the error was corrected immediately it was discovered; and

(iii) the error did not result in any loss for any client.

11.8.6   No clear guidelines can yet be given on what constitutes 'trivial', but it is suggested that the following considerations are relevant:

(a)   the amount of money involved and its significance to the client, not merely to the firm;

(b)   the frequency of occurrence of similar errors; a frequently occurring error indicates a systems deficiency and may be less easily regarded as trivial;

(c)   the extent to which any client was 'at risk' as a result of the error if the firm had ceased trading whilst the error persisted; that is, the extent to which the client was denied the protection of clients' money segregation;

(d)   whether the error was detected promptly by the firm's normal procedures, or was discovered at a later date, perhaps as a result of audit testing; and

(e)   the cause of the breach – whether it resulted from a one-off clerical error, or whether it indicates an inadequacy of the client money system or lack of understanding or competence in the staff operating the system, and is thus likely to recur.

Systems

11.8.7 The auditor needs to consider the firm's client money systems for two reasons. Firstly, to see whether the systems were adequate to enable the firm to comply with the clients money regulations throughout the year; and secondly, to obtain audit assurance on the balances of clients' free money and counterparty settlement and margin balances to enable the auditor to form an opinion on year-end compliance.

11.8.8 To determine whether the firm had adequate systems throughout the year, each requirement of the rules, as discussed in sections 11.3 to 11.7 of this chapter, needs to be considered in turn, identifying how the firm's systems meet the objective. The systems should be documented, using as a starting point at least, the firm's own documentation maintained under TSA rule 20.01f, and significant systems' changes during the year identified. 'Walk-through' tests should be carried out to ensure that the systems documentation accurately reflects the system in operation. The number of items to be 'walked through' will depend on the frequency of systems changes during the year and the 'robustness' of the system – that is, its susceptibility to unauthorised amendment. For example, a system operated by one or two unsupervised staff responsible for all elements of the system and with no real segregation of duties is more likely to be changed without authorisation than a closely supervised and fully segregated system where all procedures are clearly documented. Staff turnover is also a relevant factor.

Systems controls

11.8.9 A formal assessment of the strength of internal control should be made of those controls relevant to the accuracy and completeness of the accounting records which support the client account reconciliation, since errors in these will affect the opinion on year-end compliance. Testing the satisfactory operation of these controls, as distinct from the walk-through tests verifying the accuracy of the documentation of the system, will be necessary if reliance is placed on the controls.

11.8.10 Controls throughout the settlement system, dealt with in detail in other chapters, are relevant to the accuracy of clients money records. These include:

— bargain capture;
— receipts;

— payments;
— clients ledgers;
— stock transfer;
— market and Talisman ledgers;
— dividends and rights claims.

In addition, the following control objectives are specific to client money.

11.8.11 *Control objective: Client's free money balances are clearly identified in the client ledger*
Possible errors under this heading are:

- reconciliation of clients money is incorrectly performed;
- money is paid out of a client bank account in excess of the client money held for that client.

11.8.12 Control procedures that may exist to enable client money balances to be identified easily include:

— separate account maintained for each client for free money and settlement money;
— free money is 'flagged' as such within each client's account by the computer accounting system.

11.8.13 *Control objective: Journal entries between different clients' accounts, and between clients' free money and settlement money, are properly controlled*
A possible error under this heading is:

- amounts transferred from one client's ledger account to another in breach of the rules.

11.8.14 Control procedures which may exist to ensure that all journals are properly controlled include:

— proper documentation of all journal entries
— authorisation required for all journals before posting.

11.8.15 *Control objective: Client bank account reconciliations are properly carried out*
Possible errors under this heading are:

- reconciling items not properly identified;
- reconciling items not corrected promptly.

1.8.16   Control procedures which may exist to ensure that all client bank account reconciliations are properly carried out include:

— client bank account reconciliations and required balance calculations are carried out independently of cashiers and clients' ledger personnel;
— all reconciling items are investigated and explanations noted, and correcting entries initiated where necessary;
— reconciliations are reviewed by a senior official for full disposal of all errors detected.

1.8.17   *Control objective: All client bank accounts are properly controlled*
Possible errors under this heading are:

• new client bank accounts opened outside the client money control procedures;
• client bank accounts that are infrequently used are overlooked.

1.8.18   Control procedures which may exist to ensure that all client bank accounts are properly controlled include:

— opening of new client bank accounts approved by a senior official and properly documented;
— full and up-to-date list of all client bank accounts maintained.

1.8.19   *Control objective: Interest calculations are correctly carried out*
Possible errors under this heading include:

• interest paid at incorrect rate;
• interest calculated on incorrect balances;
• interest not paid or credited to some clients;
• tax treatment of interest incorrect.

1.8.20   Control procedures which may exist to ensure that interest calculations are correct include:

— independent check on interest calculations;
— comparison prepared between interest earned on client bank accounts and interest paid to clients, and significant differences investigated.

Substantive testing

1.8.21   The substantive testing to support the opinion on year-end compliance with the rules falls into two main categories.

11.8.22 Firstly, all reconciliations of client bank account cash books to bank statements must be checked (including all settlement and margin accounts). All reconciling items must be checked, and any that are not merely timing differences between cash book entries and bank statement entry should be noted as breaches and their subsequent correction checked. Such breaches must be considered for inclusion in the audit report to TSA unless they satisfy all three tests of triviality, prompt correction and absence of loss to any client.

11.8.23 The agreement of the total client account balances (excluding settlement and margin accounts but including all client deposit accounts) to the clients' ledger free-money balances must also be checked; again, all differences and reconciling items represent potential breaches of the rules and must be considered for inclusion in the audit report.

11.8.24 The formula calculations for UK and foreign settlement account, and the balancing of the margin accounts, must also be checked and reconciling items investigated.

11.8.25 Each bank account must also be checked to ensure that the bank is an approved bank within the rules definition and that the account complies with the statutory trust requirement referred to above. In the case of overseas bank accounts, the existence of the client agreements required by TSA rules 100.03c and 100.03f must be checked.

11.8.26 Secondly, the accuracy and completeness of the ledger balances forming part of the reconciliation must be tested. These include:

— client free money balances;
— other client ledger balances;
— market counterparty and Talisman balances;
— stock delivery records;
— futures and option positions (both client and market).

11.8.27 Much of the verification required to ensure completeness will have been carried out as part of the statutory audit work for the financial statements. Additional testing may be required in the following areas:

(i) receipts and payments of client money;
(ii) transfers from client bank accounts of commission due to the firm;
(iii) other transfers between client bank accounts, and between a client bank account and a firm's account; and
(iv) interest calculations, and testing to ensure that all interest due is either paid to a client or credited to his account.

The extent of any additional testing required will also depend on the strength of internal controls relating to these records, as considered above.

Disclosure in accounts

1.8.28   It is normal practice to exclude from the firm's balance sheet the client free money held in client bank accounts, together with the corresponding liabilities to the clients, since the firm is acting solely as trustee in relation to this money. Some firms may wish to show the amount of client money in a note to the financial statements, but this is not considered strictly necessary. Consistent with this treatment, interest received and paid on client free money should be shown net in the profit and loss account.

1.8.29   However, because of the pooling and intermingling that arises in the settlement and margin accounts, it is considered that client settlement money and margin money should be included on the firm's balance sheet (under a separate heading and not included with the firm's own bank balances), as well as the corresponding client balances.

1.8.30   An accounting policy note should summarise the treatment of client free money and client settlement and margin money.

12 Safe Custody and Nominee Shareholders

12.1 Introduction

12.1.1 Safe custody securities are defined by TSA as:

'all securities which are not the property of the firm but for which the firm, or any nominee company controlled by the firm, is accountable and are held in safe custody or have been paid for in full by a counterparty . . .'

12.1.2 In practical terms, safe custody is the service offered by firms whereby they retain their customers' securities in safe-keeping. In its simplest form, this arises where the firm purchases shares on the instructions of a customer and that customer then requests that, instead of those shares being delivered to him or his bank, they are held on his behalf by the firm, either on the firm's premises or at the firm's custodian.

12.1.3 More often, however, registerable shares will not be registered in the name of the customer but a nominee name, normally a non-trading nominee company owned by the firm. The customer's beneficial right to the shares may simply be evidenced by the contract note and subsequent despatch of regular statements by the firm.

12.1.4 Safe custody is a service which is often used by 'settle on balance' (SOB) customers as a way of easing the settlement process. Thus, when a customer sells a security, the firm does not need to wait for the stock to be delivered by the customer before it can make settlement. Instead, a transfer can be made out of the client's safe custody holdings with the firm for onward delivery to the market. Indeed, some firms may insist that they keep a customer's securities for safe-keeping as a condition of dealing. This ensures that the firm knows what securities an individual owns, which in turn means that short selling by the customer without the knowledge of the firm is made less likely. As explained in chapter 9, short selling can represent a significant credit risk to firms.

12.2 Nominee companies

12.2.1 A nominee company is a company which, whilst not being the beneficial owner of a particular security or securities, permits them to be registered in its name and acts as trustee for the beneficial owner.

12.2.2 TSA rule 100.01 allows safe custody securities to be registered in a number of ways, the overall objective of which is to clearly identify assets belonging to customers of the firm and to distinguish them from those belonging to the firm. Under the rules of TSA, any nominee company in whose name safe custody securities are registered must be controlled by the TSA member firm or a bank and is usually, therefore, a subsidiary of the member firm or part of the same group. This separation of customers' assets is one of the fundamental requirements for firms operating safe custody arrangements under the Financial Services Act (FSA) 1986.

12.3 Safe custody depositories

12.3.1 A firm may keep all of its safe custody securities on its premises. However, unless holdings are fairly small and dealing volumes are low, this may prove to be impractical. Therefore, it is highly likely that a firm will keep stock in depositories at various locations depending on where its counterparties (both customers and market) are situated. The keeping of overseas stocks in local depositories often provides the means of solving timing problems in respect of delivery, and eases the settlement process for the sale and purchase of such stocks.

12.3.2 Where third party depositories, such as banks are used, all securities must be kept in specially designated safe custody accounts. Specific rules in relation to safe custody assets and accounts apply to all SRO members with minor differences in the detailed rules of each SRO. For example, the rules of TSA require that where safe custody securities are not kept in the physical possession of the firm, they must be kept with an eligible custodian. In the case of business customers and market professionals, this means any person whom the firm reasonably believes can provide safe custody services. For other (i.e. private) clients, eligible custodians are restricted to one of:

— a branch of an *Approved Bank*; or
— an *Approved Depository*; or
— a member of an *RIE or DIE*; or
— any other person approved by TSA.

12.3.3 The above are defined in section 1 of the Financial Regulations of TSA as follows:

(i) *Aproved Bank* – 'an authorised institution under the Banking Act 1987 or the overseas parent or subsidiary company of such an institution'.

(ii) *Approved Depository* – 'shall be as set out in a list issued from time to time by the Association (TSA)'. This list at present includes such organisations as CEDEL in Luxembourg, SEPONs in the UK and the Depository Trust Company in New York.

(iii) *Regulated Clearing Firm* – 'shall mean a clearing firm regulated under the provisions of the FSA 1986'. (See chapter 24 for further details on clearing firms).

12.3.4 It is important to ensure that only eligible custodians (as defined above) are used. If there is any doubt as to whether a custodian is eligible, the regulatory authorities should be contacted and guidance sought. It is also important to ensure that any securities deposited with third parties are held free of all liens and charges, unless the beneficial owner of the stock has given written permission for the securities to be pledged (for example with loan account transactions as described in chapter 9).

12.3.5 Rule 100.01(d) of TSA's financial regulations requires that a written agreement must be in place between the firm and each custodian used by the firm for safe custody to the effect that:

(i) the eligible custodian is not to part with any documents or certificates deposited with it other than to the firm or on the firm's instructions;

(ii) documents and certificates shall be held in such a manner that it is readily apparent that the investments to which they relate do not belong to the firm or to an affiliate of the firm; and

(iii) the eligible custodian will, not less frequently than once in every six months and on the request of the firm, prepare and deliver to the firm a statement made up, as at a date specified by the firm. This statement should detail the documents of title or certificates which were held by the eligible custodian for the firm, the amount of that investment and, where the investment is a registerable investment, the amount held in each different customer's name.

12.3.6 It is also necessary for the eligible custodian to acknowledge to the firm in writing that it will not have any lien or right of retention over certificates placed in its custody, or any right to sell any of those securities.

12.4 Accounting

12.4.1 The only amounts in respect of safe custody securities which would normally appear in the firm's or, in certain instances, its nominee company's books of account, are fee income from customers for the safe-custody service and the operating expenses in respect of that service. However, it should be noted that, in most cases, nominee companies within the Securities Industry are dormant and the income and expenses involved in the safe custody operation are dealt with in the books of the parent firm.

12.4.2 The normal controls over income and expenditure should be in place to ensure that all income receivable is in fact received and all expenses are properly incurred. Consequently, the safe custody of securities has little direct impact on the firm's accounts although, because of the fiduciary responsibility for the firm, controls over clients assets' and the effectiveness of those controls are of the utmost importance. The audit requirements in this area therefore arise mainly from the SRO rules relating to the adequacy of the safe custody accounting records.

12.4.3 TSA Financial Regulations 20.01c(v) and 20.02a(vi) describe in general terms the records that are required:

> *20.01c(v)* – 'the records shall be maintained in a manner such that they disclose, or are capable of disclosing, in a prompt and appropriate fashion, the financial and business information which will enable management to safeguard the assets of the firm, including assets belonging to counterparties and other persons for which the firm is responsible;'
> *20.02a(vi)* – 'the accounting records shall, in particular, contain an up-to-date record of all investments or documents of title in the possession or the control of the firm showing the physical location, the beneficial owner, the purpose for which they are held and whether they are subject to any charge.'

12.4.4 More specifically, a proper system of accounting for safe custody securities should enable management to identify:

— the overall amount of assets held on behalf of customers;
— the number and description of each class of security held in safe custody;
— the number of each class of security held at each depository;
— the number of each class of security held on behalf of each customer.

12.4.5 In practice, all safe custody securities, whether held in the name of the firm or its nominee company, will be recorded in a combination of the following ways:

— holdings listed by stock showing the depository where the stock is held;
— holdings listed by stock for each individual customer in customer order;
— holdings listed by depository showing all stock held at each depository.

12.4.6　This can require three safe custody registers, by depot, by customer, and security. As stock is usually registered in the name of the firm or its nominee company, it is not always necessary to allocate each individual customer's stock to a particular depot. If a firm only has a relatively small number of safe custody holdings, it may be practical to maintain the information in a single register. However, the firm may find it convenient to analyse its safe custody records further where the stock of overseas customers is kept in depots in their country of residence. There can be no prescriptive way in which safe custody records should be kept and the extent of the records will vary between firms according to the nature of their business.

12.4.7　There are at least two bases on which safe custody records can be updated. The records may be updated as soon as the customer has dealt (thus giving a portfolio, rather than a true safe custody position) which can be effected by the safe custody department receiving a copy of every contract note relating to dealings by safe custody customers. However, the rules of the SROs require the true, safe custody position to be known and hence firms must adopt the alternative of updating the safe custody records to show the physical movement of securities as confirmed by the depot. Ideally, the records should show *both* positions so that reconciliations between customers' portfolios and stocks physic-ally held at depots can be easily and promptly performed; such information will also be required to carry out the reconciliations of safe custody records required under the rules of the SROs.

12.5　Audit

12.5.1　Safe custody holdings only have a limited direct effect on the firm's financial statements. Apart from the related expenditure and income, the main implication is that a liability may arise on stocks the firm has been holding on behalf of a customer, but which have been lost. Bearer stocks certificates, if lost, will usually be covered by an insurance claim provided the firm can apply sufficient evidence to its insurers to establish the claim. On the other hand, lost, registered stock certificates will normally be replaced by a new certificate issued by the company's registrars against an indemnity from the firm. This indemnity gives rise to a contingent liability. Hence, the only statutory audit reporting objective is that adequate but not excessive provisions have been made against any safe custody securities which have been lost. In practice, experience has shown that claims against such indemnities are exceedingly rare, but this does not obviate the need to consider such matters.

2.5.2 Most of the audit work on safe custody is aimed at meeting the additional reporting objectives as set out in the rules of the relevant SRO. In the case of TSA, these are contained in the Financial Regulations and are that:

(i) all customers' securities deposited by the firm with third parties are held in specially designated safe custody accounts and are held free of all lien (rule 100.01a(ii));

(ii) the firm has the necessary letters of agreement with eligible custodians (rule 10.01(d)) (this rule was implemented in June 1990 and certain transitional reliefs are available);

(iii) the firm's records are complete, accurate and comply with rules 20.01c(v) and 20.02a(vi);

(iv) the firm has, on at least two occasions during their financial year, agreed the records of all securities for which it or its nominee company is responsible against physical stock or certificates of holdings obtained from third parties (rule 100.01f(i));

(v) or if the firm has not followed the requirements of (iv) above, the firm has obtained TSA consent to use the rolling stock check reconciliation method and on at least two occasions during the accounting period has agreed its records to either the physical stock of securities of a particular issuer which rank *pari passu* with one another (ensuring that all assets are so inspected during the accounting period) or to certificates of holdings obtained from third parties (rule 100.01(g)(ii);

(vi) the firm has on at least one occasion during the financial period sent all customers a statement of their assets for which the firm is accountable (rule 100.01(h));

(vii) the firm was in compliance with the rules at year-end, i.e. all stocks held at the year-end are held in compliance with rule 100.01. In certain circumstances, it may be possible to rely on systems work and earlier stock checks to provide some evidence in this area.

2.5.3 As a result of obtaining the necessary audit evidence that these objectives have been met, the auditor should be able to report without qualification under rule 90.03d (ii), that, 'the systems for the safe

213

custody, identification and control of documents of title have been adequate throughout the financial year and include reconciliations between the records maintained by the firm and statements and confirmations from bankers and other custodians at appropriate intervals'.

12.5.4　Whilst it would normally be expected that one of the reconcilations referred to in 12.5.2(iv) above will be carried out at the balance sheet date, a firm may have carried out the detailed reconciliations of safe custody holdings at a date other than the balance sheet date. Hence, the work carried out by the firm may not provide direct evidence on any lost securities at the reporting date. However, if the firm has introduced the control procedures necessary to meet all of the systems' objectives stated above, it is less likely to misplace stock and the results of reconciliations during the year may give sufficient comfort at the year-end.

12.5.5　The results of the system's assessment and the outcome of reconciliations performed during the year will indicate the level of substantive work required to verify year-end safe custody holdings. In theory, if adequate control procedures were in place for the whole period and the working papers of the circularisations have been properly prepared and retained, little year-end testing will be necessary. It is where the auditor cannot satisfy himself in this respect that detailed year-end substantive testing will be required.

12.5.6　Many of the control procedures detailed below will only be in evidence at a specific time during the year when the circularisations and reconciliations are being conducted. In order to verify the procedures, the auditor may need to attend at these times. Other elements of internal control, such as the existence of letters of authority regarding eligible custodians, can be sample-tested to confirm their effective operation. The following control objectives are relevant for the audit of safe custody securities.

12.5.7　*Control objective: Safe custody securities are all held in specially designated accounts and are free of lien*
Possible errors under this heading are:

- client property is being used to secure liabilities of the firm;
- depots are established at short notice leading to the use of inappropriate custodians.

12.5.8　Control procedures which may exist to ensure that safe custody securities are all held in specifically designated accounts and free of lien include:

— prohibition of staff opening third party depository accounts without passing relevant details to senior designated management;

— depositories only used where they have confirmed in writing their willingness and ability to comply with relevant conditions;
— maintenance of a register of depositories;
— regular (e.g. monthly) reports to designated senior management of all depositories used for holding customers' assets.

12.5.9   *Control objective: All customers' holdings are completely and accurately recorded*
Possible errors under this heading are:

• customers' holdings excluded from the safe custody records;
• safe custody holdings incorrectly recorded.

2.5.10   Control procedures which may exist to ensure that all customers' holdings are completely and accurately recorded include:

— segregation of duties between record-keeping and stock-handling;
— record-keepers receive copies of all contract notes in respect of safe custody customers;
— record-keepers receive advice notes of physical movement from internal and external depots.
— periodic checks from records to holdings by persons independent of recording or custody function (bi-annual checks are required by most SROs, under which all securities must be counted at the same date. However, permission can be sought to conduct rolling stock counts, provided suitable controls against 'teeming and lading' are in existence; all holdings in a particular stock must be counted and reconciled at the same date, but different dates used for different stocks);
— full details recorded of all discrepancies arising from reconciliations and their resolution retained by a senior employee;
— review by senior staff of all disposal notes for possible discrepancies;
— inclusion of all securities held on behalf of customers, i.e. agreement not restricted to securities held in or to the order of the nominee company;
— periodic negative circularisation of all customers by persons independent of recording or custody functions. Note that a statement must be sent annually to all safe custody customers. Although this is the responsibility of the firm, all responses by customers should be reviewed for audit purposes.

2.5.11   *Control objective: The periodic despatch of statement to safe custody customers is performed in a satisfactory and controlled manner*
Possible errors under this heading are:

• inaccurate information is entered on the statements;

- some customers not circularised;
- queried replies not followed up.

12.5.12 Control procedures which may exist to prevent these errors include:

— letters sent as soon as possible after the date at which balances were struck;
— letters prepared and despatched by staff independent of recording and custody functions;
— list of all customers being circularised given to account executives to review for completeness;
— any cases where an account executive does not want a letter sent are noted and approved by senior management;
— letters include all assets held for each customer, and not merely those held in or to the order of the nominee company;
— letters give the name of a senior employee to whom any queries should be addressed. This individual should be responsible for monitoring all queries and ensuring that satisfactory explanations are obtained;
— a copy of each letter despatched is retained;
— a senior employee is responsible for checking off completed letters on a master list and overseeing despatch.
— letters clearly state date as at which balances are struck and where securities are held.
— letters clearly ask to check information and write back if incorrect.
— where letters are sent showing portfolio details rather than physical holdings, reconciliations are prepared between the portfolio and physical records as at the circularisation date.

12.5.13 *Control objective: Where customers' stock is held at an eligible custodian, the required notifications have been made*
Possible errors under this heading are:

- recognised custodian not informed of the status of the securities lodged with it and so not aware of its responsibilities.

12.5.14 Control procedures which may exist to prevent such errors include:

— co-ordination, by designated senior management, of all requests to set up new depots;
— review of these requests to ensure that the agreement with the custodian is obtained;
— maintenance of a register of depots.

Analytical review

2.5.15 Because of the nature of the operations of the industry there is likely to be little scope for analytical review in this area.

Substantive testing

2.5.16 The level of substantive testing will be determined by the level of evidence for compliance with the regulatory requirements arising from the systems work carried out. If controls are seen to be strong, significant reductions in the level of substantive testing can usually be made. Equally, as the TSA requirement is for the auditor to report on the operation of systems 'throughout the financial year' (*see* paragraph 12.5.3) it will, in most circumstances, not be possible to obtain the necessary audit evidence by year-end substantive testing alone.

2.5.17 The accuracy of the safe custody records can be appraised by a mixture of reviewing work performed by the firm (with vouching on a sample basis) and the auditor's own work, in particular:

  (i) agreeing the records to certificates supplied by third parties and to the customer circularisation. Work will usually be on a test basis (such as all stocks A–F). It is essential that the audit work takes into account the possibility of 'teeming and lading', and it will therefore generally be advisable to verify all holdings in one stock at the same point in time;
  (ii) reconciling the movement on the dealing accounts of a sample of customers to the movements appearing on their safe custody records;
  (iii) ensuring that a sample of safe custody customers are included within the auditor's circularisation of customer's balances; and
  (iv) ensuring that all safe custody depots are circularised and 'free of lien' is confirmed.

2.5.18 The completeness of the records is more difficult to ascertain. A simple failure to record a stock movement would be identified by the comparison of records with holdings, although suppression of a trade (or creation of a spurious trade) could be used to conceal a fraudulent or negligent loss of stock – a loss which, if large enough may affect the 'true and fair' opinion expressed in the audit report. A test on dealing account movements will give considerable comfort on the completeness of the records and this should be supplemented by the inclusion of a sample of nominee company customers in the auditor's positive circularisation of customer balances.

The audit of nominee companies

12.5.19   Most nominee companies will be non-trading and dormant for accounting purposes. All expenses and income will be accounted for in the parent firm. The only requirement over and above the statutory requirements for such companies is in respect of the systems' report on the safe custody procedures of the nominee company. In most cases these procedures will be operated by the parent firm and therefore will be dealt with above. However, the rules of TSA require an additional audit report to be submitted for nominee companies (rule 90.07b, Financial Regulations of TSA).

13 Taxation

13.1 Introduction

13.1.1 A securities business is likely to be treated as carrying on a trade for tax purposes in the same way as any other commercial entity, and therefore, if it is a company, it will be liable to corporation tax under the normal rules. Similarly, businesses operating as partnerships or as branches of overseas organisations will be liable to UK tax on their profits in the normal way.

13.1.2 However, a securities business is also likely to become involved in a number of other tax matters that are more specifically related to its particular industry such as the complications of franked investment income on dividend positions arising from trading in UK shares, the responsibility to collect tax on dividends and interest received on behalf of customers, and acting as the collector of stamp duty and stamp duty reserve tax on transactions by customers. The impact of VAT can also cause problems, because agency commissions relating to the purchase and sale of securities and the sale of securities as principal are generally exempt from VAT.

13.1.3 This chapter describes the main points relating to the taxation of securities businesses where these differ from those applicable to businesses generally, and also sets out some matters of audit significance. It does not purport to be a taxation textbook and therefore only gives a bare outline of the matters arising.

13.2 Corporation tax

13.2.1 Generally, the corporation tax liability of a securities business will be computed in the same manner as for any other entity. However, there are a number of matters where careful consideration is required.

219

Dealing profit

13.2.2   Profits and losses on dealing in investments will generally form part of
the trade of a securities business and will therefore normally be taxed
under Schedule D. As we have already discussed in chapter 3, a
securities business acting as a market maker or active principal dealer in
securities will generally compute its dealing profits on the basis of
'marking to market' all investment dealing positions held at the balance
sheet date, and will treat all profits so computed as being 'realised' for
the purposes of the Companies Act 1985. This treatment will usually be
accepted by the Inland Revenue as forming a proper basis for the
computation of taxable profits, provided that the valuation policy is
consistently and properly applied. In particular, the Inland Revenue
may examine closely any positions where the valuation is below the
quoted bid price (for long positions) or above the quoted offer price (for
short positions). Such 'abnormal' valuations will only be accepted where
it can be demonstrated that the position was significantly larger than
transactions then taking place within the market.

13.2.3   However, it is open to the tax paying business to argue that the normal
tax principles applying to the valuation of trading stock should apply,
i.e. that taxation should be computed on the basis of carrying long
positions at the lower of cost and net realisable value and short positions
at the higher of sale price and net cost of closing the position. This will
only be accepted by the Inland Revenue where the policy has been
consistently applied by the business. Where tax computations are
prepared on this basis, a deferred tax provision will be required on the
difference between accounts valuation and tax valuation.

13.2.4   Where a securities business only deals very occasionally in securities on
its own account, or where it sells fixed asset investments such as
subsidiaries, then the profits will generally be taxed under the Capital
Gains Tax rules.

Foreign exchange dealing

13.2.5   Where a securities business carries out foreign exchange dealing as part of
its normal operations, any profits or losses arising will be treated as forming part of the profits under Schedule D Case I. In practice, no adjustment
will need to be made for any unrealised gains or losses on open foreign
currency contracts and positions on the balance sheet date, which will be
brought into the profit and loss account on a mark to market basis.

13.2.6   Where a business obtains subordinated loans or other permanent capital
denominated in foreign currency, any exchange gain or loss arising

thereon in a period, reflected in the profit and loss account, must be excluded from the computation of taxable profits.

Dealing in futures and options

13.2.7 Provided that the business is trading in futures and options dealt on recognised exchanges, the profits and losses arising will be taxed in the same manner as other dealing profits, described in paragraph 13.2.2 above. Where over-the-counter options (such as 'traditional' options on the Stock Exchange) are concerned, the Revenue will normally seek to tax profits on the basis that premiums received are taxable at the time of the bargain, without any allowance for unrealised losses on open positions.

13.2.8 Where the business undertakes transactions in options or futures to hedge positions in other securities, it is unlikely that the tax treatment of the hedges will follow the accounting treatment and such transactions will need careful analysis for tax purposes.

Dividends receivable and payable

13.2.9 For a securities business that only deals in securities for its own account from time to time, and which is not a recognised market maker under the rules of the ISE, the treatment of dividends received or receivable on investment positions held is the same as for any other company: dividends received are not subject to corporation tax or standard rate income tax in the hands of the recipient business, although they are 'grossed up' for the purposes of accounts presentation, with the amount of the tax credit included within the tax charge for the period.

13.2.10 For corporate businesses, such dividends will be reported as franked investment income in the quarterly CT61 returns, and will be available to reduce the amount of ACT due on any dividends paid by the business to its shareholders.

13.2.11 For an unincorporated business, the individual proprietor(s) will be subject to appropriate higher rate tax on any dividends received.

13.2.12 To the extent that a business holds a short dealing position over the ex-dividend date of a security, then the business will be obliged to make a payment in lieu of the dividend to the buyer of the shares and to make a payment to the Inland Revenue of the amount of the notional tax credit.

13.2.13 Similar returns will be required for unfranked investment income on long or short positions in bonds and other interest-paying securities, although such items will be taxable in the hand of the recipient business.

13.2.14   Different procedures apply in the case of a market maker recognised as such by the Inland Revenue (defined under section 737(6) of Taxes Act 1988, in relation to securities of a particular kind as a person who:

(a) holds himself out at all times in compliance with the rules of the ISE as willing to buy and sell securities of that kind at a price specified by him; and

(b) is recognised as doing so by the Council of the ISE.

13.2.15   To recognise the pivotal role such entities play in maintaining the underlying liquidity of the stock market, the Inland Revenue have granted market makers the ability to offset dividends received on long positions in some securities against payments in lieu of dividends paid on short positions in other securities. The arrangements by which this operates are set out in the 'Bull and Bear Dividend Agreement' (BBDA) available from the Inland Revenue. These arrangements are inevitably complex, to cater for all the different combinations of types of receipts and payments that can arise, not least because the agreement also covers the treatment of dividends relating to companies resident in overseas tax jurisdictions. Care should be taken that these arrangements are only applied to securities in which the business is a registered market maker, as dividends on non-market making securities are not covered by the BBDA.

13.2.16   *For dividends on UK companies, the BBDA operates broadly as follows:* In each CT61 quarterly return period, the market maker is allowed to offset all dividends received on long positions against dividends paid on short positions. It should be noted that the CT61 forms are completed on a cash basis, even though accounts will be prepared on an accruals basis, with dividends being recognised in the financial statement on the ex-dividend date.

13.2.17   Any net surplus dividend received is reported as franked investment income on the CT61 in the normal manner, while any net dividend paid in a return period is reported as if it were a distribution paid by the business to its shareholders, i.e. as a franked payment. The normal rules about surplus franked payments and surplus franked investment income apply. Similar arrangements operate in relation to interest payments on positions in loan stocks etc.

3.2.18 Particular arrangements apply to dividend claims made to, or from, customers or market counterparties, which are discussed more fully in paragraph 13.3.1 below.

Stock borrowing

3.2.19 Where a registered market maker borrows or lends stock through an approved Stock Exchange money broker, borrowing or lending will be ignored for tax purposes. However, where a market maker borrows or lends stock in any other case, or where any broker-dealer borrows or lends stock, then such unapproved stock loans are treated for tax purposes as purchases or sales, as appropriate. Since the business is likely to be taxed on gains or losses as part of trading profit under Schedule D Case I, and long or short positions will in any event normally be valued for tax purposes at market value, then treatment of stock loans as purchases or sales is unlikely to change the actual tax liability for the period. Care should be taken, however, where the business is subject to the Capital Gains Tax rules or is preparing tax computations on the basis of realised gains only. Similarly, care should be taken that businesses with non-approved borrowings and lendings do not get caught by the dividend-washing rules.

Interest

3.2.20 Interest is generally brought into the accounts for tax purposes on an accruals basis, whether it is payable or receivable on bank loans/ deposits, balances owed to, or from, money brokers, customers etc., provided the interest is a trading receipt or a trading expense. However, normal schedule rules apply to interest on debentures, or long-term subordinated loans and the like, where relief will only be given where interest has actually been paid during the period.

3.2.21 It is increasingly common for securities businesses to pay interest to customers in respect of surplus funds held by the business, such money normally being treated as 'client money' for the purposes of the rules of SIB and the SROs. The extent to which the business can pay this interest gross has not yet been fully established, but at present the generally accepted basis is that interest on such funds is not yearly interest and is outside the Composite Rate Tax (CRT) scheme, and therefore can properly be paid gross. The position that is likely to exist once CRT is abolished in April 1991 is not yet known.

Bad debt and other provisions

3.2.22 It is not normal practice for securities businesses to make general provisions against bad debts or other losses arising from unsettled securities transactions, but to make specific provisions where there is a clear indication that the counterparty is unable to settle. However, some businesses have established general provisions to cover, for example, anticipated irrecoverable amounts arising from safe custody discrepancies or accounting backlogs generally. Since a securities business is subject to the general rules relating to provisions, which effectively only allow tax relief for specific provisions, any general provision will not attract tax relief until an actual loss has crystallised. Naturally, any specific provision against a counterparty balance that is properly assessed to be irrecoverable at the end of an accounting period will be allowed for tax purposes, although such provisions must take account of the likely value of any collateral or other security that the business holds.

Bonuses

13.2.23 In some areas of the securities industry, it is common practice for a substantial part of the remuneration of employees to be paid in the form of bonuses or profit shares. Accordingly, in years where profits are particularly high, the business may set aside a certain part of those profits to pay an element of bonus in periods when profits are low or non-existent. In accordance with the general tax rules on provisions for bonuses (introduced by the Finance Act 1989), the Revenue will disallow relief for sums set aside for future bonuses, unless it can be demonstrated that the bonuses were in fact paid within the statutory period after the end of the accounting period. In any event, the auditor would normally expect to see any such accrued bonuses paid promptly to ensure their validity as an expense of the year in question; but tax problems can arise with deferred bonus schemes paid to ensure staff loyalty.

International transfer pricing

13.2.24 The growth in trading in securities on a regional or global basis has led to a large number of UK securities businesses establishing operations outside the UK and vice versa, with extensive transactions between the various national offices/businesses. There is an almost infinite variety of ways in which these global transactions take place dependent on the style of management and methods of operational control, the particular business carried out by the organisation and its customers, and the countries in which business is carried out. No specific guidance can, therefore, be given on the tax implications of such arrangements. However, this is an area where both the UK Revenue and overseas tax authorities are concerned to protect the interests of their national Exchequer. Therefore, care should be taken to review the arrangements

Double taxation relief

3.2.25   As for any business, securities businesses are entitled to relief in respect of foreign taxes suffered on foreign income, which will principally comprise withholding taxes on interest and dividends received from holdings in overseas companies, held as part of the trading operations of the business.

3.2.26   Relief will be given either via the appropriate tax treaty or via unilateral relief. The amount of relief is restricted to the UK taxation attributable to each item of income.

3.2.27   Where the business is a recognised market maker in overseas securities and it applies the BBDA to dividends and interest on those securities, the double taxation relief will apply only on the net income at each particular rate of withholding tax.

UK branches and residence

3.2.28   Where a company is resident in the UK for taxation purposes, all of its profits and gains will be chargeable to UK tax irrespective of the geographical source of those profits, whether these profits are also taxed by other national authorities, and whether the profits are repatriated to the UK. These rules therefore apply to securities businesses as for any other. Residence for UK tax purposes, for a company incorporated abroad, is determined by reference to the location of its central management and control, and this is usually taken to be where the major decisions of the company are taken or where its board meetings take place. These tests are not wholly objective and therefore this is a matter which may require careful consideration. A company incorporated in the UK is resident here, with only a few exceptions.

3.2.29   If a securities business established outside the UK carries out any trade through a branch in the UK, then the profit arising from that trade will be subject to UK corporation tax. The branch will also be subject to UK tax on chargeable gains made on the disposal of assets located within the UK and used for the purposes of the branch's trade. Again, there can be a degree of subjectivity in deciding whether or not the overseas business is, in fact, carrying out a trade in the UK. It should be noted that the seeking of authorisation under the Financial Services Act may well be regarded as an indication that the business is trading within the UK. This is not, however, a conclusive test, since an overseas business might require authorisation even if it has no physical presence in the UK, for example if it needed to service UK customers. Thus, the extent to which the profits of an overseas business may be subject to UK taxation will require careful consideration.

13.2.30   If it is established that the overseas business does have a UK branch liable to UK corporation tax, the profits of the branch for tax purposes will be computed on the basis that the branch is an independent entity, trading on an arm's length basis with its head office and other related operations. This will necessitate adjustments to the profits or losses shown by the management accounts of the branch to reflect both the terms of trading with the head office (commission sharing, settlement charges etc.) and also the treatment as notional share capital of at least a proportion of what might be an interest-bearing loan account from head office used to fund the branch activities, thus eliminating any deduction for interest on this notional share capital.

Deferred tax

13.2.31   The principles of determining whether or not any provision should be made for deferred tax liabilities are the same for a securities business as for any other commercial enterprise. The main timing differences that are likely to arise are those relating to:

— fixed assets and the different rates of depreciation compared with tax writing-down allowances;
— differing methods of recognising dealing profits between financial accounts and taxable profits;
— tax relief on interest being given on an interest paid rather than an accruals basis.

The guidance contained in SSAP 15 will need to be followed in deciding whether or not full or partial provision for any timing differences is required.

13.3 Other tax issues

Inland Revenue Form SX1

13.3.1   As noted in paragraph 13.2.5 above, the Revenue have established special arrangements for market makers in relation to dividends on trading positions and related issues, known as the Bull and Bear Dividend Agreement (BBDA). As well as the treatment of dividends on the firm's own dealing positions discussed in paragraph 13.2.4 above, the BBDA covers the arrangements necessary to ensure that all buyers of securities, who need to claim a dividend through the ISE, receive the correct tax credits.

13.3.2 The precise operations of these arrangements are dictated partly by the BBDA and partly by the ISE regulations. In broad terms, the market maker has to reclaim tax vouchers from those who have sold gilt-edged securities cum-interest, but who none the less receive the interest. If the tax voucher cannot be produced, the seller is required to pay the full gross amount of interest to the market maker. The market maker will then pay the tax over to the Inland Revenue at the end of each year. Similar arrangements operate under the BBDA for dividends received after deduction of overseas tax. In the case of securities settled through Talisman, Talisman assumes responsibility for the relevant tax vouchers.

13.3.3 The method by which these sums are reported and paid over to the Revenue is by means of Form SX1 which is completed annually by the market maker, and requires an auditor's report on the accuracy of the return.

Foreign dividends

13.3.4 Securities businesses who receive dividends (or interest) on overseas securities on behalf of customers (either on safe custody holdings or on purchases) are required to ensure that the correct amount of UK tax has been deducted from each dividend or interest payment before paying it over to the customer. This means that, if no UK tax has been deducted by any UK paying-agent before receipt by the securities business, then UK tax at the basic rate of 25 per cent must be deducted by the business (after allowing credit for some or all of any withholding tax in the country of origin, in the case of dividends and interest from countries specified in a list issued by the Foreign Dividends Office). The total amount of UK tax so withheld must be paid over to the Revenue on a quarterly basis (after deducting 90 pence per £1,000 of gross dividend as a fee for collecting the tax).

Bear dividends

13.3.5 Where a customer sells a security which he does not possess (a short or bear sale), and that transaction is still open at the time the security goes ex-dividend, the Talisman system will claim an amount from the seller's broker equal to the net dividend payable on that holding, and will pay that sum to the buyer. Talisman will also produce a tax voucher for the buyer, to give him his entitlement to the tax credit on that dividend. Since this means that more dividend (and thus more tax credit) will have been received by shareholders than was actually paid by the company, the Revenue would be out-of-pocket. Accordingly, the seller's broker is obliged to claim an amount equal to the tax credit from its customer. These amounts are then paid over to the Revenue quarterly. As discussed, separate rules apply to market makers in this situation.

Stamp Duty and Stamp Duty Reserve Tax

13.3.6   Stamp Duty and its near-identical twin sister, Stamp Duty Reserve Tax (SDRT), together effectively form a tax of ½ per cent on all purchases of UK shares, convertibles etc., being an additional amount paid by the purchaser.

The only essential difference between Stamp Duty and SDRT is that the former is a tax on documents, and is therefore levied whenever a share transfer is executed. Since many purchases of securities are effected and settled without any formal share transfer needing to be registered, SDRT was introduced (in 1986) to ensure that an equivalent sum to Stamp Duty was charged on changes of beneficial ownership where there was no transfer document. Certain securities (e.g. gilt-edged stock) are exempt from both Stamp Duty and SDRT, while certain transfers (for instance purchases by charities and changes of name of owner with no beneficial change, e.g. on marriage) are subject only to a nominal rate of Stamp Duty/SDRT (50 pence). Gifts are also exempt. One further manifestation of SDRT applies on the creation of an American Depositary Receipt (ADR) from the underlying registered security, when an aggregate and once for all SDRT charge of 1.5 per cent is levied, since purchases of ADRs are exempt from SDRT.

13.3.7   Stamp Duty and SDRT can impact on a securities business in two ways – customer transactions, and transactions by the firm on its own behalf. Each of these is discussed in turn:

(i)   *Customer transactions*
Whenever a firm sells securities to a customer (as principal) or buys securities (as agent) on behalf of a customer, the firm is responsible for collecting the ½ per cent Stamp Duty/SDRT from the customer, normally by adding the sum to the contract note. The charge is made on the value of the customer's purchase: in the case of an agency bargain, this will be the consideration before commission, and for a principal deal, the price including mark-up. The firm will not usually know at the time of the bargain which of the two taxes will in fact be payable (for instance, the customer may sell the shares before the end of the account), but since they are virtually identical, this is of no significance.

The sums thus collected by the firm are paid over to the tax authorities in one of three different ways. For bargains settled through Talisman, Talisman will claim the SDRT/Stamp Duty from the firm on apportionment and pay it over to the authorities. For bargains settled outside Talisman, by delivery to the firm of a share certificate and a signed transfer deed, the transfer will have been 'stamped' by the selling broker-dealer who will pay the relevant sums to the authorities and will claim the Stamp Duty from the buying firm. All other cases (mainly those settled within the firm's own nominee) are the responsibility of the firm itself to advise the authorities of the change in beneficial ownership and to pay over the stamp duty/SDRT.

(ii) *Transactions by the firm on its own behalf*

Where a firm purchases shares for itself, it too is liable to Stamp Duty/SDRT. However, in the interests of promoting market liquidity, there are certain exceptions to this. Market makers in equities are totally exempt from the charge on securities in which they make markets, provided that the purchases are in the ordinary course of their business as a market maker.

Market makers in traded options are granted a limited exemption from the charge on purchases of the underlying equities, although the precise extent of this exemption is still the subject of debate and discussion with the Revenue. Finally, any broker-dealer is exempt, provided that he holds the security for less than seven days (on a FIFO basis) – purchases following bear sales are, however, not exempt.

13.3.8 In the 1990 Budget, it was announced that Stamp Duty and SDRT would be abolished for all securities transactions from a date to be announced. The intention is that abolition will coincide with the introduction of TAURUS, expected to be in the autumn of 1991.

VAT

13.3.9 Securities businesses are subject to VAT in broadly the same manner as any other business. However, many of the services offered by such businesses are exempt from VAT. In broad terms, commission for the purchase or sale of securities and management fees charged to unit trusts are exempt, while advisory and other management fees are standard rated. However, this analysis is complicated by the number of possible variations, for example some commissions are zero rated. Accordingly, most such business will not be able to recover all the VAT charged to them on their expenses (input VAT) and will need to negotiate appropriate special methods with Customs & Excise in order to determine the recoverable proportion of their input VAT.

13.4 Disclosure, internal control and audit

Disclosure

13.4.1 The disclosure by securities businesses relating to the charge for taxation and balances outstanding in respect of taxation and deferred taxation is entirely conventional. However, the relatively significant impact on profits, for some businesses, of dividends receivable on long securities positions may need careful consideration since the element of taxation referable to the tax credit on franked investment income will produce a sub-normal tax charge and may warrant explanation. Equally, disclosure may be necessary where the firm takes advantage of section 242 Taxes Act 1988 to reclaim the tax credit on surplus franked investment income by setting it off against losses for corporation tax purposes.

Internal control

13.4.2 It is unlikely that more than one or two people within the firm will be responsible for the preparation and submission of tax computations, the payment of tax liabilities and the maintenance of the corporation tax accounts. However, given the importance of this area, any tax payment should be carefully reviewed and monitored by appropriate senior management.

13.4.3 Internal controls are more likely to be apparent in dealing with the other tax matters referred to above, in particular Stamp Duty/SDRT and tax relating to dividends. These controls are likely to include segregation of duties between those responsible for making returns and other settlement office staff, reconciliations of the ledger balances to returns made to the tax authorities, and, in the case of Stamp Duty/SDRT, reconciliations of the total charged to customers but not yet paid over to the authorities, to the corresponding amounts reported by Talisman as potentially outstanding to them or still outstanding to other member firms on non-Talisman bargains.

Audit

13.4.4 As part of his responsibility in ensuring that the accounts as a whole give a 'true and fair view', the auditor must conclude on whether the charge for taxation and the outstanding tax balances are fairly stated. Due to the relative complexity of this aspect, the auditor is likely to draw on the skill and experience of appropriately qualified tax specialists.

13.4.5 The auditor's objectives in this area will include establishing satisfactory answers to the following questions:

- Have the current tax charge and the outstanding tax liabilities been computed correctly on the basis of the audited profit and loss account and in accordance with current tax legislation?
- Has the deferred tax charge and outstanding provision been computed in accordance with reasonable projections and assumptions about timing differences and the timing and expected likelihood of their reversal?
- Has appropriate and adequate disclosure been made in compliance with the Companies Act, SSAPs and any relevant SRO rules?
- Have all other balances due to the tax authorities been properly stated, and are there adequate procedures to comply with the requirement of Stamp Duty etc?

13.4.6 The work carried out to achieve these objectives will be the same as for the audit of commercial enterprises, and is not therefore amplified here.

13.4.7 To satisfy himself that there is no major mis-statement of the other balances due to the tax authorities, the auditor will therefore include a review of the procedures and internal controls over such matters as:

- VAT
- Form SX1 accounting
- Foreign Dividends
- Tax on Bear Dividends
- Stamp Duty

together with detailed testing as appropriate. In addition, appropriate tests will need to be carried out to support the specific opinion required by the Inland Revenue on Form SX1.

PART III

14 Market Makers and Principal Dealers

14.1 **Introduction**
14.2 **Market makers**
14.3 **Principal dealers**
14.4 **Accounting**
14.5 **Audit**
14.6 **Capital requirements**

14.1 Introduction

14.1.1   In general terms, the rationale behind the activities of market makers and principal dealers are similar in that both seek to profit from dealing in securities on their own account. However, as we discuss below, the responsibilities of each type of entity are very different.

14.1.2   A market maker is a member firm of the ISE which has committed itself to being ready to deal at all times in the range of stocks in which it is registered. This will involve quoting a bid price and an offer price at which it is prepared respectively to buy or sell shares. In return for this commitment, the market maker is allowed a range of special facilities (discussed in section 14.2 below) which are not available to other ISE member firms.

14.1.3   A principal dealer is any dealer in securities (not necessarily an ISE member firm) who buys or sells stock for his own account. There is no obligation to trade and the principal dealer need only buy or sell stock as and when he sees an opportunity to make a profit.

14.1.4   Although there are fundamental differences in the responsibilities of market makers and principal dealers, many of the accounting and therefore auditing considerations are very similar. In some respects, it can be said that a market maker is a special form of principal dealer with extra responsibilities. The distinctive features of both market makers and principal dealers are discussed respectively in sections 14.2 and 14.3 of this chapter while the accounting, auditing and regulatory capital considerations for both entities are considered in the remainder of the chapter.

14.2 Market makers

Dealing

14.2.1　As already stated, a market maker is an ISE member firm which commits itself to being always ready to deal in the range of stocks in which it is registered. This commitment is reflected in the two-way quotation to buy and sell shares published by the market maker. The way in which market makers publish their prices and the conditions under which they are prepared to deal in a particular stock are described in detail in chapter 6. The buying and selling of shares by a market maker will lead, at any given time, to the market maker holding a net long position (i.e. it has purchased more than it has sold) or a net short position (i.e. it has sold more than it has purchased) in a particular stock – these situations are commonly referred to as 'bull' and 'bear' positions respectively.

14.2.2　The market maker will base his price quotations on his reaction to many different factors. If he considers that 'good news' may be forthcoming in the near future, such as a possible bid for the company, then he may attempt to build up a bull position which may mean pushing up the price at which he is prepared to buy. Alternatively, he may predict a bad set of results in which case prices may be marked down as the shares are seen to be worth less. It should be noted that market makers will usually have their own in-house research departments to provide them with information on the companies in whose shares they trade.

14.2.3　Another factor which may affect prices is the size of the market maker's book. He may have built up a particularly large long position which would lead to heavy losses if prices fell significantly. Therefore, he may wish to reduce his position and thus will encourage investors to buy by reducing his offer price. He will also seek to dissuade investors from selling shares and therefore reduce his bid price below that quoted by his competitors. It should be noted that with the reduction in prices noted above, the spread (i.e. the difference between the bid and offer price) can widen, narrow or remain the same.

14.2.4　Market makers do not generally take large positions in a security because this creates a higher level of exposure and a risk of loss from large price movements. Market makers prefer to make money from a rapid turnover in stocks by keeping reasonably small positions and profiting from the spread (i.e. the fact that the offer price exceeds the bid price). From time to time, a market maker may decide that a particular investment is likely to appreciate in value over a medium-term view (a few days or weeks) and therefore deliberately take a large, long position in the shares. This position would normally be held separately from the day-to-day dealing operations on what is sometimes called a 'back book'.

Settlement

14.2.5 The settlement process for UK transactions is broadly the same as that outlined in earlier chapters. Equity market makers operate under the account settlement system and most transactions with member firms are settled through Talisman (discussed in chapter 7), or as residual tickets (discussed in chapter 8). Gilt-edged market makers ('GEMMs') settle this business through the CGO also discussed in chapter 8.

14.2.6 The principal, additional feature of market maker settlement relates to short positions, where the firm has sold more shares in a particular company than it has purchased. Clearly the market maker cannot deliver stock against all the sold bargains, unless either there is a mechanism for him to borrow the stock, or the market maker re-purchases the shares by adjusting his quotations to persuade investors to sell. This latter course of action is likely to result in unwarranted short-term price increases and therefore may not be conducive to the maintenance of an orderly market. ISE rules therefore permit a stock borrowing facility to be provided by moneybrokers to market makers only, which ensures that there is always sufficient stock available for delivery in the market.

14.2.7 The liquidity that this creates means that, in most cases, settlement of short positions can take place on the designated account day, and the ultimate buyer can be allocated his shares irrespective of the market maker's net position. Accordingly, the market makers are able to deal and take positions in the full confidence that they can finance and settle those positions.

14.2.8 ISE moneybrokers who lend equities and gilts are regulated jointly by the Bank of England, TSA and the ISE; those who lend only equities are regulated by TSA and the ISE. In particular, the ISE has issued a code of conduct which equity-only moneybrokers are expected to follow in their dealings with each other. The Bank of England has issued a similar code of conduct for other moneybrokers.

14.2.9 Moneybrokers play a central role in the operation of the London stock market. They do this by providing liquidity for market makers in two particular ways:

(i) where market makers are net sellers of stock (i.e. they have sold more than they have purchased), they need to borrow stock in order to be able to deliver it to all of their purchasers. They will not be paid by purchasers until they can deliver that stock; and

(ii) where market makers are net purchasers of stock (i.e. they have purchased more than they have sold), they need to be able to borrow money in order to pay for their net purchases.

14.2.10   In practice, market makers will be net sellers in some stocks and net purchasers in others, and hence, at a particular time will have a need to borrow both stock and money.

14.2.11   The moneybroker is able to provide this liquidity by matching entities which are holders of stock (i.e. large investing institutions such as pension funds and insurance companies) to those which are short of stock (i.e. market makers). In return for borrowing stock or cash, the market maker is expected to provide collateral in the form of either cash or stock, which is channelled to the stock lender via the moneybroker. Strict confidentiality is obviously necessary because of the potential effect of price-sensitive information on market maker's positions.

14.2.12   The practical mechanics of stock lending depend upon whether gilts or equities are being lent and therefore these are considered separately.

Stock lending: gilts

14.2.13   Transactions in gilts are due for settlement on the following business day and therefore stock lending operations work on a twenty-four hour cycle. The Bank of England through the Central Gilts Office (CGO) plays an important part in the process by ensuring that all lending takes place against security and by acting as a guarantor of the CGO system. The CGO system is discussed in more detail in section 8.3 of chapter 8.

14.2.14   The moneybroker maintains a record of stocks that are available for loan and at the start of any day may be contacted by a potential lender to 'ice' stock. This is effectively a preliminary reservation of stock which allows a borrower first refusal on a particular holding. By the middle of the morning the market maker's borrowing requirement based on the previous day's trading will be known and the moneybroker will be able to agree a specific stock loan. At th same time, stock previously on loan may no longer be required by the borrower, or may be needed by the lender for its own sales and so a return of stock will also be agreed.

14.2.15   To facilitate stock movements, a lender's stock is usually held in the nominee account of a bank which is a member of the CGO. Once the loan has been agreed, the lender instructs the bank to deliver the stock to the borrower via the CGO. The receipt of funds at the CGO acts as short term 'daylight' collateral for the lender and is normally replaced by gilt collateral (representing a different gilt stock in which the market maker has a long position), before the close of business on the same day.

4.2.16 Each day the loan and its collateral are revalued to ensure adequate but not excessive margin is held, and this may lead to adjusting payments or receipts moving between the borrower and the lender. If the borrower requires the collateral held by the lender, say because that particular stock has matured or been sold as part of the lending institution's own dealing activities, it is replaced by collateral with an equivalent value on the same day. As discussed above, the system operates to ensure that there is no 'daylight' exposure to the lender.

Stock lending: equities

4.2.17 In the case of equities, the mechanics of lending are governed by the fortnightly ISE account system. As in the case of gilts, the moneybroker maintains details of stock available for loan. When a stock loan is agreed, the lender sends the certificate accompanied by a signed transfer deed (provided to the lender in a standard form) to the moneybroker, who in turn lodges the certificate with Talisman.

4.2.18 Although the lender has released stock to the moneybroker, the loan does not take effect until account day, at which point stock is delivered by Talisman to the market maker. The actual process that takes place in Talisman is discussed in more detail in paragraph 7.2.20 of chapter 7. Prior to account day, the stock continues to be held by the moneybroker on the lender's behalf and can if necessary be withdrawn. On account day, the stock loan agreement comes into existence and the cash collateral passes from the market maker to the moneybroker and then on to the lender and at the same time interest on the loan begins to accrue. While it is usual for the stock loan to remain in place for the length of an account, stock can be returned by the market maker within the account.

4.2.19 The principal method of charging a market maker for the loan of stock is by means of a deduction from the rate of interest paid to him by the moneybroker for the cash given as security against the borrowed stock. Typically, the rate charged to market makers is 2 per cent for borrowing equities and 3/4 per cent for borrowing gilts, although these rates are negotiable. The moneybroker should expect to retain 1/2 per cent or 1/4 per cent respectively with the balance paid over as the lending fee to the lending institutions. Interest is calculated daily, but is normally only paid on a monthly basis.

14.2.20 Lenders of stock have to seek approval from the Bank of England and the Inland Revenue before they can lend stock through an ISE moneybroker. The reason for Inland Revenue approval is to remove the need to treat stock loans as disposals for Capital Gains Tax purposes. Written agreements must be drawn up between the stock lender and the moneybroker since the lender has no direct dealings with the ultimate borrower (the market maker). Such agreements cover the legal rights and obligations inherent in the stock lending operation and contain certain standard terms, as follows:

(a) the loan of stock is not regarded as a disposal although it involves a short-term change in registered ownership;
(b) any entitlements, such as dividends or conversion rights pertaining to stock on loan, remain the property of the lender;
(c) should a lender wish to recall stock from the borrower, the moneybroker will either borrow it from another lender or recall it from the borrowing market maker. If the stock cannot be recalled, the lender will be given the use of the funds with which the market maker secured the loan, until such time as the stock is returned; and
(d) voting rights.

14.3 Principal dealers

14.3.1 Like a market maker, a principal dealer is someone who buys or sells stock for his own account. The difference is that, whereas market makers are committed to trade at the published prices and conditions, a principal trader looks at the prices quoted and, where he considers them to be out of line with his own view of the market, buys or sells as appropriate.

14.3.2 The principal dealer may decide that a particular company's shares are undervalued or that it is a potential bid target. In this case, the dealer would purchase the shares (it should be noted that the dealer may also have customers to whom it distributes this research and who may decide to deal themselves through the firm). By taking such a view, the firm would probably be willing to hold the investment in the short- to medium-term in order to give the stock a chance to increase in value.

14.3.3 Other principal dealers may not operate on such a scientific basis and may be prepared to take a fairly short-term 'intuitive' view on a share price (e.g. in the period before a set of results are to be announced). Such trading will usually only make up a small part of any business because of the difficulty in consistently making money this way. Such trading could take place in an agency broker which permits one or more of its senior dealers to take positions in the name of the firm so long as they are limited in size, as a means of investing the return on surplus cash held within the business.

4.3.4   It should be noted that the term 'principal dealer' is also used in markets other than the ISE, such as the Eurobond Market, to describe those who are willing and able to quote prices to third parties, there being no committed 'market makers'.

4.3.5   Principal positions may also occur, for any broker-dealer, as a result of dealing errors, where for example, a bargain is transacted for the wrong number of shares and the customer repudiates it. The bargain cannot be cancelled and so the firm has to take it as its own. Such short-term trading is usually not material and is not discussed in any further detail. It should be noted that the control procedures discussed in section 14.5 below are still relevant in these circumstances.

4.3.6   Because a principal dealer in equities or gilts is prohibited from borrowing stock, bear positions can only be maintained for as long as the counterparty does not demand delivery of the stock. It should be noted that with the development of derivative markets it is possible to achieve the same financial effect as taking a short position by entering into suitable transactions in futures and options (as discussed in chapters 18 and 19).

4.3.7   The settlement process for a principal dealer will depend on whether or not he is an ISE member firm. For a member firm, settlement will be through Talisman or the residual ticket system as appropriate. A non-member firm will deal as a customer of the market maker and will usually settle on a CAD basis (i.e. against delivery of the stock as explained in chapter 9). The principal dealer might, therefore, be able to maintain short positions for long periods of time because cash settlement will only take place when stock is delivered to the market maker. However, the market maker is quite entitled to press for delivery, and it is this which limits the principal dealer's ability to maintain short positions. The market maker has an obligation to provide capital against unsettled counterparty balances (under TSA's CRR requirements which are discussed in chapter 10). If prices rise significantly, there is an associated increase in risk for the market maker and a higher regulatory capital requirement. This is likely to lead the market maker to press for delivery.

14.4 Accounting

14.4.1   Although the businesses of market making and principal dealing are different, many of the accounting considerations are similar. Therefore they are considered together below, with an indication of where differences may arise.

14.4.2   In most cases, dealers will keep their own record of positions on a 'front office' system. This is usually a memorandum record, which does not form part of the company's financial accounts and is updated as soon as a transaction has been entered into. In many organisations, the dealers' records will interface directly with the accounting/settlement records, which means that the two are updated simultaneously. The dealers' records may also include non-financial data such as implied funding costs of positions so that dealers may see quickly whether a position is profitable after taking into account funding costs.

14.4.3   Having entered into a transaction (unless dealers are themselves re-sponsible for inputting a deal to a computer screen), a dealing slip will be filled in showing, amongst other things, stock, price, counterparty, quantity and settlement terms. This slip will then be used to post the dealers' records and thence the accounting and settlement records. Where this posting does not take place automatically, it is essential that the dealers' records are reconciled to the accounting records on a regular basis.

14.4.4   The main accounting considerations relating to market making and principal dealing are considered below under three headings: valuation of positions, position agreement, and disclosure requirements.

Valuation of positions

14.4.5   The method of valuation which should be adopted was considered in section 4.10 of chapter 4, which addressed the valuation of positions at either market prices (marking to market) or at the lower of cost and market value. It is sufficient to note here that the usual method of valuation for trading securities in market makers and principal dealers is to mark to market.

Marking to market
14.4.6   The valuation of positions is considered in TSA Financial Regulations rule 30.02(ii) which states that 'where a market price is available for an investment position, it shall be valued at close-out prices. Close-out price means that long positions shall be valued at current bid price and short positions at current offer price.'

14.4.7   This achieves a measure of prudence since the market making profit (the spread between bid and offer prices) is not recognised until the position is finally closed out. It should be emphasised that this rule merely states what has been accepted practice for market makers and principal dealers for many years.

14.4.8   A valuation method frequently used by market makers is to base the valuation on prices quoted by the market maker itself, with bulls valued at his bid price and bears valued at his offer price. In other cases, these bid and offer prices may be taken directly from the best prices shown by SEAQ at the close of business. It should be emphasised that SEAQ prices are quoted for a particular size of transaction. If the position held exceeds the quoted bargain size then it may be appropriate to consider adjusting the quoted prices, and this is discussed under 14.4.10 below. If the position held is less than the quoted bargain size, then the prices quoted are usually a reasonable basis for valuation.

14.4.9   The mark to market basis has been accepted by the Inland Revenue as an appropriate basis for computing trading profits and no adjustment needs to be made to the taxable profits for 'unrealised' profits and losses at the year-end. This is discussed further in chapter 13.

Abnormal positions
14.4.10   There may be occasions when a firm has an 'abnormal' position, i.e. where it is holding a block of shares significantly larger than the quoted bargain size for the particular security. Here it may be appropriate to value the position outside the range of quoted bid and offer prices to recognise that the 'realisable value' for that holding is not the same as the quoted price, which may only be available for lots of a few thousand shares. The decision on whether or not a position is abnormal is a matter of judgement, but to be considered abnormal it will certainly require a position that is large compared with the normal market size for that security. An abnormal position could arise from a single transaction of abnormal size, or be built up in the ordinary course of trading as a result of a number of transactions of normal size.

14.4.11   The price used for such holdings should be a prudent estimate of the prices that might be achieved in closing out the position in an orderly way (i.e. not that which could be achieved by a forced sale of the entire position at very short notice) and in a reasonable timescale. It would not normally be acceptable to recognise any premium for sale to a 'special buyer' of, say, a strategic holding. Thus, an abnormal bull position may be valued at a discount of 5 per cent or more to the quoted bid price, with an abnormal bear position at a premium of a similar level.

243

14.4.12 In assessing abnormal positions, it is necessary to consider holdings on the 'back book' or held by other dealing areas, such as options dealers or corporate finance operations as well as the dealing/front book. The back book position may very occasionally be a long-term investment, in which case a lower of cost and market value basis may be appropriate. However, such positions will normally only be held for a matter of days or weeks, and thus marking to market remains appropriate. If the position is deemed to be abnormal then there may be a reduction in its estimated market value. If the aggregate of the front and back books results in an abnormal position, then adjustments to the quoted prices should be considered.

Dealing profit and loss

14.4.13 Although the valuation process is central to the dealing results of the firm, it is unlikely that the profit and loss will be posted to the accounting records from daily valuations. Rather, it is more likely that daily valuations will be approximate and be designed to give dealers information on how well they are performing and to facilitate monitoring of performance by management. Detailed valuations for the purpose of updating the accounting records are likely to be carried out less often (for example, every account or perhaps even monthly). It should be noted that errors in valuation at one account end will, due to the nature of the evaluation process, be corrected by the subsequent valuation. Methods of posting such revaluations vary across firms. The example below illustrates one way in which this is carried out.

Example

14.4.14 At the start of the account, the firm has a bull position of 50,000 nominal in ABC plc valued at £2.20 (i.e. £110,000). During the account, the following transactions take place:

Day 1 buy 25,000 at £2.15
Day 5 sell 35,000 at £2.18
Day 8 buy 15,000 at £2.12
Day 9 sell 30,000 at £2.15

The bid/offer spread at the end of the account is £2.10–£2.15.
The following trading account for dealings in ABC plc can be drawn up:

Buy			**Sell**		
	Nominal	*£*		*Nominal*	*£*
Opening balance	50,000	110,000	Day 5	35,000	76,300
Day 1	25,000	53,750	Day 9	30,000	64,500
Day 8	15,000	31,800	Loss for account	–	2,250
			Closing balance	25,000	52,500
	90,000	195,550		90,000	195,550

244

There is a closing bull position of 25,000 valued at the bid price of £2.10 (i.e. £52,500) which becomes the opening balance in the next account.

The trading account is closed down at the end of the account with a new valuation being carried forward to the next account. The loss will be posted to an overall dealing profit and loss account.

Position agreement

4.4.15   The position or 'box' agreement is a means of ensuring that the position in a stock shown by the dealers' records is matched by a physical shareholding and is therefore analogous to the stocktake in a manufacturing or retail business. Given the complexities of the settlement cycle, this matching has to encompass all aspects of the settlement position in that stock. It is an essential control feature for a market maker or principal trader in that it shows the whereabouts of the nominal amounts of each position held. It is important to ensure that all dealing positions in a particular stock are taken into account. For example the firm might have, in addition to the normal market making position, a position held on a 'back book' e.g. a large position that has been taken because of an expected rise in price.

4.4.16   A suggested pro-forma position agreement is set out below.

Pro-forma position agreement

	Nominal stock quantity
Settlement Position	
Physical stock held in office	x
Stock held by bankers/other custodians	x
Stock deposited as collateral for loans	x
Stock lent to moneybrokers	x
Stock borrowed from moneybrokers	(x)
Stock at registrars	x
Stock due to be received in respect of purchases	x
Stock due to be delivered in respect of sales	(x)
Net Settlement Position: Long (Short)	x
Dealing position	
Front book	x
Back book	x
Held by traded option dealers	x
Net dealing position: Long (Short)	x

14.4.17　As well as performing regular position agreements for all securities for control purposes, it is also necessary to perform an agreement for a specific security whenever a dividend is due to be paid, when there is a rights or bonus issue, or when a new issue moves from allotment letter form to registered form. Performing the position agreement in these circumstances ensures that the firm receives its full entitlement and can make the necessary claims where appropriate.

14.4.18　For the larger market makers and principal traders, the position agreement is likely to be a computerised process because of the volume of positions and the number of reconciling items that are likely to arise.

14.4.19　When a firm has a short position on a dividend due date for a particular stock, problems can arise in ensuring that dividends are received by the entitled party. Where a firm has sold short, but has not yet delivered the stock, the purchaser will be expecting a dividend which the company registrar will not pay out because he does not yet know of the holding. In effect, a short sale increases the total issued share capital of the company and here, the firm has to 'manufacture' a dividend and pay it away to the investor (for the taxation implications, see chapter 13).

14.4.20　Where the firm has sold short but has borrowed the stock to effect delivery, the moneybroker lending the stock will similarly require a dividend to be manufactured. Therefore the position agreement must be in sufficient detail to enable the firm correctly to manufacture dividends where appropriate.

14.4.21　Market makers often refer to stock which is held in their 'box'. This is generally used to describe stock held in their SEPON trading account (as discussed in chapter 7) and represents stock due to the firm which has been delivered into Talisman. If the firm is a bull of stock then it will remain at Talisman within the trading account. Therefore, for Talisman stocks, the firm is unlikely to handle physical stock. It will either be in the 'box' or in the course of settlement. Where the firm is a bear (i.e. a net seller), the settlement position will largely be made up of stock borrowed from moneybrokers.

14.4.22　For non-Talisman stocks and non-member firm principal dealers, physical stock certificates will be kept either in the firm's office or at a custodian where they may be used to collateralise loans. As well as items awaiting settlement, there may also be cases where stock has been settled but is in the course of being registered into the firm's name.

Disclosure requirements

4.4.23 The presentation of 'bull' and 'bear' positions is an area where the rules of TSA and the Companies Act requirements differ.

4.4.24 TSA's requirements are spelt out in the guidance notes for the completion of the various reporting statements which need to be submitted to the authorities. These require that all positions are shown 'net at valuation', arrived at on the basis discussed under (i) above. Therefore, in the various reporting statements submitted to TSA, firms must aggregate total long, less total short positions in all securities and show a single net position.

4.4.25 The Companies Act requirements are that positions should be shown net by stock (i.e. all purchases and sales in, say, ICI are netted off to show a single ICI position) – with 'bull' positions being shown as current assets and 'bear' positions as current liabilities. In addition, a further analysis of long and short positions is required between securities listed on recognised exchanges and positions which are not listed on recognised exchanges or which have been suspended from listing.

4.4.26 A second important disclosure requirement is the need to show clearly the valuation method and what market prices are used (e.g. bid, offer or mid-market). This is particularly important because, as discussed in section 4.10 of chapter 4, whereas 'marking to market' is accepted accounting practice for market makers, it is presently a departure from the statutory accounting rules laid down by the Companies Act.

4.5 Audit

4.5.1 The following audit objectives apply to both market makers and principal traders.

Statutory reporting objectives
These may be listed as:

(i) 'bull' positions represent bona fide assets to which the firm has good title; 'bear' positions are completely and accurately recorded;
(ii) 'bull and bear' positions are valued on appropriate and consistent bases;
(iii) 'bull and bear' positions are properly presented in the financial accounts in accordance with the rules of the SRO, accounting standards and the Companies Act, as appropriate.

Additional reporting objectives

These are specific matters which auditors are required to report on under the rules of TSA as follows:

(i) adequate procedures have been established for monitoring the firm's investment position risk and providing appropriate levels of management with the information necessary for them to make relevant, timely and informed decisions to control such risks (rule 90.03d(iv));

(ii) the systems for the agreement and reconciliation of securities positions with counterparties, banks and clearing houses are adequate and such procedures are carried out at appropriate intervals (rule 90.03d(i)).

14.5.2   It should be noted that these objectives are not mutually exclusive from the statutory objectives set out above. Indeed, the additional reporting objectives can usually be considered as part of the review of internal controls carried out during the assessment of the statutory objectives.

14.5.3   The audit of 'bull and bear' positions is considered below. The resulting counterparty balances are considered elsewhere (Talisman – chapter 7; residual tickets – chapter 8; CAD customers – chapter 9).

Internal control

The following control features should be considered:

14.5.4   *Control objective: All purchases and sales are properly recorded*
Possible errors under this heading are:

- validly transacted bargains excluded from the accounting records;
- bargain details incorrectly recorded (e.g. wrong stock, wrong price);
- incorrect moneys are paid away/securities delivered to counterparties;
- dealers take profitable positions for their personal account;
- mis-statement of dealing profits/losses.

14.5.5   The following control procedures may exist to ensure that purchases and sales are properly recorded:

— dealers physically segregated from, and independent of, checking department/settlement/cashiers/ accounts;
— Charm checking (chapter 7) for UK gilts/equities;
— written confirmations with counterparty for foreign stocks or special deals where no central checking, such as TRAX or SEQUAL, is possible;

— unmatched/unconfirmed bargains promptly followed up;
— check of dealing slips to stock journal;
— review by dealers of bargains recorded;
— dealers maintain up-to-date records of principal positions;
— reconciliation of dealers' records to accounting records by independent personnel;
— presence of senior management in the dealing room;
— regular agreement of balances (both monetary and stock quantities) with counterparties;
— amendments as a result of checking queries properly authorised;
— position agreement carried out regularly;
— dealers forbidden from trading for their own account without suitable approval.

14.5.6   *Control objective: All purchases and sales are genuine*
Possible errors under this heading are:

● spurious bargains recorded to conceal deficiencies of stock;
● spurious bargains booked to conceal unprofitable or unauthorised stock positions;
● bargains posted twice.

14.5.7   Controls to ensure that all purchases and sales are genuine are mainly as those detailed above. In particular the following apply:

— central checking such as Charm (chapter 7), TRAX (chapter 16), or SEQUAL (chapter 15);
— written confirmation with counterparties where no central checking is possible;
— regular agreement of balances with counterparties;
— proper analysis and authorisation for error accounts.

14.5.8   *Control objective: Physical movements of stock are only in respect of purchases, sales, properly authorised stock borrowing and collateral for authorised loans*
Possible errors under this heading are:

● securities misappropriated;
● securities used as collateral for unauthorised borrowing.

14.5.9   The following control procedures may exist to prevent such errors:

— segregation of duties between dealers/accounts/settlement areas;
— physical control over securities held on the firm's premises; inevitably this will be tempered by the need for ready access to facilitate

settlement, but access to the 'cage' or other areas where securities are held should be restricted to relevant staff. Securities should be kept overnight in a locked, fireproof cabinet;

— adequate records of securities held, distinguishing between those on the firm's premises and those held by other custodians; these should also detail all movements into and out of 'stock';

— regular checks of securities physically held against stock records (particularly for high value, high volume securities such as allotment letters);

— position agreement carried out on a regular basis and confirmed by settlement of dividends arising;

— custodians used by the firm only release securities on authorised instructions (letter or telex);

— regular checks of stocks deposited with/borrowed from money-brokers, banks etc.

14.5.10 *Control objective: Dealing positions are properly valued and the resulting profit and loss correctly reported*
Possible errors under this heading are:

- significant profits or losses are unreported;
- incorrect prices used leading to a mis-statement of profits or losses.

14.5.11 The following control procedures may exist to ensure that positions are properly valued and the resulting profit and loss correctly reported:

— review of prices by financial management independent of dealers;

— period-end valuation prices compared with dealing prices immediately prior to the valuation date;

— exception reports of all items not priced at closing SEAQ prices;

— review of reported profits/losses by individual stock and by category of stock;

— reviews of unusually large profits/losses;

— check on input of valuation prices;

— positions valued at appropriate intervals (appropriate to the size of the business);

— profit and loss for each dealer calculated and monitored on a regular basis;

— approval obtained for adjustments to the carrying value of investments (apart from the regular mark to market calculation);

— profits and losses transferred regularly to nominal accounts.

14.5.12 *Control objective: Traders are prevented from unauthorised trading beyond the scope and limitations imposed by the firm*
Possible errors under this heading are:

- transactions made at prices disadvantageous to the firm;
- positions taken in excess of prudential guidelines, exposing the firm to undesirable risk;
- deals made with counterparties who are not creditworthy.

4.5.13 The following control procedures may exist to ensure that traders are prevented from unauthorised trading beyond the scope and limitations imposed by the firm:

— prescribed bargain and position limits by dealer;
— reports produced showing positions for each dealer in excess of agreed limits;
— review by senior management of dealer-limit excess reports;
— presence of senior officials in the dealing areas;
— review by senior officials of deals transacted (usually next day);
— individual positions regularly updated;
— capability to monitor individual dealer's positions and total securities positions at any time;
— new counterparties vetted for creditworthiness;
— credit limits set for counterparties which are regularly monitored;
— hedging decisions taken centrally and independently of 'front-line' dealers.

Analytical review

4.5.14 Analytical review procedures are of little or no use in this area. Although details of turnover (i.e. purchases and sales) may be available for a particular stock, they will normally have been produced from the same accounting records as the balance sheet and profit and loss account figures. Moreover, profits are attributable both to spreads (the difference between the buying and selling prices) – which will generally be at a constant level for each category of stock (alpha, beta, etc) – and position taking, where profits arise from shifts in the prices of specific stocks. While the former will bear a close relationship to turnover, there is little that can be used to predict the latter – particularly since 'intra-day' positions can have a significant impact.

Substantive testing

4.5.15 The main areas where substantive testing will be carried out will be in verifying the valuations used by the firm; in checking the position agreement carried out by the firm at the balance sheet date; and checking the casts and extensions (i.e. ensuring that nominal × price plus accrued interest, where applicable, = valuation). The first two areas will be considered separately.

Valuations

14.5.16   The first consideration is whether the valuation method being used is reasonable, in particular whether 'marking to market' is appropriate for the size and nature of the firm's dealing operations. The second consideration is whether the valuations used by the firm are reasonable. The nature of this testing is to check prices used by the firm against available evidence, which will include:

- Comparison of prices with external information (e.g. other market makers as quoted on SEAQ, or SEDOL – as described in chapter 6). Note that for historical reasons relating to probate valuations, the spreads quoted in SEDOL are much wider than those quoted within the market, although the middle of the SEDOL range will be a good guide to the mid-market price. Therefore, SEDOL bid/offer prices should not be used for this purpose. To verify prices using SEAQ, it will usually be necessary to watch price screens at or around the close of business on the year-end date. Another useful external source of information is the financial press such as the *Financial Times* and *The Times*, (the latter gives both bid and offer prices at 5.00pm on the previous day).
- Review of actual deals transacted shortly before and after the balance sheet date to ensure that the valuation used is indicative of actual transactions. Here, care should be taken to ensure that prices were not distorted (intentionally or otherwise) by transactions in particularly small or large bargain sizes, or by transactions with related parties.

14.5.17   It will usually be necessary to accept a certain tolerance in verifying valuations since the auditor will seldom be abe to verify that a price is accurate to within less than a penny, while 1/2p on a position of two million shares would be material. It is, therefore, particularly important to identify consistent over-pricing of bull positions or under-pricing of bear positions as a means of increasing profits (or vice versa for depressing them). Small, individual under- or over-valuations applied across the trading book can lead to a substantial mis-statement of total dealing profits.

14.5.18   Particular audit problems will be posed where there have been no recent transactions in a security or where the stock has been suspended from trading. Where the firm has not transacted business recently in a particular stock, the following techniques may assist in forming an opinion on the price used:

— take the last recorded transaction before the balance sheet date and adjust by reference to the movement in the FT Actuaries Index for the relevant market sector from that date to the valuation date;

— take the first recorded transaction subsequent to the balance sheet date and adjust similarly;

— review SEDOL for actual bargains in the period around the valuation date. Note that SEDOL will give no indication as to the size of bargains, nor whether it was a purchase or a sale.

4.5.19   Where a stock is suspended from trading, it will be necessary to discover the reason for suspension and discuss with the dealers their justification for the prices used. Such discussion should take place as close as possible to the year end, to ensure dealers' recollections are as reliable as possible. The available evidence will be different in each case, although it is important not to anticipate profits where, for example, a stock is suspended pending a takeover announcement which leads to a substantially higher price when dealings recommence. Where a stock has been suspended for some period, it may be helpful to review Extel cards, or copies of the company's accounts.

'Abnormal' positions

4.5.20   A separate exercise should be carried out to review 'abnormal' positions. As discussed above, these are large holdings (taking into account the normal positions taken by the firm, the level of turnover of the stock, the quoted market 'size', etc;) where the firm may not be able to close down the position through the normal run of dealing in a reasonably short period of time. These positions should, therefore, be valued at a discount (for a bull position) and a premium (for a bear position) to the market price in order to recognise their lack of liquidity.

4.5.21   Having identified potential abnormal positions the following procedures should be performed:

● note turnover in the most recent account and ascertain how the position has arisen;

● discuss positions with senior dealers to agree on the appropriate levels of any adjustments.

This is frequently the most subjective area of the audit of positions, and therefore especial care should be taken in recording the reasons for the decision taken.

4.5.22   A further procedure is for audit staff to be present at dealers' desks on the balance sheet date. Potential 'abnormals' and any other important issues relating to valuations can be identified at that stage and discussed with dealers while the details are still fresh in their minds. This removes the need to remember specific market conditions weeks, or maybe months, later.

Position agreement

14.5.23   The purpose of the position agreement is to verify the nominal amounts for each position held (i.e. the number of shares which the firm has bought or sold). Due to the fundamental importance of the position agreement, it should have been performed by the firm at the balance sheet date and therefore the auditor should be able to base his work on the schedules prepared by the firm.

14.5.24   The number of stocks traded by a market maker or an active principal dealer is normally large, and it may, therefore, be appropriate to test the position agreement on a sample basis. This may present practical problems of sample selections in that the population to be tested is in nominal amounts and not current market value – and a superficially small position could mask a large shortfall. However, the only practical approach will be to base the sample on either the absolute monetary value of the dealing positions, or else a random selection of positions irrespective of nominal amount or value.

14.5.25   A count of securities held on the firm's premises should be carried out at the balance sheet date. As for a conventional stocktake, care should be taken with securities moving during the count. This will be a particular problem in securities with a rapid turnover (e.g. allotment letters for new issues). The sample of securities tested should include testing from book records to actual share certificates and vice versa. It is important to ensure that the description of securities precisely matches certificates held, and that certificates are in a deliverable form (e.g. where a certificate is in the name of a third party, a properly executed transfer deed is also held) and not out of date. In the case of bearer documents, it is important to ensure that all coupons relating to future payments of dividends or interest are intact.

14.5.26   Securities held by the firm's bankers or other custodians should be confirmed by circularisation. Once the appropriate certificate has been received, it will be necessary to reconcile details of holdings to the firm's records. A certificate from a recognised bank can reasonably be accepted as good audit evidence of investments held, although it is important to enquire into any charges over investments in favour of the bank or some other party and ensure that these are disclosed, as appropriate, in the financial statements of the firm.

4.5.27 Certificates obtained from non-bank third parties may require further attention. The auditor should ascertain the reason for using the depository, and also the status of the depository in terms of approval from the regulatory authorities (as discussed in chapter 12). Provided the depository is a member of a recognised overseas stock exchange, and is being used in the normal course of business, it will usually be acceptable to regard the certificate as good audit evidence.

4.5.28 Where share certificates or allotment letters are with company registrars, it may be appropriate to obtain written confirmation of the balance held with the registrar at the balance sheet date. Written confirmation should also be obtained of any stocks deposited as collateral for loans and of any stocks borrowed from, or lent to, moneybrokers or other stock lenders.

4.5.29 Reconciling items in the position agreement in respect of unsettled purchases and sales should be agreed to the relevant part of the ledger (e.g. Talisman, jobbers or tickets). The validity of these items will be verified as part of the audit work on these ledgers described elsewhere in this book.

4.5.30 The substantive work will, therefore, consist of carrying out such tests as may be necessary to verify the accuracy of the position agreement performed by the firm. This will normally entail reperforming the entire position agreement for a sample of securities. The auditor should then review items reported as disagreed and ensure either that the disagreement has been resolved or that an appropriate adjustment has been made in the accounts. It is imperative that all disagreed items are properly followed up, since disagreements may conceal stock shortfalls that would give rise to reductions in trading profit.

4.5.31 A further check on the accuracy of the dealing positions is to check the position shown by the accounting requirements to the records kept by the dealers. This will only be of benefit if the dealers maintain records independently of the accounting records and there is good segregation of duties between the dealers and settlement staff.

4.5.32 For broker dealers taking the occasional positions, either by design or as a result of dealing errors the auditor should review all ledger accounts which might contain such positions. In particular, the dealing error account should be reviewed to ensure all residual stock positions are identified.

Disclosure requirements

14.5.33   These were set out in paragraphs 14.4.23 to 14.4.26 above and the auditor's work will involve test-checking analyses prepared by the firm to ensure that they meet with the various disclosure requirements.

14.6 Capital requirements

14.6.1   As explained in chapter 3, under TSA (and other SRO) rules, firms have to provide capital against positions they are holding. This capital is known as the Position Risk Requirement (PRR) and for example, rules relating to PRR are set out in the TSA Financial Regulations, rules 62.01 to 62.40.

14.6.2   PRR in its basic form is calculated by applying a stated Percentage Risk Addition (PRA) to the value of positions held, which ranges from 10.5 per cent to 25 per cent for UK shares, and from ½ per cent upwards on gilts. All positions which are not marketable investments (as defined in section 1 of the Financial Regulations of TSA) attract a PRA of 100 per cent (i.e. the full value of the position is added to the capital requirement).

14.6.3   Market makers and active principal dealers in equities are entitled to choose to apply more sophisticated methods of computing PRR on all or part of their dealing portfolios. The basic method (known as Method 1) described above simply applies prescribed PRAs to each individual position. However, there is in practice some measure of reduction in overall risk if the market maker holds a large number of different shares. For example, if only a single position were held and the overall market fell by 10 per cent, then it is likely that the individual share would move broadly in line with the market and therefore, also fall by 10 per cent. If, however, the market maker had equal numbers of long and short positions, then if the market fell by 10 per cent, he would expect to lose money due to the fall in value of the long positions but make money due to the fall in value of the short positions. Similarly, the holder of shares in a single company would lose a lot of money if bad news about that company were published, but it is unlikely that every company would publish bad news on the same day.

14.6.4   TSA therefore allow two alternative methods for calculating PRR on equities which are complex mathematical calculations to simulate the risk reduction inherent in the diversified portfolio, provided certain laid down criteria are met. Firms which have such large portfolios will, therefore usually use computer programs to compute their PRR. It is essential that these computer programs produce a detailed print-out of the calculation so that the application of the current rules can be verified.

14.6.5   Similar, sophisticated PRR calculations are available to active dealers in gilts and other fixed income securities, and also to active traders in other investment such as warrants or options.

14.6.6   It should be noted that for GEMMs, capital adequacy is determined by the Bank of England and therefore a GEMM does not have to compute a PRR according to TSA rules. The Bank lays down its own risk calculations, but the auditor of a GEMM is not required to audit these calculations.

14.6.7   The total PRR is made up of the sum of the amounts calculated in accordance with the above mentioned TSA rules 62.01 to 62.40. The different rules relate to the various types of marketable investments that a firm may hold, until a separate rule for each type of investment such as warrants, negotiated options etc.

14.6.8   The auditor's responsibility with respect to PRR is primarily based on TSA Financial Regulations rule 90.04b which requires an opinion on whether the Firm's Statement of Total Capital Requirement as shown in the Annual Reporting Statement has been properly prepared in accordance with the rules of the Association, or the equivalent rules of the other SROs. A key element of the Total Capital Requirement is the PRR which will have been calculated by the firm in preparing the Position Risk Reporting Statement submitted to TSA. Hence the audit work on verifying the PRR element of the Total Capital Requirement will largely be centred on verifying the relevant detailed position risk reporting statement.

14.6.9   The auditor also needs to consider the adequacy of the firm's systems for calculating PRR, in particular whether they are capable of arriving at an accurate capital requirement promptly, whether there is an adequate audit trail back to the underlying accounting records and whether PRR is reviewed by senior management on a regular basis.

14.6.10   It is important that all positions maintained by a firm are assessed for PRR. The fortnightly position risk summary statement and the front sheet of the monthly position risk statement require all the different elements of PRR to be reconciled back to the balance sheet. This should provide the discipline necessary to ensure that all positions are considered for PRR; it is important to ensure that these summaries are being correctly compiled from the accounting records, and that all reconciling items can be explained.

14.6.11   The auditor's work therefore consists of firstly ensuring the adequacy of the PRR reporting system and secondly ensuring that PRR at the balance sheet date has been correctly calculated. This entails checking that all positions have been considered somewhere for PRR and then testing, on a sample basis, the calculations performed by the firm to ensure that they are in accordance with rules 62.01 to 62.40. Particular care is needed to ensure that all investment positions (including such items as swaps, over-the-counter options and other 'off balance sheet' investments) have been identified and the relevant PRR rules applied.

15 Dealing and Settlement on Overseas Stock Exchanges

15.1 Introduction
15.2 Methods of overseas dealing and settlement
15.3 Accounting
15.4 Audit
15.5 Capital requirements

15.1 Introduction

15.1.1 The most common method for a UK broker-dealer to conduct business on an overseas stock exchange is through an overseas broker based in the country where the security is traded. The UK firm then becomes a customer of the overseas broker and relies on the overseas broker to effect settlement on his behalf. It should be noted that methods of execution and settlement vary widely between different countries and exchanges. The cycle of events that takes place between the UK firm and its overseas broker is broadly similar across all markets, the main difference being in the timescale of events caused by the different settlement systems. (The eurobond market is not dealt with here since it is discussed in detail in chapter 16.)

15.2 Methods of overseas dealing and settlement

15.2.1 The execution cycle begins with the UK firm deciding to undertake a transaction in a foreign stock, as a result of:

— instructions from a customer;
— the firm wishing to deal on its own account;
— discretionary fund management by the firm.

The customer side of the transaction will be treated exactly as discussed in chapter 9 and therefore this aspect is not considered further here.

15.2.2 The firm will contact the appropriate overseas broker, either in the relevant country or through that broker's London office, and the

259

bargain will be dealt. Confirmation of the transaction and settlement details will follow. Confirmation usually takes place by telex or fax so that bargains can be agreed promptly. This is particularly important in those countries where transactions are due to settle within a few days of execution. Some overseas brokers may supply an official confirmation by post, however this cannot be relied upon where prompt settlement is required.

15.2.3 Many different settlement periods are encountered in overseas markets, from next day settlement to settlement in one month and so it is important that details are agreed with the overseas broker as soon as possible. In addition, delivery and payment instructions have to be agreed; for example the custodian or depot to or from which stock will be delivered, the currency to be used for settlement and the bank to or from whom payment will be made.

15.2.4 Firms usually maintain standard safe custody facilities and bank accounts in countries where they actively deal. This greatly eases the settlement process because it means that stock does not need to be moved between the UK and the relevant country for each bargain dealt. Indeed in many cases, this would be impossible in the time allowed. The depot will therefore hold stock to the order of the UK firm, and deliver it when it receives suitable instructions. In many cases, the depot will also be the bank at which the firm keeps its cash balances. This further eases settlement because the bank is in a position to ensure that cash is only paid away when stock is received, or that stock is only released when cash is received, thus reducing the risks associated with the settlement process.

15.2.5 Alternatively, the firm may use the overseas broker as its custodian. This also simplifies the settlement process since it reduces the number of overseas institutions that have to be instructed on a particular transaction – although it may pose unacceptable credit risks in countries where brokers are less tightly regulated. It can also cause problems where, in order to obtain the best possible price on each transaction, the UK broker uses a number of different brokers in a particular country. To comply with TSA regulations, a depot used for private customer's assets must be recognised as an eligible custodian by TSA. The process by which a firm can determine whether a custodian is eligible is discussed in chapter 12.

15.2.6 Therefore, when a bargain has been dealt, delivery and settlement instructions are telexed to the custodian bank so that it knows when to expect the stock receipt and is authorised to make a payment; alternatively the custodian bank may be given authority to deliver stock upon receipt of cash. The overseas broker will receive similar delivery/ payment instructions in order to ensure that both parties to the transaction settle correctly.

15.2.7 It should be noted that in order to minimise risk, the movement of stock and money should be simultaneous (as for CAD customers discussed in chapter 9). In some countries, this may be effected by a book-entry settlement system which means that physical stock does not move, there merely being a change in the beneficial owner of the stock as recorded in the registers of the company or the relevant clearing house. In other countries, stock still needs to be moved physically, in which case variants of the stock-note system (as exists for CAD customers in the UK) may be in operation.

15.2.8 It should be noted that book-entry settlement systems are becoming increasingly important internationally with the result that securities in many countries are either becoming 'immobilised' or 'dematerialised'. These terms can be explained as follows:

- *immobilisation* occurs when physical certificates evidencing owner- ship are stored at a central depository; changes in ownership are recorded in a book-entry system without transfer or registration of the certificates, but investors wishing to withdraw their stock from the depository can request delivery of actual certificates.

- *dematerialisation* occurs when no physical certificates are issued, all ownership of the security being recorded only in a book-entry system, and so, whilst investors will have written evidence of ownership in the form of a stock statement, they do not need to produce a certificate to effect a transfer.

15.2.9 Currently, for example, Denmark, Norway and France have total dematerialisation whilst the US, Canada and Germany are issuing securities in a partially immobilised environment. There is a general move by stock exchanges and their participants to ensure that by 1992 every leading country involved in securities markets has a central securities depository to provide participants with an efficient, low-risk method for achieving prompt and secure transaction settlement. The UK's proposal to meet this objective is the TAURUS project which is discussed in section 5.7 of chapter 5.

SEQUAL

5.2.10 SEQUAL is a trade confirmation service for international equities offered by the ISE. The SEQUAL service marks the second stage of development aimed at providing an integrated service for trading in, and settlement of, internationally traded equities. The first stage was the introduction of SEAQ International, a screen based price display service in actively traded international equities (discussed in more detail in chapter 6). SEQUAL is still very much in its infancy, and to date there has been a low take-up of its services amongst member firms. However, as more firms adapt to it, SEQUAL will move towards its eventual objective which is to match settlement and delivery instructions received from the two parties to a transaction and to pass these on to the relevant custodian banks and clearing systems. This will mark a great improvement on the current 'manual' system of trade confirmation for international transactions.

American Depositary Receipts (ADRs)

15.2.11 One particular form of financial instrument which warrants consideration is the ADR. These provide a way for shares in non-American companies to be traded within the USA without the USA investor needing to deal with the domestic settlement and registration processes, and also allows a compromise between the US investor's desire to buy shares with a high individual price (say upwards of $25) and the UK investor's desire to buy more shares with a low individual price (illustrated by the common practice of splitting shares into smaller units whenever the market price rises above £5 a share or thereabouts). An ADR is a dollar-denominated bearer document issued by a US bank or similar institution, usually in denominations of five or more of the underlying shares. The bank or similar institution will be the registered owner of the shares underlying the ADR and will account to the holder of the ADR for all dividends and other benefits arising on those shares. ADRs enable US investors to trade in non-US stocks in a cheaper and easier way than if they had to deal in the stocks direct.

15.2.12 ADRs are therefore negotiable certificates issued by a US commercial bank or similar institution, referred to as the 'depositary', for an equivalent number of foreign securities that are deposited with the depositary's foreign custodian. ADRs are registered with the US Securities and Exchange Commission by means of a listing on one of the US Stock Exchanges and trade freely like any other US security. Investors purchase and sell ADRs through their US brokers exactly as they purchase or sell securities of US companies. This means that ADR's settle on a similar five day rolling basis. Investors can deposit foreign securities directly with the depositary's custodian and request the issue of ADRs (known as 'making' an ADR). Alternatively, investors may return ADRs to the depositary for cancellation and have the underlying securities released into the local foreign market (known as 'breaking' an ADR). Making and breaking is usually subject to a fee payable to the issuing bank, and is usually undertaken by investors exploiting short-term price differences between the price of the share in London and the price of the ADR in the USA.

5.2.13 In addition, for UK securities, stamp duty of $1\frac{1}{2}$ per cent is currently payable everytime an ADR is 'made' (note that this may be abolished with the introduction of TAURUS, as discussed in chapter 13).

5.2.14 Where an investor has sold ADRs in New York and bought the underlying shares in London, there can be problems delivering the underlying stock to the depositary in time to 'make' the ADR and meet the five day rolling settlement deadline. In particular, UK account settlement procedures mean that it will usually take two to three weeks before the stock is delivered. Under these circumstances, the issuing US bank may 'pre-release' ADRs to satisfy the sale, i.e. effectively to lend the ADR to the investor in return for the provision of cash collateral. Such stock lending arrangements are usually only available to professional investors. It should be noted that as well as the pre-release method, there is also a sizeable market in ADR stock borrowing which is available to cover short ADR positions for longer periods than the pre-release method (which assumes that the ADR will be 'made' at some time).

Organisation of an overseas settlement department

5.2.15 The size and structure of an overseas settlement department and the extent to which segregation of duties is possible will depend on how actively the firm deals in foreign stocks. Where volumes are low, it is possible that one or two individuals will handle the entire settlement process. Under such circumstances, these individuals should be supervised closely by settlements management since there is little scope for effecting a suitable division of responsibilities. However, where a firm is very active in such business there will usually be specific individuals carrying out the following routines:

- *contracts* – to send out and receive confirmation telexes, ensure that bargain and settlement details match, and take care of postings to the ledgers;
- *settlements* – to prepare the settlement details which will be telexed to the overseas broker and/or custodian bank. They ensure that settlement takes place as stated and follow up problems;
- *ledger clerks* – to ensure that once settlement has taken place, the relevant details are correctly posted to the ledgers;
- *safe custody* – to keep records of stocks held at different overseas custodians and for whom they are held;

- *benefits section* – to ensure that all benefits (e.g. dividends, bonus and rights issues) are received when due and paid out to the appropriate customer;
- *control section* – to ensure that statements are received from overseas brokers, banks and custodians and are reconciled to the ledgers on a regular basis.

15.2.16   For a firm that is very active in overseas securities, these responsibilities may be further split by country. In addition, it may be necessary to employ individuals who can speak the language of the country with which they are dealing because of the need to talk to settlements staff of overseas brokers and custodian banks. Further problems can be caused by the different time zones involved, which may mean UK settlement staff working either very early or very late shifts.

Foreign exchange transactions

15.2.17   Although the customer will normally want to settle the purchase or sale of a non-UK security in sterling, the market side of the transaction will usually be settled in the currency in which the original bargain was denominated, which in most cases will not be sterling. A firm which has substantial transactions for settlement in currency will receive and pay from its own currency bank accounts. As securities may be bought in one currency and sold in another, the currency positions of a firm will fluctuate considerably leaving it with an excess in one currency (long position) and a shortage in another (short position). It will, therefore, be necessary for such a firm to monitor its long and short positions in currencies in relation to movements in rates of exchange. If positions leave the firm exposed to losses (should there be excessive movements in exchange rates), it will normally enter into transactions with foreign exchange dealers to sell or buy currencies either spot or forward. In entering into forward exchange contracts the firm will have regard to its known future settlement needs and its anticipated currency requirements.

15.2.18   Where a firm does not transact many bargains in foreign currency and does not have banking facilities in the settlement currency, it will have to enter into a transaction with a foreign exchange dealer in order for the currency to be made available on the due settlement date. In the case of a sold bargain, the firm will sell forward the currency due to be received for payment on the settlement date. The firm will inform the overseas broker bank where to deliver the securities when he has made a payment to the foreign exchange dealer. In the case of a bought bargain, the firm will buy the currency forward to be delivered to the overseas broker/custodian bank on settlement day for the account of the firm pending delivery of the stock. Settlement between the firm and foreign exchange dealer will be made in sterling. In this way, the firm fixes the exchange rate at which it will settle a transaction and therefore minimises any exposure to currency fluctuations.

5.2.19   In addition, it should be noted that the firm may be requested by a customer to enter into a foreign exchange transaction. This could occur where the customer wishes to settle in the currency in which the bargain is denominated but does not possess currency banking facilities. The customer would then require some form of foreign exchange transaction to enable him to complete settlement of the bargain which the broker dealer may offer to arrange on his behalf. Alternatively, an investor may wish to hedge against the currency risk associated with his overseas investment portfolio and, therefore, sell the appropriate currency at a forward rate.

The overseas settlement process

5.2.20   The overseas settlement process can be summarised by the following diagram:

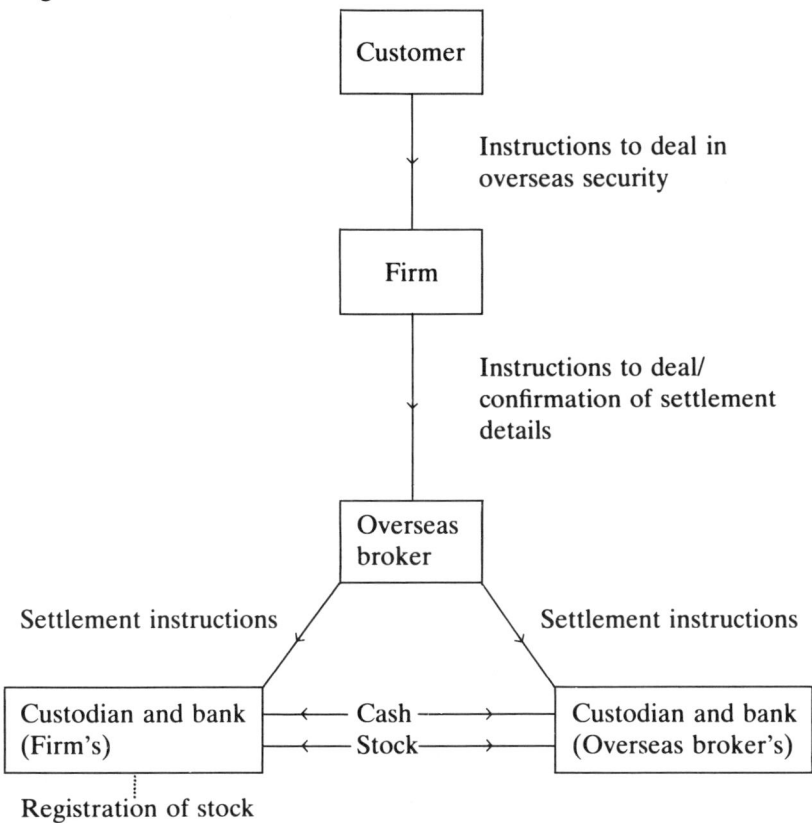

15.2.21   The following matters should be noted with regard to the settlement
           process:

           • Having been instructed by the firm and the overseas broker, the two
             overseas custodians effect settlement between each other. In many
             cases, the overseas broker may double up as custodian which simplifies
             the process.
           • Registration procedures vary across countries.
           • The customer may be holding stock at its own custodian in which case
             instructions need to be passed to that custodian as well as to the firm's
             to ensure that stock and money move simultaneously.
           • There are numerous reasons why a trade may fail to settle on time:

             — instructions not issued on time;
             — the overseas broker has not issued any instructions;
             — the instructions do not match;
             — there is not enough stock to meet the delivery;
             — insufficient funds available in the appropriate bank account.

           In these cases, the custodians will refer back to the firm/overseas broker
           for clarification.

Problems with overseas dealing and settlement

15.2.22   Dealing in overseas securities leads to a large number of potential
           settlement difficulties. These are caused by the variety of different
           dealing and settlement practices in existence around the world. As has
           already been discussed, moves are being made to bring about a more
           uniform approach to international settlement – particularly with book-
           entry stock systems and common settlement timetables. However, this
           is still some way off and, in the meantime, settlement staff need to be
           able to cope with the different procedures of different national markets.
           In addition, auditors need to be aware of these potential problems
           so that they can take them into account when considering audit
           procedures.

15.2.23   Problems may be caused by language difficulties – not all firms
           can afford to employ language experts as settlement clerks. When
           telexes and settlement details arrive in foreign languages there may be
           problems of understanding and interpreting instructions which may lead
           to incorrect settlement procedures being adopted.

15.2.24   Security is another area which needs to be carefully considered. With
           most settlement instructions being sent via telex or fax, if fraudulent
           delivery instructions are sent, stock or money could be diverted from

the firm's account. Hence, particular attention must be paid to security over telex and fax machines with special codes (such as 'test keys') in place to identify the sender. It should be noted that a number of firms use SWIFT (the international banking funds transfer system) as a means of transferring funds, which should enhance security over cash settlements.

5.2.25   There may be problems regarding the registration of stocks into the customer's name. Delays in registration may mean that the custodian bank does not actually have control of the physical stock when payment is required. There may be evidence that the firm is entitled to ownership of the stock (by some form of stock note) but it may take a considerable length of time before the registered stock can be properly delivered. In such cases, the firm must rely on information it receives from its overseas agents to ascertain whether it has control of stock.

5.2.26   Problems are often encountered in the benefits section of an overseas settlement department because, where stocks from many different countries are being dealt, it is very difficult to ensure that all benefits have been claimed and correctly paid away. In order to achieve this objective, intelligence (i.e. dividend payment dates, registration dates, payment procedures etc.) is required from all the major markets in which the firm deals. In some markets, such authoritative information is extremely difficult to obtain and in such cases the firm will have to rely on its overseas broker/custodian bank.

15.3   Accounting

15.3.1   As with any transaction, there will be a cutomer and a market posting. With bargains in foreign stocks, the market posting will be to an account with the overseas broker. Such accounts may be included as part of the customers' ledger or may be included in the cash jobbers ledger. Since overseas securities are not normally traded for sterling, the firm will need to maintain ledgers in several currencies. The maintenance of foreign currency ledgers is discussed in chapter 17 and is not considered further here.

15.3.2   For each side of every bargain, it is important at all times to know both the stock and the money position, that is to say whether or not the money or the stock components of a particular transaction has settled. It should be noted that the stock element is as important as the money component.

15.3.3   When the firm's custodian bank confirms that it has delivered or received stock, the firm's safe custody records should be updated. As

267

stated in chapter 12, these records should have been amended as soon as the bargain was transacted so that dividend claims can be made where appropriate. It should be noted that safe custody records should also show the physical stock location and therefore must be further updated when the stock movement is confirmed.

Statements from overseas counterparties

15.3.4   It has already been noted that telex and fax are the most efficient ways of ensuring that prompt settlement takes place on all bargains, although on-line systems such as SEQUAL will ease settlement in the future. However, it is essential that statements of transactions dealt and settled are received from overseas brokers so that the completeness and accuracy of the firm's accounting records can be confirmed. In addition, statements from banks and depots should be obtained by the firm on a regular basis and reconciled to the cash book and safe custody records. Internal control is improved if this control function is carried out by individuals separate from those who make the original accounting entries to the ledgers.

15.3.5   There are a number of problems relating to the receipt of statements from overseas brokers. Firstly, there may be a language problem in that the statement is in a foreign language which UK staff do not understand. Secondly, certain overseas counterparties (for example German brokers) do not send statements because, in their view, the confirmation telexes are sufficient evidence of a transaction and its settlement.

15.3.6   The language problem can be overcome by ensuring that staff are at least aware of what key words mean and, if necessary, having a language expert available to translate. Where overseas brokers do not issue statements, one approach is for the UK firm to send periodic statements to the relevant broker so that the counterparty has the opportunity to confirm the completeness and accuracy of the records. An alternative approach adopted by some firms is to accept that, so long as bargains are being settled promptly, the accounting records are complete and accurate. However, this approach cannot be regarded as entirely satisfactory.

15.3.7   The USA, Canada and certain European countries currently use settlement date accounting while the UK uses transaction date accounting. This means that while the UK firm enters transactions in the customer ledger on the day they are dealt, the overseas broker enters them on the date they are due for settlement. In between the trade date and settlement date, the overseas broker will only record these transactions in memorandum form. This means that entries appearing in the UK

268

firm's statements in one month will not appear until the following month's statement from the overseas broker.

15.3.8   Overseas broker's statements may also include depot holdings where appropriate and show dividends receivable/payable in respect of bargains and depot holdings. As noted above, these should be reconciled to the safe custody records maintained by the firm. It should be noted that if the overseas broker is not also the firm's custodian, the firm should ensure that regular statements from the custodian are received and reconciled. The minimum regulatory requirement for reconciling depot positions is discussed in chapter 12.

Accounts presentation

15.3.9   Since overseas transactions usually settle on an item by item basis, the same considerations as are applied to CAD customers, discussed in chapter 9, will apply.

15.4 Audit

15.4.1   The audit objectives for overseas broker balances are the same as for non-Talisman market balances set out in chapter 8. Here, we discuss the special considerations relating to foreign business. It should be noted that, as before, the auditor must consider both the statutory objectives and the additional reporting objectives. These latter objectives can usually be considered as part of the review of internal controls carried out during the assessment of the statutory objectives. The audit of safe custody records is discussed in chapter 12.

Internal control

15.4.2   For the following reasons, overseas settlement is often seen as a high risk area:

- few bargains dealt on overseas exchanges are checked centrally;
- the settlement procedures vary considerably across different markets; and
- the transfer of stock and money relies on authorisation by telex.

Hence, it is important that effective controls operate in this area.

15.4.3   *Control objectives*

(i)   *All bargains are completely, promptly and accurately recorded.*

(ii) *All recorded bargains are genuine.*

(iii) *All payments to, and receipts from, overseas brokers are properly recorded.*

(iv) *All stock movements are properly recorded.*

Possible errors under these headings include:

- bargains omitted from the records;
- bargains incorrectly recorded;
- spurious bargains recorded;
- spurious stock/money movements made.

15.4.4   Control procedures to prevent such errors include:

— all bargains confirmed by telex/fax, preferably on a two-way basis or via SEQUAL;

— settlement details confirmed by telex/fax with overseas broker and custodian bank;

— codes (which are only known to a small number of people) are required before a telex authorising transfer of stock or money can be sent;

— trading limits with overseas counterparties set;

— trading compared with limits reviewed regularly by senior management;

— regular reconciliation of brokers' accounts, bank accounts and safe custody depots;

— management review of reconciliations;

— segregation of duties between dealers/settlement staff;

— segregation of duties within settlements department (as far as is reasonable given the volume of transactions);

— ledger postings (of stock and money) accompanied by confirmation from overseas broker or bank.

Analytical review

15.4.5   It is unlikely that analytical review procedures will be of benefit in this area.

Substantive testing

15.4.6   One of the specific reporting requirements of TSA is for auditors to state whether 'the firm has adequate systems for the agreement and reconciliation of balances and securities positions with overseas brokers and custodians'. As can be seen from the preceding paragraphs, reconciliation procedures are essential for control over an overseas settlement department. However, it should be noted that reconciliation procedures control settlement in arrears which means that by the time errors are identified, stock or money may have already been lost. Hence security over despatch of stock and money and segregation of duties are particularly important to identify and correct errors as early as possible.

5.4.7   This reporting requirement requires the auditor to review the firm's systems for reconciling, agreeing and settling accounts with overseas brokers to ensure they are satisfactory. In particular, the auditor should consider whether reconciliations:

- are carried out regularly and are reasonably up-to-date; and
- have taken place at (or subsequent to) the end of the account immediately preceding the balance sheet date.

5.4.8   Overseas brokers often provide their statements on a calendar month basis which will not necessarily coincide with an account end. This should not present problems for the verification of the balance sheet position so long as adequate controls are in place with regard to bargain capture and settlement.

5.4.9   It is clearly important that copies of reconciliations are retained by firms so they can demonstrate the satisfactory agreement of any accounts the auditor chooses to examine. In practice, only the larger and more complex reconciliations are likely to be fully documented, the smaller reconcilations being brief annotations on statements.

5.4.10   Audit procedures will include:

- a comparison of all statements from overseas brokers with balances at the firm's balance sheet date to ensure reconciliations have been carried out;   .
- a review and test-check of the preparation of the reconciliations to ensure they are accurate and reliable;
- a review of reconciling items to ensure they are subsequently cleared. It will be necessary to consider the effect of late adjustments to the firm's books and, if material, to amend the financial statements;
- a scrutiny of brokers' statements where the firm is recording a nil balance;
- a review of the firm's working papers throughout the period to ensure that the year-end reconciliation was not a 'one-off' exercise for the auditor's benefit. Common indications of this are a large number of outstanding sundry items such as settlement differences and dividends on the year-end reconciliation;

— a review of management reporting arising from reconciliation procedures showing, *inter alia*, the date of the last reconciliation, and the number of reconciling items.

As well as a review of reconciliations as at the balance sheet date, the auditor should consider circularising all brokers who have not provided a statement and whose account has, therefore, not been reconciled.

Stock agreement

15.4.11 The procedures outlined in chapters 9 and 10 for identifying potential bad debts on customer accounts apply equally for balances in respect of overseas bargains. CRR has to be provided on foreign bargains as for UK bargains. As discussed in chapters 9 and 10, the higher the CRR, the higher the potential bad debt exposure. Therefore, if the auditor is satisfied that CRR is being calculated correctly, he may be able to limit his bad debt review to items with a high CRR. If CRR is not found to be calculated properly, then a more extensive stock agreement, (explained in chapter 10) must be performed in order to assess the adequacy of any bad debt provision. Exactly the same procedures as those discussed in chapter 10 should be performed in carrying out a stock agreement on foreign transactions.

15.4.12 The stock agreement will only cover open bargains. It is also necessary to consider the recoverability of all sundry debits (such as dividends) which may be on a customer's or overseas broker's account. A further important consideration is to ensure that all such 'sundry debits' have been identified and posted to the ledgers. As was noted above, a particular problem with trading in overseas stocks is establishing when benefits are due. Hence, the auditor must also ensure that he considers the adequacy of the relevant systems.

15.5 Capital requirements

15.5.1 These are dealt with in chapter 10 and there are no particular aspects relating specifically to overseas business.

16 The Eurobond Market

6.1 Introduction

6.1.1 The eurobond market developed in the mid 1960s as a means of enabling corporate borrowers to raise loan capital from the ever-increasing pool of eurodollars (US dollars held by non-US residents outside the domestic regulatory and tax structure of the US). As the market has matured, the range of currencies has increased and a bewildering number of variations on the basic bond structure have evolved.

6.1.2 International bonds are generally understood to be debt securities which are sold largely outside the borrower's country of residence. The term 'eurobond' is applied to any international bond issued outside the country of the currency in which the bonds are denominated, whereas 'foreign bonds' are international bonds issued in the same way as domestic bonds in the country of their currency of denomination, but by a non-resident borrower. 'Bulldog', 'Yankee' and 'Samurai' bonds are foreign bonds issued in the UK, the US and Japan respectively. Most international bonds are in bearer form.

6.1.3 The term 'bond' is a generic term used to cover all forms of medium or long-term debt security; although individual issues may be termed debentures or notes, this is of little practical significance. Interest on eurobonds is generally payable six-monthly, and the issue will be structured so that this interest is payable without deduction of with-holding tax. A bond may bear interest at a fixed rate throughout its life; or it may be a variable rate bond, where the interest is reset every interest payment date, usually based on a fixed margin above LIBOR (London Inter Bank Offered Rate) for the appropriate currency. Variable rate bonds are generally referred to as 'floating rate notes' or FRNs. Since the coupon on such FRNs is frequently readjusted to market interest rates, their market value should remain near par whatever changes in market interest rates occur, subject only to variations in the credit worthiness of the entity issuing the bond.

16.1.4 The term 'note' is commonly applied to fixed rate bonds of relatively short maturity – often one year or less, and often issued at a discount, for repayment at par, rather than bearing an interest coupon. These offer the investor a more liquid investment, whilst the borrower will usually ensure that further notes can be issued when the first tranche matures by arranging a 'note issuing facility' or 'revolving underwriting facility' with a bank which undertakes to take up further issues of the notes. The issuer thereby effectively obtains a long-term borrowing capability. More recently, such short-term notes have been issued without an underwriting facility but with the issuing bank committing itself to making a market in the notes. These notes are referred to as euro-commercial paper.

16.1.5 A fundamental characteristic of the eurobond market (which encompasses all the instruments and variations discussed above) is the absence of any physical location for the market. The main participants in the market are international banks (or their bond dealing subsidiaries) and most trading is done by telephone or telex. Although London is the main centre of market activity, the market extends round the world. Until recently, the market was largely unregulated, and had developed its own code of practice and methods of dealing and settlement. The recent implementation of the Financial Services Act in the UK has imposed the need for formal regulation of the market in this country. Bond dealing or market making operations in the UK will normally be regulated by TSA, although a lighter regulatory system than that for domestic securities has been permitted, reflecting both the fact that this market is not, and never has been, a market for the unsophisticated private investor; and also, perhaps, the fear that too stringent regulations would merely cause the market participants to move to another location where less restrictive regulations applied.

16.2 The issue of eurobonds

16.2.1 A eurobond issue is organised on behalf of the issuer by a 'lead manager' which will usually be a major euromarket bank or bank subsidiary. The issuing syndicate will also include a number of co-managers who, together with the lead manager, will assume responsibility for underwriting and placing the issue, although occasionally additional underwriters are involved. It should be noted that, unlike the domestic UK equity market, where underwriters are effectively buyers of last resort (i.e. they only buy the shares if not taken up by the investing public), in the eurobond market syndicate members buy the bonds 'firm', ready for onward sale to end investors. Most major lead managers of new issues are members of the International Primary Market Association (IPMA), formed to establish standardised terms and procedures for eurobond issues. Although neither a regulatory nor supervisory organisation, IPMA has established considerable *de facto* authority in the primary eurobond market, and most new issues of eurobonds now comply with IPMA guidelines.

6.2.2 Once the issue has been announced, but before finally agreeing the issue terms, coupon and price with the issuer, the lead manager will discuss with the co-managers their soundings of the market and the likely demand for the bonds.

6.2.3 On the offering day, usually five days after the announcement of the issue, the terms are fixed and the document constituting the offer formally signed; the issuer then becomes legally committed to the issue, having previously been able to withdraw or 'pull' it if the market soundings proved unfavourable.

6.2.4 At this point, the formal offer document is printed and distributed. The lead manager allocates the issue between the co-managers on the basis of the level of interest each has indicated, and they in turn try to place the bonds with the potential purchasers they have already identified as showing an interest in the bonds.

6.2.5 On the closing day, some twenty to thirty days after the offer is announced, payment is due by the purchasers of the bonds to the managers and by them to the issuer. Any shortfall in the placing of bonds must, at this stage, be paid for by the underwriters. On passing on the issue proceeds, both lead manager and co-manager will deduct their fees, usually a percentage of the issue price.

'Grey market'

6.2.6 Some bond dealers, not connected with the issue, will be prepared to deal in the bonds in the days between the announcement and formal offering, although at this stage details of allotments of the bonds, and some of the terms of the issue, will not have been finalised. These dealings are termed the 'grey' or 'when-issued' market.

Stabilisation

6.2.7 For a number of days after the offering day, the lead manager may carry out stabilisation operations to support the price of the newly issued bonds and to reduce their price volatility. This is done by repurchasing bonds in the market when the price appears to be falling, to give the impression of additional demand for the bonds and thus support the price, with the intention of selling the bonds again when investors' demand increases and the price strengthens. These operations must be carried out within the restrictions of the SIB stabilisation rules. These govern the notification that must be given before an issue may be stabilised, the maximum price at which stabilisation purchases may be made (broadly speaking, stabilisation purchases may be used to arrest a fall in price, but not to reverse a fall that has already occurred), and the period after the issue in which stabilisation is permitted (generally up to thirty days after closing date). If these rules are not complied with, the lead manager may be guilty of creating a false market, an offence under section 47(2) of the FSA.

16.2.8   Under IPMA guidelines, the costs of stabilisation are charged to the underwriters of the issue, up to the amount of underwriting commission they have received, with any excess borne by the lead manager. Under TSA rules for capital requirements (rule 50.05 f and g), a proportion of underwriting fees receivable must be excluded from approved assets whilst the issue is being stabilised, and any profit on the stabilisation account is excluded from capital until stabilisation is complete (though losses on stabilisation must be calculated, and provided against, daily).

16.3   Secondary market trading

16.3.1   Although many eurobonds are listed on either the ISE in London or, more usually, the Luxembourg Stock Exchange, very little trading in the bonds takes place on these exchanges. The majority of bond trading is dealt 'over the counter', by telephone or telex. Many banks and securities houses have a department or subsidiary dealing in bonds. Whilst many of these dealers are prepared to take positions in bonds from time to time, there are only a few who have established themselves as market makers, willing to buy or sell at any time, whatever the market conditions, at their quoted price. However it should be noted that these market makers are more akin to principal dealers on the ISE, since no sanctions are imposed on Eurobond market makers that do not, in fact, quote prices.

16.3.2   Price information is made available via a telecommunications system provided by Reuters, giving subscribers information on screen of the latest quotes provided by market makers. The screen quotes are indicative only, in that the market maker has no obligation to deal at the price he has quoted; however, a market maker's reputation will suffer if he regularly refuses to deal at his quoted price, unless the deal is very large (or for an odd small amount) or market conditions are particularly volatile.

6.3.3   The secondary bond market is regulated by the Association of International Bond Dealers (AIBD), located in Zurich, Switzerland, although this regulation is less formal than that of, say, the ISE. As a Designated Investment Exchange under the SIB rules, the AIBD has obligations to ensure a proper market is maintained, but there is also an awareness that the eurobond market, which developed so rapidly as a professional market largely because of the lack of formal regulation, could easily be stifled by excessively detailed regulations.

6.3.4   The AIBD has recently introduced a trade reporting and comparison system, TRAX. However, there is as yet no obligation on AIBD members to report trades to TRAX. Most UK eurobond dealers, who have an obligation under TSA rules to report trades to either AIBD or to TSA, use TRAX reporting, but few overseas eurobond dealers are as yet using the system. Its value as a deal checking and matching mechanism is thus limited.

6.3.5   Input to TRAX is generally made automatically through a direct computer link with the dealer's 'front office' bond trading system. Strong computer controls are therefore required to ensure that incorrect deal information is not transmitted. Trade mismatches identified by TRAX are generally reported within 30 minutes of the trades being input, normally enabling disputes to be resolved before prices have moved substantially.

Price

6.3.6   Although prices are quoted excluding accrued interest (known as 'clean prices'), the price paid on settlement must include interest, calculated up to the due settlement date rather than the dealing date. Interest on fixed rate bonds is normally calculated on a 360-day year, thirty-day month basis. Interest on bearer bonds is paid on the due date against the surrender of an interest 'coupon'; there is therefore no equivalent of ex-div dates. The coupons are issued with the bond and attached to the bond certificate itself. Where bonds are held in a clearing system (*see* below) the clearing system is responsible for claiming interest from the issuers and crediting it to the beneficial holder of the bonds.

16.4   Settlement

6.4.1   Eurobond transactions are normally dealt for settlement seven calendar days after trade date, and normally for delivery against payment. Most settlement of eurobonds, irrespective of the nationality of the issuer, takes place via one of the two clearing systems, Euroclear and CEDEL (based in Brussels and Luxembourg respectively). CEDEL is a private organisation owned by a large number of market participants, while Euroclear is a subsidiary of Morgan Guaranty Trust Company of New York. Although their operations differ in detail, the general principles are the same.

16.4.2   All movements of securities within the clearing system are by book-entry only; each participant opens a securities account with the clearing system which records the bonds owned by that participant. The bond certificates themselves are held in a network of depository banks and only physically move when transferred out of the clearing system.

16.4.3   Participants in the clearing system normally have both a stock account and a cash account with the clearing system. When a participant purchases bonds, they are credited to his stock account on the settlement date and the payment debited to his cash account, provided there are sufficient funds available in that account, or an appropriate overdraft facility has been arranged. Similarly, on a sale, the bonds are debited to the securities account, and credited to the purchaser's account, on settlement date on receipt by the clearing system of payment from the purchaser's bank. The payment is at the same time credited to the seller's account with the clearing system, unless instructions have been given to pay it to the seller's own bank. Thus the clearing house ensures that for all transactions stock and money settle simultaneously.

16.4.4   An electronic link between CEDEL and Euroclear enables transactions between a seller holding bonds in one clearing system and a purchaser requiring delivery in the other to be made in an equally straightforward way.

16.4.5   Instructions may be given to the clearing system for the transfer of securities and funds via computer links named Euclid (for Euroclear) and Cedcon (for CEDEL), or by authenticated telex (using a test key) or SWIFT, the international banking funds transfer system.

16.4.6   More complex delivery procedures are required if bonds are delivered from outside the clearing systems, particularly if this involves banks or depositories in different time zones. Most international bonds are in bearer form, and attached to the bond certificate itself is a sheet of interest 'coupons'. Interest payments are only made on presentation of the appropriate coupon cut from the sheet. Problems on settlement may also arise if the bonds delivered are defective in some way – for example, are damaged, or if coupons or warrants that should be attached are missing.

6.4.7 Euroclear and CEDEL also operate stock lending facilities whereby a short seller of bonds can borrow the bonds to enable delivery to be made. This facility also enables the seller of bonds where the certificates are held outside the clearing system, and which may not be immediately available, to borrow bond certificates and meet the delivery obligation on the due date, thus preventing a 'chain reaction' of failed deliveries. The lender of the bonds will be an institution or other investor holding the bonds as a long-term investment and wishing to enhance the income earned from the bonds. The lending and borrowing is all controlled by the clearing house, who also guarantee the return of bonds to the lender when required.

Warrants

6.4.8 A further important area of the eurobond market is the market in warrants. These are usually issued 'attached' to a bond issue so that the subscriber to the issue receives both bonds and warrants in a fixed ratio, but are subsequently traded separately from the bonds. Each warrant entitles the holder to purchase a fixed number of equity shares of the issuing corporation, at a fixed price per share, during a specified exercise period. The warrants thus represent a long-term option to acquire shares of the issuing corporation, and their pricing and price volatility have more in common with the options market than the bond market.

Accounting

6.4.9 The general accounting principles discussed in section 4.10 of chapter 4 relating to long and short securities positions apply equally to eurobond positions. However, given the absence of any obligation by market makers to deal at quoted prices, the marketability of eurobonds which are included in a trading book, accounted for on a mark-to-market basis, must be considered carefully.

16.5 Audit

16.5.1 The audit objectives relating to eurobond trading are similar to those for domestic securities trading operations:

Statutory reporting objectives
These may be listed as:

(i)   amounts due to and from counterparties relating to eurobond dealing are genuine and are completely and accurately included in the balance sheet;

(ii) adequate but not excessive provisions have been made for amounts which may prove to be irrecoverable;

(iii) long positions represent bona fide assets to which the firm has good title; short positions are completely and accurately recorded;

(iv) long and short positions are valued on appropriate and consistent bases;

(v) amounts due to and from counterparties, and long and short positions, are presented in the balance sheet in accordance with the rules of TSA, accounting standards and the Companies Act as appropriate; and

(vi) adequate but not excessive provision is made for any losses arising from underwriting commitments.

Additional reporting objectives

16.5.2 These are specific matters which auditors are required to report on under the Financial Regulations of TSA:

(i) the systems for the agreement and reconciliation of counterparty balances and positions are adequate and such procedures are carried out at appropriate intervals (rule 90.03d (i));

(ii) adequate procedures and controls are in operation for reporting and investigating the ageing and analysis of balances with customers (rule 90.03d (iii)); and

(iii) adequate procedures have been established for monitoring the firm's position risk exposure (including that resulting from primary market operations) and counterparty risk exposure and for providing appropriate management information (rule 90.03 d (iv)).

16.5.3 In addition, a eurobond trading operation may well hold client money, to which the requirements of chapter 11 will be relevant, and bonds may be held on behalf of customers, in which case the safe custody and customers' assets rules discussed in chapter 12 will apply.

Internal control

16.5.4 The control objectives, systems controls and audit procedures set out in chapters 9, 10, 14 and 20 are largely relevant to eurobond dealing and are not repeated here. However, the auditor needs to take account of the special features of the eurobond market as follows:

● most bond dealing operations handle a relatively small number of transactions when compared to broker-dealers dealing in equities, but these transactions are generally of high value;

- the high value of transactions has led to strict cash against delivery being operated throughout the bond market; free deliveries (delivery without corresponding payment) and free payments (payment without corresponding delivery) are exceptional;
- settlement rarely fails to occur on or very soon after the due settlement date; any transactions remaining unsettled after a few days require careful examination; and
- whilst market values are readily available for most bonds, it may be difficult to obtain values for some less actively traded bonds, particularly where there is doubt as to the creditworthiness of the issuer. Quoted prices may be of little value if an issue is not actively traded as there is no obligation on market makers to deal at their quoted prices.

16.5.5   The recently introduced TRAX system of checking provides confirmation on trades where the counterparty also reports trades on TRAX. However, many overseas counterparties do not yet do so and confirmation of deals continues to rely on the exchange of telexes and confirmation notes.

16.5.6   Input of settlement instructions to Euclid and Cedcon is usually by means of a direct computer link from the eurobond dealer's main dealing computer system, without manual intervention. It is therefore essential that strong computer controls exist over the sending of such instructions to prevent incorrect or fraudulent transmissions, in addition to the normal controls over the accurate entry of deals to the computer system.

Analytical review

16.5.7   As with other types of principal dealing operation, an analytical review approach is rarely applicable to the verification of dealing profit and losses. However, in some circumstances an analytical review comprising a comparison of interest receivable with the market value of the bonds held, may give some audit assurance on the completeness of the recording of interest receivable, since most bonds in any one currency of similar maturity are likely to have very similar yields.

Substantive testing

16.5.8   A substantive-based approach will often be applicable where there are a low number of high-value transactions. The main substantive tests would be:

(i)   agreement of stock and money balances with Euroclear and CEDEL;
(ii)   circularisation of stock and money balances with customers and other counterparties;

281

(iii) post year-end settlement of open transactions;

(iv) verification of market prices of bonds held by the firm as principal;

(v) performance of a position agreement, verifying the nominal amount of bonds held as long or short positions (chapter 14);

(vi) reconciliation of all stocks held in the firm's name on behalf of customers; and

(vii) verification of interest income received.

16.5.9 As mentioned above, settlement in the eurobond market rarely fails to occur on the due date or shortly thereafter; any transactions open at the year-end date and unsettled at the time of the audit require investigation.

16.5.10 For the valuation of the firm's own positions, market prices are generally available for most eurobonds, though these are not published daily; it may be necessary for the auditor to note prices shown on the dealer's screens at the close of business of the last dealing day of the firm's financial year. Quoted prices must always be used with a degree of caution, since they do not always indicate prices at which transactions have actually taken place and, if the market in a particular bond is very 'thin', may not be a true reflection of the value. The ability of the bond issuer to repay the bond at maturity is a crucial element in the valuation of a bond, and uncertainties as to the issuer's creditworthiness can have a substantial impact.

Disclosure requirement

16.5.11 For principal positions, the Companies Act requires an analysis between securities listed in the UK, those listed overseas and unlisted securities.

16.6 Capital requirements

16.6.1 Under TSA counterparty risk requirement (CRR) rules applicable to debt securities, a CRR will arise on settlements of bonds more than fifteen days overdue. This will be a percentage of the increase in value over the contract price in the case of securities purchased by the bond dealer, or decrease in value below the contract price in the case of securities sold by the bond dealer. In addition, the full value of any free deliveries will be included in the CRR. However, as stated above, such overdue settlement or free delivery should arise infrequently in the bond market. CRR calculations are discussed in more detail in chapter 10.

16.6.2 Long and short bond positions will attract a PRR as described in chapter 14. Special rules apply to positions in warrants and convertibles. A PRR will also arise on commitments given under note issuing facilities and similar arrangements, under rule 62.23.

16.6.3   Issuing market obligations and positions are dealt with under rule 62.33. In summary, this rule requires a PRR of 30 per cent of the basic 'Method 1' PRR applicable to the bonds (without any allowance for hedging) on any commitments entered into, after deducting sales made and underwriting commitments obtained. This applies from the beginning of the third business day after the issue is announced, until the earlier of the closing date and twenty-eight calendar days after the allotment date. Thereafter the normal PRR rules apply, except that the concentrated position requirement does not apply until thirty calendar days after the closing date.

16.6.4   Issuing market commitments, as lead manager, co-manager, underwriter or selling syndicate member, attract PRR under rule 62.33b.

17 Foreign Exchange

17.1 Introduction

17.1.1 Many broker-dealers number among their customers, entities (either institutional investors or individuals) which are based outside the United Kingdom but who wish to buy and sell securities traded in London. Similarly, as described in chapter 15, many domestic customers of a broker-dealer will wish to buy or sell securities traded on overseas markets. Both these situations are likely to result in the broker-dealer settling with his customer in one currency and settling with the market in another, which in turn means that the broker-dealer will have to become involved in foreign exchange transactions.

17.1.2 In order to account for securities transactions in foreign currencies, broker-dealers normally maintain ledgers in currencies other than sterling which enables them to record transactions to be settled in the currency of the relevant overseas market.

17.1.3 The most frequently encountered situation is where a broker-dealer buys or sells a security in a foreign currency whilst rendering the contract to the customer in sterling. This results in a situation where the broker-dealer is long or short of a particular currency. For example, if a customer placed an order for a US stock and the firm pays the US market in US dollars, but contracts with the customer in sterling, the firm would have a short position in US dollars and a long position in sterling.

17.1.4 The effect in this example is to expose the firm to the risk of movement in the exchange rate between US dollars and sterling between the contract and settlement dates. To minimise this risk, firms usually adopt one of the following procedures:

(a) for each contract involving a cross currency share deal, execute a foreign exchange deal to convert all currency proceeds or liabilities to sterling; or,

(b) execute a foreign exchange deal to convert the net of all currency assets or liabilities to sterling at the end of each day. This method can be appropriate where the nature of the firm's share dealing is such that foreign stock deals will give rise to currency positions which, to an extent, cancel each other out; or

(c) to operate a separate treasury function and actively manage positions in the currencies in which the firm most frequently deals, at the same time controlling the overall exposure within pre-set limits, with a view to profiting from exchange rate movements.

17.1.5   Generally, firms will execute foreign exchange transactions with 'foreign exchange dealers', typically banks or other securities dealers that deal in foreign currencies as part of their main business. Where the firm is buying shares in non-UK markets it may buy the relevant foreign currency from the same security dealer to generate effectively a sterling denominated purchase.

17.1.6   The number of foreign exchange transactions undertaken by a firm will, therefore, vary depending on the means by which the firm intends to control its currency exposure. If the firm decides to take positions in a currency, suitable control systems and procedures clearly need to be established.

17.1.7   The majority of firms deal in foreign exchange as an adjunct to their securities business and it is comparatively rare for a broker-dealer to deal in foreign exchange on a speculative basis. In most cases, firms will deal on a spot basis, (i.e. for settlement in two days). Forward foreign exchange contracts may be entered into to coincide with the expected settlement date of the underlying stock transaction, for example five days forward for bargains transacted on the New York Stock Exchange. Firms may also make use of 'options' contracts, where the actual settlement day for the foreign exchange contract can be chosen from within a range of dates to coincide with the actual settlement date of a particular transaction. Such contracts are more expensive but avoid the potential funding problem of being obliged to settle the foreign exchange contract without having received the foreign currency from the share transaction, should delivery be delayed.

17.1.8   Some customers, particularly large institutions, who wish to hedge their overall exposure to movements between the US dollar and sterling on the US dollar shares in their portfolio, may also deal with broker-dealers in order to take positions in foreign currency for hedging purposes but unrelated to any specific securities transaction.

17.2 Accounting

17.2.1 The accounting systems used by broker-dealers are similar to the currency accounting systems used by banks. There are two principal systems of recording transactions in foreign currencies which are commonly used, namely 'multi-currency' accounting and 'dual-currency' accounting.

Multi-currency accounting

17.2.2 In a multi-currency system, all accounting entries are recorded in the relevant currencies in which the transactions take place and in order to prepare accounts in the base currency, balances are translated at rates of exchange ruling on the accounting date. Movements between currencies are passed through inter-currency accounts known as 'trade' or 'position' accounts. The balances on the various position accounts will reflect the long and short positions held in individual currencies. When translated to the base currency, the net difference on position accounts, representing spot exchange profits and losses arising from the individual long and short currency positions in relation to the base currency, will be taken to the profit and loss account as foreign exchange income or expense.

17.2.3 It is not necessary for profit and loss account items to be converted into sterling, through a transaction with a bank. However, in practice it is usual for each item of currency income or expense to be recorded immediately in sterling, by passing it through the position accounts thus fixing the sterling equivalent. The effect of this treatment is that currency income and expense is included in the sterling accounts at the rate ruling on the date of the transaction. If, however, the net profit is held in currency and not physically converted into sterling, this may give rise to subsequent exchange gains or losses.

Dual-currency accounting

17.2.4 In a dual-currency system the base currency equivalent for each currency accounting entry is recorded simultaneously, which therefore relegates the currency entries to the status of memorandum accounting records.

17.2.5 Multi-currency accounting is probably the more widely used system in the UK, and is more suitable in cases where a large volume of business is carried on outside the base currency. Not only does the multi-currency system reduce the number of exchange differences which arise but it also, through the position accounts, allows the spot position in each currency to be calculated with ease. The principal advantage of dual-currency accounting is that a complete record of all transactions is maintained in the base currency with fewer accounting entries. However, a dual-currency system can produce large exchange differences and does not allow the currency position to be calculated as easily. With the advent of computerised accounting systems the clerical exercise of consolidating and translating currency balance sheets has been greatly simplified and this has removed the principal advantage of dual-currency accounting. Accordingly, only multi-currency accounting is considered in the rest of the chapter.

7.2.6 An example of the specific accounting entries required to record certain foreign exchange transactions is set out below.

Spot transactions

7.2.7 These are foreign exchange transactions with a value (settlement) date, two working days after the contract date. The accounting entries generated from a spot deal are usually recorded in the accounting records on the day that the deal is contracted, even though settlement is not expected until two days later. For a purchase of currency in exchange for sterling the accounting entries on the day of the deal would be:

(1) Dr Foreign Exchange Dealer A
     Cr Spot Trading Account   } in currency
     Recording of expected receipt of currency

(2) Dr Spot Trading Account
     Cr Foreign Exchange Dealer A   } in sterling
     Recording of sterling liability

For a sale of currency in exchange for sterling, the above entries would be reversed.

The corresponding entries reflecting the purchase of US dollar shares for a UK customer would be:

(3) Dr Spot Trading Account
     Cr US Broker Dealer X   } in currency
     Recording of share purchase in USA

(4) Dr Customer 1
     Cr Spot trading account   } in sterling
     Recording of share purchase by customer

Forward transactions

17.2.8 Forward deals can be transacted for settlement at any date in the future so long as it is more than two days after the transaction date, since a one- or two-day settlement period would make such a deal a spot transaction. Although there is a forward market of more than five years in certain currencies, the market is concentrated on deals maturing in less than one year. Forward foreign exchange rates are normally quoted for each month forward in terms of a premium or discount to the spot rate. The premium or discount is primarily dependent upon interest rate differentials between the relevant currencies, but other factors include the market's view of the general economic outlook.

17.2.9 Unlike banks, broker-dealers usually record forward deals in the books of account in double-entry form on the contract date, and the accounting entries are the same as those described above for a spot deal. During the course of the forward contract, the asset and liability with the foreign exchange dealer in the respective currencies are netted off, so that only the net differences between the original sterling book cost of the transaction and the sterling equivalent value of the currency position at the accounting date calculated using the relevant forward rates on that day, is reflected in the balance sheet.

17.2.10 To the extent that the firm does not eliminate all currency exposures at the end of each day, it will value its currency positions at each accounting date by reference to the appropriate spot or forward market rates. The resultant profit or loss on valuation is reflected in the profit and loss account, either by a provision for forward losses or by a debtor representing unrealised profit. The profit or loss arising on the valuation of a forward foreign currency position is normally calculated as the difference between:

   (a) the sterling equivalent value of the currency position at the accounting date calculated using the relevant forward rates on that date; and
   (b) the memorandum 'sterling book cost' of the position recorded when the transaction was originally set up.

Position accounts

17.2.11 In a multi-currency system movements between currencies are passed through for control or position accounts to be maintained. When period-end accounts are prepared, all currency balances are translated and consolidated with the sterling trial balances, and the currency control accounts will, after adjustment for profits or losses on translation, cancel each other out.

.2.12   At any time the balances on the position accounts in the sterling ledger will represent the cost of the broker's investment in the relevant currencies. For example, a sterling debit balance in the US dollar position account will indicate that the broker took a long position in that currency. However, it should be noted that exchange gains and losses will distort the relationship between the currency position account and its corresponding sterling control. This distortion is illustrated in the following example:

| | £ control | | US$ control | |
	US$	US$	£	£
Note 1		55,000	50,000	
Note 2	56,000			40,000

Note 1: The broker takes a long position in US$ at £1 = $1.10
Note 2: The dollar weakens significantly and the broker, having decided to run a small short position sells $56,000 at 1.40 (= £40,000).

.2.13   The US dollar position account in the sterling ledger still shows a debit balance, but the sterling control account in the dollar ledger is showing the broker short of currency. In reality the debit balance of £10,000 is made up of a realised exchange loss of £10,714 and a short currency position of £714 (i.e. $1,000 at 1.40).

17.3 Audit

.7.3.1   Certain aspects of trading on overseas markets are dealt with in chapter 15 on overseas stock exchanges. There are however, certain specific audit procedures which overseas dealing and foreign currency transactions require and these are set out below. There are no specific additional reporting objectives relevant to this area, other than the need to confirm the proper calculation of the PRR and CRR arising on foreign exchange transactions.

Statutory audit objectives
.7.3.2   These objectives are to ensure that:

- all foreign exchange transactions entered into are correctly recorded;
- unsettled balances arising from foreign exchange transactions are correctly disclosed in the financial statements;
- profits and losses on translation of currency positions are fairly stated;
- all income and expense translated or converted to sterling is recorded completely and accurately in the sterling records.

Occasionally brokers will carry out unmatched foreign exchange deals on behalf of their customers. In these circumstances, in addition to the above objectives, the auditor must ensure that adverse exchange rate movements have not given rise to potential bad debts.

17.3.3 *Control objective: All foreign exchange transactions are correctly recorded*
Possible errors under this heading are:

- foreign exchange deals excluded from the accounting records;
- foreign exchange deals incorrectly recorded.

17.3.4 General controls: The following general controls should identify a failure to record foreign exchange deals:

— confirmations of all deals received from foreign exchange dealers;
— regular review of contra and spot trading accounts for unmatched positions;
— regular preparation and review of bank reconciliations;
— regular scrutiny of customer and broker accounts for unidentified cash items.

17.3.5 Specific control procedures which may exist to ensure that all foreign exchange deals are completely and accurately recorded include:

— regular review of bank reconciliations, customer and market accounts for apparently unallocated cash items. This process needs to be applied to all currency ledgers to ensure both sides of a transaction are identified;
— regular review of outstanding trades to ensure that for each debit in one currency there is a credit in a second currency;
— regular positive circularisation of currency dealers with whom the firm has dealt to confirm outstanding trades are complete.

17.3.6 *Control objective: Unsettled balances arising from foreign exchange transactions are correctly disclosed in the financial statements*

17.3.7 Unsettled balances arising from foreign exchange transactions should have two elements, one in the currency being purchased and one in the currency being sold. The net of these balances represents the difference between the rate at which the deals have been contracted and the closing rate of exchange used in the accounts, effectively a net asset or a net liability due to a foreign exchange dealer. Normally, this would only be a small amount and any large balances will generally require explanation. As explained above, the net balance for each dealer is included within the balance sheet as a debtor or creditor as appropriate.

7.3.8 Control procedures which may exist to ensure that unsettled balances arising from foreign exchange transaction are correctly disclosed in the financial statements include:

— regular management review of working papers to ensure the required analysis of balances has been correctly carried out;
— review of balances by suitably senior management to ensure they are reasonable in relation to the size of net balances in individual currencies and the movements in exchange rates since the period in which outstanding deals originated.

7.3.9 *Control objective: Profits and losses on translation of currency positions are fairly stated*

7.3.10 Control procedures which may exist to ensure that profits and losses on translation of currency positions are fairly stated include:

— frequent checks of all items in each sterling control account, to ensure that they are mirrored by entries that appear in the corresponding control account in the currency ledger and that no other items exist there;
— regular preparation and review of bank reconciliations;
— regular reconciliations with overseas brokers' statements;
— review of gains and losses in each currency against rate movements and the size and nature (long/short) of the exposure.

7.3.11 *Control objective: All income translated or converted to sterling is recorded completely and accurately in the sterling records*

7.3.12 Normal audit procedures for revenue will apply but for revenues generated in currency it is important to confirm completeness since the translation or conversion of revenue items is frequently recorded by use of journal entries and thus is more susceptible to error.

7.3.13 Control procedures to ensure that all income translated or converted to sterling is recorded completely and accurately in the sterling records may include:

— establishment of strict routines for converting or translating foreign currency balances;
— restrictions on the numbers of personnel authorised to transact foreign exchange deals;
— review and authorisation of any journals relating to foreign exchange profits or losses by appropriate senior management.

Analytical review

17.3.14   Analytical review is of little practical value in this area.

Substantive tests

17.3.15   Substantive tests in the area of foreign currency include:

— verification of contracts open at the balance sheet date, by agreement to counterparty confirmations;
— circularisation of counterparties, including a sample of nil year-end balances for accounts which have been active during the year;
— verification of exchange rates used for valuation;
— checks on arithmetic;
— cut-off tests;
— review of exposures and compare with authorised limits;
— check of recording of both sterling equivalent and currency accounts into the relevant ledger accounts for a sample of deals transacted during the year;
— review of position account balances to confirm that differences on translation are reasonable in relation to exchange rate movements.

17.4   Capital requirements

17.4.1   The capital requirement relating to foreign currency are dealt with in two areas under TSA rules.

17.4.2   First, a position risk requirement (PRR) under rule 62.40, which requires a PRR of 5 per cent of the net long position in each currency, including sterling. Secondly, unsettled forward transactions in foreign currency will create a Counterparty Risk Requirement (Rule 63.14). The full workings of this rule have yet to be agreed as it is intended that it will have a similar effect to the requirements of the 'risk-asset ratio' rules applied by the Bank of England to the foreign exchange exposures of banks. TSA rule 63.14 sets out the procedure whereby a 'credit equivalent amount' (CEA) is to be calculated and a percentage of the CEA is then added to the firm's CRR.

17.4.3   The CEA calculation is intended to be a two-stage process, although only the first stage is operative at present and this consists of deducting the mark-to-market value of each contract from its book value, and adding any deficit to the CEA. The second stage of computing the CEA relates to the 'potential future exposure' of the contract and is expected to be a set percentage of the gross amount of the value of the contract. This aspect of the rules has not yet been implemented but it is proposed that this should ultimately be consistent with the corresponding requirements for banks set by the Bank of England.

18 Equity Options

18.1 Introduction

18.1.1   An option is a contract between two parties whereby one (the holder of the option) has the right, but not the obligation, to buy from (in the case of a call option) or to sell to (in the case of a put option) the other party a specified amount of a particular currency, stock, financial instrument or commodity at a specified price. This right may be exercised at any time in a specified period, after which the option expires.

18.1.2   A wide variety of options contracts are traded on various exchanges. Traded options are the most important and widely traded form of equity option on the London market. They were introduced in 1979, before which conventional (sometimes known as traditional) options were the most widespread form of option contract. Conventional options are still dealt although the market is now much smaller than the traded options market.

18.1.3   The difference between conventional and traded options is that the former is a personal contract between two persons with no transfer of the benefits arising under the contract being possible; whereas the benefits arising under a traded options contract are fully transferable via dealings on the London Traded Options Market (LTOM), which is part of the International Stock Exchange.

18.1.4   It should be noted that plans to merge LTOM and LIFFE (discussed in chapter 18) have recently been announced. At the time of writing, the process by which this merger is to be achieved has still to be decided but it is proposed to be effective before the end of 1990. The exact details of the merger were not available at the time of writing and we do not speculate on the likely implications here. Rather, we consider the main characteristics of equity options separately, characteristics which are

293

likely to remain unchanged even after the merger of the market place in which they are dealt.

18.1.5   One potentially misleading term which should be explained here is the distinction between American and European options. The term American option is used to refer to an option which can be exercised at any time during its life, whereas a European option is one which can be exercised only on a single stated date. As is discussed in more detail below, the majority of UK traded options are classified as American options. Conventional options do not fit easily into either category because they can be exercised during the life of the option, but only on certain pre-set dates.

18.2 Traded options

18.2.1   Traded options dealt on the LTOM fall into two categories – options on a single security and options on an index of securities (such as the FTSE 100 Index) which allow investors to profit from movements in overall market levels. For each type, there are two forms of option – calls and puts. A call option gives the holder the right to buy the underlying share or the index; a put option gives the holder the right to sell the underlying share or the index.

18.2.2   With traded options, the minimum unit in which an investor may deal is one 'contract', where a contract usually represents an option on 1,000 shares of the underlying security. Where the price of the underlying security is high, each contract may represent an option on 100 shares. It should be noted that a contract is not divisible.

18.2.3   The decision as to which listed shares will be included on the traded options market is taken by the LTOM Committee of the ISE. This may be upon application of the listed company, or by application of the market at large where interest in a particular stock is high.

18.2.4   A traded option contract has a limited lifespan which is determined by pre-set expiry dates which are set at successive three-month intervals. It should be noted though that a traded option contract can be exercised at any time during its lifetime, with the exception of the recently introduced 'Euro-FTSE' options on the FTSE index which can only be exercised at expiry. Traded options have a maximum life of nine months and so, at any time of the year, three of these expiry dates will be quoted. When, say, the February expiry date is reached, the February option will cease to exist and November options will be introduced, so there will then be May, August and November options available. When

294

the May expiry date is reached, options will be introduced with an expiry date of February in the following year, and so on.

18.2.5 The precise expiry date within a particular month is announced by the ISE when the options are introduced and will always be stated on contract notes. Generally, options expire on the third or fourth Wednesday of the final month of their life.

18.2.6 The price at which an option contract gives the holder the right to buy or sell the underlying security is known as the exercise or strike price. Exercise prices are fixed by the ISE in accordance with a standard scale with successive prices set at increments of between 10p and 50p depending on the actual underlying share price.

18.2.7 As an example, suppose it is June and traded options in a particular company are to be listed for the first time. This company has been allocated a February, May, August, November cycle and has a current share price of 270p. The standard scale of exercise prices around this price is: 220, 240, 260, 280, 300.

18.2.8 At the time of initial listing, the operative expiry dates will be August, November and February and for each of these dates, exercise prices of 260p and 280p will be set. These are set according to the standard scale so that one exercise price (260p) is below the share price and the other (280p) is above it. Therefore, the following call and put options will be available:

August	November	February
260	260	260
280	280	280

18.2.9 All the options on a particular underlying security, which have the same expiry date and exercise price, are known as 'series'. If the price of the underlying security was to fall below 260p, three more series, one for each of the three outstanding expiry months, would be introduced at the next price down, i.e. 240p. Similarly, if the share price rose above 280p, then August, November and February 300p series would be introduced (in accordance with the standard scale).

18.2.10 The price of a traded option is known as the premium. The premium is quoted in terms of an option on a single share of the underlying security. Therefore, if an investor purchases a single contract in a security where the number of shares relating to a contract is 1,000, the price he will pay is 1,000 × premium (plus dealing costs). Premiums are determined, like share prices, by the market forces of supply and demand.

18.2.11　The pricing of option contracts is a complex subject with numerous mathematical models available which attempt to predict premiums based on known data. Two key factors in determining the price of a particular option contract are the exercise price and the price of the underlying security. As an example, suppose we have a security whose underlying share price is 200p. A call option with a strike price of 180p is clearly worth more than a call option with a strike price of 220p.

18.2.12　If the price of the underlying security is seen to be volatile, there is a greater possibility that the price will rise above 220p. Hence premiums for volatile stocks are likely to be higher than for non-volatile stocks. A further factor determining the likelihood of an option being profitable is the time to expiry. The longer the period until expiry, the more chance there is that the option will make a profit (because the share price has longer to move above or below the relevant exercise price) and hence the higher the premium is likely to be. All of these factors and more are used in the mathematical models referred to above.

18.3　Dealing

18.3.1　A typical traded option transaction might be as follows. Assume that at the beginning of June, XYZ plc shares stand at 290p and an investor takes the view that the shares are likely to rise over the next few weeks. He therefore decides to buy one XYZ plc August 300 call option contract. His broker goes to the market and buys the contract for him at, say, 14p. This costs the investor £140 (plus dealing expenses) and means that he has acquired the right to buy 1,000 XYZ plc shares at 300p each at any time up until the expiry date of the option in August.

18.3.2　The fact that the broker was able to make the transaction means that there is someone in the market who takes the opposite view to our investor. This individual has sold (or written) the August 300 call option and hence will receive the option premium. If the investor decides to exercise his option then the writer of the option has to deliver the stock at 300p either from his own portfolio or by purchase in the market if he has written the option uncovered or 'naked'. If the price of the stock rises above 300p, the purchaser will be able to make a profit by selling at the then current price; if the underlying share price does not reach the exercise price (or in practice, the exercise price plus the option premium), it is not worthwhile for the purchaser to exercise his option and the writer makes a profit represented by the premium he has received.

18.3.3　The gearing effect of options can be demonstrated by extending the above example. Suppose that the price of the shares was to rise during the life of the August option to 320p. If that happened, the option would also rise to, say, 28p and the investor could sell the option for a 100 per cent profit without ever owning the underlying shares. We can compare the profit made on the option transaction with the movement in the share price:

— XYZ plc August 300 call options cost 14p
— shares rise from 290p to 320p
— options rise from 14p to 28p
— shares rise 10.3%
— options rise 100%

18.3.4   The feature distinguishing options trading from trading in the under-lying stock is the limited life of options contracts. In dealing in the underlying security, the investor is not faced with a pre-set time scale over which his expectations must be achieved. The hope is always for shares to reach the target price as quickly as possible, but a series of events which delays that process is not critical since the investor still has ownership of a tangible asset. In options transactions, time acts against the buyer as the asset wastes away, each day eroding its value.

18.3.5   The example given has dealt with the purchase of a call option. If, conversely, the investor thought that the price was going to fall, he could buy one XYZ plc August 300 put option contract. This gives him the right to sell 1,000 shares at 300p at any time up until the expiry date of the option in August. In all other respects, put options are similar to call options.

18.3.6   It should be noted that the purchaser of an option does not have to exercise his option in order to realise a profit. Indeed, most traded options contracts are never exercised because it is actually simpler (and cheaper) for investors to make their money by trading solely in the options. Hence they will take their profit (or indeed cut their losses) by selling the options back to the market. This is possible because as the option becomes more profitable to the holder, the premium will rise by the process of supply and demand.

18.3.7   Conversely, the writer of an option can buy his options back from the market rather than wait for them to be exercised. It should be emphasised that writing call options without owning the underlying stock (known as 'uncovered' or 'naked' writing) carries a higher level of risk because, as is discussed below, the writer can be called upon to deliver the stock at any time during the life of the contract and his potential loss is therefore theoretically unlimited.

18.3.8   If at any time an option holder wishes to acquire the underlying shares
          to which his option entitles him, he may do so by instructing his broker
          to issue an 'Exercise notice' and the shares will be delivered to him in
          return for payment of the exercise price of the option plus the
          appropriate dealing expenses. This process is discussed in more detail in
          section 18.4 below.

18.3.9   The market making system for traded options is similar to that which
          exists for equities (discussed in chapter 14). There are market makers to
          whom the brokers go when they have customers who wish to buy or sell
          options. Therefore, there is no need to find another customer who holds
          the opposite view before being able to enter into a traded option
          contract. Market makers quote a bid/offer spread at which they are
          prepared to buy or sell a particular series and they will generally quote
          prices for all series that are available at a particular time. The London
          traded options market operates on the former stock exchange trading
          floor, with bargains struck by 'open outcry'. The market in a class of
          options is made by the 'Crowd', composed of market makers, brokers,
          the pitch official and the board official. There is a pitch official and a
          board official for each option. The pitch official is responsible for
          ensuring the orderly conduct of the trading in that option, whilst the
          board official is responsible for the transaction of public limit orders in
          that option.

18.4 Settlement

18.4.1   Settlement of traded options transactions is made through a central
          clearing house called LOCH (London Options Clearing House) which is a
          wholly owned subsidiary of the ISE. LOCH operates a full clearing house,
          rather than merely facilitating settlement like Talisman by standing as a
          principal between the counterparties to an option transaction; it
          matches bargains, settles premiums and ensures that when options are
          exercised, stock is passed between the correct counterparties (it should
          be noted that stock settlement is still effected through Talisman).

18.4.2   Once the buying and selling firms have transacted a bargain on the floor
          of the Exchange, the benefits and obligations of the two parties to the
          transaction are assumed by LOCH and the two parties subsequently
          have no further communication with each other. Moreover, LOCH
          accepts full financial responsibility to both parties, so that if one side
          defaults the other is still able to obtain the benefit of their rights under
          the contract. This is very similar to the guarantee given by ICCH to
          financial futures transactions dealt on LIFFE which is discussed in more
          detail in chapter 18.

18.4.3 For every holder (i.e. purchaser) of an option contract there must be an equivalent writer. LOCH acts as a register for these open contracts and if a holder exercises a contract, LOCH appoints, by a process of random selection, a writer of a contract in the same series to deliver or receive the underlying shares. Thus the option may well not be exercised against the original counterparty.

18.4.4 It should also be noted that broker-dealers can have varying degrees of involvement with LOCH as either clearing members, clearing agents or public order members:

(a) Clearing members are firms which carry out business on their own and their customers' behalf and which are responsible for the settlement of that business with LOCH.
(b) Clearing agents are firms which not only settle their own trans-actions with LOCH but also those of other brokers who do not have the capital or experience to take responsibility for their own business with LOCH.
(c) Public order members (POMs) are firms which do not have clearing membership of LOCH, and thus settle their business through a nominated clearing agent.

18.4.5 It is administratively convenient for many firms to settle through a clearing agent since this means that they do not need to keep the detailed records which are required to control the risks associated with traded options dealing. In summary, the POM delegates the settlement of traded options transactions to the clearing agent and merely has to react to instructions from the agent in respect of payment for premiums and margins. However, as discussed below, the POM cannot completely avoid responsibility for control over its traded options business and has to maintain certain records.

Checking, clearing and settlement

18.4.6 A new trade matching system has recently been introduced on the floor of the LTOM. Whilst each party to a trade is still required to fill in a dealing slip and have it time stamped in the 'pitch', these are now placed in a trade registration system (TRS) box. These slips are collected at approximately fifteen-minute intervals by ISE staff and input to a computer checking system, which involves the matching of bought contracts with those which have been written. Instead of the five 'passes' each day previously carried out to identify unmatched bargains, the TRS system allows clearers to obtain trade matching information on demand via computer terminals. All transactions in traded options contracts must be matched on the day of the trade and firms are required to make available, at all times, responsible personnel for the resolution of bargain queries.

18.4.7   By 8.00 a.m. on the following morning LOCH makes available to all clearing members a statement detailing the amounts payable or receivable as a result of bargains transacted the previous day. Amounts payable or receivable will be made up of premiums, fees, VAT and margin requirements (discussed in section 18.5 below). Amounts due to LOCH must be paid by 10.00 a.m. whilst payments from LOCH are made available to member firms from 11.00 a.m.

18.4.8   It is important to realise that there are no certificates for traded options as there are for the underlying shares. LOCH and each clearing member or clearing agent maintains a record of open option contracts; for the customer evidence of the existence of the option is a contract note and his broker's statement.

18.4.9   All customers who have dealt in traded options are expected to settle by 9.45 a.m. the following day. If a customer has purchased options, he will be expected to pay the premium, clearing fee (passed on to LOCH or the clearing agent as appropriate), commission (due to the firm), PTM levy (due to the ISE) and any related VAT. If a customer has written an option then he will receive the premium less clearing fee, commission, VAT and any margin requirement.

Settlement of bargains resulting from the exercise of options

18.4.10   The holder of an option contract wishing to exercise his option must first inform his broker. The firm will then complete an 'exercise notice', which is a formal notification to LOCH that the holder of an option wishes to buy or sell the underlying stock at the exercise price in accordance with the terms of the option contract. Upon receipt of the exercise notice, LOCH assigns it to a firm which has a position as a writer of option contracts in the series concerned. This assignment is carried out by a computerised process of random selection, and is followed by an 'assignment notice' being sent to the appropriate firm. An assignment notice is formal notification from LOCH requiring a writer to fulfil his contractual obligation to buy or sell the underlying security. A firm receiving an assignment notice then allocates it to a customer holding a position as a writer. This has to be done by a system of random selection previously approved by the ISE.

18.4.11   Once a writer has received an assignment notice from LOCH he must sell the underlying security to the buyer, in the case of a call option, or buy the underlying security, in the case of a put option.

18.4.12 On the business day following the submission of an exercise notice to LOCH, a contract note for the purchase or sale of the underlying security will be issued to the exerciser by his broker. Similarly, a contract note will be issued to the investor assigned against by his firm. These bargains will then be settled on the appropriate account day, usually through the Talisman settlement system.

18.5 Margin and collateral

18.5.1 The writer of an option enters into an obligation to either receive or deliver shares at a fixed price. In order to ensure that writers can meet their obligations, they are required to pass over collateral (often referred to as margin) to LOCH. Purchasers of options have no risk beyond the option premium which they have paid and therefore are not required to provide margin.

18.5.2 Margin is lodged with LOCH through the writer's broker and may be in a number of different forms such as:

- cash;
- shares underlying any traded option, any 'alpha' security, or convertible securities and ADRs relating thereto;
- UK and US gilts, Treasury bills and certain other fixed interest stocks;
- other assets approved by the ISE.

18.5.3 There are a number of rules for calculating how much margin is required which are set out in the *Traded Option Users' Manual*, issued by the ISE. The basic rule for writers of options is that the margin is calculated by taking 20 per cent of the current share price of the underlying security and adjusting this figure by reference to the exercise price of the option. This adjustment reflects the extent to which the option stands 'in' or 'out' of the money. An 'in the money' option is one that is in profit for the purchaser; an 'out of the money' option is one that is making a loss for the purchaser. Margin requirements can be illustrated by the following examples:

Margin calculation 'in the money'

ABC plc 50p Ords – underlying share price	250p
Investor writes one 240p call option contract.	
The margin required therefore consists of:	
(i) 20% of underlying share price (250p x 20%)	50p
(ii) Adjustment to reflect exercise price below share price: 250p − 240p	10p
	60p
Margin per contract 1000 × 60p	£600

301

18.5.4   In the example, ABC plc shares are standing at 250p in the market. The customer who has written one call contract with an exercise price of 240p has sold the right to buy from him 1000 shares in ABC plc at 240p. The purchaser of the option is actually in profit at the moment (i.e. he can purchase shares worth 250p for 240p by exercising his option) and so is 'in the money'. In order to ensure that the writer can fulfil his obligations, he has to deposit margin worth £600.

18.5.5   By contrast, if the investor had written not the 240p call but the 260p call:

> *Margin calculation 'out of the money'*
>
> | | |
> |---|---:|
> | ABC plc 50p Ord – underlying share price | 250p |
> | | |
> | Investor writes one 260p call option contract. The margin required therefore consists of: | |
> | (i) 20% of underlying share price (250p × 20%) | 50p |
> | (ii) Adjustment to reflect exercise price above share price: 250p − 260p | (10p) |
> | | 40p |
> | Margin per contract 1000 × 40p | £ 400 |

18.5.6   The calculation of the first element remains unchanged; however in this example, the call option is 'out of the money' – in the hands of the purchaser of the option, the right to buy an asset at 260p which is only worth 250p has no intrinsic value. For this reason the writer of the option is given the benefit of the 10p difference which is subtracted from the margin requirement.

18.5.7   Writers' margin requirements are recalculated daily in the light of the movement in the underlying share price. It should be noted that these are *minimum* margin requirements that are demanded by LOCH from a member firm. It is the broker's responsibility to collect this margin from its customers and it may, therefore, be sensible for the broker to ensure that a customer writing options has free funds in excess of the minimum requirement at the time of the transaction. This avoids the situation where the firm has to finance its customers' requirements because of delays in collecting margin. By requiring from the investor a somewhat higher figure than the margin required by LOCH, the firm has a buffer against further margin calls should the option price rapidly move against the writer.

18.5.8   In many cases, firms and their customers find it more convenient to use stock as margin rather than cash. Stock can be lodged with the ISE to the order of LOCH and will be revalued (with a suitable discount or 'haircut') on a daily basis. If the value of the stock pledged is in excess of the current margin, it gives the customer scope for meeting increased requirements. For the customer, LOCH becomes a form of safe custody depot, and for the firm it means that regular margin calls on the customer are not required.

8.5.9   There are varying procedures across the market for dealing with margin once it has been collected from the customer.

8.5.10 A common practice is for clearing members to provide a bank guarantee to LOCH to cover all margins required in respect of their business. The firm then retains all margin which it has collected from its customers. This means that, so long as the total margin requirement of the firm does not exceed the bank guarantee, regular movements of cash between the firm and LOCH to cover margin changes are not required. This greatly eases the administrative process of collecting and controlling margin, although the firm still needs to ensure that it collects sufficient margin from its customers to cover their individual requirements. Moreover, the cash margins received must be held in a client money bank account (see chapter 11).

8.5.11 Many firms still choose to lodge their customers' collateral with LOCH. This ensures that it is kept separate from other stock held on a customer's behalf and also makes it less likely that the stock will be accidentally transferred back to the customer when it should still be pledged.

8.5.12 For POMs, the treatment of margin will depend on the requirements of their clearing agent. The POM will deposit any collateral received from customers with his Agent who will in turn deposit it to the order of LOCH. The POM will usually rely on his clearing agent to inform him when there is a shortfall on an individual customer's account. In this case, the clearing agent will collect any shortfall from the POM, who is then responsible for collecting this from his customer. Alternatively there may be a bank guarantee from the POM to his clearing agent covering potential shortfalls.

8.5.13 Whichever of these procedures is followed, there is a common requirement to maintain collateral ledgers which state clearly what assets have been pledged by customers and where they are held. This is discussed further in section 18.7 of this chapter.

18.6   Conventional options

18.6.1 Conventional or traditional options were the only permitted form of options before the introduction of traded options. Nowadays, they make up only a very small proportion of total options business transacted and are principally dealt in stocks where traded options are not available. As more stocks become quoted on the traded options market, turnover in conventional options is likely to decrease further. Due to the relatively minor role played by conventional options, it is only intended to describe them in overview.

18.6.2   Conventional options are personal contracts between the 'giver' and the 'taker' of option moneys. The giver is the purchaser and the taker is the writer of the option. Options are granted for a three-month period with settlement of the premium not usually taking place until the seventh account day subsequent to the date of dealing. The option can be exercised on the penultimate day of each account prior to the expiry date.

18.6.3   Due to the small size of the conventional options market, there are currently very few organisations willing to make a market in them. Investors wishing to deal in conventional options will first contact their broker who will, in turn, contact a market maker and enter into a transaction at a negotiated price.

18.6.4   Options can be for 'the put', 'the call' or 'the double'. The first provides the giver of option money the right to sell shares at a pre-determined price; the second provides the giver the right to purchase shares at a pre-determined price; and the third provides the giver with the right to buy or sell shares at a pre-determined price. 'The double' may seem to mean that the giver of the option money cannot lose, i.e. he can choose whether to buy or sell the stock depending on how its price has moved. In practice, this is not often the case since the option premium is likely to be quite high and, in order to achieve a profit, the price must have moved from the exercise price by more than the premium. Hence, although 'doubles' are always likely to be exercised, profitability is not guaranteed to the giver of the option money.

18.6.5   A typical conventional option deal might be 'given 62p for the call, 2,000 ABC @ 870p'. This means that the customer pays a sum of £1,240 (2,000 @ 62p) plus commission in return for the right to purchase 2,000 ABC shares at £8.70. In this example, the option money (the price paid for the option) is 62p, and the striking price (the price at which the option can be exercised) is £8.70. The giver of the premium will only exercise his option if the underlying share price rises above £8.70. Having paid 62p for each option, the giver will only be in profit if the underlying share price rises above £9.32.

8.6.6   The option money becomes due on the settlement day of the account in which the option is exercised or when it is allowed to lapse, whichever is the later. This can mean that the premium is not paid for three months after the deal was entered into, although some firms require their customers to pay as if for a normal purchase of shares.

8.6.7   If the giver of options money wishes to exercise his option, he must notify his broker who, in turn, must notify the market maker (prior to 2.45 p.m.) on any 'declaration day' during the life of the option. On declaration, a contract note will be issued for the purchase or sale of securities (as appropriate) at the striking price. If an option has not been exercised by the expiry date, then it is deemed to have been abandoned.

8.6.8   It should be noted that the benefits arising under a conventional options contract cannot be transferred, in contrast to traded options.

8.6.9   Where a customer is a taker of option money, there are no formal requirements for him to provide any 'margin' in the event of the market price of the underlying security moving against him. It is therefore prudent for firms to set up procedures to ensure that the potential loss to a customer taking option money is monitored and that appropriate steps are taken if the potential loss becomes excessive in relation to the client's resources. However, at present there is no industry norm in this regard.

8.7   Accounting for traded options

Traded options

8.7.1   It is only proposed to consider in detail accounting for options within clearing firms (who deal directly with LOCH) and POMs (who deal through clearing agents). Clearing agents are few in number and their accounting records are complex since all positions must be analysed by POM and therein by customer. This means that their accounting records will be similar to, but more detailed than, those of a clearing firm.

8.7.2   The procedures are broadly the same for clearing firms and POMs, except that the source of the information received varies according to whether the recipient is a clearing firm (receiving information direct from LOCH) or a POM (receiving information from his clearing agent).

8.7.3   As a simplified example, assume that a customer writes five contracts at a premium of 14p. LOCH charges £1 per contract, in addition to which the clearing firm charges 1.5 per cent commission to its customer (note that this example ignores VAT).

			£
Premium: 14p × 1,000 × 5	=		700.00
LOCH charges	=		5.00
Firm's commission 1½% × £700	=		10.05
			684.95

The posting that the firm should make for this transaction is:

Dr LOCH	695.00	
Cr customer		684.95
Cr commission		10.05

18.7.4   If the firm was a POM then the only difference is that the debit will be to the clearing agent's account, and the charges will be higher since they will need to cover the clearing agent's fees as well as those for LOCH.

18.7.5   The customer is required to settle his account on the next business day. The balance with LOCH/clearing agent will be the net of all purchased and written options dealt by the firm on the previous day and is also required to settle on the next day. Hence an important control is that the LOCH/clearing agent account clears down to zero on a daily basis.

18.7.6   Even though all monetary balances in respect of traded options should clear the day after the bargain was dealt, it is still very important for firms to maintain a record of all open options positions. This is so that it can monitor risk on written options and can confirm that a customer is entitled to exercise an option when he gives the necessary instructions.

18.7.7   Best practice with respect to accounting for traded options is set out in appendix 3 of the *Traded Options Users' Manual* and is summarised below.

18.7.8   With written options, the records should show how the option is being margined, for example by a deposit of stock, by cash, by a guarantee, or whether a spread or a straddle is in place thereby reducing any requirement.

18.7.9   A detailed collateral ledger should also be kept, cross-referenced to the records of open positions. This ledger should show, in respect of each customer, all collateral received for written options and where this collateral is being kept. Underlying stock which is received as collateral may be passed to the ISE to the order of LOCH (either directly for clearing firms, or through the clearing agent for POMs) or may be kept at the firm's bank or other safe custody depots. In these circumstances the stock must be clearly designated as belonging to a customer and as being pledged against traded option margin requirements.

3.7.10 Any cash received as margin from a customer may either be passed to LOCH/clearing agent or, where part of such margin is retained by the firm, be held in a separately designated customer's collateral bank account. In this case, the firm must ensure that it is in compliance with the client money rules with respect to margined transactions. This is considered in more detail in section 11.6 of chapter 11.

3.7.11 On a daily basis, the clearing firm will receive a listing of open positions and the corresponding margin requirements from LOCH. This information only shows total open positions in a particular stock with no analysis by customer. This is why the firm's own records need to be detailed, in particular showing the exposure to each customer. The clearing firm must be able to calculate margin requirements on each customer's open positions on a daily basis. Given that clearing firms are likely to have a large number of customers, and that margin calculations can be complex, the maintenance of open positions and calculation of margin requirements are normally computerised.

3.7.12 The clearing firm should agree open positions between its records and those produced by LOCH. This may not be an easy exercise because LOCH gives the net position in a particular series across all customers. Accordingly, the firm has to total all positions shown in its records in order to agree to LOCH. This exercise should be carried out periodically as a check on the completeness and accuracy of the firm's own records on which the margin requirements of its customers are based.

3.7.13 For POMs, the information received from the clearing agent is likely to be far more dtailed than that produced by LOCH. In particular, it will be in customer order and will show margin requirements and collateral pledged. Hence, it is less important for the POM to maintain his own detailed record of open positions.

3.7.14 It is important for both POMs and their clearing agents to maintain a detailed collateral ledger which is regularly agreed to reports produced by LOCH or, in the case of a POM, its clearing agent. For clearing firms the collateral ledger should be regularly cross-referenced to total margin requirements in order to ensure that shortfalls do not arise on individual customer accounts.

3.7.15 It should be noted that under TSA and ISE rules, firms must ensure that they have two separate letters in which customers acknowledge that they understand the risk involved in dealing in options. An example of the letter of authority required under ISE rules in given in section 8 of the *Traded Options Users' Manual* which must be signed by the customer before he commences dealing. This letter must be lodged with the Central Registry of the Options Market not later than thirty days after the date of the customer's signature. The letter required under TSA rules is the normal client agreement letter and risk warning which firms must have under the conduct of business rules and is not a specific requirement for options customers.

18.7.16 Both POMs and clearing firms should set out clearly in their client agreement letters that they have the right to close down traded option positions where the customer can be reasonably expected not to be able to fulfil the terms of the option contract. One source of evidence for such a view would be the failure to pay margin. In closing down a written option contract, the firm purchases in the market the options on behalf of the customer and thereby realises the loss which the customer must bear.

Disclosure of options balances and related matters

18.7.17 There are few specific disclosure requirements with respect to traded options. The balances on customer accounts should be treated in the same way as other items in these accounts as discussed in chapter 9. In practice, many firms maintain a separate account for customers' traded options transactions, with the balance on the account representing transactions entered into on the previous day. The balance with LOCH or the clearing agent will be treated as a market balance.

18.7.18 The only particular point of note relates to the treatment of margin calls made on customers which have not been paid. It will generally be appropriate to show this claim as a debtor with the corresponding credit included within counterparty creditors.

18.7.19 Special requirements relate to client money on margined transactions and these are considered in detail in section 11.6 of chapter 11.

18.7.20 The existence of any guarantees which have been given by the firm to LOCH or its clearing agent should be disclosed as contingent liabilities.

Conventional options

18.7.21 As explained above, option moneys are not payable until the later of declaration or expiry. Therefore, it is important to keep balances represented by option moneys separate from balances arising from other dealing activities. Such balances should only be transferred to ordinary dealing accounts on the appropriate settlement day.

8.7.22 It is also important to ensure that customers settle their option moneys on the due date. Some firms adopt a policy of requiring givers of option money to settle the balance on the next account day, notwithstanding the fact that settlement is not due until declaration or expiry. This method has the benefit of reducing the possibility of bad debts when, for example, the share price moves against the giver thereby rendering the option worthless.

8.7.23 Usually option moneys due to, or from, the option market maker are recorded in the residual jobbers ledger where they will remain as open items until they become due for settlement. Once the option money becomes due for settlement, it will be settled directly with the market maker.

Disclosure

8.7.24 Conventional option transactions give rise to no special requirements, other than those discussed in chapter 9 on customer balances and chapter 8 on residual jobbers ledger balances.

18.8 Audit

18.8.1 There are two types of objectives that should be addressed by the auditor of a firm transacting options business for customers on an agency basis as set out below. The audit of options business where the firm is trading for its own account is considered in paragraphs 18.8.23 to 18.8.27.

Statutory reporting objectives
18.8.2 These may be listed as:

(i) debtors and creditors with respect to options business are genuine and are completely and accurately included in the balance sheet;
(ii) adequate but not excessive provisions have been made for amounts which may prove to be irrecoverable;
(iii) balances and other information in respect of options business are presented in the balance sheet in accordance with the rules of TSA, accounting standards and the Companies Act as appropriate.

Additional reporting objectives
18.8.3 These are specific matters which auditors are required to report on under the rules of the Financial Regulations of TSA as follows:

(i) the systems for the agreement and reconciliation of options balances are adequate and such procedures are carried out at appropriate intervals (rule 90.03d (i));

(ii) adequate procedures and controls are in operation for reporting and investigating the ageing and analysis of options balances (rule 90.03d (iii));

(iii) adequate procedures have been established for monitoring the firm's counterparty risk exposures and providing appropriate levels of management with the information necessary for them to make relevant, timely and informed decisions to control such risks (rule 90.03d (iv).

It is also necessary for the auditor to consider adherence to client money rules as applied to margined transactions. This is dealt with in detail in chapter 11 on client money and is not repeated here.

18.8.4 Since options are simply another form of financial instrument that customers may deal in, much of the audit work set out in chapter 9 on customer balances is also relevant here. As a result, only the special considerations relating to options transactions – in particular the higher risk aspects of written options – are considered here. It should be noted that the 'market' side of the audit is greatly simplified by the fact that there will only ever be one market counterparty, either LOCH or, for a POM, the clearing agent.

Internal control

18.8.5 For the audit of customer balances a list of control objectives is set out in chapter 9, in particular with respect to the completeness and accuracy of postings and with respect to credit control. Due to the specific risks associated with written options, the credit control function is especially important, and additional control features to those discussed in chapter 9 are as follows:

18.8.6 *Control objectives*

(i) All options bargains are completely and accurately recorded.
(ii) All recorded options bargains are genuine.
(iii) All payments to, and receipts from, LOCH/clearing agents are properly recorded.

Possible errors under these headings, relating to options, are:

- option bargains omitted from the records;
- option details incorrectly recorded in the records;

- spurious options recorded which reduce the recorded risk (e.g. spurious spreads);
- options bargains posted twice;
- options bargains recorded in the wrong customer account.

18.8.7   Control procedures to prevent such errors include:

— all unmatched transactions followed up;
— daily reconciliation of the LOCH/clearing agent account and proof that it clears to zero;
— record kept by the firm of all open positions for each customer;
— contract notes sent out for all options bargains;
— statements of open option positions (purchased and written) sent to customers on a regular basis;
— regular agreement of aggregate open positions to LOCH/clearing agent reports;
— segregation of duties between option dealers/option settlement department;
— regular bank reconciliations.

18.8.8   *Control objective: Adequate margin is provided by customers who write options*
Possible errors under this heading are:

- one customer's margin being used to secure another customer's requirement;
- insufficient margin leading to an exposure for the firm;
- margin held in unsuitable form.

18.8.9   The following control procedures may exist to ensure that adequate margin is provided by customers who write options:

— up-to-date register of traded options customers maintained;
— all of the required letters are in place before a customer can deal in traded options;
— collateral ledger kept;
— regular agreement of collateral ledger to LOCH/clearing agent reports;
— segregation of duties between option dealers/option settlement staff;
— customer margin set at levels over and above the minimum required by LOCH;
— margin conditions set out in customer agreement letter;
— margin requirements calculated daily;
— margin calculations (and calls) made during the day when large price movements take place;

— regular check that margin requirements adequately met by collateral pledged;
— all margin shortfalls over a preset limit or a certain age reported to management;
— collateral ledger regularly reviewed by senior management for suitability of margin;
— surplus cash traded option margins are held in separately designated customers' collateral bank accounts;
— open position closed out on the instructions of senior management when a margin shortfall persists;
— summaries of margin pledged versus margin required regularly produced and reviewed by senior management.

Analytical review

18.8.10   It is unlikely that analytical review type procedures will be of much use in this area.

Substantive testing

18.8.11   The main areas of substantive testing are:

(i)   direct confirmation from LOCH/clearing agent of balances, open positions, collateral held and collateral due;
(ii) a circularisation of traded options customers (covering open positions and collateral); and
(iii) ensuring that adequate margin has been pledged by customers.

These tests all aim at proving that positions are correctly recorded and that adequate margin has been pledged by customers.

Confirmation from LOCH/clearing agent
18.8.12   To verify the firm's records of options transactions, the auditor should obtain a listing of open positions, balances and collateral pledged from a third party source. For the audit of a clearing member, this is obtained directly from LOCH whereas for the audit of a POM, this should be requested from the firm's clearing agent. The request for confirmation of open positions and collateral should be signed by a suitable authority within the firm and despatched at least two weeks prior to the balance sheet date.

18.8.13   With the statement from LOCH, the total position in each option series will have to be reconciled to the individual customers' positions according to the firm's records. The statement from the clearing agent will usually be split by customer and so no further analysis is required.

Circularisation of traded options customers

8.8.14 This should be carried out as part of the circularisation of customers discussed in chapter 9. It should be ensured that a representative sample of traded option customers are included in the overall population. It is important that all open positions (whether purchased or written) and all margin held (whether or not actually pledged) in respect of a particular customer are included in the letter.

8.8.15 These circularisations provide evidence that:
(a) all positions are completely and accurately recorded in the firm's records; and
(b) all positions and margins are in respect of bona fide customers.

Adequacy of margin

8.8.16 Having determined the overall completeness and accuracy of the firm's records with respect to traded options positions and collateral pledged, it is then necessary to ensure that individual customers have provided the firm with sufficient margin.

8.8.17 As noted in the list of control procedures, firms should produce regular reports of margin pledged versus margin required which are circulated for review by senior management. If one of these reports has been prepared at the balance sheet date, it will be necessary to test-check its compilation and then enquire into any margin shortfalls. The test-check of the compilation of this report will involve agreeing the calculation of the margin requirement for a sample of customers with open positions and also ensuring that any collateral provided has been correctly valued and aggregated with any cash paid in arriving at the total margin put up by the customer. Particular care may be needed where margin calls are satisfied by a transfer from the customer's main dealing account, since the traded options records may indicate an adequate margin position, but the firm is exposed due to an incorrect debit in the main account.

8.8.18 If such a report is not produced, the auditor will first need to consider whether the firm's systems of monitoring and controlling counterparty risk are adequate. Next, the auditor will need to consider whether positions are adequately margined. This will mean requesting the firm to produce a report on margin requirements as at the balance sheet date and test-checking this as discussed above. It is important that the production of such a report is discussed with the firm at the planning stage to ensure that it is available at the appropriate time. Having arrived at a listing of margin shortfalls, the auditor should consider these as he would any other potential bad debt.

The audit of conventional options

18.8.19 The considerations set out above for traded options will broadly apply to conventional options. The main features are set out below.

Internal control

18.8.20 *Control objective: Conventional option dealings are properly conducted, recorded and controlled*
The following procedures may exist as a means of controlling the conventional options business (in addition to the controls with respect to bargain capture and credit control set out in chapter 9):

— balances representing conventional option moneys kept separate from other customer accounts;
— customers required to settle conventional options moneys on or before the due date;
— monitoring of each customer's potential loss arising on unexpired positions;
— bargains with customers matched regularly with bargains open with option dealers.

Analytical review

18.8.21 There is little scope for analytical review procedures in this area.

Substantive testing

18.8.22 Particular features of the audit of conventional options are as follows:

(a) 'Stock Agreement' (a misnomer since, with options there is no stock) – for all customers (CAD and SOB), the option account should be analysed into the component bargains, and it should be checked that for each open bargain there is a corresponding open item with the market maker, and vice versa. For all instances where this is not the case, explanations should be obtained.
(b) Circularisation of customers and the conventional options market makers to confirm open positions and premiums due.
(c) Review of the adequacy of provisions for bad debts which can arise in two instances:
    (i) givers of option money (debit balances) – if the share price moves so as to render exercise unprofitable, the customer might be unable/unwilling to settle the option moneys due. This can be audited by means of verifying post-balance sheet settlement; and

(ii) takers of option money (credit balances) – if the option is exercised against the customer, he may be required to purchase (or sell) the stock in the market to close his position, resulting in a net loss which he may be unable to settle. A review should be made of all options open at the balance sheet date which are exercised subsequently in order to identify any such losses. In addition, a review should be made of the potential exposure on any options still open when the audit field work is completed.

Principal dealing in traded options

8.8.23   A firm may deal on its own account in traded options for three main purposes, firstly as a committed market maker in the traded options market, secondly as an adjunct to the firm's existing market making activities (e.g. where an equity market maker uses options to hedge positions) and thirdly where the firm chooses to use surplus cash resources to make a short-term investment.

8.8.24   In the first two instances, the firm should control and operate its options dealing in the same way as a normal market maker in equities (*see* chapter 14). In the third instance, the firm should ensure that, as for any other short-term investments, senior management is aware of, and approves, positions taken. Audit procedures should follow those adopted for any other short-term investment.

8.8.25   Where a firm has material balances in respect of traded options dealing on its own account, it should disclose in its financial statements the accounting policies adopted for the valuation of traded options positions.

8.8.26   The value of traded options positions will be audited as for normal bull and bear positions. Where positions are marked to market, or for investments, where the lower of cost and market value is appropriate, it will be necessary to review the firm's stated accounting policy with respect to traded options dealing, to determine whether it is appropriate to the circumstances of the individual firm and whether it is consistent with that adopted in previous years.

8.8.27   The valuation policy adopted for positions in options contracts will depend on whether they are being used to hedge some other instrument or are being used purely as a trading instrument. This is discussed in more detail in section 4.10 of chapter 4.

18.9 Capital requirements

18.9.1 Where a firm transacts business in traded options, there are two areas where it requires regulatory capital under TSA's rules. Where all business is transacted on behalf of customers, only CRR is relevant. Where the firm also transacts options business on its own behalf, there will be the need to consider PRR.

CRR

18.9.2 TSA rule 63.12 states that where:

(i) a firm has purchased on behalf of a customer an option where the customer has no liability to make any payment other than the initial purchase price of the option; and

(ii) more than one business day has passed since the settlement date of that purchase; and

(iii) the amount owed to the firm in connection with the purchase exceeds the realisable market value of the option;

the amount of the excess shall be added to the CRR.

18.9.3 Where a firm purchases a traditional option, either on its own account or on behalf of a customer, and does not pass the premium over to the writer, the CRR is zero. In all other cases, the amount of the traditional option premium passed to the writer shall be added to the CRR. Usually this means that CRR does not arise until after the settlement day of the premium.

Margined transactions

18.9.4 TSA rule 63.13 states that an amount equal to the total of margins recoverable from customers but not yet paid shall be added to the CRR, except that those balances which have been outstanding for less than five business days shall be excluded. If the aggregate of any margin-business customer's collateral and his equity balance results in a net amount that is owed to the firm, that amount shall be added to the CRR to the extent that it is not secured.

PRR

18.9.5 There are a variety of complex rules relating to PRR which are applied according to the nature of trading within the firm under consideration. Rule 62.20b of the Financial Regulations of TSA sets out the normal PRR requirement for Traded Options. However, there are a number of alternative treatments which may be available if the options meet certain requirements or are being used to hedge other positions, further details on these are set out in TSA rules 62.02, 62.08, 62.15, and 62.40.

Other considerations

18.9.6   It should be noted that where a firm is a clearing member of LOCH, it may give a guarantee to LOCH in respect of outstanding margins as described above. Under TSA Financial Regulations rule 50.08, the amount of any guarantees given by the firm must be reported to TSA and a deduction from capital may be made having regard to the nature of the guarantee. It is understood that where guarantees, such as a guarantee to LOCH in respect of margins, are normal market practice (effectively required to enable trading to be settled on an organised basis), then currently TSA make no deduction from capital. However, it is necessary to write to TSA under the requirements of rule 50.08 to have this confirmed. The auditor should therefore ensure that he inspects the correspondence between the firm and TSA to ensure the correct deduction from capital is made.

19 Financial Futures and Options

19.1 Introduction

19.1.1 The London International Financial Futures Exchange (LIFFE) was opened during 1982 in the Royal Exchange building in the City of London. The market provides facilities for dealing in financial futures and options contracts for a variety of different financial instruments (e.g. government bonds and foreign currencies) and financial indicators (e.g. interest rates and stock indices). Such contracts were first developed in Chicago and their success there meant that demand grew for a similar market in London. One of the main reasons for the success of such markets is the continuing volatility of exchange rates and interest rates against which, as will be shown below, financial futures and options can provide protection.

19.1.2 The success of first the US futures markets and then LIFFE has subsequently led to other financial futures markets opening around the world (principally in Singapore, Japan, Canada and Australia).

19.1.3 There are two broad categories of transactions which may be dealt on LIFFE:

(i) money market related transactions in interest rate or exchange rate contracts; and
(ii) stockmarket related transactions in government bonds or the FTSE 100 Index.

19.1.4 Two financial futures contracts and their related options contracts of particular relevance to the securities industry, are those based on UK government bonds (gilts) and the FTSE 100 Index and these are considered in detail in sections 19.2 and 19.3 below. Both categories of transactions are traded and settled in a similar way although the contract specifications are somewhat different. Precise details of the contracts currently traded can be obtained from LIFFE.

19.1.5   As noted in chapter 18, plans have been announced to merge LTOM and LIFFE, with full-scale integration expected in late 1990. The exact details of the merger were not available at the time of writing and we do not speculate here on the likely implications. Rather, we consider the main characteristics of financial futures and options, characteristics which are likely to remain unchanged even after the merger of the market place in which they are dealt.

19.2 Financial futures

19.2.1   A financial futures contract is an exchange-traded contract for the delivery of standardised amounts of the underlying financial instrument at a future date. The price for the financial instrument is agreed on the day the contract is bought or sold and gains or losses are incurred as a result of subsequent price fluctuations. Unlike foward contracts, future contracts are readily tradeable, reflecting the standardisation of contract terms.

19.2.2   The purchase or sale of a financial futures contract is, therefore, a commitment to make or take delivery of a specific financial instrument, at a pre-determined date in the future, for which the price is established at the time of the initial transaction. Transactions are actually entered into through 'open outcry' on the floor of LIFFE.

19.2.3   Contracts are standardised which means that participants can buy and sell them freely on LIFFE with precise knowledge of the contracts being traded.

19.2.4   The contract specifies both the type of the financial instrument and its 'quality' in terms of such matters as coupon rate and maturity. The instruments specified must be delivered at or during a specified month in the future (known as delivery date) – usually in a cycle of March, June, September and December. Exact delivery details vary according to the nature of the instrument – for example, a number of different actual gilts are deliverable in settlement of a gilts future, with complex price adjustments required. For contracts based on (for example) the FTSE 100 index no physical delivery can take place, and settlement is based on a cash payment calculated on the movement in the index.

19.2.5   Although contracts are traded between the buyer and the seller on the exchange floor, each has an obligation not to the other, but to the

319

central futures clearing house which, for LIFFE, is the ICCH (the International Commodities Clearing House) which is discussed in section 19.4 below. This feature ensures that the futures market is largely free of credit risk.

19.2.6   Participants may offset equal numbers of bought and sold contracts of the same type and delivery month and thereby close out a position without actually communicating with the original counterparty. The transaction is simply closed down once it has been notified to ICCH. This means that individuals do not actually need to take or make delivery on contracts. Indeed, as will be seen in the examples below, for some types of futures contracts such as stock index futures, delivery is impossible.

19.2.7   As the market price moves, holders of open futures contracts will see corresponding profits and losses arising on their positions. The standard nature of each futures contract makes such gains and losses easy to measure. Movements are tracked in terms of minimum price fluctuations allowed by LIFFE which are known as 'ticks' and which carry a fixed value for each contract type.
   For example:

- for gilts, the minimum price fluctuation is $\frac{1}{32}$ per £1 nominal. As the nominal value of each gilt futures contract is worth £50,000, the tick is worth £15.625 (i.e. £50,000 $\times$ $\frac{1}{32}$ $\times$ $\frac{1}{100}$). This means that the change in the value of a contract is £15.625 for each tick price movement;
- for the FTSE 100 Index futures contract, the minimum price movement, or tick, is one point on the value of the Index and each tick has a stipulated value of £25. This means that, if an individual buys one contract, then for every 1.0 increase in the index the individual makes a profit of £25.

Uses of financial futures

19.2.8   There are two reasons for entering into a financial futures transaction: either as part of a hedging strategy or for pure trading. Hedging may be used to reduce the risk of loss through adverse price movements in interest rates or share prices and is effected by taking a position that is equal and opposite to an existing or anticipated position in the future. In the following simplified example, we show how futures may be used to cover a position exposed to the risk of upward movement in the equity markets.

19.2.9   Suppose that it is 1 May, and an investment manager considers that the market will rise prior to 1 August when he is due to receive £5m to purchase a diversified portfolio of equities. He can get the benefit of investing this sum at today's market level by buying sufficient FTSE 100 Index futures contracts.

On 1 May, the September contract (the nearest contract following the target date of 1 August) is priced at 2,000.00. This means that one contract is worth £50,000 (i.e. the price of the index is 2,000.00, which is 2,000 ticks, each of which is worth £25). Hence the Manager needs to purchase 100 contracts (because 100 × £50,000 = £5m).

Let us suppose that equity prices do rise and by 1 August, the FTSE 100 Index and the September futures contract both stand at 2,200.0 (i.e. both have increased by 10 per cent).

The value of each futures contract has increased to £55,000 (i.e. 2,200.0 × £25). Hence 100 contracts are worth £5.5m.

Our investment manager will then sell his futures contracts and realise a £0.5m profit. This added to the £5m anticipated receipt, leaves him with £5.5m to invest.

The FTSE 100 Index has risen by 10 per cent, and the funds available to the manager have risen by 10 per cent which means he has benefited from the rising stock markets without having directly owned any stock over the period.

9.2.10 Trading in financial futures contracts enables individuals to seek profits from rises or falls in interest rate or stock markets without necessarily having to buy or sell the underlying financial instrument. It can be seen from the worked example above that our investment manager could equally have been a trader taking the view that equity prices were about to rise. If the opposite view was taken, that prices were about to fall, then the trader would instead sell the FTSE 100 Index contract.

9.2.11 Practically, it would be impossible for anything to be delivered with respect to the FTSE 100 Index futures contract since this would require fractional quantities of each of the 100 shares whose prices form the Index. This means that if a contract has not been closed down by expiry, then at expiry, it will be closed down automatically by LIFFE with the investor having to settle in cash the net profit or loss.

19.3 Financial options

19.3.1 As explained in Chapter 18 an option contract gives the purchaser the right, but not the obligation, to assume a position in the relevant financial instrument or futures contract, at a set exercise price at some time in the future. In return for this right the purchaser pays a premium to the seller (otherwise known as the writer) of the option.

19.3.2   The difference between an options contract and a futures contract is that a futures contract carries a commitment to purchase or sell some financial instrument, whereas an options contract conveys merely the right (which need not be exercised) to assume such a position.

19.3.3   LIFFE options are very similar to traded options (discussed in detail in chapter 18) in that the purchaser of an option has losses limited to the value of the premium, but unlimited potential for profits. For option writers the reverse is true with profits limited to the premium but scope for unlimited losses.

19.3.4   As for traded options, there are call options (which give the purchaser the right to take up a long position in the underlying financial instrument) and put options (which entitles the purchaser to assume a short position).
    There are two broad types of option traded on LIFFE:

(i)   options on futures which give the option purchaser the right to assume a long or short position in a particular financial futures contract; and
(ii)   options on physical cash which give the option purchaser the right to buy or sell a particular currency.

LIFFE's option contracts have expiry dates in a cycle of March, June, September and December and as for traded options, each expiry date will have a number of exercise prices for both call and put options.

19.3.5   One of the main features of LIFFE options is that the premium is not paid 'up front' as is the case with ISE traded options. There is a requirement for an 'initial margin' payment, see paragraph 19.4.7. Further payments are only made by the purchaser if the market price of the option declines. In addition, LIFFE does not require the full potential loss to be provided as margin. Risk factors are set by LIFFE for each type of option contract, and reductions in margin are allowed, based on these factors. These features give a considerable cash flow benefit for a LIFFE option purchaser as compared with other types of option (particularly ISE traded options).

19.4   The operation of the market

Users of the market

19.4.1   The main users of LIFFE are individuals and institutions who wish to use financial futures and options to reduce their financial risk. A particular feature of the market is the presence on the trading floor of 'locals' – individuals trading on their own account, frequently providing market liquidity by taking short-term positions.

Execution

19.4.2   Orders may be originated either by firms dealing on their own account or by customers who communicate their orders via a member firm of LIFFE. The order is transmitted to the trader's booth on the floor of LIFFE and from there to the traders on the floor (known as the 'pit') who execute the order by open outcry. Details of the executed order are sent back to the member's booth. The order will be confirmed with the customer and entered onto the computerised matching system. Matched orders are registered into the clearing system, whilst unmatched orders are referred back to the member firms so that the necessary corrections can be made. All confirmed trades are published on the trading floor throughout the day.

19.4.3   Figure 19.1 summarises the execution cycle on LIFFE.

Clearing

19.4.4   Following confirmation and registration of a transaction, the contract between the buyer and seller is replaced by two different contracts:

(i)   one between the clearing house and the buyer; and
(ii) one between the clearing house and the seller.

Thus a process of novation takes place whereby the clearing house substitutes itself for each counterparty and becomes the seller to each buyer and the buyer to each seller. As mentioned above, the clearing house for LIFFE is the ICCH which is owned by the UK clearing banks.

19.4.5   The clearing cycle is summarised by Figure 19.2.

19.4.6   There are a number of different classes of membership of LIFFE:

(i)   *Individual clearing members* – who only clear their own transactions;
(ii) *General clearing members* – who can clear other members' transactions as well as their own;
(iii) *Non-clearing members* – who must clear their transactions through a general clearing member;
(iv) *Public order members* – any member (clearing or non-clearing) who can enter into transactions on behalf of customers;

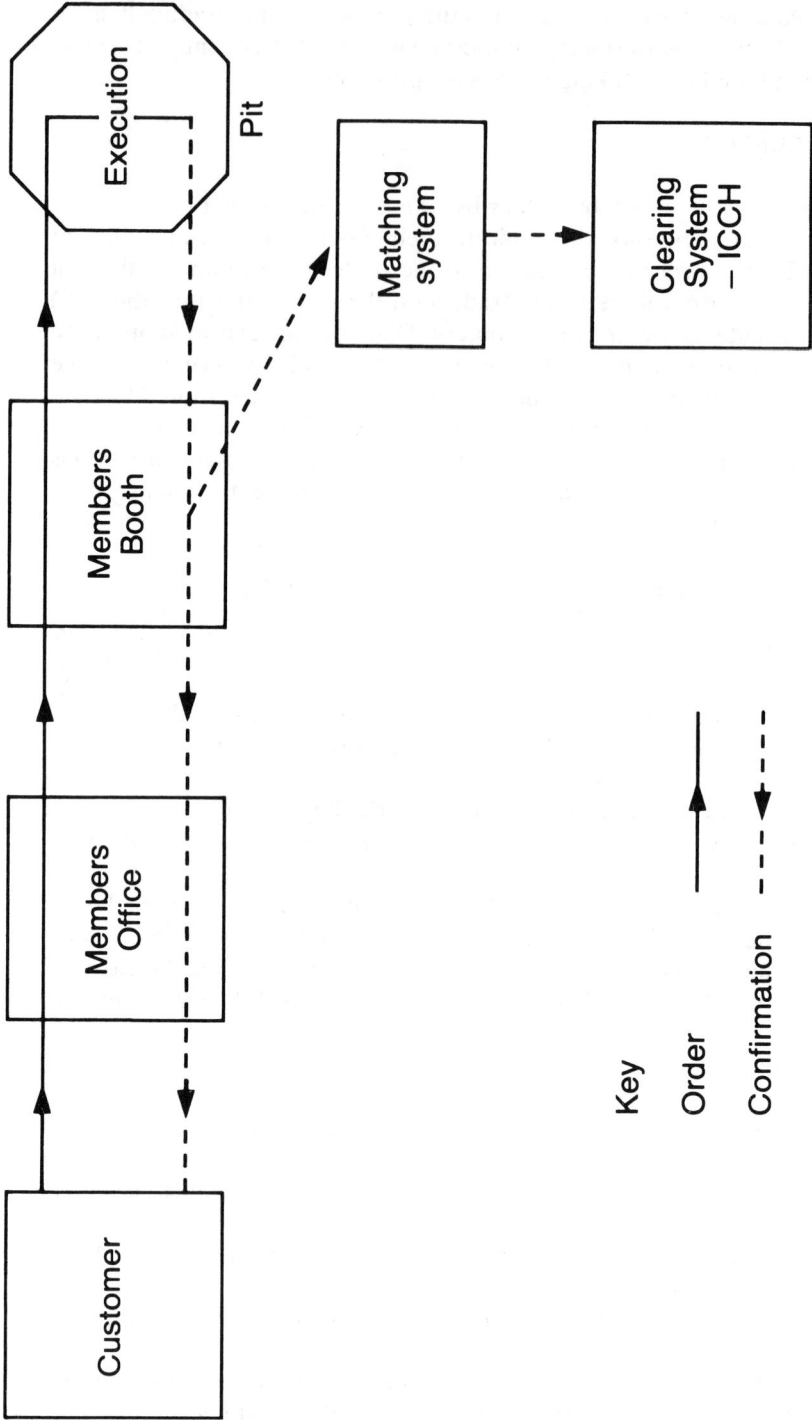

Figure 19.1 The execution cycle

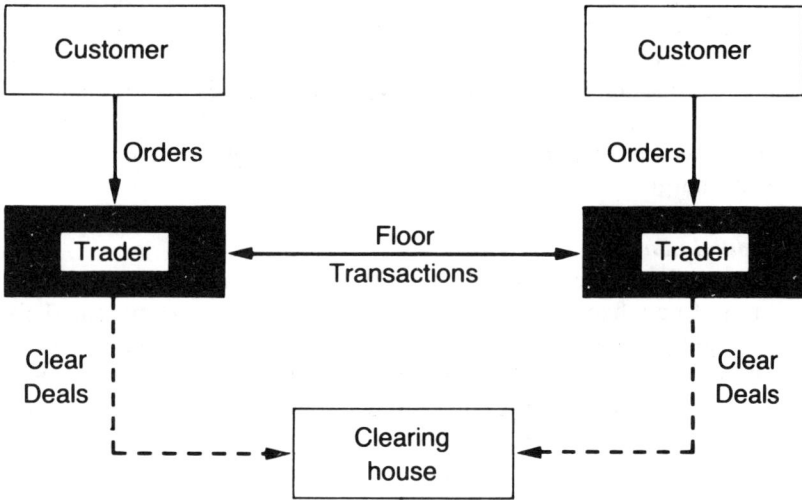

Figure 19.2 The clearing cycle

(v) *'Locals'* – a term given to LIFFE members who are only permitted to deal with other members on the floor of LIFFE. They cannot deal with or on behalf of customers.

In order to become any form of clearing member, various conditions laid down by LIFFE and ICCH must be satisfied. These conditions include minimum financial requirements.

Margin requirements

19.4.7   Margins are payable on futures and options contracts by both buyer and seller. Margin funds are held by ICCH as a means of ensuring each counterparty's ability to meet its obligations to the market, thereby enabling ICCH to provide its guarantee. As already noted above, ICCH effectively guarantees every transaction carried out on LIFFE and its willingness and ability to undertake this role depends on the financial discipline it can impose on market participants. This discipline is imposed by way of performance deposits or margin. There are three types of margin:

(i) *Initial margin*
For each transaction registered with ICCH, clearing members have to put up a fixed initial (otherwise known as deposit) margin. This margin provides an initial buffer against the risk of the contract not being honoured. ICCH could be forced to close out a contract at the current market price and could sustain a loss arising from price changes during the current day's trading. The level of initial margin varies across different contracts and reflects the price volatility of the underlying financial instrument or indicator.

(ii) *Variation margin*
This is calculated on a daily basis and represents the potential loss adjusted by the risk factor for that type of option, based on prices prevailing at the close of the previous day.

(iii) *Settlement margin*
This is the release of margin upon the closing out of a futures or an options contract. It simply reflects the difference between the price at which the contract was closed out and the previous day's variation margin.

19.4.8   As noted above, initial margin is intended to protect ICCH against the exposure arising in the period between the contract being dishonoured and the contract being closed. As variation margin is paid daily, this period is usually quite short (one or two days). Hence, the initial margin can be relatively small compared to the variation margin which is based on profits or losses arising from price movements over the life of the contract. Examples of the various types of margin and the way in which they are calculated are given in exhibit 1.

Daily settlement

19.4.9 As noted above, open financial futures and options contracts are marked to market on a daily basis and the profit or loss for the day paid over by way of variation margin. This is added to any initial margin required on new contracts and any initial and settlement margin due to be paid back on closed contracts. This gives the net cash settlement which is calculated and settled on a daily basis. Settlement of margin with ICCH in respect of the previous day's transactions is due by 10.00a.m. on the following business day.

19.4.10 There are various ways in which the firm can satisfy its margin requirements with ICCH, of which the most straightforward is to pay margins as and when due. Two other common methods are to obtain a bank guarantee (in which case the firm will need to pay a fee to its bankers and interest to ICCH on the margins due), or to place a cash deposit with ICCH of sufficient size to cover the likely amounts of margin (in which case the firm will receive interest on the unused portion of the margin). The choice between the various methods will depend on cash flows, financial cost and administrative simplicity.

19.4.11 Customers in turn are required to meet margin calls made by their public order member. It should be noted that margin requirements set by ICCH will be the minimum that a customer should ever 'put up'. Typically, firms require their customers to 'put up' more than this (either cash or some other form of collateral such as stock or a bank guarantee), to ensure that credit risk to the firm is minimised.

19.4.12 It should be noted that there are special rules which apply to client money relating to 'margined transactions'. These are defined as transactions in options, futures or other 'contracts for differences' where the customer may be required to pay margin. All client money relating to margined transactions must pass through a special client-margin bank account and must be reconciled and controlled on a daily basis. The detailed requirements are set out in section 11.6 of chapter 11 on clients' money.

Delivery/exercise of contracts

19.4.13 Most futures contracts which have not been closed out before their maturity date have to be delivered. The only exceptions are contracts such as index futures, where there is no underlying instrument and thus delivery is impossible, in which case the contract is closed down automatically by LIFFE at expiry and settled for cash. The mechanics of the delivery process vary for different types of contract; for the detailed arrangements reference should be made to the contract specifications provided by LIFFE. For all types of contracts, ICCH ascertains and advises the details of the contracts to be delivered and controls the process which makes up delivery.

19.4.14   The exercise of a call option on a futures position causes a long position to be assigned to the option purchaser and a corresponding short position to be assigned to the option writer. Conversely, the exercise of a put option on a futures position causes a short position to be assigned to the option purchaser and a corresponding long position to be assigned to the option writer. Assignment takes place at the option exercise price with the resulting futures position then being marked to market in the usual way.

19.4.15   It should be noted that the exercise of options contracts is far more common than delivery of futures contracts. One reason for this is that option contracts traded on LIFFE are exercisable over the life of the option, right up to expiry rather than only at the delivery date (as is the case with futures). The exercise of an option on cash is more complex and reference should be made to the contract specifications provided by LIFFE.

19.4.16   Upon exercise, the value of an option, by definition, is zero. Hence, the value of the option just prior to exercise has to be paid over as settlement margin. The option premium is therefore paid over partly as variation margin during the life of the option and partly as settlement margin upon exercise.

19.5 Accounting

19.5.1   We can illustrate the nature of the accounting for financial futures and options by way of a worked example and this is given in exhibit 1 to this chapter. A number of points about the nature of the accounting records need to be considered.

(i)   The only accounting entries will be in respect of margin payments/ receipts to and from customers and the clearing house. These are usually accounted for on a cash basis.

(ii)   The clearing house only monitors the net position of the firm and so does not give the positions of individual customers. Therefore, it is vital that the firm keeps separate records of each customer's positions.

(iii) The clearing house calculates margin based on the overall net position of the firm and all its customers. Therefore, the firm must be able to calculate margin requirements on each customer's position and keep this margin separate from other balances relating to that customer.

19.5.2 Where a firm does not deal directly with the clearing house but settles through a clearing agent, the accounting requirements are likely to be much reduced because the maintenance of open positions and margin requirements by customer will be carried out by the clearing agent. Nevertheless, a record will still need to be kept of customers' margin which has been passed over to the clearing agent. Here, something similar to the collateral ledger, discussed in chapter 18 on traded options, is usually maintained.

19.5.3 To describe the operation of the various accounts involved, the accounting entries for a series of transactions are set out in exhibit 1. The example is based around dealings in the long gilt contract which has a nominal value of £50,000; however, the principles illustrated by this example apply to all types of financial futures and options contracts.

19.5.4 From the worked example, it will be seen that, as a minimum, the following accounting records should be maintained:

(i) customer margin accounts (which may be split between initial and variation margin, especially where the firm prefers to keep initial margin intact);
(ii) clearing house margin account;
(iii) clearing house settlement account to which amounts relating to the closure of contracts are posted. Payment will be made out of this account to customers as they close out their position.

These records will be extended to show the firm's margin where the firm also enters into financial futures and options transactions on its own account.

19.5.5 It is generally accepted as best practice that all balances relating to futures transactions, in respect of a particular customer, should be kept separate from all his other balances.

Regulatory authorities

19.5.6 The relevant SRO for future and options business is usually the AFBD. However, a firm whose main business is in securities but which also carries on futures and options business may in certain circumstances be regulated by TSA for both securities business and futures and options business.

Accounts presentation

19.5.7 As already stated, most of the accounting balances likely to arise from financial futures and options are in respect of margins. It will be necessary to gross up customer balances in respect of margin monies due from customers but not yet paid. The simplest way to effect this will be to calculate the amount due from customers and to debit a 'customer margin due' account, and credit the normal customer margin account. Balances with the clearing house/clearing agent simply represent margins paid to that entity. They should be treated as for any other counterparty balance.

19.5.8 It should also be noted that AFBD lays down strict disclosure requirements (Financial Statements Rules 8.12 to 8.22) which member firms need to follow in preparing their financial returns.

19.6 Audit

19.6.1 If the firm being audited is regulated by TSA, the same objectives as for traded options, set out in section 18.8 of chapter 18, will apply here. There is the usual split between statutory reporting objectives and additional (i.e. regulatory) reporting objectives. The review of systems required for the additional reporting objectives should usually be carried out as part of the review of internal controls which is performed during the assessment of the statutory type objectives.

19.6.2 If the firm is regulated by the AFBD, the nature of the opinion required from the auditor is a little different to that required by TSA. These requirements are set out in rule 8.29 of the AFBD rulebook and can be summarised as follows:

    (i)   the financial statements and the statement of financial resources have been prepared in line with the detailed Financial Statements Rules (rules 8.12 to 8.22);

    (ii)   the balance sheet and profit and loss account agree with the accounting records;

    (iii)   the accounting records have been kept in line with the Financial Records Rules (rules 8.1 to 8.11);

    (iv)   all information and explanations necessary for the audit have been obtained;

    (v)   the client money rules have been complied with (section 7);

(vi)   the firm has resources of at least the minimum required by the rules;

(vii) the client property rules have been complied with (rules 19.5.46 to 19.5.48); and

(viii) the financial statements show a true and fair view.

19.6.3   All of the above have to be specifically reported on and hence it is important for the auditor to consider each in turn. Many of the requirements are broadly similar to the TSA requirements. The main difference lies with the detailed accounting records requirements which are set out in AFBD rules 8.8 to 8.10. Although many of these requirements are common sense in nature, they are detailed and in assessing the adequacy of the records, the auditor should use the rules as a checklist.

19.6.4   The rationale behind the remainder of the audit work is similar to that for TSA members even though the detailed requirements are slightly different. Therefore, it is not intended to ascribe the audit procedures discussed below to a particular rulebook.

19.6.5   It should be noted that financial futures and options are just additional types of financial instruments that customers may deal in. Therefore, much of the audit work set out in chapter 9 on customer balances is also relevant here. For this reason, only the special features of financial futures and options are dealt with, in particular the need to ensure that accounts are adequately margined. In addition, the work is simplified in comparison with other securities trading due to the fact that there will only ever be one market counterparty, either the ICCH or the clearing agent.

19.6.6   As noted in paragraph 19.4.12 above, the detailed requirements in respect of client money will be applicable and these are discussed in detail in section 11.6 of chapter 11. In addition, it is probable that firms will be holding customers' non-cash assets as margin, and in this case the requirements set out in chapter 12, on safe custody, should also be considered.

Internal control

19.6.7   A list of control objectives in respect of customer balances has already been given in chapter 9, and these should be referred to as appropriate. Additional considerations are as follows.

19.6.8 *Control objectives*
(i) All bargains are completely and accurately recorded.
(ii) All recorded bargains are genuine.
(iii) All payments to, and receipts from the ICCH/clearing agent are properly recorded.

Possible errors under these headings, relating to financial futures and options, are:

- contracts omitted from the records;
- contracts incorrectly recorded in the records;
- contracts recorded in the wrong customer account;
- spurious closing contracts recorded, thereby reducing the recorded risk;
- contracts posted twice.

19.6.9 Control procedures to prevent such errors include:

— all unmatched deals followed up on a daily basis;
— contract notes sent to customers for all deals done;
— daily reconciliation of ICCH/clearing agent account to the firm's records (both for margin and positions);
— segregation of duties between futures dealers and futures settlement staff;
— regular bank reconciliations;
— statements sent to customers on a regular basis detailing all open positions in financial options and futures.

19.6.10 *Control objective: Adequate margin is provided by customers for all open contracts*
Possible errors under this heading are:

- one customer's margin being used to secure another customer's requirement;
- rapid price movements leading to sudden, large margin requirements;
- insufficient margin received leading to a potential exposure to the firm;
- margin held in an unsuitable form.

19.6.11 The following control procedures may exist to ensure that adequate margin, in the proper form, is provided by customers on all open contracts:

— collateral ledger maintained;
— collateral ledger regularly reviewed by senior management for suitability of margin;

- margin requirements calculated daily;
- daily check to ensure that margin requirements are adequately met by collateral pledged;
- in-house limits set for individual customers and dealers beyond which management approval to deal is required;
- margin over and above the minimum imposed by ICCH/clearing agent required by the firm;
- clients' margins paid into the firm are kept separate from other clients' funds;
- intra-day margins calculations can be and are carried out when large price movements take place;
- margin requirements clearly set out in the customer agreement letter (which should be in place before a customer starts dealing in financial futures), including the right of the firm to close down open positions at the expense of the customer if margin due is not paid;
- contracts are closed down when a margin shortfall persists;
- summaries of margin pledged versus margin required, and exception reports of overdue margins regularly produced and reviewed by senior management.

Analytical review

9.6.12 It is unlikely that analytical review procedures will be of benefit in this area.

Substantive testing

9.6.13 The main areas of substantive testing are:

(i) confirmation from ICCH/clearing agent;
(ii) circularisation of customers who deal in financial futures and options (covering both open positions and margin); and
(iii) ensuring that adequate margin has been received from customers.

These all aim at proving that positions are completely and accurately recorded and that adequate margin has been received from customers.

Confirmation from ICCH/clearing agent
9.6.14 The purpose of obtaining this confirmation is to obtain a listing of open positions, margins paid and cash balances from a third party source. The request for confirmation should be signed by a suitable authority within the firm and despatched at least two weeks prior to the balance sheet date. Having obtained such a listing of open positions, they should be reconciled to the open positions of individual customers, as shown in the firm's records.

19.6.15   When the firm relies on a clearing agent for settlement of its futures business, the agent will usually provide detailed position reports together with the margin requirements and actual margin received analysed by customer. In this case, it will simply be necessary to agree the balances on the individual margin accounts back to the records kept by the firm. This will either be to actual balances on the ledger, or, where margin is passed directly to the clearing agent, to a collateral ledger. However, care should be taken to ensure that margin received from any client in excess of his requirement has not been applied against another client's deficit. Where two customers are connected and the firm wishes to make such an offset, it should ensure it has written agreements from the customers concerned.

Circularisation of customers dealing in futures

19.6.16   A representative sample of financial futures and options customers should be included in the overall population of customers circularised, as discussed in chapter 9. It is important that all open positions and margin received in respect of a particular customer are included.

19.6.17   These details will either be taken from the firm's own records or from position statements provided by the firm's clearing agent. It may be that the firm simply sends statements provided by the clearing firm direct to its customers. If this is the case, these statements should be accompanied by a letter asking the customer to confirm directly to the auditors that the statement is correct.

19.6.18   These circularisations referred to in paragraphs 19.6.14 to 19.6.17 are aimed at providing evidence that:

(a) all positions (whether set out in the firm's own records or on statements provided by the firm's clearing agent) are completely and accurately recorded; and
(b) all positions and margins are in respect of bona fide customers with no 'cross pledging' of margin or offsetting of one customer's positions with another.

Adequacy of margin

19.6.19   Having determined the completeness and accuracy of the firm's records with respect to futures positions and margin pledged, it is then necessary to ensure that individual customers have pledged sufficient margin on their accounts.

19.6.20   As noted in the lists of control procedures, firms should regularly produce reports of margin received from customers compared to the margin required. So long as they have been suitably test-checked, these reports can be used to identify customers with a shortfall at the balance sheet date.

.6.21 A firm which is a clearing member of ICCH will need to calculate (daily) the margin requirement on the account of each customer. As these firms are likely to have a large number of such customers, and the margin calculations can be complex, this process is likely to be computerised (indeed software packages are available for the maintenance of open positions and the calculation of margin requirements). In such cases, the auditor should test-check a sample of margin calculations and then compare the requirement with the total margin received, according to the customer's margin account. This will involve verifying the initial margin and then checking the prices used in calculating the variation margin to the financial press.

.6.22 For non-clearing members, all of the required information should be supplied by the clearing agent in the form of position and margin statements. These should be produced for each customer of the firm and should enable shortfalls to be identified easily.

.6.23 Having arrived at a listing of margin shortfalls, the auditor should consider these as he would any other potential bad debt.

Disclosure requirements

.6.24 The only balances arising in the accounting records from a financial futures or options transaction are the margin accounts. Firms will receive margin in from customers and pay it away either to ICCH or to its clearing agent. Amounts paid away will not necessarily be the same as amounts received. This may be because the firm requests extra margin (over and above the minimum) from its customers, but only pays away the minimum amount requested by ICCH or the clearing agent. In addition, for clearing members, as is illustrated in the worked example in exhibit 1, the amount paid away to ICCH is calculated by reference to the net positions of the firm rather than on individual customer accounts.

.6.25 If the firm simply passes cash received from customers straight to the clearing agent without cashing the cheques, then these amounts will not appear in the accounts. Here, entries only arise where margin is overdue and the firm has been debited by the clearing agent. This debit will then be shown as an amount due from that particular customer.

19.6.26 Where the firm retains the margin itself and only passes over a net requirement to ICCH, these amounts should be grossed up in the accounts (i.e. receipts from customers shown as credits, and payments to ICCH as debits).

19.6.27 The actual disclosure requirements are discussed in section 19.5 above. The auditor should ascertain how the firm accounts for margin paid and received and consider whether the approach adopted is reasonable. Having done this, it is necessary to test-check the accounts' analyses to determine whether they have been correctly prepared.

Principal dealing in financial futures and options

19.6.28 A firm may deal on its own account in financial futures for three main reasons: firstly as a committed market maker in the financial futures market, secondly as an adjunct to the firm's existing market making activities (e.g. where a gilt market maker uses futures to hedge gilt positions) and thirdly where the firm chooses to use surplus cash resources to make a relatively short-term investment.

19.6.29 In the first two instances, the firm should control and operate its futures dealing in the same way as any other market maker (*see* chapter 14). In the third instance, the firm should ensure that, as for short-term investments, senior management is aware of, and authorises, any positions taken.

19.6.30 The only area that requires specific consideration is the balance sheet treatment of financial futures dealings by the firm as principal. Where a firm deals on its own account it should include the following information in its financial statements:

- the accounting policy adopted with regard to LIFFE accounts;
- balances relating to margin and unrealised profits and losses on positions would not be separately disclosed unless material.

19.6.31 It will be necessary to review the firm's stated accounting policy with respect to the valuation of financial futures dealing in order to determine whether it is appropriate to the circumstances of the individual firm and whether it is consistent with that adopted in previous years. The valuation of futures contracts will depend on whether they are being used for hedging purposes or are being used purely as a trading instrument. This is discussed in more detail in section 4.10, chapter 4.

9.7 Capital requirements

9.7.1   For a TSA regulated firm, there are two areas where capital may need to be provided in respect of financial futures and options transactions:

(i)   where customers have entered into such transactions, CRR may need to be provided; and

(ii) where the firm has entered into such transactions on its own account, PRR will need to be provided.

CRR

9.7.2   The detailed rules are exactly the same as for traded options since both are covered by TSA Financial Regulations rule 63.13 in respect of margined transactions. In particular, an amount equal to the total of margins recoverable from customers shall be added to the CRR except for those balances which have been outstanding for five days or less. If the aggregate of any margin business customer's collateral and his equity balance results in an amount that is owed to the firm, that amount shall be added to the CRR to the extent that it is not secured.

PRR

9.7.3   As with traded options, there are a variety of complex rules relating to PRR. The simplest method, and one which, in consequence, is adopted quite widely in practice is that prescribed by TSA Financial Regulations Rule 62.19b which states that where futures contracts are traded on a recognised investment exchange (of which LIFFE is one), the PRR shall be equal to 100 per cent of the initial margin required to be deposited under the rules of the exchange. Various other treatments are possible, but these are dependent on hedging and various other situations which usually only occur in principal traders and market makers. These are complex and, in such cases, the appropriate rules should be referred to.

Other considerations

9.7.4   Where a firm is a clearing member of LIFFE, it will normally be required to give a guarantee to the clearing house. Alternatively, the firm may have provided a guarantee to its LIFFE subsidiary in favour of the clearing house. Under TSA Financial Regulations rule 50.08, the amount of any guarantees given by the firm must be reported to TSA. In this case, a deduction from capital has to be made on a basis to be determined by TSA, having regard to the nature of the guarantee and to whether assets have been pledged by the firm in respect of the guarantee. Accordingly, the auditor should review the correspondence between the firm and TSA to ensure that TSA have been advised of the guarantee and that the correct adjustment is being made to capital.

19.7.5 For an AFBD regulated firm, the capital requirements are set out in the Financial Resources Rules (rules 8.22 to 8.41). The auditor is required to report on whether the firm has the minimum financial resources as at the balance sheet date, as required by the rules, as well as reporting on the proper calculation of those resources.

Exhibit 1 Accounting for financial futures and options – worked example

Underlying transactions

Day 1	Customer A buys	6 lots of June long-gilt contracts at 106-12
Day 2	Customer B sells	10 lots of June long-gilt contracts at 106-02
Day 3	Customer A sells	6 lots of June long-gilt contracts at 105-04
Day 3	Customer B buys	10 lots of June long-gilt contracts at 104-30

Other relevant information

(i) Initial margin is £1,000 per contract.
(ii) The firm clears its own trades and hence settles directly with the clearing house.
(iii) Note that prices are in £ per £100 nominal with the two digits after the dash representing one tick or 32nd of a £ per £100 nominal.
(iv) End of day valuations

	Day 1	Day 2
June contract	106-04	105-20

Day 1

(i) Customer A buys 6 lots of the June contract at 106-12. This is recorded in the memorandum open position records which will not form part of the double entry system.
(ii) The firm requests customer A to put up initial margin of £6,000 (6 lots of £1,000). It may actually request a higher figure – the £1,000 is the minimum imposed by the clearing house.
(iii) At the end of the day, all positions are valued to determine the amount of variation margin payable.

338

	Position	Dealing Price	Valuation Price	Change in value Profit/(loss)
Customer A	+6 June	106-12	106-04	(£750)

The change in value is a loss to the customer resulting from the fall in the price of the contract by 8 'ticks', giving an overall loss:
6 contracts × 50,000 × $\frac{1}{32}$ × $\frac{1}{100}$ × 8 = £750; this is requested from customer A (request made at beginning of day 2).

(iv) This is matched by the firm's position with the clearing house. The clearing house requests payment by 10.00 a.m. on day 2 of the initial margin and the 'loss' in respect of day 1.

(v) No cash has moved on day 1 and so no entries are made to the accounting records.

Day 2

(i) The firm pays £6,750 cash to the clearing house (being initial and variation margin requested for the previous day). The entry to the accounting records is:

Dr Clearing house margin account	6,750	
Cr Cash		6,750

(ii) The firm requests customer A to pay £750 as variation margin relating to day 1.

(iii) Customer A pays £6,000 initial margin. The entry to the accounting records is:

Dr Cash	6,000	
Cr Customer A initial margin account		6,000

(iv) Customer B sells 10 lots of June contracts at 106-02. This is recorded in the firm's memorandum open-position records.

(v) The firm requests customer B to put up initial margin of £10,000 (10 lots at £1,000).

(vi) The firm's position with the clearing house has now altered. Since the clearing house looks at the net position of the firm, it will treat the 6 lots of June contracts purchased on day 1 as being closed out and 4 more contracts as being sold.

The closing out of the 6 contracts gives rise to a profit and loss calculation:

		£
Bought 6 June contracts at 106.12		319,125.00
Sold 6 June contracts at 106.02		318,187.50

	Loss	937.50

(vii)   The net clearing house position is valued at the end of day 2.

Position	Dealing Price	Valuation Price	Change in value Increase/(decrease)
-4 June	106-02	105-20	£875

	£
The settlement is calculated as follows:	
Initial margin	4,000
Change in value	(875)
	3,125
Existing balance on margin account	(6,750)
	3,625
Loss on closure of 6 June contracts (per (vi) above)	(937.50)
Due from the clearing house	2,687.50

(viii) The open positions of the customers are valued:

Position	Dealing Price	Valuation Price	Change in value Profit/(loss)
Customer A +6 June	106-12	105-20	(2,250)

	£
Initial margin	6,000
Valuation loss on position	2,250
Margin required	8,250
Cash received	(6,000)
Margin requested but not yet received	(750)
Additional margin requested	1,500

	Position	Dealing Price	Valuation Price	Change in value Profit/(Loss)
Customer B	-10 June	106-02	105-20	2,187

	£
Initial margin	10,000
Valuation Profit on positions	(2,187)
Margin required	7,813

Day 3

(i)   The firm receives £2,687.50 from the clearing house. This is split between margin and settlement and the following entry made in the accounting records.

Dr Cash	2,687.50	
Dr Clearing house settlement account	937.50	
CR Clearing house margin account		3,625

(ii)   Customer A pays £750 variation margin requested on day 2. The entry to the accounting records is:

Dr Cash	750	
Cr Customer A variation margin		750

(iii) The firm requests customer A to pay £1,500 as variation margin relating to day 2.

(iv)   Customer B pays £10,000 initial margin. The entry to the accounting records is:

Dr Cash	10,000	
Cr Customer B initial margin account		10,000

(v)   The firm could pay back to customer B £2,187 relating to the closing valuation of his positions on day 2. Policies of individual firms vary on this and here we will assume that this does not happen because of the desire to keep initial margin intact. Depending on the nature of the customer and policy of the firm, interest may be paid on this surplus.

(vi)   Customer A closes down his 6 June contracts at 105-04. The firm calculates the profit/loss from the customer's dealings:

341

	£
Bought 6 June contracts at 106-12	319,125
Sold 6 June contracts at 105-04	315,375
Loss	3,750
Commission for the firm (say £100 per lot 'round turn')	600
Amount due from customer A	4,350

Calculation of settlement margin for customer A

	£
Initial margin paid	6,000
Variation margin paid	750
Variation margin requested but	
not yet paid	1,500
	8,250
Amount due on closed contracts (as above)	(4,350)
Amount due to be repaid to customer A	£ 3,900

(vii) Customer B closes down his 10 June contracts at 104-30. The firm calculates the profit/loss from the customer's dealings:

	£
Sold 10 June contracts at 106-02	530,312.50
Bought 10 June contracts at 104-30	524,687.50
Profit	5,625
Commission for the firm (£100 per	
lot 'round turn')	(1,000)
Amount due to customer B	4,625

Calculation of settlement margin for customer B

	£
Initial margin paid	10,000
Amount due on closed contracts (as above)	4,625
Amount due to be repaid to Customer B	14,625

(viii) The clearing house position is closed down as follows:

	£
Sold 4 June contracts at 106-02 (day 2)	212,125
Sold 6 June contracts at 105-04	315,375
Bought 10 June contracts at 104-30	524,687.50
Profit	2,812.50

(ix) The clearing house position is valued at the end of day 3:

	£
Initial margin	–
Existing balance on margin account	(3,125)
Profit on closures	(2,812.50)
Amount due to the firm from the clearing house	5,937.50

Day 4

(i) The clearing house pays the firm £5,937.50. This is split between margin and settlement and the following entry is made in the accounting records:

Dr Cash	5,937.50	
Cr Clearing house margin account		3,125
Cr Clearing house settlement account		2,812.50

(ii) Customer A pays the firm £1,500 being variation margin requested on day 3. The entry to the accounting records is:

Dr Cash	1,500	
Cr Customer A variation margin account		1,500

(iii) The firm repays to customer A £3,900. The entry to the accounting records is:

Dr Initial margin account – customer A	6,000	
Dr Variation margin account – customer A	2,250	
Cr Clearing house settlement account		3,750
Cr Commission		600
Cr Cash		3,900

343

(iv) The firm repays to customer B £14,625. The entry to the accounting records is:

Dr Initial margin – customer B	10,000	
Dr Clearing house settlement account	5,625	
Cr Commission		1,000
Cr Cash		14,625

Postings to the accounting records

Clearing house margin account

Day 2 (i)	6,750	Day 3 (i)	3,625
		Day 4 (i)	3,125

Clearing house settlement account

Day 3 (i)	937.5	Day 4 (i)	2,812.5
Day 4 (iv)	5,625.0	Day 4 (iii)	3,750
	6,562.5		6,562.5

Customer A initial margin account

Day 4 (iii)	6,000	Day 2 (iii)	6,000

Customer B variation margin account

Day 4 (iii)	2,250	Day 3 (ii)	750
		Day 4 (ii)	1,500

Customer A initial margin account

Day 4 (iv)	10,000	Day 3 (iv)	10,000

Cash

Day 2 (iii)	6,000	Day 2 (i)	6,750
Day 3 (i)	2,687.5	Day 4 (iii)	3,900
Day 3 (ii)	750	Day 4 (iv)	14,625
Day 3 (iv)	10,000	Balance c/f	1,600
Day 4 (i)	5,937.5		
Day 4 (ii)	1,500		
	26,875		26,875

Commission

Profit and loss a/c	1,600	Day 4 (iii)	600
		Day 4 (iv)	1,000

20 Corporate Finance within the Securities Industry

20.1 **Introduction**
20.2 **The role of the broker-dealer**
20.3 **Audit**
20.4 **Capital requirements**

20.1 Introduction

20.1.1 Corporate finance is a term which covers a wide spectrum of activities within the securities industry. The range of these activities is illustrated by the definitions of corporate finance as set out in paragraph 2 of rule 1090 of TSA's *Conduct of Business Rules* which can be summarised as follows:

(a) an offering of investments whether by the issuer or otherwise and whether to the public or not;

(b) a listing of investments, or an admission of investments to dealings, on any investment exchange or a suspension or discontinuance of, or other matter arising from, any such listing or admission to dealings;

(c) (i) an exchange, conversion, redemption, purchase, re-issue or cancellation of any investments;

(ii) an alteration of the terms of any investments;

(iii) a reduction of capital (including for this purpose any share premium account or capital redemption reserve fund or similar reserve) or scheme of arrangement or similar operation concerning or affecting any investments;

(d) a takeover or related operation;

(e) any form of merger, demerger, division, reconstruction or re-organisation concerning any investments or business;

(f) an acquisition or disposal of a business or control of any company;

(g) a default or anticipated default, or event having the consequences of a default, in respect of any investments and any insolvency or prospective insolvency;

(h) providing, arranging or advising about any kind of financing, re-financing, rescheduling or reorganisation of debt or any transfer of debt, in each case otherwise than in connection with the purchase of investments by or for a private customer or a discretionary customer of the firm concerned;

(i) the establishment of a new business or the expansion of an existing business;

(j) general corporate or general financial advice or general assistance in relation to the affairs of a company or any of its associates; including in particular advice or assistance as to borrowing profile, capital requirements, investment and foreign exchange policies, share incentive schemes, investor relations, general meetings and proxy solicitation, board composition and management structure.

20.1.2 These activities are extremely wide reaching and several different professional advisers are usually required when any form of corporate finance activity is being contemplated.

20.1.3 The key factor in the appointment of all advisers, but especially the lead adviser, is that they should be respected within the financial community so that they add credibility to whatever exercise is being proposed. Many of the largest and most respected corporate finance advisers operate within banking institutions (sometimes known as merchant or investment banks). This is because 'financial clout' can be important when it comes to raising finance, especially when, as discussed below, it comes to underwriting an issue. Since the number of large issues is relatively small, banks tend to build up expertise and hence become more likely to obtain similar referrals in the future. It should be noted that firms of accountants and high street banks increasingly provide corporate finance advice to smaller businesses.

20.1.4 Other professional advisers include reporting accountants (who prepare reports on the financial position of a company covering the nature of its business, management and systems, substantiate profit forecasts and consider other financial matters); lawyers (who prepare any formal sale/merger agreements and ensure that all legal requirements are met); broker-dealers (discussed below); and valuers (who value major assets).

20.1.5 It is clear therefore, that the term corporate finance covers a wide range of activities. In section 20.2, corporate finance is discussed as it impinges on the securities industry. The audit and capital implications of such corporate finance activities are considered in sections 20.3 and 20.4.

20.1.6 Before considering the role of broker-dealers in corporate finance, it is important to understand the framework and rules under which corporate finance business is conducted. The City Code on Takeovers and Mergers operates principally to ensure fair and equal treatment of all

346

shareholders in relation to takeovers. It also provides an orderly framework within which takeovers are conducted.

20.1.7　The code represents the collective opinion of those involved professionally in the field of takeovers, as to good business standards and how fairness to shareholders can be achieved. It is issued and enforced by the Panel on Takeovers and Mergers. The responsibilities described in the code apply most directly to those engaged in the securities markets, although they also apply to all professional advisers insofar as they advise on the transactions in question. The code applies to offers for all listed or unlisted public companies considered by the panel to be resident in the UK, the Channel Islands or the Isle of Man. It also has a limited application to private companies.

20.1.8　It should be noted that the code does not have the force of law. However, the SROs require their members to comply with it and indeed, any organisations or individuals who do not conduct themselves in accordance with the code are likely to find that, by way of sanction, the facilities of the markets in which they conduct business are withheld from them.

20.1.9　The code is based upon a number of general principles, which are statements of good standards of commercial behaviour. They are expressed in broad, general terms. The code does not define the precise extent of, or the limitations on, their application. They are applied in accordance with their underlying purpose and may be modified or relaxed as the panel sees fit. In addition to the general principles, the code also contains a series of rules, some of which are expansions of general principles and examples of their application, whilst others are provisions governing specific aspects of takeover procedure. As with the general principles, the rules are interpreted to achieve their underlying purpose and so their spirit, as well as their letter, should be observed.

20.2　The role of the broker-dealer

20.2.1　Broker-dealers have significant roles to play in the corporate finance field, and after the merchant bank, probably the most wide-ranging. Indeed, the broker-dealer may even be the lead adviser if it is large enough and carries enough weight in the financial community.

20.2.2　The range of activities for such firms can be summarised as follows:

(i)　liaison with the ISE with regard to formal application for listing, public announcements and trading arrangements;

(ii) gauging market reaction to possible flotations or takeovers, in particular for generating interest and determining what price will be acceptable to the market. This can be done by informal discussions with large potential shareholders and other market operators with whom the firm will be in daily contact;

(iii) putting together a sub-underwriting syndicate (possibly the individuals referred to above) in order to ensure that none of the shares are left unsold. This aspect is discussed in more detail below;

(iv) in a takeover situation, taking instructions from the company or its lead adviser to purchase as many shares as possible in the target company as quickly as possible, so that the risk of an increasing share price (and thus the costs of the takeover) is minimised. This is known as a 'dawn raid' and the broker-dealer is usually in the best position to carry it out because of its contacts with the market and with shareholders of the target company;

(v) in connection with flotations, they may recommend the company, and/or the sector to customers. In addition they operate as a channel of information on the company to customers and shareholders.

20.2.3 There are a number of ways in which a broker-dealer may be paid for providing these services:

(a) a fee for putting together a sub-underwriting syndicate (usually a flat percentage of the total amount of the issue underwritten – 1/4 per cent is usual);

(b) a fee for that part of the underwriting risk they take on themselves (*see* paragraph 20.2.8 below);

(c) a flat fee for the processing work as regards the ISE, including formal applications for listing, public announcements and trading arrangements;

(d) a fee for general corporate finance advice; and

(e) commissions generated through dealings in the market in the shares of the company concerned. For a recently floated company, the sponsoring firm may be seen as a leading market maker for the securities of that company and hence may gain a large proportion of the transactions in the stock.

20.2.4 Items (a) to (c) will usually be fixed fees. If the firm is likely to earn a significant amount from commissions or market making, the fee for corporate finance advice may be reduced accordingly.

Underwriting and sub-underwriting

20.2.5 Underwriting is a form of insurance and is designed to ensure that the company will receive the funds it needs even if the share issue does not prove popular with the public. In return for a fee, the underwriter undertakes to purchase all the shares that are not subscribed for by the investors.

20.2.6　The firm which takes the lead in underwriting an issue may be a merchant bank, a broker-dealer, or some other financial institution. The lead underwriter will not usually wish to take on all the risk itself and hence will want to contract out some of that risk, a process known as 'sub-underwriting'. As noted in paragraph 20.1.3 above, the lead underwriter may need significant 'financial clout' in case the issue cannot be sub-underwritten. This will mean it has to take the whole risk of underwriting onto its own books so as not to jeopardise the issue. Banks tend to dominate in this aspect of the corporate finance field because they have resources to guarantee the success of an issue by underwriting the whole of it.

20.2.7　The lead underwriter is required to sign a contract by which he is committed to take up 100 per cent of the underwriting. However, prior to signing, he will usually wait for formal replies from the institutions invited to sub-underwrite in order to minimise his own risk. If the lead underwriter is large enough and is sufficiently confident about an issue, he may sign the underwriting contract before completing the sub-underwriting.

20.2.8　Broker-dealers are well placed to put together a sub-underwriting syndicate because, as noted above, they can gauge market reaction to an issue and the level of investment interest in the shares. The firm identifies institutions who may be interested in joining the sub-underwriting syndicate. This may eventually be made up of other broker-dealers, merchant banks, unit trusts, fund managers and other market professionals. The aim is that even if there is a disappointing level of public response, the sub-underwriters will provide the company with a reasonable spread of investors. The sub-underwriter will receive a fee which will be a percentage (usually 1 1/4 per cent to 1 1/2 per cent) of the risk assumed. The fee will also depend on the length of the exposure period which varies according to the type of issue being underwritten.

20.2.9　If the issue is fully subscribed, all underwriters are released from their obligations and are paid their fee. If the issue is under-subscribed, sub-underwriters are required to take up any shortfall in proportion to their commitment. In such a case, the opening market price is likely to be weak (because all investor demand was fully satisfied by the issue) which means that sub-underwriters will be left with over-priced stock. Losses can be substantial and can often exceed the fees earned on a number of successful issues.

20.2.10   The risk that underwriters run of having to take up shares varies in different circumstances. The highest level of risk arises on flotations where shares are open to subscription by the general public. Adverse publicity or general economic circumstances around the time of the issue can lead to significant under-subscription by the public. Conversely, rights issues are offered to existing shareholders and so the chances of under-subscription are less, although the higher the price of the rights in relation to the price of the existing shares, the more likely it is that under-subscription will occur.

Confidentiality and conflicts of interest

20.2.11   It is clear that corporate finance activities generate price-sensitive information which could benefit individuals if they became aware of it. Therefore, it is important that all such information is kept confidential both within the firm and externally. As well as benefiting individuals, such information could be used to the advantage of another part of the firm. This is a particular risk where firms have market making operations and/or fund management operations in addition to a corporate finance department.

20.2.12   In particular, the agency business department of such a firm may be appointed as broker to a company contemplating a takeover. This is clearly price-sensitive information from which the market making department could benefit, in that it could purchase the shares of the target company and profit from the rise in prices following the announcement of the bid. Alternatively, if the broker-dealer has a fund management operation, the fund managers could purchase the stock on behalf of their customers in advance of the bid.

20.2.13   This problem of keeping confidential information segregated becomes even more acute when merchant banks, agency brokers and market makers are combined into a single company, or 'integrated house'. Here, it is very important that 'chinese walls' are established between the various departments to ensure that price-sensitive information does not unfairly benefit other parts of the company. Such integrated houses are usually determined to be seen to be maintaining strong 'chinese walls', since they are otherwise likely to lose substantial amounts of business because their clients perceive that they are unable to control the conflicts of interest inherent in their business.

Venture capital

20.2.14   Another significant area of corporate finance which impinges upon the securities industry is venture capital. This may be through broker-dealers which sponsor venture capital activities, or through specialist venture capital operators. The funds for such finance may come from investors who wish to participate in the potentially large returns that the venture capital field can bring, and the broker-dealer often acts as a fund manager for these investors.

.2.15 Venture capital comprises finance provided for a wide range of transactions ranging from large management buy-outs from public groups to arranging investment under the Business Expansion Scheme. However, traditionally it is recognised as finance for 'greenfield' businesses which require considerable sums for development but lack the track record necessary for a full listing or a USM flotation. Venture capital is often raised with a view to a market flotation at some future date, with capital frequently issued in the form of a number of different classes of equity shares with varying rights, together with a high proportion of debt.

20.3 Audit

0.3.1 There are three main areas which should be considered when auditing corporate finance activity within a broker-dealer:

(i) the completeness and accuracy of fee income;
(ii) the extent of any contingent liabilities on underwriting commitments; and
(iii) the valuation of any investments taken on as a result of corporate finance activity (ranging from underwriting commitments to venture capital operations).

0.3.2 It should also be noted that a firm engaging in venture capital activities may be holding client money (i.e. customer subscribed funds which are held pending investment in venture capital projects). In this case, the audit considerations are as set out in chapter 11 on client money.

Fee income

0.3.3 Corporate finance activity typically results in fees which are credited to the profit and loss account. A particular consideration is that many broker-dealers account for fees on a cash basis and therefore there is scope for errors arising from delayed invoicing or from a failure to pay in cheques received.

0.3.4 Hence an important part of the audit work consists of ensuring that fees for all deals which have been completed, have been accrued for in the profit and loss account. There are a number of procedures which can be utilised to judge whether income has been brought into accounts in the correct financial year:

— a review of the work in progress of the corporate finance department in the period up to the balance sheet date to ensure that fees have been rendered for all completed transactions;
— a review of the financial press for announcements of deals where the firm is an adviser;
— a review of the corporate finance working and correpondence files;
— discussions with corporate finance management.

20.3.5   It should be noted that it can be difficult to perform this work because of the confidentiality of the information and the reluctance of corporate finance management to discuss these matters in any detail. However, because corporate finance income, and even individual fees, can be very significant, it is important that they are accounted for on a consistent basis. Therefore, this is an area which is often best covered by a senior member of the audit team.

Underwriting commitments

20.3.6   A further audit consideration is the existence of underwriting commitments at the balance sheet date which may subsequently result in a loss to the firm.

20.3.7   Underwriting commitments which have crystallised before the balance sheet date will result in tangible investment positions in the balance sheet and the valuation aspects of these are discussed below. The principal audit objective for these items is to ensure that any income from the underwriting commitment has been correctly accrued in the financial statements.

Internal control

20.3.8   The following control feature should be considered with respect to underwriting commitments:

20.3.9   *Control objective: Underwriting activities are controlled in such a way as to prevent unauthorised commitments or commitments in excess of specified limits*
The following control procedures may exist to meet these objectives:

— authorisation from suitably senior management required before an underwriting commitment is made;
— a record kept of all outstanding underwriting commitments;

— outstanding commitments are regularly reviewed and any prospective losses reported to senior management;
— all relevant legal and settlement data reviewed by suitably senior management.

.3.10 By considering these control features, the auditor will ensure that procedures are in place to monitor the firm's investment position risk and provide appropriate levels of management with the information necessary for them to control such risks. This is a regulatory audit objective on which the auditor is required to report under TSA Financial Regulations rule 90.03d(iv) and therefore a specific review of such matters needs to be made.

Analytical review

.3.11 There is little scope for analytical review procedures in this area.

Substantive testing

.3.12 Substantive testing will involve reviewing outstanding underwriting commitments and determining whether there are any related liabilities at the balance sheet date. This will involve looking at outstanding commitments and seeing which ones actually lead to the firm having to purchase stock for which the market value is less than the underwritten price.

.3.13 If the forced purchase of stock subsequent to the balance sheet date results in a material loss, then it should be provided for in the period in which the underwriting commitment was entered into. In this case, any income arising from the underwriting should be accrued in the same period.

.3.14 It should be noted that it is also normal practice to quantify all underwriting commitments at the balance sheet date in a contingent liability note. This note would normally refer to the capital commitment, but would only refer to any loss arising in the subsequent period if it were material.

Valuation of investments

.3.15 There are two types of investment which a broker-dealer may acquire as a result of its corporate finance activity:

(a) securities quoted on an exchange with a readily available market price; and

353

(b) unquoted securities for which an independent market value is not readily available.

20.3.16   The audit objective is to ensure that investments are reasonably valued. There are various methods which can be used to value such investments, commonly the lower of cost and market value through to cost less a provision for any permanent diminution in value. The merits of these approaches are discussed in more detail in section 4.10 of chapter 4.

20.3.17   For quoted securities, market value is the price for which the investment could be sold at the relevant date. Many of the factors set out in chapter 14 on market makers and principal dealers will apply in determining the acceptability of the valuations used. Unquoted investments typically arise from venture capital activities where shares are spread across a small number of investors and hence are highly illiquid. Such companies will typically make losses in their initial years, especially where high gearing means very high levels of interest payments, for example in the case of management buy-outs.

20.3.18   It is therefore necessary to consider whether investments are likely to become profitable by reviewing management projections and actual progress to date. It is usual for major investors in venture capital schemes to ensure that they participate in the running of their investment through representation on the board of directors. Therefore, they would expect to receive regular management information and to attend board meetings.

20.3.19   Assessing the following matters will frequently be the only way in which a judgement can be made on whether or not a permanent diminution in value has occurred:

— working capital requirements;
— cash flow forecasts;
— comparison of actual performance to business plan;
— review of order books;
— evaluation of business levels.

20.4   Capital requirements

20.4.1   The only SRO which specifically recognises corporate finance activities as a separate category of membership is TSA, under whose rules firms have to provide CRR and PRR relating to their underwriting commitments.

20.4.2 The requirements for PRR are set out in TSA rule 62.33 under the heading 'issuing market'. The issuing market refers to transactions in securities carried out by managers, underwriters or members of a selling syndicate usually in the period between the pledging of an underwriting commitment and the actual allotment date of the securities.

20.4.3 It should be noted that rule 62.33 allows for a number of different issuing market situations:

(i) Domestic offerings (any offering directed primarily at investors in the UK and which uses methods normal in the UK domestic capital markets), in particular:
— underwriting of new securities where securities are already traded;
— underwriting where securities are not already traded;
— commitments to purchase new securities or existing securities which are new to the market;
— underwriting and commitments to purchase existing securities where the securities are already traded.
(ii) International offerings (any offering not classed as a domestic offering), in particular:
— bought deals (where the firm, on its own, gives an outright commitment to the issuer or seller to purchase or subscribe for the securities to be offered);
— pre-priced deals (an international offering, other than a bought deal, all the pricing terms of which have been fixed);
— open-priced deals (any international offering, which is neither a bought deal nor a pre-priced deal).

20.4.4 It is important to be able to classify the underwriting commitment into one of the above categories. The detailed provisions of the rules are complex and detailed and are not set out here. Reference should be made to the TSA rulebook as appropriate.

20.4.5 It is also necessary to consider issuing market transactions in the calculation of CRR. It is probable that, when a firm has to honour its underwriting commitments, a 'free delivery' (as defined in chapter 10) will take place. This is because the firm has to settle money due on the purchase well before the stock can be delivered. The normal CRR rules only give a three-day 'period of grace' before a free delivery has to be provided for; however, TSA rule 63.04b(iii) recognises that it is unreasonable to expect delivery in the issuing market to take place this quickly and therefore allows an addition to be made to CRR equal to the following percentages of the total value of the cash involved:

Number of business days after closing date	Equities per cent	Debt Securities per cent
0–5	0	0
6–10	0	50
11–20	25	100
21–30	50	100
over 30	100	100

It should be noted that the closing date is the date on which payment for the securities is due to be made to the issuer or seller.

Underwriting commissions

20.4.6   The only other area where corporate finance activities may have a bearing on capital is in respect of underwriting commissions receivable. The detailed requirements are set out in TSA rule 50.05(f),(g) and (h).

20.4.7   The main provisions of rules 50.05(f) and (g) relate to international offerings where stabilisation is taking place. Stabilisation is discussed in chapter 16 on the eurobond market.

20.4.8   Debtors relating to underwriting commissions receivable on domestic offerings are treated as non-approved assets if they have been outstanding for more than thirty days from when they were due to be received. The same provisions also apply to management fees receivable on a new offering if they have not been received within thirty days after the closing of the offer (rule 50.05(h)).

Corporate finance advisory firms

20.4.9   Section 11 of TSA Financial Regulations applies to corporate finance advisory firms and to venture capital firms. For advisory and venture capital firms whose activities are defined by paragraph 2 of rule 1090 of the Conduct of Business Rules (summarised in section 20.1 of this chapter), which do not handle client money, and only invest their own funds, rules 110 and 111 set out separate capital and audit requirements.

20.4.10   There are varying capital requirements for advisory firms and venture capital firms which depend on the exact nature of the firm's business. Generally, these are substantially less onerous than those which apply to broker-dealers and reference should be made to the rules as appropriate.

20.4.11   Advisory and venture capital firms have to submit to TSA annually, within three months of the balance sheet date, financial statements drawn up in accordance with appropriate company law.

.4.12   For corporate finance advisory firms, the financial statements must contain a report by the firm's auditors stating:

(i)   whether or not the audit was conducted in accordance with approved Auditing Standards;
(ii)   whether or not the financial statements give a 'true and fair view' of the state of affairs of the firm at the balance sheet date and the result for the period then ended; and
(iii)   whether or not the financial statements comply with the Companies Act.

.4.13   The auditors of venture capital firms have to produce a similar TSA audit report as for broker-dealers. Where certain aspects are not applicable (e.g. in respect of client money or property), then suitable reference needs to be made to this in the audit report.

21 Financial Intermediaries

21.1 Introduction

21.1.1 An intermediary is defined, for example, by TSA as 'a person (other than a market professional) requesting a firm to deal or give investment advice for a particular client of his, consistent with the terms of the intermediary's customer document with the firm, and on the basis that the firm will be responsible to the ultimate customer for the execution of the order, or for the advice as if that ultimate customer had been a direct customer of the firm'.

21.1.2 This TSA definition describes the type of financial intermediary which perhaps immediately springs to mind in relation to the securities industry, although it is restrictive in that such a financial intermediary would not be responsible for the execution of the customer's order. In the TSA definition, the intermediary is envisaged as acting as no more than an introducer between the customer and the organisation which actually executes the transaction. Whilst a financial intermediary may well act on this basis, a large number are in practice responsible for ensuring the execution of their customer's transactions even though they themselves are not executing those transactions. For instance, in the case of the purchase of shares, the intermediary would place the order with a broker-dealer on behalf of his customer and be responsible to his customer for ensuring that the transaction is executed and the shares received.

21.1.3 The customers of such financial intermediaries are often private individuals or smaller corporations who require objective and impartial advice on a wide range of their financial affairs, including such matters as:

— investment advice;
— pension and insurance planning;

358

— personal tax planning.

21.1.4　These customers are looking for a single integrated source of guidance on the wide range of products and services in the market, in order to manage their financial affairs. Whilst some customers may wish to be involved in their 'day-to-day' investment decisions, others will leave the decisions to the financial intermediary who will manage their assets on a discretionary basis (effectively acting as an investment manager – *see* chapter 22).

21.1.5　Many financial intermediaries will offer this broad range of financial services tailored to the customer's requirements and not just the purchase or sale of shares. However, some financial intermediaries are not able or willing to provide the broad spectrum of services, and restrict their activities, for example to insurance related products.

21.1.6　Indeed, some financial intermediaries act solely as representatives of specific insurance companies and under the FSA are only allowed to sell the products of that particular company.

21.1.7　Others, who are not affiliated in any way, offer independent advice. These 'independent financial advisers' are required to have sufficient knowledge of all the products available to ensure that, given the customer's investment objectives and circumstances, they can provide best advice. The majority of financial intermediaries are members of the Financial Intermediaries, Managers and Brokers Regulatory Association (FIMBRA) and the impact of the rules and regulations of that SRO are considered below.

Other financial intermediaries, specialising in providing services related to insurance, may be registered with the Insurance Brokers Registration Council (IBRC), rather than with FIMBRA. Currently, organisations who carry on insurance business which requires regulation under the FSA may register and have that business regulated under the IBRC as long as it constitutes no more than 25 per cent of their turnover.

21.2　FIMBRA membership categories

21.2.1　FIMBRA has eight different categories of membership, which for financial resources purposes fall into three bands A, B and C. The eight categories A1 through to C3 are set out in FIMBRA rule 1.2.1 and are considered below.

21.2.2   Category A1 members are able to provide investment advice but are not allowed to arrange or effect transactions relating to investments, or act as an investment manager.

21.2.3   A2 members can arrange and effect transactions in respect of a restrictive range of investments but only where they do not hold clients' money or assets. These restrictions are set out in FIMBRA rule 1.2.2 and effectively only allow transactions in relation to life policies, pension contracts, collective investment schemes such as unit trusts, applications in respect of new issues and the sale of other readily realisable investments in order to provide funds to purchase any of the above.

21.2.4   Category B1 members can, subject to two restrictions, arrange and effect transaction in investments of any kind other than in respect of discretionary managed funds. The first restriction is that they do not hold clients' money or assets. The second is that for transactions other than those relating to life policies, pension contracts, collective investment schemes and business expansion schemes, a clearing firm accepts primary responsibility for the performance of the member's obligations in connection with those transactions.

21.2.5   B2 members can arrange and effect the same restricted range of transactions as A2 members but can hold clients' money or assets and act as a broker-fund adviser, but only for funds or investments issued by a life office.

21.2.6   Category B3 members can arrange and effect the same range of transactions as B2 members and, in addition can, act as a broker-fund advisor or discretionary investment manager but only in relation to collective investment schemes, and any funds or investments issued by a life office.

21.2.7   Category C1 members are able to arrange and effect transactions within the same restrictions as B1 members but are able to hold clients' money and assets.

21.2.8   Category C2 covers those members of FIMBRA who act as investment managers but not in so restricted a way as to fall within category B3. Such C2 members must not hold clients' money or assets and the assets of each fund must be held by a bank or custodian appointed by the client to whom specific instructions have been given to release money or assets only in restricted circumstances.

21.2.9   Category C3 covers all other FIMBRA members and allows for the arranging and effecting of transactions relating to investments and/or acting as an investment manager in such a manner as not to fall within any of the above categories.

21.3 Accounting

21.3.1 FIMBRA requires all members to keep proper accounting records and, as with TSA, the FIMBRA rules go further than the Companies Act in defining what constitutes adequate accounting records. The detailed requirements are set out in FIMBRA rule 10 to which reference should be made. In broad terms, these rules state that accounting records should be sufficient to:

(a) show all transactions carried out and disclose with reasonable accuracy the financial position of the member at any point in time;
(b) disclose whether the member is complying with the Financial Resources rules of FIMBRA;
(c) enable the member to prepare the financial reports and the six-monthly questionnaires required by FIMBRA.

21.3.2 All records and working papers created to meet the above requirements must be retained for a period of seven years from the date on which they are prepared. In most circumstances, the records for the most recent two years should be held at the place of business of the FIMBRA member.

21.3.3 Whilst FIMBRA requires annual financial statements to be submitted to it within four months of the year-end, it does not require accounts produced under the requirements of the Companies Act to be submitted as a matter of course.

21.3.4 FIMBRA does however, require its members to produce management accounts although these are not required to be submitted. It is recognised by FIMBRA that the diversity of member firms makes it difficult to be prescriptive as to what such management accounts must contain. However, in general terms FIMBRA states that management accounts should:

— demonstrate compliance with the financial resources requirements;
— be prepared at least quarterly;
— be 'accurate'.

21.3.5 As discussed above, FIMBRA have eight different categories of membership and three different levels of rules for financial reporting and financial resources purposes. This section deals with the reporting requirements of the different categories of FIMBRA members but

361

should be read in conjunction with the details regarding categories of membership and the relevant financial resources requirements for each category.

21.3.6   Category A1 or A2 members do not have to submit annual financial statements to FIMBRA. Rather, following a rules amendment in May 1989, they are required to submit an 'annual financial declaration' and to ensure a position of continuing solvency. In essence, this requires that the member must be able to meet its liabilities as they fall due.

21.3.7   Category B1, B2 and B3 members are required to submit annual financial statements to FIMBRA within four months of the accounting reference date. These statements must be in the FIMBRA prescribed format and accompanied by a audit report from the member's auditors.

21.3.8   Category C1, C2 and C3 members are required to submit audited financial statements annually and are also required to submit quarterly financial statements. In addition, category C3 members must submit monthly financial statements. Neither the quarterly nor monthly financial statements need be accompanied by an auditors' report.

21.3.9   It should be noted that in the case of category C members, the annual financial statement must contain a reconciliation of the amounts shown in the annual profit and loss account with the sum of the amounts shown in the quarterly profit and loss accounts submitted to FIMBRA during the year.

21.3.10   The format of the balance sheet and profit and loss accounts required by FIMBRA are set out in appendix 5 (part 3) of the FIMBRA rulebook. The format is broadly similar to the requirements of the Companies Act except that:

— only the 'vertical' format of both the balance sheet and profit and loss account is allowed;
— more disclosure categories are required;
— the financial statements must be in sterling;
— whilst there is no specific requirement for notes to the accounts, there is a requirement to disclose any additional information and explanations necessary for the accounts to give 'a true and fair view.'

21.3.11   It has been mentioned that category A1 and A2 members are required to submit a half-year and a year-end questionnaire and a similar requirement applies to category B and C members. The questionnaire is confirmation by the management of the member that they have adhered to certain key aspects of the FIMBRA rules. There is no requirement

362

for the auditor to review or approve the questionnaire before submission. The format of this questionnaire is set out in Appendix 5 part 4 of the FIMBRA rulebook and covers such matters as:

— preparation of quarterly financial statements (management accounts);
— outstanding legal proceedings;
— reconciliation of suspense accounts;
— submission of VAT returns.

21.4 FIMBRA financial resources requirements

21.4.1 All members of FIMBRA are required to have capital of at least £1,000, either as issued and fully paid share capital in the case of an incorporated member, or in the form of proprietors' or partners' capital accounts in the case of an unincorporated member.

21.4.2 The financial resources requirement for category A members of FIMBRA is set out in rule 9.5.2. A FIMBRA member in category A1 or A2 must have a financial position of continuing solvency. These members are required to sign and submit an annual financial declaration (set out in section 3, Part 3 of Appendix 5 of the FIMBRA rulebook) that, to the best of the member's knowledge and belief, it can meet its liabilities as they fall due.

21.4.3 The financial resources requirement for category B members in rule 12.2(1) is much more complicated than that for category A. FIMBRA rule 12.2.(1) requires category B members to have a minimum of:

(i)   net tangible worth of £2,500; and
(ii) adjusted net current assets of £1; and
(iii) adjusted capital of 4/52nd of relevant annual expenditure.

21.4.4 The above fraction of adjusted capital increases to 8/52nds in the case of a member authorised to carry on business solely or partly within category B(3). The test for category B members of FIMBRA is a three-part test and the member must meet all three requirements.

21.4.5 The financial resources requirement of category C members of FIMBRA is that the member's liquid capital (as defined by FIMBRA rule 12.2.(2)) must be at least equal to the greater of:

(i) £5,000; and
(ii) 4/52nds of relevant annual expenditure.

21.4.6   The requirement is increased to £10,000 and 13/52nds in the case of a member authorised to carry on business solely or partly within category C(3).

21.4.7   Further analysis of the requirement of the above rules is not set out in this book as the large amount of detail and the changes to the rules which can take place make it preferable for the reader to refer directly to the appropriate sections of the FIMBRA rulebook. Details of the relevant definitions are set out in the following FIMBRA rules:

> Rule 12.3 *Relevant Annual Expenditure*
> Rule 12.5 *Net Tangible Worth*
> Rule 12.6 *Adjusted Net Current Assets*
> Rule 12.7 *Adjusted Capital*
> Rule 12.8 *Liquid Capital*

21.5 Audit

21.5.1   The operations of financial intermediaries in the securities markets will be similar to those of members of TSA and IMRO and hence the audit approaches described elsewhere in this book will in most cases be applicable. The detailed requirements of the auditor's report in respect of a category B or C member are set out in section 13.3 of the FIMBRA rulebook and the auditor will need to organise his work to provide appropriate evidence for each of the opinions required in that report.

21.5.2   Two distinct types of FIMBRA member can be identified; those who hold clients' money, customers' assets or both and those that do not; the audit work required will be considerably greater for the former category. Clients' money is discussed in chapter 11 and, whilst that chapter considers the audit of clients' money from the viewpoint of a member of TSA, the other SROs' clients' money rules, including those of FIMBRA, are very similar, being based on those set by the SIB. It is envisaged therefore, that with only minor amendment the audit work set out in chapter 11 will be applicable to a FIMBRA member holding clients' money.

21.5.3   Customers' assets are discussed in chapter 12 'Safe Custody and Nominee Shareholders'. There will be minor differences in the detailed audit work to take account of FIMBRA rule 14 on customers' assets, but chapter 12 should provide the basis for the audit work required on a FIMBRA member who holds customers' assets.

21.5.4 Due to the wide diversity of operations of FIMBRA members, it is difficult to be prescriptive in the audit work required. However, apart from the audit work necessary to meet the Companies Act requirements, the following additional points need to be considered:

(i) testing of the financial aspects of the FIMBRA rules with appropriate compliance and substantive tests tailored to the systems of the client;

(ii) testing of clients' money and safe custody systems. Care should be taken that, where the category of FIMBRA membership prohibits the holding of clients' money or clients' assets, checks have taken place to ensure that there has been no breach.

21.5.5 The auditor may also gain evidence from the procedures and controls set up by the client to meet FIMBRA rule 4.19 which requires members to:

• establish procedures to ensure compliance with all FIMBRA rules;
• set out such procedures in writing (unless the number of authorised persons carrying on the investment business is ten or less);
• appoint a compliance officer to carry out a review of the compliance procedures at least annually to ensure they are effective.

A certificate of compliance (or details of failure to comply) has then to be submitted by the member to FIMBRA.

21.5.6 It is possible that, for larger firms with detailed procedures manuals, the work carried out in the review of compliance procedures may be sufficiently well documented to provide some element of audit evidence. Consideration should be given to that possibility at the audit planning stage.

21.5.7 A review, at the commencement of the audit, of the non-financial aspects of compliance (probably initially by discussion with the compliance officer) may provide a useful indication of whether problems have been encountered by the member during the period.

22 Investment Management

22.1 Introduction

22.1.1 Investment management, at its broadest level, is the function of taking decisions on the investment of funds, the re-investment of the subsequent income and gains derived from those assets and the continuing review of those assets resulting in the sale of holdings and the purchase of others, in order to maximise their value over a period of time, subject to a pre-determined level of risk. Investment management can, therefore, include the deployment of funds into any form of investment such as property, works of art, foreign currencies and commodities as well as securities. One subdivision of investment management, dealing solely with the deployment of investment into securities, is commonly known as fund management, although the two terms are sometimes used synonymously.

22.1.2 Investment management is carried out by a wide variety of organisations including:

- *In-house teams* – staff employed by an organisation for the management of an investment portfolio owned by that organisation. For example, a large pension fund (or a business setting up a pension scheme on behalf of its employees) might employ a team of investment managers to invest pension contributions in order to minimise the cost to the employing company of paying the defined level of benefits to the retired employees of the company, as and when they fall due. Alternatively, an insurance company will employ staff to invest the receipts from the writing of insurance business, to maximise the return on those funds until any claims have to be paid out.
- *Merchant banks and stockbrokers* – organisations offering a service to customers whereby funds owned by customers will be managed in accordance with their instructions covering the overall investment goals, the acceptable level of risk in the portfolio etc., in order to maximise the value of the portfolio or the income derived therefrom.

366

- *Managers of collective investment schemes* – investment trusts and unit trusts exist to provide the means whereby investors can benefit from a wide spread of risks, by investing in a greater number of securities than would be economic for the individual's own direct investment or by being able to make investments that would not be accessible to individual investors (e.g. investing in commercial property development). The manager of the collective investment scheme will frequently assume the responsibility of managing the investments owned by the scheme.
- *Specialist firms* – who may either be independent or subsidiaries of a larger organisation (e.g. a merchant bank) with the specific role of managing investments. Specialist firms will normally act on a discretionary basis for the portfolios under their control, and will normally execute transactions themselves or through broker-dealers.

2.1.3   What is common to all except the first group noted above is that the investment manager does not become the owner of the portfolios that he manages. The portfolio remains the property of the customer but is managed on his behalf.

2.1.4   This chapter is primarily concerned with the audit of an investment management business; that is an entity whose main function is the management of investments on behalf of others, and therefore does not address the audit considerations for collective investment schemes themselves. Such schemes are subject to detailed regulations by the Department of Trade and Industry and by the Securities and Investment Board. The audit and accounting consideration for such schemes are too extensive to be covered by this book.

2.1.5   The following groups may use the services of an investment management business:

- trustees of pension funds;
- insurance companies;
- collective investment schemes (unit trusts, investments trusts);
- companies investing surplus funds;
- charities;
- trusts (for example, the trustees of a trust set up as a result of a will to provide income for the widow of the settlor before settling the capital on his children);
- private investors.

2.1.6   By far the largest users, by value, of the services of investment managers are pension funds, insurance companies and collective investment schemes (known together as 'institutional investors') although there are a greater number of private investors.

22.1.7   The specialist investment manager has seen rapid growth in recent years mainly for the following reasons:

- published performance statistics of fund managers showing favourable average rates of return over varying periods in relation to the All Share Index and other investment performance measures;
- the individual investor's perceived inability to out-perform the share indices and the returns achieved by fund managers due to:
  — rapidly changing market conditions
  — lack of research facilities and ability to predict movement in the market
  — lack of dealing skills and familiarity with the market;
- increased willingness on the part of private investors to move away from traditional fixed interest investments into equity investments in order to increase returns;
- the ability of fund managers to carry out transactions on a block basis for more than one customer, thereby reducing the cost to individual investors;
- overall, a far simpler method of investment; and
- the inability of market settlement systems to process large volumes of small transactions.

22.1.8   Investment managers make use of all available means of investment dependent on the objectives of particular customers. This encompasses direct investment in equities, fixed interest securities, property and so on, investment in derivative markets such as options and futures – both on securities and commodities, and investment in collective investment schemes. The latter is particularly common where the manager is investing funds on behalf of private investors.

22.2   The investment of funds

22.2.1   Funds are invested on behalf of a customer on the following principal bases:

- *discretionary* – where the customer gives the manager complete control over asset allocation and stock selection within defined parameters;
- *advisory* – where the manager does not have the authority to change the portfolio without prior reference to the customer, but where the manager recommends changes which the customer may, or may not, accept.

There can be many variations on these, broad classifications to suit the needs of individual customers.

2.2.2 Institutional investors tend to employ managers on a discretionary basis whilst private investors are more likely to require an advisory service.

2.2.3 The decision by an institutional or corporate investor to use the services of a particular investment manager is generally based on the performance of the manager over recent years. This performance, or return on funds invested, is firstly compared with the returns published for a variety of investments available in the market, e.g. the All Share Index, and then against the performance of other investment managers.

2.2.4 The types of fund management available can be broken down as follows:

- *Balanced management* – funds which may be invested in all classes of securities, e.g., UK and foreign equities or UK and foreign bonds. The investment manager will make his selection depending on the customer's desire for capital growth or income or a combination of both, and the level of risk that the customer is prepared to accept.
- *Specialist management* – funds whose investment is restricted to, for example, fixed-interest stocks or non-UK equities. This will normally be a service requested by a sophisticated customer who can take his own decisions on the level of funds to be allocated to a particular sector, but who is not sufficiently knowledgeable to choose particular shares within that sector;
- *Passive management* – funds which are invested in proportion to the constituent stocks of a particular index, e.g., the FT All Share Index of UK equities so that, in theory, the fund's performance will track the relevant index without any switching of investments and thus have much lower dealing costs.

2.2.5 The decision as to which stocks a fund will purchase is generally made after reference to three sources of information:

- *In-house* research, where the manager has an internal research facility which he can call upon in making his investment decisions;
- *Bought-in* research, where the manager does not have in-house facilities available to him or where his own research does not cover all areas of potential investment. He will buy research from an external source such as a broker or a specialist research firm;
- *Broker* research, where the fund manager is sent the research material produced by stockbroking firms without charge, in the hope of generating business for the stockbroker.

Types of research

22.2.6   The types of research which a manager will obtain from the above sources include the following:

- *Broad economic* – how the researcher believes an economy will 'move' in the future, in terms of such factors as a country's balance of payments, exchange rates, inflation rates and interest rates. From this information a manager will hope to gain a 'feel' for the economy in which his proposed investments will perform and how changes in the economy may affect those investments. This enables the manager to determine the extent to which his funds should be invested in shares, property or cash and in which countries.
- *Sectors* – how the researcher believes a particular sector of the economy e.g. the automotive industry, or the banking industry, will perform in the short and medium term. The analyst will provide certain indicators in respect of each sector such as expected demand for the sector's goods or services and whether that particular sector will flourish or decline in the forecast period.
- *Company* – having reviewed the sector analysis provided by the analyst, the manager will then request research on the major companies in that sector covering matters such as forecast profitability, share price, price/earnings ratio, dividend yields and other general comments. This information will assist the fund manager in selecting individual investments in a chosen sector.

Remuneration

22.2.7   Income for an investment manager may be derived from various sources:

- *Fees* – based on the value of funds under management, which may be charged as an initial fee when the funds are passed over to the manager (particularly common with collective investment schemes) or on a periodic basis, or both.
- *Commission* – on the value of securities traded, which is typically only earned when the fund manager is also a broker-dealer.
- *Introductory commission* – when the manager receives a commission for allocating funds to another fund manager, particularly a collective investment scheme.
- *Administration charge* – where the fund manager is responsible for the safe-keeping of investments and the collection of income thereon, and he charges a fee for this work.

2.2.8   In recent years, a new form of 'income' has emerged in the form of 'soft' commissions. These arise where the broker-dealer agrees to pay certain expenses (such as the cost of bought-in research) of the fund manager who, in return, agrees to provide the broker with a pre-determined level of commission income by transacting investment business through it. This commission income will be a multiple (normally between one and two) of the expenses paid on behalf of the fund manager. This means that expenses of the fund manager are allocated directly to the funds under his control by way of the commission charged on share purchases and sales. It may also mean that services are made available which the fund manager could not afford if they had to be paid for directly by him.

2.2.9   This practice is acceptable to the regulatory authorities providing that the arrangements are disclosed to the underlying customers, that the fund being charged with the commission is actually benefiting from the expenses incurred, and that the broker used provides 'best execution' on the investment business transacted.

22.3 Conduct of business and dealing procedures

Customer agreements

2.3.1   It is important for the fund manager to know the overall investment aims of his customers, and to be granted formal authority to deal on the behalf of customers. Therefore, agreements should be in place between the manager and his customers setting out the terms and conditions of their relationship. It should be noted that this is also required by the SROs.

2.3.2   The major items which should be included in this agreement are laid down by the relevant SROs and include:

- duration of the arrangement;
- required notice of termination for both parties;
- level of fees, commissions and administrative charges to be levied by the manager;
- the funds to be invested;
- investment objectives;
  — capital growth
  — income
  — balanced
- level of risk;
- basis of investment;
  — discretionary
  — advisory

371

- the type of investment fund to be used;
  — balanced
  — specialised
  — passive
- frequency of statement and portfolio valuations;
- who will hold the title documents;
- who will exercise the voting rights attached to securities held on the customer's behalf;
- signatures of both parties.

Dealing procedures

22.3.3   Having received the signed customer agreement letter, the investment manager is ready to begin dealing on behalf of his customer. At this initial stage, the customer may deposit cash with the manager, or may transfer an existing portfolio. If the arrangement is to be advisory, with the customer or the manager arranging execution through a separate broker-dealer, the customer will advise the manager of existing holdings. If the role is to be advisory, then there may be occasions when the customer decides on a particular transaction on his own initiative, and the customer may then give an 'execution only' order to the investment manager. However, to protect himself from subsequent criticism from either the regulators or a customer who has lost money by making his own decisions, the manager will in such cases usually seek to satisfy himself that the decision is not incompatible with the rest of the customer's portfolio.

22.3.4   For discretionary arrangements, the investment manager will ensure that he has sufficient funds before deciding to make an investment, which may require the disposal of an existing stock in the portfolio. The fund manager will then contact a broker-dealer in order to execute the transaction.

22.3.5   The broker-dealer will raise a contract note (usually in the name of the customer, not the fund manager) which will be sent to the fund manager for onward transmission to the customer, often accompanied by an advice note from the investment manager. The bargain will be settled on the appropriate account day either from funds held on behalf of the customer by the fund manager or by the bank or trustee holding the assets on behalf of the customer.

22.3.6   In order to ease the settlement process, investment managers often provide nominee facilities in order to hold securities for their customers. This also means that the manager is able to ensure that the customer does not dispose of stock in the portfolio without first informing him. As noted in section 22.5 below, it is important that reconciliations of dealing records to safe custody records are performed at regular intervals by the investment manager.

2.3.7 Many customers of investment managers (particularly pension funds and collective investment schemes) do not give the investment manager the right to hold or receive investments or dividends on behalf of the customer, and instead have their assets held by a bank or other custodian on their behalf. The manager merely instructs the bank to pay or receive funds to, or from, the broker when a transaction takes place.

2.3.8 However, many investment managers hold significant amounts of client property (both money and stock) over which strict control needs to be maintained, and in such cases many of the procedures and controls noted in chapter 12 on safe custody and in chapter 11 on client money are relevant.

2.3.9 When investment managers deal, it is important that portfolio records are updated promptly. Having decided to deal, the investment manager will raise a dealing slip which will form the basis for updating the portfolio records. Updating may be delayed until a contract note has been received from the broker (usually on the next business day), particularly if there is any doubt as to the level of commission and other charges that will be levied by the broker. This delay ensures that the manager updates his records accurately.

2.3.10 Most investment managers now maintain computerised portfolio records. The software packages available are usually connected directly to a share valuation service such as Extel or Datastream. This enables holdings to be valued on a daily basis, and also ensures that the investment manager can be aware of the disposition and performance of each fund under his control, at any given time, in order to deal with customer enquiries and for monitoring purposes.

2.3.11 There are various other conduct of business rules and matters of business practice which apply to the conduct of investment management business and these are summarised below.

Statements of account

2.3.12 On a regular basis, a manager must provide each customer with a statement of account setting out the customer's portfolio, including details of cost and current valuation for each item. The valuation statement will also include details of income earned on the portfolio. This income may either be paid away to the customer at, for example,

373

six-monthly intervals or may be accumulated with the rest of the fund. Where the investment manager charges a fee based on the value of funds under management, a fee invoice may accompany the valuation statement. As, and when, changes to the portfolio are made, contract notes and advices will usually be sent to the customer. These may be accompanied by a letter from the manager explaining why the deal was transacted and how it fits with the customer's investment objectives.

Allocation of investments

22.3.13   A proportion of any fund will usually be kept in gilt-edged securities, short-term deposits, cash or equivalent securities in order to provide an available source of liquid funds for investment opportunities. In addition, investment managers prefer their funds not to be biased towards a particular stock (e.g. over 10 per cent of the total portfolio) because the performance of the fund will then be dependent, to a large extent, on the performance of that stock. This will usually be covered by the customer agreement letter, but the rules provide an underlying code of practice.

Churning

22.3.14   Where the remuneration of the investment manager arises from commission based on the value of securities traded, it is important that the manager does not generate income by excessive and unnecessary levels of trading (known as 'churning'). One way of preventing this is for the investment manager to communicate with customers at the time statements are despatched, explaining the rationale behind investments made in the period. In addition, there should be an independent review of trading activities on customers' accounts by personnel within the investment manager's business to ensure that churning is not taking place.

Allocation of bargains

22.3.15   One of the reasons for the growth in investment management activity in recent years is the ability of managers to carry out transactions on a block basis for more than one customer, thereby spreading the cost. The SROs have strict rules on when such aggregation of deals can take place and on how and when the resultant trades should be allocated to the accounts of the individual customers. These rules are designed to ensure that no one customer is disadvantaged, and that the fund manager is not able to change allocations subsequently so that, for example, losses in particular portfolios can be disguised. Generally, firms should have systems to ensure that, when a transaction has been effected, the

374

employees responsible for the transaction allocate it by, at the latest, the same time on the next working day.

Complaints procedure

.3.16 It is a requirement of the SROs that all fund managers (and, indeed, all investment businesses) establish a formal complaints procedure which is disseminated to all staff. The procedures should ensure that the customer is advised of his rights to complain to the SRO if he is not satisfied with the response he receives from the firm. The procedure should also ensure that senior management is informed immediately any complaint is received, and provided with copies of any relevant papers and the ultimate resolution as soon as is practicable thereafter. Letters of complaint should be acknowledged promptly and a response also prepared promptly. Due to the discretionary nature of much of an investment manager's activities, it is important that customers are kept fully aware of the performance of their investments and that there is an established procedure for dealing with complaints.

'Chinese walls'

.3.17 This expression relates to the means established within a single company or a securities trading group to ensure that the effect of conflicts of interest are minimised and that confidential information held by one part is not abused (for instance, the fund manager should not be influenced in voting for or against a takeover because a group company is advising the bidder). Chinese walls are also discussed in chapter 20 on corporate finance. The 'terms of business dealings' for a fund manager which is also part of a group of securities companies should make clear to customers in their agreement letters the nature of conflicts of interest that may arise, and the steps that are taken to prevent conflicts affecting the customer; in particular, setting out the conditions under which one company of the group may deal with another.

22.4 Regulatory and capital requirements

2.4.1 The majority of investment managers are regulated by the Investment Managers Regulatory Organisation Ltd (IMRO). Its members are principally engaged in the management of investments for private investors, unit trusts and pension funds. In certain situations, where fund management is not the principal business carried out by the manager, another SRO such as FIMBRA or TSA may be appropriate. Since the majority of investment managers are regulated by IMRO, only IMRO's rules are considered here, although the rules of TSA and FIMBRA are broadly similar.

22.4.2   IMRO's rulebook includes the following principal sections that affect the day-to-day activities of IMRO members:

— chapter 3 – Customer agreement;
— chapter 4 – Conduct of business;
— chapter 5 – Financial requirements.

22.4.3   Chapter 3 requires a written agreement with each customer. The nature of the agreement depends on the customer's status and the typical contents are set out in section 22.3 above.

22.4.4   Chapter 4 covers conduct of business and deals with matters such as:

— independence;
— best advice and best execution;
— remuneration/commission;
— allocation of transactions;
— investments not readily realisable;
— record keeping.

22.4.5   Most of these rules are designed to ensure fair play for the customer. However, the best advice and best execution rules are crucial and in practice will be very closely monitored by IMRO and by senior management in the firm.

22.4.6   Chapter 5 covers financial requirements, in particular:

— accounting records;
— financial statements;
— financial resources;
— audit requirements;
— financial notification.

22.5 Audit

22.5.1   The auditor of a fund manager will need to consider both statutory audit objectives and additional reporting requirements as discussed earlier in this book.

22.5.2   The regulators for a fund management business all require the auditor to report on the 'adequacy of systems for the control of the accounting records' and therefore, the auditor will need to review all aspects of the firm's control procedures, whether or not he seeks to rely on them for the purposes of his statutory report.

2.5.3 Similarly, IMRO's rules state that systems shall not be deemed to be adequate unless the firm has properly documented them, as well as the relevant control procedures. Therefore, the auditor must review the existence and accuracy of this documentation.

2.5.4 One aspect of the audit opinion not considered in detail in this section is that relating to the capital requirement and financial resources. The detailed IMRO capital requirements are set out in their rulebook and the audit work required is simply a test-check of the various analyses and calculations.

AUDIT STRATEGY BY MAJOR AREAS OF THE BUSINESS

New customer procedures

2.5.5 *Control objective: that there is a valid and appropriate letter of agreement for each customer setting out the terms and conditions of trading which is complied with for all advice given*

2.5.6 The following control procedures may exist to meet this objective:

— all enquiries logged, together with date of enquiry;
— source of introduction logged;
— standard 'know your customer' questionnaires filled in for all customers;
— standard customer agreement letters exist and are despatched as appropriate, according to the results of the 'know your customer' questionnaire;
— before accepting the customer, designated senior management approve the details and ensure that the signed letter is in place;
— trading forbidden without the aforementioned approval and signed agreement letter;
— customer agreement letters reviewed at least once a year for continued applicability;
— register of customers maintained which includes date of receipt of signed agreement letter;
— independent review of portfolios and transactions on a periodic basis for compliance with customer agreement letter;
— details of existing investments of new customers passed to the investment manager and recorded;
— share certificates held by new customers passed to the investment manager for safe custody.

2.5.7 Substantive testing under this heading is designed primarily to ensure that there have been no breaches of the conduct of business rules which might give grounds for successful litigation by an aggrieved customer. It will therefore consist of:

— ensuring that, for a sample of new customers introduced during the year, a signed, valid agreement letter was in place prior to dealing;
— reviewing a sample of customer portfolios for consistency with customer agreements;
— reviewing the 'compliance review' carried out by the firm's compliance officer – this review is a requirement of the SROs' rulebooks and is effectively an internal audit of the firm's compliance with the conduct of business rules.

Dealing procedures

22.5.8   *Control objectives: details of dealing are correctly input into the portfolio records; dealers' portfolio records agree with the safe custody records; 'churning' is prevented; dealings are in line with the dealer's knowledge of the customer and his investment objectives*

22.5.9   The following control procedures may exist to meet these objectives:

— dealing slip matched to contract note received from broker;
— portfolio records regularly reconciled to safe custody records and reconciliations reviewed by senior management;
— all transactions notified to customers promptly, together with an explanation from the investment manager of the rationale behind the transaction;
— review by senior management of dealings on accounts to ensure that 'churning' is not taking place;
— regular contact with customers to ensure that the 'know your customer' requirements are still being met;
— regular (i.e. at least annual) 'know your customer' update questionnaires filled in.

22.5.10   If control procedures in this area are weak it may be appropriate to carry out substantive testing under this heading, for example to review a sample of customer accounts in an attempt to detect churning, or a circularisation of customers to check compliance with the customer agreement letter and ensure that customers are generally content with the investment manager. Specific work on the agreement of dealing records to safe custody records is discussed below.

Recording of customer portfolios

22.5.11   *Control objective: to ensure that an adequate system is operating to record and maintain customer portfolios*

.5.12   The following control procedures may exist to meet this objective:

— customer portfolios are only updated after validation of the bargain
  (e.g. by comparison to a contract note issued by the broker)
— customer portfolios are regularly reconciled to safe custody records
  (this is a key process for ensuring that records are properly maintained, and will need to take into account unsettled bargains where
  stock is still due to or from the broker). Ideally this should be
  carried out by staff independent from the dealing and safe custody
  department
— customer portfolios are connected to automatic valuation updating
  services (e.g. Extel or Datastream)
— performance of portfolios is regularly monitored
— customers regularly informed of the performance of their portfolio
— procedures are established to deal with customers' complaints regarding their portfolios
— valuation updating and monitoring is carried out by staff independent of the fund manager (although valuations should still be
  reviewed by fund managers for accuracy).

.5.13   Substantive testing under this heading should be designed to test on a
sample basis the posting of transactions to ensure that correct bargains
are being recorded on the proper portfolios.

Safe custody and cash holdings

.5.14   *Control objective: securities and cash balances held on behalf of*
customers are properly controlled

.5.15   The bulk of a customer's portfolio will usually be in the form of
securities, with a proportion in the form of cash. The investment
manager will usually wish to keep these assets under his control in order
to ensure swift settlement and also to ensure that customers do not
dispose of stock without informing him.

.5.16   There are specific requirements for customer assets in the IMRO
rulebook (chapter 5, appendix 4) and the auditor must report on
whether the firm was in compliance with these rules at the year end.

.5.17   The IMRO requirements are broadly similar to the TSA requirements,
which are discussed in detail in chapter 12 on safe custody and chapter
11 on client money. The control procedures, key controls and substantive audit procedures relating to customers' assets are as set out in these
chapters and are not repeated here.

Settlement

22.5.18   *Control objective: to ensure that deals are properly settled*

22.5.19   For the most part, settlement problems should not arise for fund managers since they are allocated a specific level of funds for investment, and therefore should only undertake deals within the resources of funds available.

22.5.20   However, certain control procedures may be relevant, not least to ensure that the firm is properly supervising its dealers and settlement staff:

— purchases not carried out by fund managers without liquid funds being available to settle the transaction;
— the use of one customer's funds to settle another customer's trades is strictly prohibited;
— settlement procedures are carried out by staff independent of the fund managers;
— memorandum settlement accounts maintained to monitor the settlement process where the fund manager is not responsible for settlement;
— overdue settlement from customer's funds (i.e. insufficient cash to settle) reported to senior management promptly;
— stock undelivered by brokers is regularly pursued.

22.5.21   Substantive procedures will consist primarily of ensuring that settlement balances at the year-end are settled promptly. As a check on the completeness and accuracy of the accounting records, a circularisation of brokers used by the investment manager should be carried out.

Collection of income on behalf of customers

22.5.22   *Control objective: to ensure that all dividends and other benefits receivable on behalf of customers are received when due, correctly apportioned to each customer and dealt with according to the wishes of the customer (either accumulated with the rest of the fund or paid away)*

22.5.23   The collection of dividends and other benefits is usually the responsibility of the safe custody department whose task is to ensure that the investment manager's nominee shareholding receives all dividends that it is entitled to. In addition, it is their responsibility to ensure that dividends and other benefits are correctly apportioned to individual customers with the relevant stock in their portfolio. In order to carry this out satisfactorily, all of the controls detailed above on the safe custody function need to be in place. It will also be necessary to ensure that benefits on purchases, where the purchase is not registered in time to receive the benefit from the registrar, are properly claimed from the selling broker.

2.5.24 Control procedures which may exist under this heading are:
— dividends are credited to customers as soon as they fall due;
— where a dividend has not been received on a holding for more than a year (for UK stocks, more than three months for overseas stocks), since either the holding was purchased or the last dividend was paid, enquiries are made into whether a dividend has fallen due but not been paid;
— for each bank advice/dividend warrant received on a nominee holding, a reconciliation is performed to the holdings of individual customers entitled to a share of the dividend.

2.5.25 Substantive testing will be based on selecting a sample of stocks and determining for these stocks the dividend or other benefits payable per share (from SEDOL, the FT or Extel cards). Using the firm's portfolio records, calculate total dividend due (which can be agreed to the bank advice/dividend warrant) and agree the payment due to each customer. By reference to the customer's agreement letter, ensure that the dividend or other benefit is then correctly dealt with (i.e. either reinvested or paid away).

Collection of fee income

2.5.26 *Control objective: fees/commissions are charged on a regular basis in accordance with the terms stated in customer agreement letters*

2.5.27 The following control procedures may exist to meet this objective:
— for customers charged a fee, the invoice is despatched with the portfolio valuation, which is prepared at regular intervals;
— fee notes are prepared and despatched independently of the fund manager;
— checklists of customers are maintained to ensure the completeness of income collection;
— customer accounts are flagged by the computer system according to the nature of charging (as per their agreement letter);
— invoice calculation is reviewed to ensure their proper preparation and consistency with expected portfolio details.

2.5.28 The substantive work under this heading will involve selecting a sample of customers and ensuring that they have been charged during the year in accordance with the terms stated in the agreement letter. Where the last charge was not at the balance sheet date, the accuracy of accruals for income will also have to be tested. Finally, the recoverability of all debtors will have to be assessed. This should be straightforward since invoices are usually charged to the customer account and recovered from the funds held by the manager.

23 Clearing Firms

23.1 **Introduction**
23.2 **Roles and responsibilities**
23.3 **Audit**

23.1 Introduction

23.1.1   An increasingly common practice within the securities industry is for firms to make use of clearing firms ('clearers') to handle their back-office processing. This can provide considerable benefits in terms of risk-management, flexibility of costs, expertise, and range of services provided. At one end of the spectrum, the clearing firm will execute bargains transacted by the introducing firm, issue contract notes, settle bargains and provide all necessary working capital for the settlement process and may even take a degree of financial responsibility for any bad debts that may be experienced. At the other extreme, the clearing firm simply provides the clerical support staff to enable settlement to take place in much the same way as firms make use of bureaux for payroll production.

23.1.2   The extent to which the Financial Services Act applies to clearing firms has been the subject of considerable debate, and it is generally suggested that where the clearing firm merely provides an element of computing and clerical staff support, it does not carry on investment business and has no need to be regulated.

23.1.3   TSA recognise the following three broad categories of clearing firm:

- *Model A mark 1* – a firm which accepts responsibility as agent, using the introducing firm's money, for general back office administration – the processing of bargains originated by the introducing firm. In addition, such a firm may act as dealing agent for the introducing firm and hence be responsible for the execution of bargains.
- *Model A mark 2* – a firm which provides the same services as a model A mark 1 firm except that it uses its own money, relying on reimbursement on a daily basis from its introducing firm.
- *Model B* – a firm which accepts primary responsibility for the performance of obligations undertaken by the introducing firm, i.e. it carries and clears the counterparty accounts of one or more introducing firms, assumes the entire settlement responsibility, and subject to the clearing agreement, incurs the legal liability and the responsibility

for the contracted relationship with both client and market counter-parties.

23.1.4   An introducing firm may be defined as a firm which enters into arrangements with one or more clearing firms in relation to transactions entered into by the firm. The main distinguishing feature between model A and model B clearers is that with the former, the clearer assumes no legal responsibility for completion of bargains to either customer or market. With the latter, the clearer takes full legal responsibility for each trade, once transacted. Therefore, the user of a model A clearer will show unsettled balances on its own balance sheet, and retains formal responsibility to its own regulator for client money and client property, while the user of a model B service will pass all these responsibilities to the clearer and will show no customer balances on its own balance sheet.

23.1.5   One other category of clearing firm is the 'derivative clearer'. These are firms which provide a clearing service for derivative instruments (i.e. futures and options). These have been discussed in chapters 18 and 19 and are not considered further here.

23.1.6   Before considering in more detail the roles and responsibilities of the introducing firm and its clearer, it is worth discussing some of the practical benefits which arise from the relationship:

- *cost control* – the introducing firm will have a more definite basis for business planning without the large fixed costs associated with maintaining a settlements office (although most clearers charge set-up costs which can be substantial). Clearers' charges are more likely to be closely related to bargain volumes and business types;
- *resources* – the use of a clearing firm removes the problem of resourcing a back office with the right level of skills at a reasonable cost. They are particularly attractive to new businesses;
- *systems* – the introducing firm will usually have access to a more powerful computing facility able to cope with a range of business activities, markets and the burden of regulatory changes.

23.1.7   However, it is also necessary to be aware of some of the problems which can arise in the relationship:

- *expectations* – introducing firms may have unreasonably high expectations of their clearing firms, compared with an in-house back office;
- *security of the clearing firm* – the financial strength and continuing existence of a clearing firm is an important consideration for an introducing firm. A loss of confidence in a clearer or operational

difficulties in settlement will create serious problems for the introducing firm;

- *management controls* – as is discussed below, transferring the back office to an outside agency does not remove the need for effective controls – indeed it strengthens this requirement;
- *interface with customers* – the level of interface between the clearing firm and the customers of the introducing firm must be carefully established in order to minimise the risk of losing the confidence of those customers.
- *compliance with regulations* – the introducing firm remains ultimately responsible for ensuring that all the requirements of the SRO regulations are met for the business it transacts, and must be able to obtain adequate information and confirmations from the clearer to verify this.

23.2 Roles and responsibilities

23.2.1 At present, the predominant type of clearer in the UK is the model A firm. The roles and responsibilities of the model A marks 1 and 2 are broadly similar, the main difference being that the mark 1 clearer has control over certain bank accounts of the introducing firm. Mark 2 clearers rely on a daily reimbursement from the introducing firm and so do not control bank accounts of the introducing firm.

23.2.2 The usual sequence of events with a model A clearer is as follows:

- the introducing firm reports transactions to the clearer, by fax or by direct input;
- the clearer processes the transaction, submits details to the ISE for checking and sends a contract note to the customer;
- the clearer advises the introducing firm of checking queries which require the attention of the originating dealer;
- the clearer processes sold bargain documentation from the customer for delivery to the ISE. Stock may come direct from the customer, via the introducing firm, or from safe custody holdings kept by the clearer or by the introducing firm – the exact detail depends on the agreement between the clearer and the introducing firm;
- the clearer advises the ISE of relevant registration details for bought bargains;
- the clearer receives cheques from customers;
- the clearer settles with the ISE and with customers and draws down cash from the introducing firm as appropriate.

23.2.3 The clearer has responsibility for the maintenance of the customer ledgers and will usually only refer to the introducing firm when it is necessary to contact a customer to resolve a problem. The clearer also has responsibility for the market ledgers, both Talisman and jobbers/ ticket ledger balances. It should be noted that the cycle described in paragraph 23.2.2 only relates to UK bargains. Transactions dealt on overseas exchanges are more complex – and follow broadly the procedures described in chapter 15.

23.2.4   The model A clearer will therefore maintain detailed ledgers on behalf of each of the introducing firms that it services. These ledgers will include customer, market, cash and nominal (i.e. commission and interest) balances. There may be also a 'capital' account representing cash passed between the clearer and the introducing firm. This account should match an equal and opposite balance in the introducing firm's ledgers being of the nature of an inter-branch control account. It should be noted that the introducing firm will not usually duplicate the records kept by the clearer. The clearer will be responsible for all the normal control and reconciliation functions for the ledgers and balances under its control – as described in the earlier chapters of this book.

23.2.5   The comprehensive nature of the accounting and settlement records kept by the clearer means that it will usually have the day-to-day responsibility for ensuring that the various regulatory requirements relating to financial controls, such as reconciling client money (as discussed in chapter 11) and calculating CRR (as discussed in chapter 10) are met. However, it is the ultimate responsibility of the introducing firm to comply with TSA rules and therefore the relevant reconciliations and calculations should be received and reviewed by the introducing firm on a regular basis.

23.2.6   The use of a model A clearer therefore reduces the introducing firm's back office to that of a liaison role, consisting largely of:

— resolving checking queries;
— maintaining a customer database;
— management control;
— cash control;
— submitting regulatory returns.

23.2.7   The more comprehensive model B clearing service, where the clearing firm assumes legal responsibility for all transactions, will involve the introducing firm with less work. Here, the introducing firm will simply record commission income and any clearing charges payable, as a net balance due from the clearing firm, and will not maintain any detailed record of customer or market balances outstanding.

23.3 Audit

User of model B clearer

23.3.1 The audit implications for firms using clearing services naturally depend on the sort of service being used. The more comprehensive model B service will usually take the form of the clearing firm assuming legal responsibility for all transactions, with the introducing firm simply recording commission income and any clearing charges payable, as a net balance due from the clearing firm. If the introducing firm retains some residual responsibility for bad debts then this may need to be disclosed as a contingent liability. For the auditor, the use of the comprehensive service will normally simplify matters since the financial statements will not include any unsettled business and the 'systems' on which the auditor needs to report to the SRO are within the clearing firm, and not the responsibility of the auditor's client.

User of model A clearer

23.3.2 However, where the clearing firm is providing the model A service, the problems are rather more complex. In this situation, legal responsibility for settlement remains with the introducing firm and therefore all unsettled transactions will need to be included on that firm's balance sheet. Similarly, the introducing firm retains the obligations to TSA to maintain adequate controls over its business including proper systems for client money, although the actual operation of those systems will largely be carried out by the clearing firm. This gives an immediate, practical problem to the auditor of the introducing firm as he is required to report on the systems of his client, but the majority of those systems are designed and operated by a third party with whom the auditor has no relationship, and who is likely to object to allowing a variety of unrelated auditors access to his offices and staff.

23.3.3 Accordingly, the method that has been adopted is for the auditor of the clearing firm to issue a report to the various introducing firms using its services, covering those systems aspects that are under the control of the clearing firm. The format of this report not only expresses the appropriate opinions, but should also set out the key control objectives and the procedures that exist within the clearing firm to achieve those objectives.

23.3.4 Once the auditor of the introducing firm receives this report, he will need to ensure that he audits all other systems aspects which remain the responsibility of the introducing firm. It should be noted that the period covered by the report, issued by the clearing firm's auditor, may not necessarily coincide with the period being audited. It will generally be appropriate for the auditor of the introducing firm to refer in his report to TSA the reliance placed on the report received from the clearing firm's auditor. An example of such a report is set out in appendix 1 of this book.

23.3.5   The extent of any additional audit work carried out will depend on the range of services offered by the clearing firm. In the case of a model A clearer, providing the full range of settlement services (including safe custody), the following procedures should be considered by the auditor of the introducing firm, to conclude on the adequacy of its systems and internal controls.

Front office

23.3.6   Here, it will be necessary to consider the adequacy of controls over bargain capture and processing, in particular:

— completeness of data (i.e. dealing slips) submitted to the clearing firm;
— authorisation controls over standing data amendments;
— management review of clearing firm output (e.g. bargain journals);
— response to checking queries.

Back office

23.3.7   A great deal of audit reliance will be placed on the report received from the auditor of the clearing firm. However, it is still necessary for the auditor of the introducing firm to report on the monitoring of the capital requirement, and on the safe-keeping of client money and property. This will involve:

● ensuring that the introducing firm is being provided with regular reconciliations in respect of both free and settlement client money and that appropriate notifications have been given to banks (as discussed in chapter 11);
● ensuring that daily CRR reports are received and reviewed, along with any other types of capital requirements arising from the firm's business;
● ensuring that all the relevant client property reconciliations (as discussed in chapter 12) are being provided to the introducing firm and that these are reviewed and action taken as appropriate.

23.3.8   In addition, the auditor should ensure that the introducing firm is monitoring key parts of the clearer's work, i.e:

- ensuring that important reconciliations (e.g. Talisman, banks and unanalysed 'internal' accounts) are being provided by the clearing firm and reviewed by suitable management in the introducing firm;
- ensuring that client-ageing reports are reviewed and followed up by the introducing firm.

23.3.9   Even though the auditor of the introducing firm has to place a great deal of reliance on the clearing firm's auditor for his report on systems and controls, it is still his sole responsibility to report on the truth and fairness of the financial statements produced by the introducing firm.

23.3.10   The procedures carried out at the balance sheet date by the introducing firm's auditor should therefore be no different to where a clearing firm is not being used. It is important for the auditor to obtain a complete set of the records produced by the clearing firm at the balance sheet date. These records will provide the basis for carrying out the audit procedures set out in previous chapters, i.e. circularisation, reconciliations, subsequent receipt of cash and so on.

APPENDICES

APPENDICES

Appendix 1 Unqualified Reports for TSA, IMRO, FIMBRA and AFBD

Specimen audit report to TSA for an incorporated member firm

The Securities Association Limited
The Stock Exchange Building
London EC2N 1HP

Date of report

Dear Sirs

A Broker Limited (The Company)
Accounts For The Period From [date] to [date]

In accordance with rules 90.03 and 90.04 of the Financial Regulations of The Securities Association (The Association), we report as follows:

Rule 90.03

(a) We have audited the financial statements of the company on pages [X] to [X] in accordance with approved Auditing Standards.
(b) We have received all the information and explanations which we consider necessary for the purposes of our audit.
(c) In our opinion:
    (i)   the financial statements give a true and fair view of the state of affairs of the company at [balance sheet date] and of the profit and source and application of funds for the period then ended;
    (ii) proper accounting records appropriate to the business conducted by the company have been maintained by it during the period ended [balance sheet date];
    (iii) proper returns adequate for the purposes of our audit have been received from branches not visited by us;
    (iv) the financial statements are in accordance with the accounting records.

(d) The management of the Firm are responsible for establishing and maintaining adequate accounting and internal control systems. In fulfilling that responsibility, estimates and judgements must be made to assess the expected benefits and related costs of management information and of control procedures. The objective is to provide reasonable, but not absolute, assurance that assets are safeguarded against loss from unauthorised use or disposition, that transactions are executed in accordance with established authorisation procedures and are recorded properly, and to enable the management to conduct the business in a prudent manner. Because of inherent limitations in any accounting and internal control system, errors or irregularities may nevertheless occur and not be detected. Also, projection of any evaluation of the systems to future periods is subject to the risk that management information and control procedures may become inadequate because of changes in conditions or that the degree of compliance with those procedures may deteriorate.

In the context of the matters referred to above in our opinion, during the period ended [balance sheet date]:

(i) the systems for the agreement and reconciliation of balances and securities positions with counterparties, banks and clearing houses were adequate and such procedures were carried out at appropriate intervals;

(ii) the systems for the safe custody, identification and control of documents of title were adequate and included reconciliations between the records maintained by the company and statements and confirmations from bankers and other custodians at appropriate intervals;

(iii) adequate procedures and controls were in operation for reporting and investigating the ageing and analysis of balances with counterparties;

(iv) adequate procedures had been established for monitoring the company's investment position risk and counterparty risk exposures and providing appropriate levels of management with the information necessary for them to make relevant, timely and informed decisions to control such risks.

(e) We have examined the statements on pages [X] to [X] reconciling the financial position shown in the audited balance sheet with the company's Quarterly Reporting Statement as of the same date. In our opinion, the reconciliation has been properly prepared.

(f) We have examined the calculation of adjusted annual expenditure set out on page [X]. In our opinion the calculation has been properly prepared in accordance with rule 61.03 based on the results for the period.

(g) In our opinion, throughout the period ended [balance sheet date], the company had adequate systems to have enabled it to comply with the appropriate client money and property rules (Section 10 of the Financial Regulations of the Association), having regard to the inherent limitations of any accounting and internal control systems, the nature and scale of the company's business and the need for cost effectiveness in the design of such systems.

In our opinion, the company was in compliance with the requirements of that Section at [balance sheet date], disregarding trivial breaches of rules 100.02 to 100.10 which were rectified immediately upon discovery and which caused no loss to any counterparty of the company.

Rule 90.04

We have examined the company's Annual Reporting Statement made up at [balance sheet date] which is appended hereto and initialled by us for the purpose of identification only. In our opinion:
(a) the company's Statement of Qualifying Capital as shown in the Annual Reporting Statement at [balance sheet date] has been properly prepared in accordance with the rules of the Association in effect at that date;
(b) the company's Statement of Total Capital Requirement as shown in the Annual Reporting Statement at [balance sheet date] has been properly prepared in accordance with the rules of the Association in effect at that date.

Yours faithfully

Chartered Accountants

Specimen audit report to TSA for an incorporated member firm using a model A mark 1 clearing firm

The Securities Association Limited
The Stock Exchange Building
London EC2N 1HP

Date of report

Dear Sirs

A Broker Limited (The Company)
Accounts for the period from [date] to [date]

In accordance with rules 90.03 and 90.04 of the Financial Regulations of The Securities Association (The Association), we report as follows

Rule 90.03

(a) We have audited the financial statements of the company on pages [X] to [X] in accordance with approved Auditing Standards.
(b) We have received all the information and explanations which we consider necessary for the purposes of our audit.
(c) In our opinion:
   (i)   the financial statements give a true and fair view of the state of affairs of the company at [balance sheet date] and of the profit and source and application of funds for the period then ended;
   (ii) proper accounting records appropriate to the business conducted by the company have been maintained by it during the period;
   (iii) the financial statements are in accordance with the accounting records.
(d) The company uses the services of a clearing firm model A mark 1 (as defined by rule 10). For the purpose of reporting under paragraph (d) and (g) of rule 90.03, the clearing firm and its auditors have agreed with the Enforcement Division of the Association that an annual report will be provided to the customers of the clearing firm. The last such report was dated [date] and covered the period [start date] to [end date].

The management of the Firm are responsible for establishing and maintaining adequate accounting and internal control systems. In fulfilling that responsiblility, estimates and judgements must be made to assess the expected benefits and related costs of management information and of control procedures. The objective is to provide reasonable, but not absolute, assurance that assets are safeguarded against loss from unauthorised use or disposition, that transactions are executed in accordance with established authorisation procedures and are recorded properly, and to enable the management to conduct the business in a prudent manner. Because of inherent limitations in any accounting and internal control system, errors or irregularities may nevertheless occur and not be detected. Also, projection of any evaluation of the systems to future periods is subject to the risk that management information and control procedures may become inadequate because of changes in conditions or that the degree of compliance with those procedures may deteriorate.

In the context of the matters referred to above and based on the aforementioned report, during the period to [end date] for those

396

systems operated by the clearing firm and to [balance sheet date] for those systems operated directly by the company, in our opinion:

  (i)   the systems for the agreement and reconciliation of balances and securities positions with counterparties, banks and clearing houses were adequate and such procedures were carried out at appropriate intervals;

  (ii)   the systems for the safe custody, identification and control of documents of title were adequate and included reconciliations between the records maintained by the company and statements and confirmations from bankers and other custodians at appropriate intervals;

  (iii) adequate procedures and controls were in operation for reporting and investigating the ageing and analysis of balances with counterparties;

  (iv) adequate procedures had been established for monitoring the company's investment position risk and counterparty risk exposures and providing appropriate levels of management with the information necessary for them to make relevant, timely and informed decisions to control such risks.

(e) We have examined the statements on pages [X] to [X] reconciling the financial position shown in the audited balance sheet with the company's Quarterly Reporting Statement as of the same date. In our opinion, the reconciliation has been properly prepared.

(f) We have examined the calculation of adjusted, annual expenditure set out on page [X]. In our opinion the calculation has been properly prepared in accordance with rule 61.03 based on the results for the period.

(g) In our opinion, throughout the period ended [balance sheet date], the company had adequate systems to have enabled it to comply with the appropriate client money and property rules (section 10 of the Financial Regulations of the Association), having regard to the inherent limitations of any accounting and internal control systems, the nature and scale of the company's business, the need for cost–effectiveness in the design of such systems and having regard to the aforementioned report from the clearing firm's auditor.

In our opinion, the company was in compliance with the requirements of that Section at [balance sheet date], disregarding trivial breaches of rules 100.02 to 100.10 which were rectified immediately upon discovery and which caused no loss to any counterparty of the company.

We have examined the company's Annual Reporting Statement made up at [balance sheet date] which is appended hereto and initialled by us for the purpose of identification only. In our opinion:

(a) the company's Statement of Qualifying Capital as shown in the Annual Reporting Statement at [balance sheet date] has been properly prepared in accordance with the rules of the Association in effect at that date;

(b) the company's Statement of Total Capital Requirement as shown in the Annual Reporting Statement at [balance sheet date] has been properly prepared in accordance with the rules of the Association in effect at that date.

Yours faithfully

Chartered Accountants

Specimen audit report to IMRO for an incorporated member firm

The Investment Management Regulatory
Organisation Limited
Broadwalk House
5 Appold Street
London EC2A 2LL

Date of report

Dear Sirs

An Investment Management Company Limited (The Company)
Membership Reference Number ....
Accounts For The Period From [date] to [date]

In accordance with rule 5.05 and Appendix 9 of the Financial Regulations of the Investment Management Regulatory Organisation Limited (IMRO), we report as follows:

(i) A copy of the Statutory Companies Act accounts for the year ended [balance sheet date] are enclosed separately.

(ii) We have audited the Annual Financial Statements of the company

398

set out on pages [X] to [X], with the exception of the figure for funds under management on page [X], together with the supplementary information on pages [X] and [X] and our audit has been conducted in accordance with Auditing Standards.

(iii) In our opinion:

(a) the Annual Financial Statements have been properly prepared in accordance with the Financial Statements rules of IMRO and the company's accounting policies have been consistently applied within the Annual Financial Statements;

(b) & the Annual Financial Statements together with the sup-
(c) plementary information and enclosed statutory accounts give a true and fair view of the state of affairs of the company at [balance sheet date] and of the profit and source and application of funds for the year then ended;

(d) the company's Financial Resources Requirement as set out on page [X] has been properly calculated as at the balance sheet date in accordance with the Financial Resources rules of IMRO;

(e) the company's Financial Resources as set out on page [X] have been properly calculated as at the balance sheet date in accordance with the Financial Resources Rules of IMRO and exceed the company's Financial Resources Requirement as shown on page [X];

(f) the balance sheet and profit and loss account are in agreement with the company's accounting records;

(g) during the year, proper accounting records have been kept and adequate systems for control have been maintained by the company as required by the Accounting Records Rules of IMRO, having regard to the inherent limitations of any accounting and internal control systems, the nature and scale of the company's business and the need for cost–effectiveness in the design of such systems;

(h) during the period ended [balance sheet date], reconciliations of clients' money and customers' assets have been performed by the company in accordance with the Accounting Records Rules of IMRO;

(i) the company was in compliance with the Customers' Assets Rules of IMRO at the year end;

(j) all information and explanations necessary for the purpose of our audit have been obtained.

In connection with the matters referred to in paragraph (iii)(g) above, you should note that the management of the member firm are responsible for establishing and maintaining adequate accounting and internal control systems. In fulfilling that responsibility, estimates and judgements must be made to assess the expected benefits and related costs of management information and of control procedures. The objective is to provide reasonable, but not absolute, assurance that assets are safeguarded against loss from unauthorised use or disposition, that transactions are executed in accordance with established authorisation procedures and are recorded properly, and to enable the management to conduct the business in a prudent manner. Because of inherent limitations in any accounting and internal control system, errors or irregularities may nevertheless occur and not be detected. Also, projection of any evaluation of the systems to future periods is subject to the risk that management information and control procedures may become inadequate because of changes in conditions or that the degree of compliance with those procedures may deteriorate.

Yours faithfully

Chartered Accountants

Specimen audit report to FIMBRA for an incorporated member firm

The Financial Intermediaries Managers
and Brokers Regulatory Association
Hertsmere House
Hartsmere Road
London E14 4AB

Date of report

Dear Sirs

A Financial Intermediary Limited (The Company)
Licence No ....
Accounts For The Period From [date] to [date]

In accordance with rule 13.3 of the Financial Intermediaries, Managers and Brokers Regulatory Association we report as follows:
(i) We have audited the financial statements of the company Limited set out in pages [X] to [X] in accordance with Auditing Standards.
(ii) To the best of our knowledge and belief we have obtained all necessary information and explanations required for the purposes of our audit.

(iii) In our opinion:
   (a) proper accounting records appropriate to the business carried on by the company have been maintained during the financial year and proper returns adequate for the purposes of the audit have been received from branches not visited by ourselves;
   (b) the balance sheet and the profit and loss account are in agreement with the accounting records and returns;
   (c) the annual financial statements have been prepared in accordance with rule 11 (financial reporting), so as to give a true and fair view of the state of the affairs of the company as at [balance sheet date] and of the profit and source and application of funds for the year then ended;
   (d) the reconciliation referred to in rule 11.4.1(4) has been properly prepared;
   (e) the statement of financial resources has been prepared and calculated in accordance with the applicable provisions of rules 11 and 12:
   (f) the company had, as at [balance sheet date], financial resources of at least the minimum which it was required to have at that date in order to comply with rule 12 (financial resources);
   (g) during the period ended [balance sheet date], the company has adequate systems to have enabled it to comply with rules 14.1 to 14.3 and to carry out, with reasonable accuracy, the reconciliations required by rules 10.2.4 and 10.2.5 at any time, and was in compliance with rules 10.2.4 and 10.2.5 as at [date], the date of the most recent reconciliation carried out in the financial year;
   (h) during the period ended [balance sheet date] the company had adequate systems to have enabled it to comply with rule 14.4 (Client's Money), and was in compliance with that rule as at the annual and half-yearly accounting reference dates, and as at [date] being the date selected at random during the year, disregarding trivial breaches which were rectified immediately upon discovery, and which caused no loss to any counterparty of the firm.

In connection with the matters referred to in paragraphs (iii)(g) and (h) above, you should note that the management of the member firm are responsible for establishing and maintaining adequate accounting and internal control systems. In fulfilling that responsibility, estimates and judgements must be made to assess the expected benefits and related costs of management information and of control procedures. The objective is to provide reasonable, but not absolute, assurance that assets are safeguarded against loss from unauthorised use or disposition, that transactions are executed in accordance with established authorisation procedures and are recorded properly, and to enable the management to conduct the business in a prudent manner. Because of inherent limitations in any accounting and internal control system, errors or irregularities may nevertheless occur and not be detected. Also, projection of any evaluation of the systems to future periods is subject to the risk that management information and control procedures may become inadequate because of changes in conditions or that the degree of compliance with those procedures may deteriorate.

Yours faithfully

Chartered Accountants

Specimen audit report to AFBD for an incorporated member firm

The Association of Futures Brokers
and Dealers Limited
Plantation House
5–8 Mincing Lane
London EC3M 3DX

Date of report

Dear Sirs

A Futures Broker Limited (The Company)
Licence No ....
Accounts For The Period From [date] to [date]

In accordance with rule 8.25.2 of the Association of Futures Brokers and Dealers Limited (AFBD) we report as follows:
(i)   A copy of the Statutory Companies Act accounts of the company for the period ending [balance sheet date] is enclosed separately.
(ii) We have audited the financial statements of the company set out on pages [X] to [X] in accordance with Auditing Standards.
(iii) In our opinion:
    (a) the annual financial statements have been properly prepared in accordance with the Financial Statements Rule of AFBD; the

company's accounting policies are in accordance with rule 8.22 and have been consistently applied within the annual financial statements;

(b) the annual financial statements together with the enclosed statutory accounts give a true and fair view of the state of affairs of the company as at [balance sheet date] and of the profit and source and application of funds for the period ending on that date;

(c) the company's statement of financial resources has been properly drawn up in accordance with the Financial Statements Rules;

(d) the company's balance sheet and profit and loss account are in agreement with the company's accounting records;

(e) the company's accounting records have been kept in accordance with the Financial Record Rules;

(f) the company was in compliance with the Client Money Rules as at [balance sheet date].

(g) all information and explanations which to the best of our knowledge and belief were necessary for the purpose of our audit have been obtained:

(h) the company had at the balance sheet date financial resources of least the minimum which it was required to have under rule 8.32.

(i) having regard to the inherent limitations of any accounting and internal control systems, the nature and scale of the company's business and the need for cost effectiveness in the design of such systems, during the period ended [balance sheet date], the company had adequate systems to enable it to:

  (i) comply with the requirements of the client money rules throughout that period;

  (ii) identify documents of title and documents evidencing title to investments held in safekeeping for the company's customers in accordance with rule 5.47;

  (iii) at any time carry out the reconciliations specified in rule 8.7; and

(j) as at [balance sheet date] (the most recent reconciliation date) the firm has complied with the requirements of rules 5.47 and 8.7.1.

In connection with the matters referred to in paragraph (iii)(i) above, you should note that the management of the member firm are responsible for establishing and maintaining adequate accounting and internal control systems. In fulfilling that responsibility, estimates and judgements must be made to assess the expected benefits and related costs of management information and of control procedures. The objective is to provide reasonable, but not absolute, assurance that assets are safeguarded against loss from unauthorised use or disposition, that transactions are executed in accordance with established authorisation procedures and are recorded properly, and to enable the management to conduct the business in a prudent manner. Because of inherent limitations in any accounting and internal control system, errors or irregularities may nevertheless occur and not be detected. Also, projection of any evaluation of the systems to future periods is subject to the risk that management information and control procedures may become inadequate because of changes in conditions or that the degree of compliance with those procedures may deteriorate.

Yours faithfully

Chartered Accountants

Appendix 2 Specimen Letter Of Engagement For An Incorporated Member Firm Of TSA

The Directors
A Broker Limited

Date

Dear Sirs

The purpose of this letter is to set out the basis on which we act as auditors of the company and the respective areas of responsibility of the board of the company and of ourselves.

1. Audit

1.1 Our function as auditors under the Companies Act 1985 (the Companies Act or the Act) and the Financial Regulations of The Securities Association (TSA) is to examine the annual financial statements of the company presented to us by the directors and to report to the members and to TSA thereon.

Companies Act reporting responsibilities

1.2 Our responsibility under the Companies Act is to report to the members of the company whether, in our professional opinion, the annual financial statements give a true and fair view of the state of the company's affairs at the balance sheet date and the profit or loss for the accounting period then ended, and comply with the requirements of the Act.

1.3 We are also required by law to consider the following matters and to report on any in respect of which we are not satisfied:

405

(i) whether proper accounting records have been kept by the company and proper returns adequate for our audit have been received from branches not visited by us;

(ii) whether the company's balance sheet and profit and loss account are in agreement with the accounting records and returns;

(iii) whether we have obtained all the information and explanations which we think necessary for the purposes of our audit; and

(iv) whether the information in the directors' report is consistent with that in the audited financial statements.

1.4 In addition, there are certain other matter which, according to the circumstances, may need to be dealt with in our report. For example, where the financial statements do not give full details of directors' remuneration or of transactions with the company, the Companies Act requires us to disclose such matters in our report.

TSA reporting responsibilities

1.5 Under the Financial Regulations of TSA, we must include within the scope of our examination the company's Annual Reporting Statement made up to the audited balance sheet date and the statement reconciling the financial position shown in the balance sheet to the Quarterly Reporting Statement made up at the balance sheet date. This will in practice involve a reconciliation between the Quarterly Reporting Statement and the Annual Reporting Statement to deal with figure refinements and in certain circumstances a further reconciliation between the Annual Reporting Statement and the audited accounts where, for example, there are netting or other differences of presentation. The preparation of the Quarterly Reporting Statement, the Annual Reporting Statement and the reconciliation is the responsibility of the directors.

1.6 We have a responsibility to report expressly to TSA on the following:

(a) that the audit was conducted in accordance with Auditing Standards;

(b) that we have received all the information and explanations which we considered necessary for the purposes of our audit;

(c) whether in our opinion:
   (i) the financial statements give a true and fair view of the state of affairs of the company at the balance sheet date and the result for the period ended on that date;
   (ii) proper accounting records appropriate to the business conducted by the company have been maintained during the year;
   (iii) proper returns adequate for the purposes of our audit have been received from branches not visited by us.

(d) whether the financial statements are in accordance with the accounting records;

(e) whether in our opinion:

   (i) the systems for the agreement and reconciliation of balances with banks and counterparties and of securities positions with counterparties and clearing houses are adequate and such procedures are carried out at appropriate intervals;

   (ii) the systems for the safe custody, identification and control of documents of title are adequate and include reconciliations between the records maintained by the company and statements and confirmations from bankers and other custodians at appropriate intervals;

   (iii) adequate procedures and controls are in operation for reporting and investigating the ageing and analysis of balances with counterparties;

   (iv) adequate procedures have been established for monitoring the company's Investment Position Risk and Counterparty Risk exposures and providing appropriate levels of management with the information necessary for them to make relevant, timely and informed decisions to control such risks;

(f) that we have examined the statement reconciling the financial position shown in the audited balance sheet with the balance sheet shown in the company's Reporting Statement as of the same date and that, in our opinion, the reconciliation has been properly prepared;

(g) whether in our opinion the company has adequate systems to have enabled it to comply with section 10 of the financial regulations throughout the financial year, and that the company was in compliance with the requirements of section 10 of the regulations at the date at which the balance sheet was prepared, disregarding trivial breaches of rules 100.02–100.10 which were rectified upon discovery and which have caused no loss to any counterparty of the company;

(h) whether in our opinion:

   (i) the company's Statement of Qualifying Capital as shown in the Reporting Statement at the balance sheet date has been properly prepared in accordance with the rules of TSA;

   (ii) the company's Statement of Total Capital Requirement as shown in the Reporting Statement at the balance sheet date has been properly prepared in accordance with the rules of TSA.

Professional reporting responsibilities

1.7 We have a professional responsibility, as chartered accountants, to report if the financial statements do not comply in any material respect with relevant Statements of Standard Accounting Practice, which are issued from time to time by The Institute of Chartered Accountants in conjunction with other UK accountancy bodies, unless that non-compliance is in our opinion justified in the circumstances.

1.8 We shall additionally report, both to the members and to TSA, that the statement of source and application of funds included in the financial statements gives a true and fair view.

Conduct of the audit

1.9 To enable us to form our opinion, we shall, in accordance with the Auditing Standards approved by our Institute and other UK accountancy bodies;

(i) review the company's accounting system in order to assess its adequacy as a basis for the preparation of the financial statements. We shall report to you in writing any material weaknesses or other points of interest which have come to our notice and which we think should be brought to your attention. As our audit work does not necessarily include a comprehensive review of all procedures, our comments should not be regarded as a complete report;

(ii) make such tests and enquiries as we consider necessary for the purposes of our audit. These will include tests on the existence, ownership and valuation of assets and liabilities and on the day-to-day transactions of the company, but their nature and extent will vary according to our assessment of the adequacy of the company's accounting system. As part of our normal audit procedures, we may request the directors to provide written confirmation of certain information and explanations we receive in the course of our audit where such information cannot be otherwise substantiated; and

(iii) review the financial statements, the Directors' Report and any other documents or statements issued with the accounts in conjunction with the conclusions drawn from our tests and enquiries.

1.10 We are given by the Companies Act and the Financial Regulations of TSA a right of access to the accounting and other records of the company and are entitled to require from the officers of the company such information and explanations as we think necessary for the performance of our duties as auditors.

1.11 In accordance with rule 80.01 of the Financial Regulations of TSA, our audit work shall be carried out in the course of two separate visits to the company's premises; one such visit shall be during the period subject to audit and shall include a review of the company's accounting records and systems of internal control. Both visits shall be followed by a meeting between us and the management of the company at which we shall inform the management of significant matters which have arisen during the audit visit. However, no such meeting need be held if we inform you, in writing, that in our opinion no significant matters have arisen. Further regular meetings will be held to discuss the implications of any changes made to accounting systems and internal controls.

1.12   Our responsibility as auditors is related solely to financial controls and records and does not extend to other parts of the system of internal control; moreover it is related solely to the period under audit and not subsequently.

Responsibilities of the Directors

1.13   As directors, you are solely responsible for ensuring compliance with the requirements of the Companies Act and the financial regulations of TSA relating to the maintenance of adequate accounting records and for establishing and maintaining a system of internal accounting control, including the procedures for safeguarding clients' money and securities. In fulfilling this responsibility, management must make estimates and judgements to assess the expected benefits and related costs of control procedures. It needs to be borne in mind that the objectives of a system and the related procedures are to provide management with reasonable, but not absolute, assurance that assets for which the company has responsibility are safeguarded against loss from misappropriation, unauthorised use or removal; and similarly to provide such assurance that transactions are executed in accordance with established authorisation arrangements and are recorded properly and comprehensively to permit the preparation of financial statements in accordance with the statutory and regulatory requirements. Nevertheless, any system of internal accounting control and the related procedures will contain inherent limitations. In consequence, errors or irregularities may occur and not be detected while there is the risk that presently satisfactory systems may become inadequate in future because of changes in conditions or that the degree of compliance with them may deteriorate.

1.14   It is also your responsibility to prepare financial statements complying with the Companies Act and the Financial Regulations of TSA. In the event that we are asked to provide services additional to audit, your responsibilities are unchanged.

1.15 You are also responsible, under the Regulations, for making the required returns to TSA and for keeping TSA informed about the affairs of the company in accordance with the Notification Rules (rule 90.09). Nevertheless, under section 109(1) of the Financial Services Act 1986 we are entitled as auditors to make a report direct to TSA without your knowledge or consent, although it is envisaged that the need to make such a report will arise only very rarely, in circumstances where we consider that in order to safeguard the collective interests of investors, such a report must be made.

Other matters relating to the audit

1.16 You have authorised us, in accordance with rules 80.01 and 80.02 of the financial regulations of TSA, to supply such information or opinions to TSA as it may request from time to time, and to communicate to TSA any information or opinion on a matter of which we become aware in our capacity as auditors of the company and which is relevant to the regulatory functions of TSA; and to supply to any external accountants, appointed by TSA to report on a matter relating to the company, such information as they request.

1.17 We appreciate that, in common with many businesses of a similar size and organisation, the company's system of control over transactions will be dependent on the close involvement of the directors.

In planning and performing our audit work we shall take account of this supervision; we may ask additionally for written confirmation that all the transactions of the company have been reflected in the books and records, and our audit report may refer to this confirmation.

1.18 When any significant changes in the company's accounting system are contemplated, particularly if these changes involve the introduction or extension of computer applications, we would be grateful if you would advise us, in advance, in order that we may assess the extent to which the proposed changes affect the system or produce any auditing difficulties.

1.19 The responsibility for the prevention and detection of irregularities and fraud rests with yourselves. We shall endeavour to plan our audit so that we have a reasonable expectation of detecting material misstatements in the financial statements or accounting records resulting from irregularities or fraud, but our examination should not be relied upon to disclose irregularities and frauds which may exist. If you so require, we can of course carry out specific investigations into suspected defalcations or irregularities.

1.20   Under rule 90.03 of the Financial Regulations of TSA you are required to make available to us all Reporting Returns sent to TSA. Please forward a copy of each Quarterly Reporting Statement to us, for purposes of information only, as soon as it is submitted to TSA, together with the corresponding Position Risk statement.

1.21   In addition, please send to us a copy of any notification made to TSA under the Notification Rules (rule 90.09) and also TSA's acknowledgement of its receipt and their response.

1.22   We shall not be treated as having notice, for the purposes of our audit responsibilities, of information provided to members of our firm other than those engaged on the audit (for example, information provided in connection with accounting, taxation and other services) and therefore any matters of relevance to us in our position as auditors must be brought specifically to our attention in that capacity.

2. Fees

2.1   Our fees are computed on the basis of the time spent on your affairs by partners and staff. Unless otherwise agreed, our fees will be charged separately for each class of work mentioned above and will be billed at monthly intervals during the course of the audit or other assignment.

2.2   Fees rendered are due for payment immediately.

3. Terms of appointment

3.1   The terms set out in this memorandum, once agreed, shall remain effective from one period of office to another until replaced.

3.2   You have notified us, or by means of this letter are notifying us, that our resignation, removal or retirement as auditors requires written notification by us to TSA and you have authorised us, in such eventuality, to advise TSA of any circumstances connected with our resignation, removal or retirement which we consider should be brought to its attention.

3.3   If, for any reason, we become ineligible to act as auditors of the company we shall tender our resignation forthwith and notify TSA accordingly.

We should be grateful if you could confirm your agreement to the terms of this letter in writing, or by signing and returning a copy of this letter.

Yours faithfully

For and on behalf of A Broker Ltd

Date

Minuted by the Board

Date

Index

Index references are to chapter and paragraph numbers.

415

418

419